INSIDE

3D STUDIO MAX 2

VOLUME II

MODELING AND MATERIALS

TED BOARDMAN
JEREMY HUBBELL

New
Riders

New Riders Publishing, Indianapolis, Indiana

Inside 3D Studio MAX 2 Volume II: Modeling and Materials

International Standard Book Number: 1-56205-864-9

Library of Congress Catalog Card Number: 97-80887

Printed in the United States of America

First Printing: April, 1998

00 99 98   4   3   2   1

Trademarks

PUBLISHER	Jordon Gold
EXECUTIVE EDITOR	Alicia Buckley
MANAGING EDITOR	Brice Gosnell

ACQUISITIONS EDITOR
Michelle Reed

DEVELOPMENT EDITORS
Laura Frey
Linda Laflamme

SOFTWARE DEVELOPMENT SPECIALIST
Adam Swetnam

PROJECT EDITOR
Kathryn Purdum

COPY EDITOR
Michael Brumitt

TECHNICAL EDITOR
David Marks

COVER ART
Jeremy Hubbell

COVER DESIGNER
Dan Armstrong

BOOK DESIGNER
Louisa Klucsnik

INDEXER
Greg Pearson

PRODUCTION
Michael Henry
Linda Knose
Tim Osborn
Elizabeth SanMiguel
Staci Somers
Mark Wachle

About the Authors

Ted Boardman skipped college. After completing a two year Voc-Tech drafting program, he spent a short stint in the Infantry in Korea, and then went to Europe to travel before settling in to work. That European trip lasted 3 years and included jobs ranging from Architectural Drafter for Daimler-Benz in Stuttgart, Germany to all-around-man at the Adambraeu Brewery in Innsbruck, Austria. Work and travel time were divided equally during those years.

On returning to the U.S. in the mid-seventies, he traveled and skied awhile before starting an architectural service specializing in hand-cut post and beam structures around the country. That business was suspended for another European visit and a 6 month trip around India and Sri Lanka, overland across Afghanistan and Iran and then back to Germany.

Back in the U.S., the business returned to post and beam design and construction and full service architectural design, only to be interrupted to deliver sailing yachts to and from the Caribbean and New England in the spring and fall.

Ted introduced AutoCAD into his practice in 1983 with Version 1.4 and eventually converted his business to presentation and animation services with the release of 3D Studio. He started training in AutoCAD in the mid-80s.

His business is now primarily training users of 3D Studio Max around the world, and writing books and training guides on 3D Studio Max and VIZ. Ted is a Kinetix Authorized Training Specialist.

Jeremy Hubbell is the Design Products Marketing Manager at Kinetix. Within the Design Visualization group, Jeremy is responsible for the development and implementation of various marketing components of 3D Studio VIZ and its associated family of products. Prior to his current role, Jeremy was the Senior 3D Studio MAX instructor. He served on both the 3D Studio MAX and VIZ development teams as the worldwide training liason. He also implemented the Kinetix Training Specialist program designed for 3D Studio experts who wanted to instruct others on the intricacies of the 3D Studio family of products. Prior to joining the former Autodesk Multimedia Division in 1994, Jeremy was an Autodesk reseller in his hometown of New Orleans. He currently resides in San Francisco.

Dedication

Ted Boardman—I would like to dedicate this book to Sally Turner, my longtime sweetheart.

Jeremy Hubbell—For my family back home in New Orleans.

Acknowledgments

Ted Boardman—I would like to thank Alicia Buckley, Laura Frey, Linda LaFlamme, Michele Newcomb, and the staff at New Riders for a very professional environment and for their support during the writing process. I'd like to especially thank David Marks at Kinetix for a great job of technical editing and for the extra mile he went to offer suggestions for making the book better.

Jeremy Hubbell—First and foremost, I'd like to acknowledge the love and dedication of my family. Without their support and encouragement, my contribution to this book may never have happened. I also want to take a moment to thank the great team that helped me put this book together. Alicia, for being both nice and vicious at the same time, Laura for being the practical one, and Linda for keeping my "wonderful" grammar and style skills in check. A big thanks must also go to David Marks for making sure both Ted and I didn't insert our feet into our mouths on technical issues. Lastly, thanks to the Yost Group for envisioning such an incredible product.

Contents at a Glance

Table of Contents

Introduction

WELCOME...

...to Inside 3D Studio MAX 2, Volume II: Modeling and

Materials*! As a MAX user, you are probably as excited as we*

are about Release 2. After all, with 1000 new features, who

wouldn't be ready to dive in and start exploring?

As you start to get into MAX R2, however, you may find that there is just so much to use that you haven't the foggiest idea of where to start—much less on how to be productive with this incredible tool. The MAX R2 documentation is certainly an adequate reference, but we both knew that users thirsted for more.

In our experience as instructors, our students regularly begged for tips, tricks, and techniques that would make them "power users." So we said, "Why not put it in a book?" What you hold in your hands right now contains the fruits of our labor. If you're interested in finding out more about the intricacies of modeling, working with materials, or achieving the best rendering effects, then this book is for you.

Out of the Box, into the Book

While writing the book, we purposely avoided using any third-party plug-in routines within the exercises. Our intention is that you should be able to execute the exercises with 3D Studio MAX R2 as it comes out of the shipping box. We feel it is important to be familiar with the enhanced capability of MAX R2 and to understand what you can accomplish with the built-in tools. Understanding the functionality of the program will make you more productive and will make writing useful custom routines using MAXScript easier.

Read the Books in the Box

We set out to write a book that takes users beyond what's covered in the MAX documentation. Although there is some overlap in places, many discussions and exercises talk far above what the MAX reference material covers. That being said, it's strongly recommended that you take the time to do the MAX tutorials before tackling this book. You'll find that you'll get much more out of the book that way.

Real-World, Real Work Examples

We have tried to use everyday, real-world examples in the exercises throughout the book. We understand that it is fun to create flashy, deep space scenes crawling with slimy aliens in full battle mode, but most of us have a need to create more immediate, practical renderings and animations. This doesn't mean that you should not be creative. We have tried to emphasize the need to add that extra edge of realism to your scenes, that thin patina of reality that we see and take for granted in our everyday world. You need to train yourself to "see" the world around you as it really exists and to use the principles put forth in these chapters and exercises to simulate the details most people overlook.

Productivity Is the Key

It was important for us to try to write these exercises to make you, the MAX R2 user, more productive in your work. Extreme realism and beauty are noble goals in creating renderings and animations, but except for the few of you who are true artists, if it can't be accomplished on time and on budget, then you won't win many friends in the workplace. We have tried, where appropriate, to use the most efficient method of creating any given effect. Always keep in mind that the quickest and easiest method may not be the most productive in the long run. Try to anticipate future editing needs and adapt your work habits accordingly.

Try More Than the Steps

The book's exercises should be executed with some thought. The intention is not to teach you how to read or follow instructions—an exercise has value only if you learn something from it. The exercises have been tested and will work if you follow the steps carefully. Take the time to think, however, and take notes on the process or concept being introduced so that you can apply it to your own work. Simply performing the steps, getting the desired results, and moving on to the next exercise is not particularly helpful in the learning process.

The Book's Organization

When browsing through the book, you'll notice that it is divided into three distinct sections. The first is a comprehensive discussion on modeling techniques in various industries. Even though the subject material addresses using MAX in different industries, don't limit yourself to just your profession. There are many more helpful techniques contained in other chapters that may help you.

The second section covers materials. Here we focus not only on the features of the Material Editor, but also on how to make the most of them. Some discussions you'll find straightforward and practical, while others require a more "out there" way of thinking that's often required when using the Material Editor.

The third section is on rendering. While "rendering" is a bit nebulous, the chapters cover many aspects of rendering, from cameras and lighting techniques to using the new Lens Effects built into MAX R2.

Building Up: One Chapter at a Time

The chapters within the three major sections are arranged to build on each other. This is especially the case for each of the three "Concepts" chapters at the beginning of each section. These chapters set the tone for the rest of the section and provide a good foundation for the material to come. This isn't to say that you should read each chapter one after the other. Of course, feel free to jump around!

Let the Fun Begin!

We hope that you enjoy and value the material presented in this book. As authors and instructors, we know the importance of having good reference material. It's our desire to provide the MAX user community with the best possible information about using this product to its fullest. Enjoy the ride!

Sincerely,

Ted Boardman & Jeremy Hubbell

Part I

MODELING METHODS

Chapter 1

MODELING CONCEPTS

At the heart of an animator's job is the ability to build and manipulate 3D models. The tools that an animator uses can vary a great deal, but the end result is the same—a quality 3D model that fits the particular job. If you're reading this book, you've either chosen 3D Studio MAX R2 as your tool or you're at least considering it. Lucky for you!

As of MAX R2, 3D Studio has entered what many people call the "big leagues" of 3D animation. Although 3D Studio has been the tool of choice for thousands of animators for many years, MAX R2 can now serve the needs of just about anybody wanting to do 3D modeling and animation. You now have the ability to choose between three different modeling methods, Polygonal, Patch, and NURBS, in the base package. You can further extend the software with plug-ins, but there's little need to do so unless you have specific requirements that MAX cannot meet out-of-the-box.

This first chapter explores what's possible in modeling technology as it relates to 3D Studio MAX. You'll see how the three modeling methods are defined as well as how they work. Perhaps most importantly, you'll see what methods work best in a given situation. Specifically, this chapter covers:

- Modeling technologies and methods

- Strengths and weaknesses of each modeling type

- Choosing the right modeling type

- Picking a place to start your model

Modeling Methods

As mentioned before, MAX R2 incorporates three types of modeling: Polygonal, Patch, and NURBS. With three different technologies at your disposal, the possibilities are endless. However, knowing how each works, as well as its strengths and weaknesses, can help you in choosing the right one for the job. It's important to point out that although the three technologies are functionally different, they should not be treated as separate parts of MAX. Where possible, you should try to merge them in your model. There's nothing wrong or taboo with mixing polygons and NURBS, for instance. What matters is the end result—no matter how you get there.

In this section, you'll explore the various modeling methods as well as their strengths and where they fall short. If you're new to modeling in 3D, this is a great place to find out what modeling types might work for your project. If you're already a seasoned animator, this section should serve as a reference for your day-to-day modeling tasks.

Polygonal Modeling

Polygonal modeling has been around for quite a while—and rightly so. It makes sense. The geometry you see on your screen is made up of little interconnecting triangles, called *faces*, of various sizes and orientations. By arranging the faces, you can build from the very simple 3D model to the very complex. Polygonal models are also easily animated. By altering the size and orientation of the faces, you can produce simple animations, such as bends or twists, or more complex animations, such as morphing.

The principle of detail is straightforward, too: The more faces you have in a given location, the more detail there is. By adding more detail, you can shape the model. Take the example in Figure 1.1. You can see the 3D model of a tire represented two different ways. The one on the left is a simple Polygonal model, the tire on the right represents a more detailed model.

FIGURE 1.1

The difference in detail of polygonal representations of a tire. The more detailed model on the right requires more faces but looks much better when rendered close up.

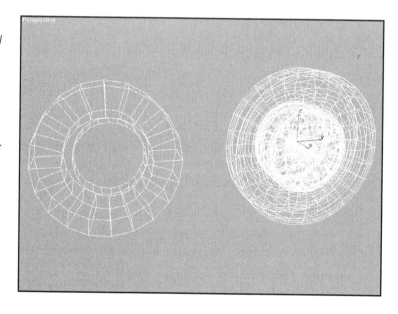

Figure 1.2 points out an interesting thing about detail and Polygonal models. We'll use the tires as an example again. As you get closer, you can notice the difference in detail levels much more easily. However, the further you get from the geometry, the tires begin to look very similar. Remember this bit of information. You'll need it when you design scenes.

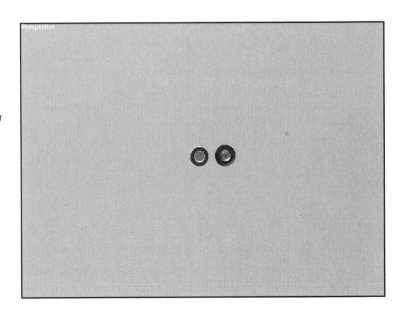

Faces, Edges, and Vertices

To get a better idea of how Polygonal models work, it's good to understand the building blocks of a Polygonal object. As discussed before, Polygonal objects are constructed by arranging triangles of various sizes and orientations, called faces. Each face is made up of three sides (or *edges*) and at the ends of each edge are points known as *vertices*. Figure 1.3 shows the breakdown of a face.

The construction of Polygonal models essentially involves the connecting of vertices. If all of the faces of a model share an edge with at least three other faces, the model is said to be *closed*. If a model contains faces that do not share edges, the model can be considered *open*. Most Polygonal models you'll deal with daily will be closed. The only time that you'll desire to have an open model is if you plan to fill the open area with another object.

A good use of open Polygonal models is for Planar mapped surfaces such as:

- Flat ground planes
- Floors and ceilings
- Backdrops
- Pictures or posters
- Trees and bushes

FIGURE 1.3

The construction of a face on a Polygonal object.

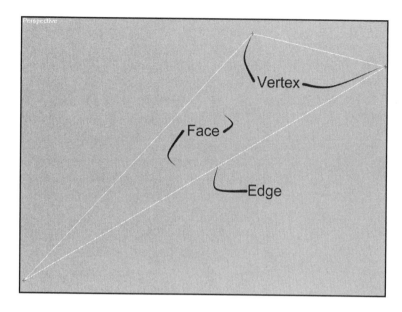

Polygonal Modeling Uses

You can use polygons to model just about anything. As a matter of fact, there's not much you can't model using polygons. With enough detail, you can create any surface. However, some models lend themselves to being created by polygons more than others. For instance, models that tend to be more squared off can be most effectively modeled through polygons. Architectural models come to mind most often. Due to the fact that many angles on objects—walls, windows, doors, and even most interior furniture—are right angles, Polygonal models work best. Figure 1.4 shows an example of a model built entirely from Polygonal objects using MAX.

Polygonal Modeling Shortcomings

As mentioned previously, detail on Polygonal objects requires more faces. As face count increases, MAX's performance begins to degrade. Don't worry, though! On a decent workstation, it takes thousands of faces to notice *any* degradation in performance. It just means that you'll have to be careful when building geometry. A common mistake for beginning animators is to build everything with high detail. As you'll discover later on in this book, it's not always necessary to model everything with lots of detail. There are many workarounds and short cuts for designing a great looking scene without all the extra detail.

FIGURE 1.4

A ceiling fan modeled using Polygonal modeling techniques.

Along the lines of the detail problem is the ability to edit detailed models. Due to the large number of faces in detailed areas of a Polygonal model, making small changes can often be a significant challenge. Even with all of MAX's selection tools and editing capabilities, you'll find that getting into the nooks and crannies of a detailed mesh can be tough. Figure 1.5 shows the challenges that detailed meshes present with respect to editing. Where do you start?

Patch Modeling

Patches, short for Bezier patches, represent another surface modeling technology available in MAX. Rather than being constructed from faces, patches are defined by their boundaries. This means that the locations of the boundaries exist and how they're oriented control the interior of the patch.

The interior of the patch is governed by the *Bezier technology*. Bezier technology allows for smooth areas within the interior of the patch. Across the patch is a series of interconnecting points called a *Lattice*. The position of the Lattice points define the curvature of the surface. Although the Lattice is itself not editable without applying an Edit Patch modifier, it allows you to see the way a patch is constructed rather easily. Figure 1.6 shows what Patch modeling can be used for.

FIGURE 1.5

A highly detailed model of the Titanic. The model presents a serious challenge for any animator who wishes to make changes to the Polygonal mesh.

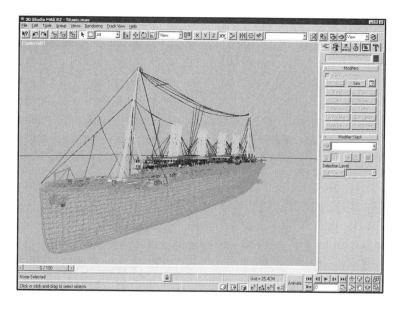

FIGURE 1.6

A 3D Patch surface. The smoothness of the geometry is directly related to the Bezier technology built into the patches.

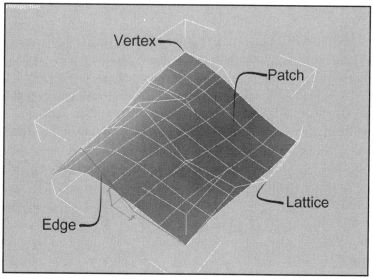

A huge benefit of Patch models is their capability to represent smooth surfaces easily. Unlike Polygonal models, Patch models require less detail to represent smoother, more contoured shapes.

Patches, Edges, and Vertices

Patches are made up of components similarly named as a Polygonal model's. First, a Patch model is actually made up of several smaller patches. Patch's surfaces, in MAX R2, are defined as four-sided surfaces. Each side is referred to as an *edge*. Each corner of a patch has a point called a *vertex*. Lastly, there is a *Lattice* that defines the overall shape of the patch itself. Figure 1.6 shows the components of a Patch model. Although the naming scheme is similar to polygonal models, that's where the similarity ends.

The vertices of a patch have *Bezier tangent handles*, very similar to the Bezier splines that you can create within MAX.

NOTE

Bezier splines are curves defined by control points, using parametric polynomial mathematics, which only affect the local region of the curve and not regions beyond control points on either side. Bezier was a French mathematician.

The tangent handles of patch vertices control the overall curvature of the patch around the area of the vertex. By manipulating the vertex's handles, you can alter the shape of the patch from that corner. An important note about Bezier handle control: the handle alters only the shape of the patch it is associated with. It does not alter the shape of neighboring patches. This is a crucial difference between patches and NURBS objects, discussed later in this chapter.

You use edges of patches to alter the shape of a patch along a specific edge or to define where you want to add patches onto the existing patch. This is primarily how patches work—by propagation. By adding adjoining patches to existing patches, you can build complex surfaces easily.

Patches themselves can be defined by either a *Quadrilateral surface* or by a *triangular patch*. Triangular patches work best for corners or places where a Patch surface may need to come to a peak. For general-purpose use, however, a quadrilateral patch, or *QuadPatch*, works best.

A feature that both patches and NURBS surfaces share is their capability to have relatively low detail models in the viewports and then render higher detail versions. This feature, called Surface Approximation, allows you to specify both the viewport and rendering quality of a model. In Figure 1.7, the model of a shoe in MAX viewports is about 300 faces. In the rendering, it is about 9200 faces! This makes building and editing both patch and NURBS surfaces very easy—and detailed.

FIGURE 1.7

A shaded viewport with a smooth patch model. The rendered model has 30 times more faces.

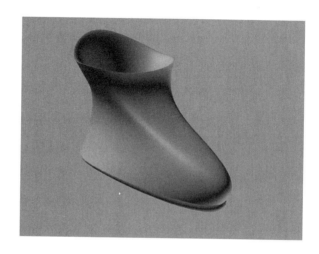

Patch Modeling Uses

Patches can be used to model mostly smooth surfaces. Although the technology can do edges very easily, that type of modeling is best suited for a Polygonal model. Creating organic shapes is very easy. For the most part, you'll need to think about building objects from a center point outward. Through patch propagation, you'll simply add more and more patches as you build outward. Eventually, you'll end up with a smooth, flowing surface with no seams.

Patch Modeling Shortcomings

Patch models have some limitations associated with them that can present problems if you're used to modeling a specific way. For instance, if you like to build an object using defining shapes such as a Loft object, you'll be unable to accomplish this. Patches can be built from primitives, or *Patch grids*, and that's it. You can, however, convert a Polygonal object to a Patch surface by applying the EditPatch modifier. Doing this turns your Polygonal mesh into one big patch with a ton of vertices. For the most part, this is impractical except for on the simplest of Polygonal meshes.

NURBS Modeling

Perhaps the most popular modeling technology to come around has been NURBS (Non-Uniform Rational B-Spline) modeling. Simply put, NURBS modeling excels at smooth surfaces but can also do sharp edges very well. It seems as if everyone is using NURBS to build their 3D models—from characters to cars. Like patches, NURBS allow you to create complex detail that is rendered but not necessarily displayed in the viewports. This means that both the construction and editing of NURBS surfaces is fairly straightforward. Figure 1.8 shows a model built with NURBS surfaces.

FIGURE 1.8

The front end of an F-16. The entire model was built in MAX R2 using NURBS curves and U-Loft surfaces. Thanks to Yoi Hibino for the model.

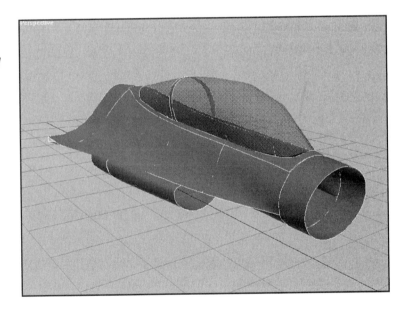

Surfaces, Curves, Points, and CVs

NURBS surfaces are defined by a series of curves and control points. Depending on the type of surface or curve you use, your editing capabilities differ somewhat. Let's first start by talking about the different curves and their Control points.

NURBS curves can be defined by either *points* or *CVs* (Control Vertices). The closest comparison for points is vertices. Points actually lie on the curve itself and directly control the shape of the curve. CVs are a bit different. Instead of lying directly on a curve, CVs are actually part of a lattice that acts more like a magnet. As you move the CVs around on a NURBS curve, they push and pull on the curve itself. CVs also have weights that control the influence of the CV on the curve. All CVs have independent weights that can be edited both in a static nature and over time. Figure 1.9 shows the difference between a Point curve and CV curve.

FIGURE 1.9

The curve on the left is defined by points and the curve on the right is defined by CVs. Notice that the CVs don't lie directly on the curve.

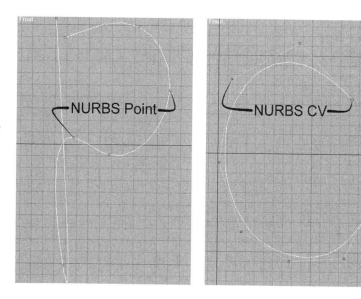

Later on, you'll see that MAX's standard primitives can all be converted into NURBS surfaces. However, this isn't as straightforward with NURBS curves. The Exercise 1.1 takes you through the steps of creating a standard Bezier spline shape and converting it into a NURBS curve.

EXERCISE 1.1: CREATING A NURBS CURVE FROM A STANDARD SPLINE

1. Open 01max01.max from the CD-ROM. This is a standard spline shape.

2. Click the Shapes button in the Create panel. Click the Shapes pull-down menu and choose NURBS Curves.

3. Draw either a small point curve or a CV curve next to the spline shape.

4. Go to the Modify panel, click the Attach button, and then choose the spline shape.

5. The NURBS curve converts the spline shape into a NURBS CV curve. Turn on Sub-Object mode and switch to Curve mode.

6. Select the small NURBS curve and then press the Delete key.

7. Turn off Sub-Object mode. You now have a NURBS curve based on a standard Bezier spline.

WARNING

Exercise 1.1 also points out a limitation of using this method of converting splines into NURBS curves. The NURBS curves shape created is heavily segmented. You'll have to use the Join function to connect all the points of the spline to fix this. Currently, there's no way around this problem.

Curves can act as the building blocks of a NURBS surface, but you can also build straight NURBS surfaces much like patches. You can create either a *Point surface* or a *CV surface*. Which one you use depends on how you like to model. CVs act like your finger pressing on a lump of clay to shape it into a model. Points act like pinpoint pressure on a gel-filled object; it affects both that point as well as the immediate surrounding areas. As you can see from Figure 1.10, moving a point on a Point surface directly affects the surrounding areas of the surface. A CV surface behaves a bit differently. Not only does the CV need to be pulled much higher, it also doesn't have the same affect on the surrounding areas as the point does. The CV surface tends to "gravitate" to the CV. The Point surface seems to push and pull from the point that was moved.

NOTE

All the standard primitives can be converted into NURBS surfaces by going to the Modify panel, clicking the Edit Stack button and choosing Convert to NURBS Surface. This only works if no modifiers have been applied to the primitive.

FIGURE 1.10

The figure on the left is a Point surface with one point moved up. The figure on right uses a CV surface with the same edit operation applied. Notice the end result.

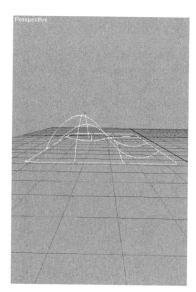
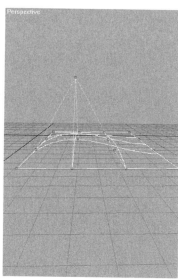

NURBS Modeling Uses

If you can dream it, you can build it using NURBS. The primary benefit of the NURBS method is that it has the modeling and editing flexibility of a Polygonal model, but it doesn't rely on complex meshes for detailed surfaces. In this respect, it's much like using a Patch surface. You can model simply using curves to define surfaces. Those surfaces look rather low-detail in the viewports but can render at a much higher level of complexity.

Many animators use NURBS to build characters. This is primarily because NURBS can give you both smooth, contoured surfaces and keep mesh detail relatively low. Characters tend to be very complex so using NURBS can significantly increase performance versus the same model in polygonal form.

Car manufacturers seem to be in love with NURBS modeling. Have you noticed how many smooth-looking cars are on the road these days? Much of this is due to the fact that they're adopting CAD design packages that model with NURBS technology. Although MAX is capable of conceptual modeling objects like cars, there is currently no way to export NURBS data from MAX R2. This means that the benefit of NURBS is lost as soon as the model is exported—this includes exporting to a format that supports NURBS, such as DWG.

NURBS Modeling Shortcomings

When speaking of shortcomings of NURBS models, it's difficult to point out serious problems. NURBS models, for all intents and purposes, work in almost every situation. However, there is one area where NURBS just can't compete with polygons—simplicity.

NURBS models are designed to be complex eventually. If you build a foundation based on complexity, you can rule out any type of simple modeling. For instance, if you model a box, copy it, and then convert box to a polygonal mesh and the other to a NURBS surface, you might be surprised. The polygonal mesh is eight faces. The NURBS box is 34. That means that a simple model like a box has already over four times as many faces.

Aside from the complexity issue, you could point to the fact that it's very difficult to extrude sections of a NURBS model at right angles. For the most part, NURBS models want to have curvature. That means that even if a model looks like it has right angles, close inspection shows that it does, in fact, have some smoothness around the edges.

Getting Started

Now that you're more familiar with the three modeling technologies within MAX R2, it's time to start modeling! Wait a minute, though. Where do you start? Before building, ask yourself three questions:

- **What's the easiest way to build this model?** There are so many ways to model in MAX that you can usually approach a modeling problem from many different angles. Determining which one is "best" is based mainly on your knowledge of the software. For instance, do you feel comfortable modeling with NURBS or perhaps Booleans? Whatever the case, you'll need to decide this before proceeding.

- **Which modeling technology will work the best?** Depending on the situation, you'll need to evaluate which modeling type works best. Polygonal modeling works best for low detail or more rigid looking models. Patches and NURBS work well for more complex and organic models.

- **What's the final output supposed to be?** If your model is going to be examined either in a still frame or very closely during the course of an animation, you either want to take the complex modeling approach or use high-resolution bitmaps for textures. For models that are moving quickly through a frame of animation or are in the distance, lower detail should be your choice.

The Right Modeling Method for the Job

Asking the question "Which modeling technology will work best," is a lot easier than answering it. You've got all these choices. So, how *do* you pick the right modeling technology for your object? A recap of the key characteristics of each modeling method should help you decide. Think about your model's requirements, then compare them to the lists that follow.

Polygons

The key points to remember about using polygons are:

- Great for low detail

- Great for architectural models

- High detail meshes equal more computer resource usage

- Not good for low-detail organic meshes

Patches

When considering patches, remember several points:

- Great for smooth or organic surfaces modeling

- Work well for most complex models

- Require a "building out" mentality

- Variable level detail through surface approximation feature

NURBS

The strengths and weaknesses of the NURBS method are:

- Nearly a catch-all for modeling

- Works great for high-detail smooth models

- Building block mentality: start with simple shapes and construct more complex surface from them

- Does not work well for more rigid-looking surfaces

NURBS for Simple Shapes

Because NURBS can actually incorporate simple shapes to build complex geometry, there are some handy techniques that you can use when you're building NURBS objects.

When using Point curves, you can reduce the overall amount of computing resources taken up by the model by keeping the number of points relatively low. In other words, don't add any extra points if the shape doesn't need it. Like splines, however, NURBS curves need extra points if you need more detail. The curves will *not* render smoothly unless you add points to them. It's not until a NURBS curve becomes a surface does it actually render smoothly—as part of the surface instead of an independent spline.

Remember that you can convert normal Bezier splines into NURBS curves by using the attachment method covered in Exercise 1.1. However, most attached splines require that you use the Join command to connect all the broken points.

NURBS for Complex Geometry

When starting out with or eventually working with complex NURBS surfaces, you'll find that it's best to work one section at a time. Complex NURBS models tend to slow MAX down quite a bit. There's no way around this except to hide sections of the model that you're not working on.

The Right Place to Start

After you've decided, at least tentatively, on which modeling method to use, you can begin to figure out how to model your design. Whether you opted for Polygons, NURBS, or a combination, you'll next need to determine where on your model is the right place to start.

When looking for a starting point, ask yourself, "Where is the foundation?" For an architectural design, it's often the actual foundation or at least a floor plan. Rarely would you start to build a house by constructing the roof first. For a character, you'd usually start at the center of gravity and work outward. For a mechanical design, you'd often start with the smaller, essential component and build outward. Whatever your situation calls for, it's safe to say that starting from some foundation point for modeling is the most sure-fire way to begin the modeling process.

Building Your Model

Once you've gone through all the labors of preparing to build your model, you're finally ready to get started. Don't worry, the set up is not always a long, involved process. You can usually do most of the pre-work in a few minutes. In order to understand the modeling process from top to bottom, you're going to build a model step-by-step in the Exercise 1.2 series. This way, you can see the whole process. For now, we'll not worry about materials, just the model itself.

You've been asked to design a jet engine. Whether you're an animator, an architectural modeler, or a mechanical designer, you'll find some value from this exercise series. Spin it anyway you want. Maybe you're designing a CG jet engine that will be attached to a live-action jet that will explode. Perhaps you're a designer trying to conceptually model a new engine mount or maybe you're trying to check jet-way clearances at the new concourse of an airport. See, you can find a case for this exercise! The completed jet engine is shown in Figure 1.11.

FIGURE 1.11

The completed model of a jet engine that will be constructed over the next several sections.

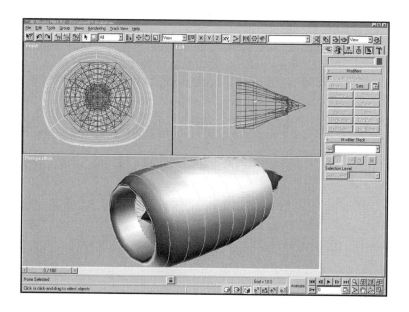

Start from a Basic Shape

The most obvious way to build something that already exists is to trace it in MAX. Fortunately, in MAX R2, you can now load different images into each viewport. This makes tracing the profile curves of the jet engine fairly easy to do. This also helps ensure that the model is based on the real thing.

In this case, you have two photographs of a Boeing 737 jet engine. The pictures were taken on a ramp at an airport in Malaysia and then scanned in. Where you get your photographs, however, is completely dependent on your resources. Sometimes you can find pictures on the Web to use as references; sometimes you can find stock photography CD-ROMs that have what you're looking for. In any case, just make sure you have the rights to use it if you plan to publish the MAX scene and the supporting photographs.

One photograph is a frontal shot of the engine. The other is a side view. You'll use the side photograph in the left viewport and the frontal photograph in the, well, front viewport.

TIP

Photographs are a great way to start building any model. Sometimes it's a good idea to mark significant points on them once you've scanned them in. Edges you wish to trace or significant points to match would be good items to point out specifically in a photograph.

Looking at the photographs of the jet engine in Figure 1.12, it should be fairly obvious which type of modeling technology you should use. If it's not too clear, just look at the shape of the engine. For the most part, it's a circular shape with a flattened bottom. Although you could use a Loft object to build this model, a NURBS U-Loft would work best. It gives you the ability to get nice, round geometry in your renderings while having lower, more manageable detail in your viewports. It also allows you to build other objects, like the engine mount, from the contours of the engine.

FIGURE 1.12

The photographs that you'll use to trace the profile of the jet engine for the exercise.

EXERCISE 1.2.1: TRACING THE CURVES OF THE ENGINE

1. Open 01max02.max from the CD-ROM. The MAX file contains a viewport layout with the two views along the top and a perspective view on the bottom.

2. Go to the Create panel and click the Shapes button. Select NURBS curves from the Shape Type pulldown menu.

3. Activate the front viewport and make it full-screen by pressing W.

4. Click Point Curve.

5. In the viewport, trace the lightest edge of the engine intake—basically the front-most edge of the engine itself. Place points at the 12, 1:30, 3, 4:30, 6, 7:30, 9, and 10:30 positions. Click the point at 12 o'clock again to close the curve.

6. Your curve may be a little rough. Go to the Modify panel and click the Sub-Object button. Use the Move command to position the points so that the curve matches up with the front edge of the engine intake.

7. When you're done editing the points, turn off the Sub-Object button and click the Scale button in the top toolbar.

8. While holding down the Shift key, select and scale a copy of the curve so that it's at the outside diameter of the engine.

9. Repeat the process but scale the curve inward this time so that it matches the outside of the dark area of the engine's intake.

10. Use Sub-Object mode on both curves to position the points on the curve, such that the curves line up with the outermost diameter of the engine and the outer edge of the dark intake area.

11. Turn off Sub-Object mode. Your curves should look like the curves in Figure 1.13.

FIGURE 1.13

The result from Exercise 1.2.1. The curves should line up with the corresponding areas of the engine in the photograph.

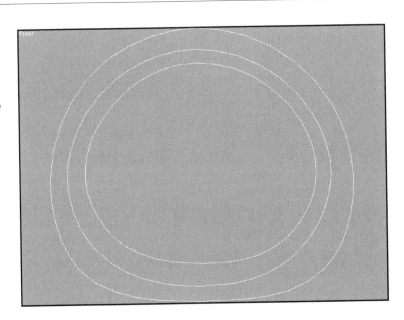

Use Curves as Starting Points

Now that you've got some shapes to work with, it's time to begin building the model. Because NURBS curves are the building blocks of NURBS surfaces, you can use the curves you already have to build the rest of the jet.

Curves, with respect to NURBS and U-Lofts, act as cross sections—much like in a Loft object. You'll be able to use the outermost cross-section to define the shape of the engine cowling. By copying and scaling that cross-section, you can define the shape of the cowling from the front of the engine backwards. To get the an idea of the size of the cross-sections, you'll need to switch to the Left viewport. You'll use the side view to determine the scale of the cross-sections.

In this next exercise, you'll use simple copy and pasting operations to build the skeletal shell of the engine cowling. By building and orienting the cross-sections in the left viewport, you'll set up the overall scale of the engine correctly. After you're done with the left viewport, there's no real need to show the background images anymore.

EXERCISE 1.2.2: BUILDING THE ENGINE'S CROSS-SECTIONS

1. Load 01max03.max from the CD-ROM. Select the outermost curve.

2. Press L to switch the full-screen viewport to the left viewport. Activate the Move command in the top toolbar and constrain to the X axis.

3. While holding down the Shift key, move a copy of the outermost curve so that it intersects between the letters "B" and "O" in the Boeing logo. When prompted for number of copies, choose 8.

4. Select all the curves and move them down on the Y axis so that the leftmost curve is centered on the engine. (It can be approximate.)

5. Use the Scale command to scale each cross-sectional curve so that it's the proper size for the given location.

6. Move the curve designed for the forward-most part of the engine. The name is Curve01 if you want to select by name. You can also move the innermost curve (Curve03) toward the back of the engine image slightly.

You now have the completed cross-sections positioned correctly for the engine cowling. The result of Exercise 1.2.2 is shown in Figure 1.14. The curves need to be attached into one object and converted into a surface before you can properly loft the model itself. You'll do this plus surface the model in the next exercise.

FIGURE 1.14

The completed result from Exercise 1.2.2. The NURBS curves serve as cross-section surfaces.

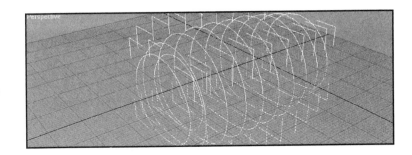

EXERCISE 1.2.3: SURFACING THE ENGINE

1. Open the 01max04.max from the CD-ROM. This is the completed file from the last exercises containing the cross-sections for the engine.

2. Select any curve. Click the Attach Multiple button in the Modify panel.

3. Select all the curves in the list and choose the Attach button in the Attach Multiple dialog box.

4. Click the Edit Stack button and choose Convert to: NURBS Surface. The cross-sections will flash. This does not change the look of the model but prepares the cross-sections to be surfaced.

5. Scroll down to the bottom of the Modify panel and expand the Create Surfaces section. Click the U-Loft button.

6. Click the last curve on the back of the engine. Progressively click all the way to the front of the engine to the inner curve representing the intake. Note, you can back up if you make a mistake by pressing the Backspace key. Right-click to exit U-Loft mode.

7. Render the Perspective viewport. You'll notice that the geometry isn't all that smooth. You can fix this by altering the Surface Approximation values.

8. Expand the Surface Approximation rollout. Click the Renderer radio button.

9. Make sure Curvature is selected and set Distance and Angle to 0.5 and 5.0, respectively.

10. Rerender the scene. The end result is much more smooth.

As you can see from Figure 1.15, the jet engine is starting to take shape. You have the cowling that's complete, but now you're missing the intake fan as well as the exhaust port. (We won't model a complete NURBS engine in this book.)

TIP

The sharp seam visible on the top of the engine cowling can be eliminated by opening the Surface Approximation rollout and checking Mesh Parameters/Parametric. The default settings of 2 U and V Steps should be sufficient.

FIGURE 1.15
The final rendered result from Exercise 1.2.3 or the surfaced jet engine.

Use Primitives

Although you could use more NURBS surfaces to build the rest of the engine, the components are simple enough to be built from the standard primitives available in MAX R2.

In the final portion of this exercise, you'll add in the remaining geometry using regular primitives and modifiers. This isn't done so much to demonstrate how to model with primitives, but rather to show that combinations of modeling technologies can produce an end result.

EXERCISE 1.2.4: ADDING THE REMAINING GEOMETRY

1. Open the file, 01max05.max, from the CD-ROM. This is the completed engine cowling from Exercise 1.2.3.

2. In the Display Panel, click Unhide All. This unhides the basic geometry that you'll use to build the intake fan and exhaust port.

3. Click the Fan Blade in the front viewport.

4. Click the Coordinate System pulldown menu and choose Pick. Click the FanCone object.

5. In the Transform Coordinate flyout, choose Transform Coordinate Center, make sure the front viewport is active, and then click the Array button.

6. In the Rotate row, click the right arrow button to the right of Rotate to activate the Totals fields. Enter 360 in the Z degrees field. In the Array Dimensions area, enter 40 in the Count field to the right of 1D, then click OK.

7. You'll now have fan blades surrounding the cone. Now you can create the engine's exhaust port. Select the Exhaust Port object and go to the Modify Panel.

8. Apply the Edit Patch Modifier and, in the left view, select all the right-most vertices.

9. Select the Uniform Scale button. Verify that Use Selection Center is selected and scale the selection to taper the end of the cylinder about 50 percent of the original size.

TIP ———————————————————————————————

You can see the scaling amounts for the X, Y, and Z axes in the fields just above the Snap icons while you are scaling.

10. In the Front viewport, pick the center vertex of the Exhaust Port. Hit the Spacebar to lock the selection set.

TIP ———————————————————————————————

If you pick several times near the center you will be able to toggle between the left center vertex and the right center vertex of the Exhaust Port. You can see when you have the right-most center vertex selected by watching the left viewport.

11. Drag it slightly to the right of the engine to create the tip extending from the exhaust port. Hit Spacebar to unlock the selection set.

12. Render the perspective viewport to see the final result. Try rendering different angles to see the engine from different sides.

You Did It

Congratulations, you've taken a concept from start to finish to produce a very accurate model of a 737 engine. If you're an animator, go blow it up! If you're an architect, go do your study. If you're a mechanical designer, see if it fits on the wing properly. In other words, go have fun!

The point of this exercise series is to show you the complete modeling process from beginning to end. You can certainly take the model much further than it's at right now. For instance, feel free to add an engine mount—or even the internal components of the engine. It's up to you at this point. The final result is shown in Figure 1.16.

FIGURE 1.16

The final result showing the completed 737 engine. The result is from using NURBS, Polygonal, and Patch models.

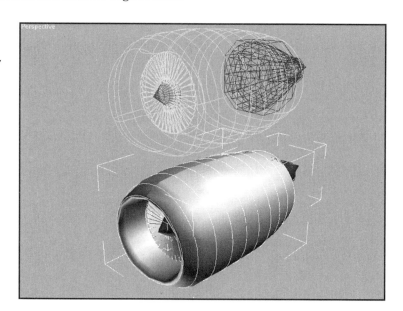

In Practice: Modeling Concepts

- **Polygonal modeling excels at low detail or architectural models.** Because polygonal models are made up of faces, you'll find that they're very easy to edit and animate when you're working on a relatively low-detail model.

- **Patch modeling is for smooth models being built from the foundation outward.** Patch modeling works by attaching small grids, called patches, which are based on Bezier spline technology. This provides for smooth rendered surfaces with relatively low detail geometry in the viewports.

- **NURBS modeling works best for complex, smooth, or organic surfaces.** Because NURBS models are just as smooth as patches, you'll find they work well for complex models. Unlike patches, NURBS surfaces can be built from defining curves that allow you to construct your surfaces based on simple objects instead of small patches.

- **Use combinations of all three for best result.** Although using each modeling technology separately works well, using a combination of all three can often produce the best results. Because patch and NURBS surfaces are close in their behavior, there's no need to use both at the same time. More than likely, once you get comfortable with NURBS, you'll be able to leave Patch modeling behind.

Chapter 2

ARCHITECTURAL MODELING

Although many of the concepts of modeling are the same for mechanical, character, and architectural projects, some are very useful to the architectural community, as you'll see in this chapter. A clear understanding of these, the options available, and when to use them will make the process of creating 3D worlds productive and cost-effective. Most architects assume, for example, that the entire model has to be in one file, complete to the same detail as the working CAD drawings. In this chapter, you will learn concepts of:

- Using several smaller files

- Keeping detail to only that which can be seen at the viewing distance

- Using mapped materials instead of mesh objects to create the illusion of detail

- Controlling the level of complexity in lofted objects

Before You Build

Learning to model effectively in 3D Studio MAX R2 is much like learning a foreign language or learning music. At first, everything may seem overwhelming. Terminology is completely new, concepts and work methods appear to make no sense, and people expect you to produce a masterwork after a week with the program. Do not become discouraged. Start slowly with small, manageable projects and work your way into more complexity. Following two simple guidelines will help you in all your projects: Make a storyboard and keep your scenes compact.

In this section you will look at:

- Storyboarding an Architectural Scene

- Compact, Efficient Modeling Concepts

Make a Storyboard

A most important step in the process is planning. Create a storyboard, a graphical outline of the scene or animation project, before you turn the computer on. The storyboard can be simple or complex, but it must contain all the issues important to the project at hand. The storyboard should be signed off by you and the client before any work is started. Figure 2.1 is a sample storyboard you will use for the modeling in this chapter.

Most storyboards, such as one for an architectural walkthrough, contain some of following information:

- Starting camera viewpoint

- Subsequent camera view sketches

- Transition information from one scene to the next

- Timing information notation

- Lighting detail information

- Color information (Pantone numbers can be a good starting point)

- Material assignments

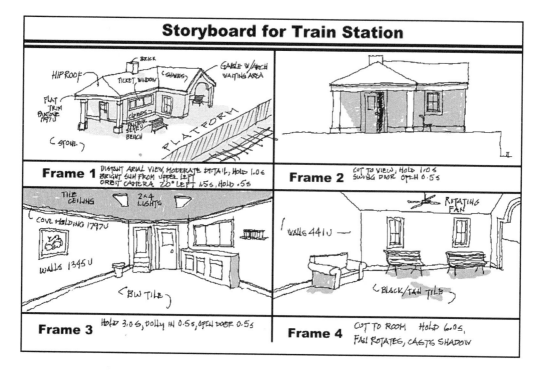

FIGURE 2.1

A sample storyboard.

This storyboard is neither the most complete nor the simplest, but serves as an example. You will have to determine the detail necessary for each project based on the complexity of the scene and the levels of trust and understanding between you and the client.

WARNING

Do not skip the storyboard under any circumstances!

Compact Models

A key factor to always keep in mind during the modeling process is that the number of polygon faces and vertices that an object contains has a profound effect on your computer resources. The more complex an object is the slower your system will react during the creation and rendering process. It is imperative to keep the face/vertex count to a minimum in each scene. For more information, see the "How Much Detail is Enough?" section later in this chapter. Several methods for keeping the models small are:

- Break up large scenes into smaller files
- Do not create or import objects that will not be seen
- Do not create detail too small for the viewing resolution
- When using Primitive Objects, reduce the number of segments
- When lofting objects, use Optimize or appropriately reduce path and shape steps
- When importing objects, use the Optimize modifier

Modeling Exercises

Whether or not architecture is your chosen profession, you will often be called upon to create buildings or structures, real or fantasy, for backdrops to your scenes. We will present some of the concepts of creating structures with 3D Studio MAX R2 and offer some helpful tips and methods for making the process more productive. In this section, you will first learn the concepts, so you can apply them to specific methods of modeling in the chapter's later projects.

There are essentially three approaches you can take to create buildings and structures:

- Start with 2D floor plan views and extrude for wall height
- Start with 2D wall elevation views and extrude for wall thickness
- Start with 3D CAD models

In a typical architectural office, the method of modeling you choose often depends on the comfort level of those performing the work. You should, however, familiarize yourself with all three methods to have a variety of tools options. There is no right or wrong way of creating 3D presentations and the last thing you want to do is to rely on only one method of modeling scenes. In the real world, you will use a combination of methods.

Think of it as buying a large set of mechanics tools. You get several cabinets (software packages), each with several drawers (menus and panels). Each drawer is filled with unusual tools (commands and modifiers). Until you familiarize yourself with as many tools as possible and have a feel for where they are and when best to use them, there is no way you can fix a car in a productive and cost-effective manner.

Even though you have the tools to model incredible detail, however, keep in mind that not all detail has to be modeled. 3D Studio MAX R2 has the tools to create the illusion of 3D geometry when none exists and a productive office must know when it is appropriate to *simulate* complex geometry instead of modeling it. Some 3D Studio MAX tools for simulating geometry are:

■ Bump Mapping

■ Opacity Mapping

■ Environmental Backgrounds

For more detail on using materials to simulate geometry see Chapter 9, "Designing Naturally Occurring Materials," and Chapter 10, "Designing Man Made Materials."

T IP

A couple of helpful books for anyone creating buildings and everyday household objects are the student or professional versions of *Architectural Graphics Standards* by Ramsey/Sleeper (John Wiley and Sons) and *The Architect's Portable Handbook* by Pat Guthrie (McGraw-Hill). For years the professional version of *Architectural Graphics Standards* has been the bible for architects and builders as a reference for the determining sizes of almost everything you can imagine from restaurant equipment, to sports field layout, to standard construction methods.

The best way to understand the basics of architectural modeling, is to see them in action. In the exercises that follow, you will model a small country train station. While the example exercises are simple, the same concepts are applicable to the largest projects. Some of the concepts covered include:

- Setting up your workspace

- Extruding a 2D plan for height

- Extruding a 2D elevation for thickness

- Creating soft furniture with the Meshsmooth modifier

- Building a street lamp with Bevel Profile modifier

- Making cove molding by lofting a shape on a path

- Designing cove molding with the Lathe modifier

Setting Up Your Workspace

Just as a doctor wouldn't start an operation without scrubbing up, you shouldn't begin modeling without preparing your working file. In this exercise, you will set up a 3D Studio MAX file with some basic units and snap settings, and then save the file to be used as a prototype for future projects. Any settings you make in this prototype will automatically be loaded any time you open a new file or perform a File/Reset. The file works similarly to AutoCAD prototype files, except you can have only one prototype in 3D Studio MAX R2.

TIP

You could have files on your hard drive with various settings but no mesh objects and simply open them, then Save As a new working file.

You could also create custom 3DSMAX.INI files and create desktop shortcuts pointing to the custom files with the 3DSMAX.EXE –I option.

The prototype's settings provide the much needed precision for architectural modeling: Using the proper Units settings and Grid Spacing enables you to create 2D or 3D models that are accurate to the nearest 1/100 of an inch.

Setting Units and Grid Settings

Although this may be a basic operation to many of you, some people over-look these settings and struggle with inaccuracy in creating and placing objects. Making these settings is a vital step in production.

T IP

If you are comfortable with Unit Settings, Grid Spacing, and prototypes, feel free to skip this exercise and move on to the next section.

EXERCISE 2.1: SETTING UNITS AND GRID SPACING

1. From the Views pull-down menu, click Units Setup.

2. In the Units Setup dialog (Figure 2.2), pick US Standard and choose Feet w/Fractional Inches from the list. Leave the other values at their defaults and press OK.

FIGURE 2.2

Units Setup dialog box.

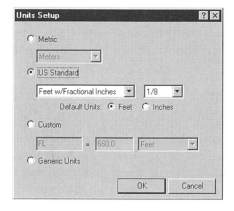

3. From the Views pull-down menu, click Grid and Snap Settings.

4. In the Grid and Snap Settings dialog, pick the Home Grid tab.

5. Type 0′6″ in the Grid Spacing field, and 8 in the Major Line Every Nth field and close the dialog. (See Figure 2.3.)

FIGURE 2.3

Grid and Snap
Settings dialog box.

6. From the File pull-down menu, choose Save As, and save the file in the \3DSMAX2\SCENES subdirectory with the filename MAXSTART. MAX. Now, MAX automatically loads the settings information each time you open a new file or choose File/Reset from the pull-down menus.

You can now use the Snap and Osnap tools to control object creation or object transforms to the degree set in the Grid Spacing field. The settings can quickly be adjusted by right clicking any of the Snap icons at the bottom of the screen and changing the settings.

Object Naming

Take the time to devise a well-thought out naming scheme for all objects in your scenes. Do not use the default Box01, Cylinder01, Line01 names assigned by 3D Studio MAX. You will quickly become lost and inefficient without standardized object naming conventions. 3D Studio MAX enables case-sensitive sorting in the Select by Name dialog box (see Figure 2.4). Take advantage of this option; it can increase productivity by keeping your important objects near the top of the list.

One possible naming scenario might be:

■ OBJECT_NAME: Use all caps for important animated objects

■ Objectname: Use inital caps for stationary objects

■ pathname: Use all lower case for 2D objects

FIGURE 2.4

Select by Name dialog box with Case Sensitive option checked.

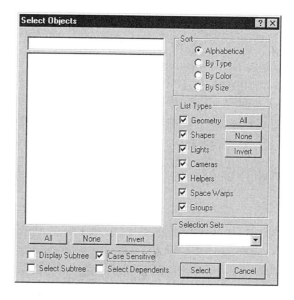

TIP

If, perhaps, you have 200 "important" objects in your scene but are working consistently with only 15 of them, you can temporarily rename the 15 objects by prefixing the name with a numeral to force it to the top of the list. For example, when you make "pathname" "1pathname," it floats to the top of the list for easy access.

Before you move on to your first building project, take a moment to review the important preliminaries you learned in this section, such as how to:

- Set the Snap option and turn Snap on and off for greater accuracy in creating and transforming object.

- How to use Snap Overrides when you require a single pick that is not a currently checked option.

- How to adjust the visible Grid Spacing on the World Grid plane as an aid to layout and editing of an architectural scene.

- How to set up naming conventions to streamline object selection in large scenes.

Extrude 2D Plan Views for Wall Height

In this section's exercises, you will open a MAX file containing two identical columns of 2D shapes in the Top viewport to begin work on your train station. The shapes are *compound* shapes; in other words, shapes made up of more than one spline.

You will use the 2D shapes to create 3D walls, a roof, interior trim, a bench, and a lamppost. Two methods of wall creation are presented; extruding a floor plan (a view from above) to a height and extruding wall elevations (front view, side view, and so on with window and door openings) to a given thickness.

You will take advantage of 3D Studio Max R2's ability to use References, or clone objects. These are objects with a one way link back to the original. When you change the original, the Reference changes, but you can change the Reference (such as adding an Extrude modifier, for example) without having it pass the changes back up to the original.

The shapes in the right column of the Top viewport are Reference clones of the originals in the left column.

This process allows easy editing of the original 2D shapes in the left column, later in the exercise, to affect the 3D objects created by modifying the Reference clones.

T IP

If you're familiar with AutoCAD, you'll be pleased to learn that when lofting or extruding, MAX handles compound shapes in a manner similar to ACAD's "normal" hatching mode. For nested, non-overlapping splines in a single shape, 3D Studio MAX starts at the outer spline and creates a solid mesh to the next internal spline. From the first internal spline, MAX creates a void to the next internal spline and continues creating solid, void, solid, as deeply as the splines are nested.

We highly recommend you use this to your advantage by creating complex cross-section shapes with little system overhead, then lofting or extruding into the final 3D object.

You can create compound shapes by using the Start New Shape checkbox when drawing 2D primitives or by collapsing shapes to an Editable Spline and using the Attach option to combine individual shapes into one.

For now, you will work with only the shapes in the right-hand column, which were cloned from the original shapes in the left-hand column using the Reference option. You will take advantage of this process later in Exercise 2.8 to edit the 3D objects.

Note

A *Reference* contains a one-way link to the original. Modifications to the original are passed to the clone, but changes to the clone are not passed back to the original.

In this exercise, you will use a 2D compound shape of a floor plan with two 2D columns at the front. You will apply an Extrude modifier to extrude in the positive Z-axis to the wall's height. You will be extruding a Reference clone of an original shape to help make editing easier in later exercises.

EXERCISE 2.2: EXTRUDING A FLOOR PLAN SHAPE TO A HEIGHT

1. Open the file called \CH2_2DOR.MAX on the CD-ROM. It should appear similar to Figure 2.5:

FIGURE 2.5

*Open CH2_2DOR.
MAX.*

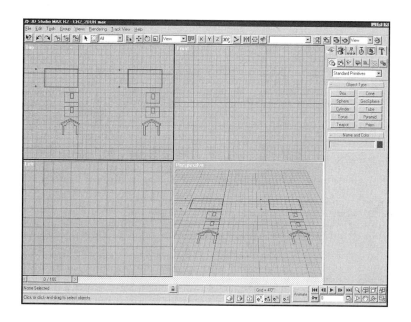

2. In the Top viewport, select the top object in the right-hand column or press H and choose ticketplan_ref from the list in the Select by Name dialog.

3. In the Modify panel, click the Extrude modifier and type 9′0″ in the Amount parameter field. Name the new object TICKET_BOOTH.

   Congratulations, you just built four walls, six inches thick, and two one-foot square columns, all 9′0″ tall.

4. In the Tools pull-down menu, click Display Floater to call up the new Display Floater floating dialog, which has options for hiding and freezing objects in the display (see Figure 2.6).

FIGURE 2.6

Display Floater dialog box.

5. In the Display Floater's Hide column, click Unselected to hide everything but the TICKET_BOOTH object.

NOTE

If, for some reason, you did not have the TICKET_BOOTH selected, choose Unhide All in the Display Floater, select the object, and choose Hide and Unselected again.

6. Click the Zoom Extents All icon to fill the viewports with the new walls and columns.

7. Save this file as STATION13.MAX.

As a result of this exercise, you have four walls cleanly mitered at the corners, but they lack window and door openings. When using this technique, remember that the 2D floor plan shape must be imported from a CAD program or created in MAX R2.

Next, you'll have to cut out the window and door openings with 3D Boolean operations. 3D Boolean operations in 3D Studio MAX are not always reliable and sometimes fail at apparently simple tasks. Some of their other drawbacks are:

- 3D Booleans add greatly to system overhead.

- 3D Boolean operations can create long thin faces in a mesh object.

- 3D Boolean operations can disrupt smoothing groups and welded vertices.

In their defense, some advantages of 3D Boolean operations are:

- 3D Booleans can be used to cut openings in curved walls.

- 3D Booleans can be used at anytime in the modeling process.

- 3D Boolean operands can be animated.

Using 3D Booleans can be stressful, so use them when you have no other reasonable option. In the next exercise, you will perform a few simple 3D Boolean subtractions to cut out door and window openings. You will then learn some methods of increasing the likelihood of success in more complex situations.

EXERCISE 2.3: CUTTING DOOR AND WINDOW OPENINGS WITH 3D BOOLEANS

1. Right-click in the Front viewport to active it, and type W to Maximize the viewport to full display.

2. Click to turn on the 3D Snap icon, then right-click on the icon to bring up the Grid and Snap Settings Dialog. Check only Grid Points in the Snaps tab.

3. In the Create panel, click Box and click a Grid Point 1'0" below the base of the walls. Next, drag up and to the right to create a box with a Length of 8'0", a Width of 3'0", and a Height of 3'0". Name the object

door3x7. You can use the box you just created to cut out 3′0″ × 7′0″ door openings by copying it around the scene. Using a box that obviously overlaps the bottom edge of the wall insures that no faces will be left behind to create a sill or threshhold.

4. Starting at the same height as the top of the door3x7 object, create a box with a length of 4′0″, a width of 8′0″, and a height of 3′0″. Name the object ticketwind.

5. Next to ticketwind, at the same height, create a box with a 5′0″ length, a 2′6″ width, and a 2′6″ height. Name this object dhwind. Press W to return to four viewports. The viewport should appear similar to Figure 2.7

FIGURE 2.7

3D Boolean operands for doors and window openings.

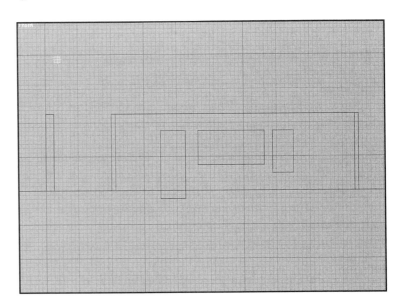

6. In the Top viewport, copy and arrange the objects in a similar layout as shown in Figure 2.8: two windows on the back wall, one door on each of the left and right walls, and the ticketwind on the front wall.

TIP

If you want to position the door and windows exactly, move them using Snap mode to the corner of a wall or other known position, then click and right-click the Select and Move transform icon, and type in exact offset distances. In 3D Studio MAX R2, you can also find the Transform Floater in the Tools pull-down menu.

FIGURE 2.8

*3D Boolean operands
for doors and window
openings.*

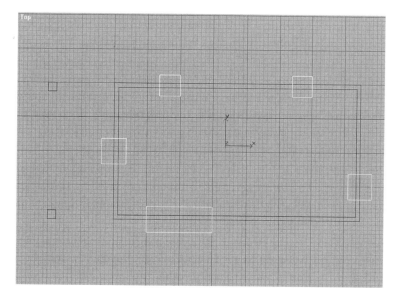

7. Maximize the Perspective viewport and select TICKET_BOOTH.

TIP

For Boolean Subtractions, such as those in the exercise, select the object that will remain after the process. With Boolean Union and Intersect, the order you pick is not important.

WARNING

Prior to any Boolean operation, *always* select the Hold operation from the Edit pulldown menu to insure that you can use Edit/Fetch to return the model to its present state if the Boolean goes awry.

8. In the Create/Geometry panel, click Standard Primitives, choose Compound Objects from the list, and click the Boolean button.

9. TICKET_BOOTH, the selected object, is operand A. Click the Pick Operand B button and, in the Perspective viewport, pick one of the window objects on the back wall.

WARNING

Operand B should disappear and leave a clean opening in the wall. At this point, it is important to right-click in the active viewport to clear the Boolean operation.

10. Pick Boolean in the Object Type pulldown, click the Pick Operand B button and pick one of the other door or window objects in the Perspective viewport.

11. Save the file as STATION01.MAX by clicking the plus icon to the right of File Name: in the "Save File As" dialog. This creates a new incremental file, leaving your previously saved file intact, in case you need to go back to it.

TIP

If you have trouble picking the object you want, press H after clicking the Pick Operand B button and select the object by name.

So far, everything is working predictably; you have walls with two window openings. In the background, however, 3D Studio MAX is working hard to keep track of the Boolean processes. If you continue repeating Step 10 above, you may be able to subtract the doors and windows in this simple scene without any problems. However, if the scene is any more complex, the process would soon fail and you would get unwanted and possibly difficult to correct results. (Do not forget to Edit/Hold for each Boolean operation.)

In this exercise, you have seen how to:

■ Create and position objects to be used as Boolean operands to cut door and window openings from extruded floor plans.

■ Perform an initial Boolean operation and, upon completion, exit the Boolean process by right-clicking in a viewport before starting a new Boolean operation.

■ Use the Hold option in the Edit pulldown menu before each Boolean operation as a safety feature if the operation fails.

In Exercise 2.4, you simplify the amount of information that 3D Studio MAX has to keep track of, therefore increasing the chances greatly of successful Boolean operations and freeing system resources at the same time. If you choose to work with the extruded floor plan method of creating walls, an architectural scene will become very cumbersome with the many Boolean operations required to punch door and window openings, and you will soon deplete system resources.

TIP

We highly recommend that you perform these next steps after each Boolean operation to avoid many frustrations.

EXERCISE 2.4: CLEANING UP THE BOOLEAN PROCESS

1. Select TICKET_BOOTH if it isn't already selected.

2. In the Modify panel, expand the Modifier Stack rollout. In the rollout, click the Edit Stack icon and choose Editable Mesh from the Convert To list. You now have a simple mesh object that appears the same but doesn't have the overhead of the Boolean operations.

3. In the Create/Geometry panel, click Standard Primitives, choose Compound Objects from the list, and click the Boolean button.

4. TICKET_BOOTH, the selected object, is Operand A. Click the Pick Operand B button and, in the Perspective viewport, pick one of the remaining door or window objects.

5. Pick Boolean in the Object Type rollout, click the Pick Operand B button, and pick one of the other door or window objects in the Perspective viewport.

6. Repeat Steps 1 through 5 and create the remaining door and window openings in your walls. TICKET_BOOTH should appear similar to Figure 2.9.

TIP

If you have a large structure to create with this method, it is relatively easy to write a 3D Studio MAX R2 MaxScript to simplify the steps.

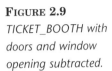

FIGURE 2.9
TICKET_BOOTH with doors and window opening subtracted.

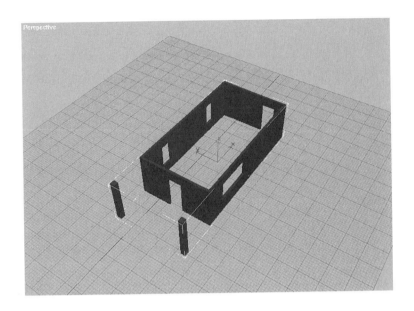

7. Save this file as STATION02.MAX by clicking the plus icon in the "Save File As" dialog.

In this exercise you have learned to collapse a Boolean object to a simplified editable mesh object to increase the likelihood of successful future Boolean operations and to save system resources.

Extrude 2D Elevation Views for Wall Thickness

There's more than one way to build a train station. In this section, you will take a different approach to creating the structure. Many of the steps may be the same, but you will build the walls from the 2D elevation and align the 3D walls in space. This would be analogous to building a pre-stressed concrete tilt-up structure.

TIP

We personally try to use this method as much as possible for its efficiency and the extra control it affords during the editing process.

EXERCISE 2.5: EXTRUDING AN ELEVATION SHAPE TO A WALL THICKNESS

1. From the Tools pull-down menu, click Display Floater, and click the All button in the Unhide section.

2. Type W to switch to four viewports and click the Zoom Extents All icon.

3. Select the waitfront_elev_ref object.

4. In the Modify panel, click Extrude modifier and type 0'6" in the Amount field. Rename the object WALL_WAITFRONT.

5. Repeat Steps 3 and 4 for the other two wall shapes and name them WALL_WAITBACK and WALL_WAITLEFT. Do not extrude gab-trim_elev_ref, yet. The Perspective viewport should appear similar to Figure 2.10.

FIGURE 2.10

Waiting room walls extruded to 6" thickness.

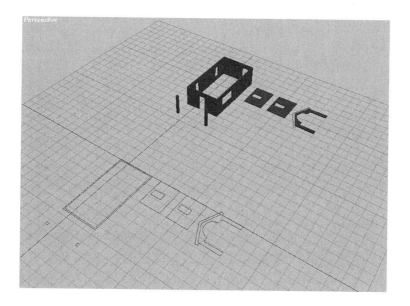

6. Select the four 3D wall objects, and use Hide Unselected to hide everything else in the scene.

7. Maximize the Perspective viewport, and choose Zoom Extents All.

02.01

8. Save this file as STATION03.MAX. You have created new walls in this exercise by extruding the 2D shape of the wall elevation, complete with window and door openings, in one simple step. You extruded a Reference of the original 2D shape to allow easier editing in a later exercise.

The prefab walls have been delivered to the building site and now you need to put them up. In Exercise 2.6, you will use Align and Normal Align to "throw" the walls through 3D space and into position. Normal Align uses the face normals to align one object to another and is easier to use in the Perspective viewport. Align uses bounding edges, centers, or pivot points to align objects and may be used in any viewport comfortably.

N OTE

The X,Y,Z-axis directions used by Align are dependent on the active viewport and the active Reference Coordinate System.

EXERCISE 2.6: ALIGNING THE WALLS IN 3D SPACE BY FACE NORMAL

1. In the Perspective viewport, select WALL_WAITFRONT.

2. Click and hold on the Align icon, and click the Normal Align flyout.

3. Click WALL_WAITFRONT and hold the mouse button down, then move the mouse a little. You will see a blue normal vector.

4. Position the blue normal vector anywhere on the top surface of the wall and release the mouse button.

5. Click anywhere on the TICKET_BOOTH inside back wall (opposite the column end), and hold the mouse button. You will see a green normal vector.

6. Position the green normal vector anywhere on the wall surface. Release the mouse button, and WALL_WAITFRONT flips up and aligns itself with the two selected surfaces in the same plane. Check the Flip Normal checkbox in the Normal Align dialog so the wall is right side up. Click OK.

7. Repeat Steps 1 through 6 for the WALL_WAITBACK object. Repeat them again for the WALL_WAITLEFT object, but normal align it with the ticket window's wall. Also, check the Flip Normal checkbox in the Normal Align dialog so the wall is right side up. Your scene should look similar to Figure 2.11.

FIGURE 2.11

Extruded walls flipped with Normal Align to TICKET_BOOTH.

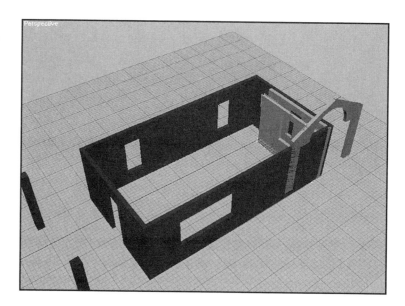

8. Save this file as STATION04.MAX

TIP

Take the time to become proficient with the Normal Align command and its options. It can save a lot of steps by moving an object through 3D space and "sticking" it onto the surface of another object. You can put skylights on sloped roof, a picture or trim on walls, or a box on the surface of a dome quickly and easily.

Exercise 2.7 uses the Align command to finish what you started in Exercise 2.6. Align enables more accuracy than Normal Align but does not flip objects as it aligns them. You will first align the bottom edges, then align the walls into final position.

EXERCISE 2.7: ALIGNING OBJECTS WITHOUT FLIPPING

1. In the Perspective viewport, select WALL_WAITBACK.

2. Click the Normal Align icon, hold the mouse button down and click the Align flyout.

3. Pick TICKET_BOOTH as the target object, and the Align Selection dialog appears. Check the Z Position checkbox.

4. Pick Current Object:Minimum and Target Object:Minimum. This aligns the walls using the World coordinate system and matches the extreme edges in the negative Z direction.

5. Click the Apply button in the Align Selection dialog box to reset the Align values, which allows a new alignment without leaving the command.

6. Check the Y Position checkbox and pick Current Object:Maximum and Target Object:Minimum. Click the Apply button.

7. Check the X Position checkbox and pick Current Object:Maximum and Target Object:Maximum. Click the OK button to finish the alignment process for this wall.

8. Repeat the process for the two remaining wall objects. Aligning first WALL_WAITLEFT to WALL_WAITBACK, then WALL_WAITFRONT to WALL_WAITLEFT. Each alignment builds on a wall in the correct position. The aligned walls should look similar to those in Figure 2.12.

NOTE

The walls in this exercise are named with the assumption that the columned overhang is at the "front" of the station.

The viewport labels "front," "right," and so on are generic and do not necessarily have anything to do with a building layout.

9. Save this file as STATION05.MAX

TIP

The Align command is one of the most powerful productivity tools in 3D Studio MAX, yet it is overlooked by many users. Practice using it; the time you spend will be rewarded. Keep in mind that the current viewport and current Reference Coordinate System affect which direction the X, Y, Z Axis points. Experiment with all the options of this command.

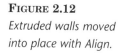

FIGURE 2.12

Extruded walls moved into place with Align.

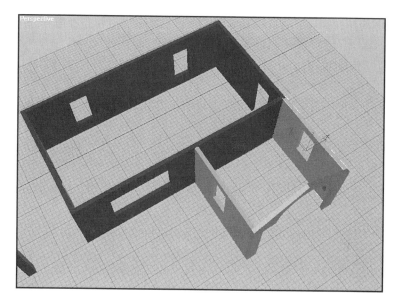

In Exercises 2.6 and 2.7, you aligned 3D walls lying flat in the "ground plane" by flipping them in space with the Normal Align command, then positioned the walls by aligning with existing objects in the scene. With this method, you can quickly assemble a building after positioning a few key walls.

The Reference Clone Editing Shortcut

Exercise 2.8 highlights one of the biggest advantages of working from the 2D elevation. As you may recall from Exercise 2.2, the 2D shapes in the right-hand column are created with the Clone/Reference option that enables a one way link between the original and its Reference. Take advantage of this and edit the 2D shapes in the left-hand column to change the extruded walls. To prepare for the exercise, unhide all objects and maximize the Perspective viewport to see both the 3D walls and the 2D Shapes in the left-hand column. It should look similar to Figure 2.13.

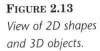

FIGURE 2.13

View of 2D shapes and 3D objects.

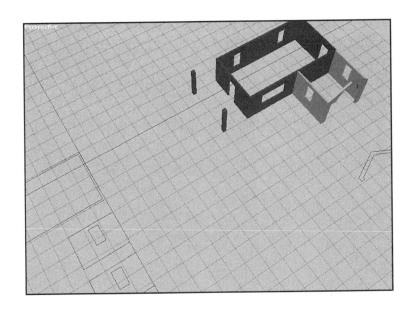

EXERCISE 2.8: EDITING REFERENCE CLONE OBJECTS

1. In the Perspective viewport, select waitfront_elev in the left column.

2. In the Modify panel, click Sub-Object and choose Spline from the list.

3. In the Perspective viewport, pick the window rectangle Spline. It should highlight red.

4. Click Select and Move, click Restrict to X-Axis, and move the spline back and forth. Observe the rectangle in waitback_elev and the window openings in the 3D walls moving at the same time.

WARNING

The Restrict to Axis constraints have no effect if Snap is turned on in default mode. Right-click the Snap icon, click Options tab, and check Use Axis Constraints or just turn Snaps off.

5. Save this file as STATION06.MAX.

TIP

Working in this manner enables easy access to 2D wall elements that, when modified, affect the reference walls in the same way. It does not matter where these 3D walls are located or their orientation to the original shape. This same editing method can be used on animation paths as well.

Notice that if you try this with the plan 2D shape the reference link is no longer valid. It was broken by collapsing the Boolean operations into an Editable Mesh.

Exercise 2.8 introduced you to the concept of editing a "skeleton" of original 2D wall elevation shapes to affect the Referenced 3D wall. It eliminates the need to find a particular wall and align a Grid plane before making edits such as moving window or door openings.

You will use the concepts from Exercise 2.8 in Exercise 2.9 to create a bent wood bench with extruded shapes for the same editing flexibility.

EXERCISE 2.9: CREATING EDITABLE BENT WOOD BENCHES

1. In the Top viewport, zoom in to the waitfront_elev shape. (This is just for a size reference.)

2. Using Create/Shape/Line, design a 2D shape similar to the bench profile shape shown in Figure 2.14. Name the object benchprofile. (Alternately, you can also bring in BNCHPROF.MAX from the CD-ROM using File/Merge.)

FIGURE 2.14

Compound Shape made from three splines.

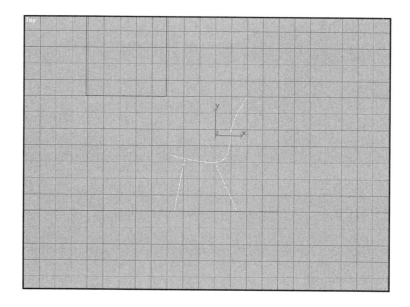

T IP

The 2D shape has to be created as one shape containing three splines. Use the Start New Shape button when creating this object.

3. With the Shift key held down, select and move benchprofile off to the right, near the 3D walls. Release the mouse button and choose Reference in the Clone Options dialog and name it benchprofile_ref. Click OK to exit the dialog.

4. Click and right-click Select and Rotate, and type 90 in the Absolute: World X-axis field.

5. In the Modify panel, click Extrude and type 8′0″ in the Amount field. Name the object BENCH01. It should appear similar to the one in Figure 2.15.

FIGURE 2.15

Bench extruded from compound shape.

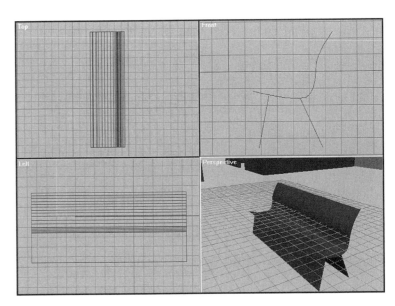

TIP

These benches should not be the central focus of the train station; therefore, they can be simple. In a later exercise, you will use materials to make them look more realistic. Do not create a lot of incredibly detailed benches that will only slow the process and add no relevant information.

6. Use the Align command to align the bottom of the bench legs with the bottom of a 3D wall, then Move it into any position in the Top viewport.

7. Save this file as STATION07.MAX

Creating Soft Furniture with Meshsmooth

Many times during architectural modeling you need to have soft or *organic* objects. In Exercise 2.10, you will create a sofa with a face level editing method and you will use the Meshsmooth modifier to round or soften the edges. This method can be applied to all sorts of organic objects:

- Soft furniture

- Cushions and pillows

- Trees

- Rocks

- Low resolution people and animals

- Low resolution vehicles

The advantages to using this Meshsmooth modeling method are:

- Easy to use

- Low face/vertex count for complex objects

- Easy to edit

The disadvantages to modeling with Meshsmooth are:

- Inaccurate, you have no exact control over the smoothing. Use lofting, extruding, sub-object editing for more accuracy.

- Modifier requires some overhead (it should be collapsed in Edit Stack to reduce complexity).

EXERCISE 2.10: CREATING A SOFA WITH MESHSMOOTH

1. In the Top viewport, create a box with Length=3'0", Width=7'0", and Height=1'6".

2. Set Segments to Length=3, Width=6, and Height=2. Name the object SOFA01.

3. In the Modify panel, click Edit Stack and choose Editable Mesh for Convert To.

4. Click the Sub-Object button, choose Face.

5. Check the Ignore Backfaces checkbox.

6. Holding the Crtl key, pick in the middle of each visible edge, square polygon up the left, across the back, and down the right. This leaves 8 out of 18 square polygons that will become the cushion.

7. Hit the Spacebar to lock the selection set.

8. In the Modify panel, enter 12 in the Extrusion amount field. This extrudes the selected faces, adding new side faces.

9. Hit Spacebar to unlock the selection. Click Sub-Object to exit sub-object mode. The sofa shape should appear similar to the one in Figure 2.16.

FIGURE 2.16

The sofa with extruded faces.

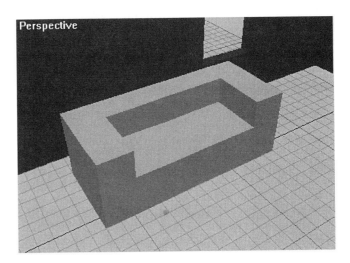

10. In the Modify panel, click More and choose the Meshsmooth modifier.

11. Set Meshsmooth's parameters to Strength=0.2, Relax Value=0.5, and Iterations=2, with Smooth Result checked on. These settings are a starting point; adjust the values to get the result you want.

12. In the Modify panel, click More and choose the Optimize modifier. With the default Optimize settings the sofa should drop from around 3000 faces to around 475, a significant savings.

13. In the Modify panel, click Edit Stack, and choose Collapse All. Click OK at the warning dialog. The sofa is now a simple Editable Mesh object taking up almost no computer resources. The finished object should appear similar to the one in Figure 2.17.

FIGURE 2.17

*Sofa with
Meshsmooth and
Optimize modifiers.*

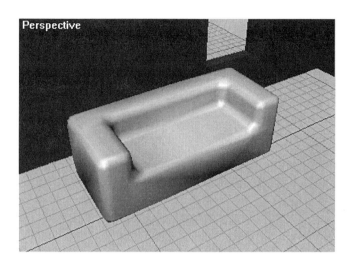

Perspective

14. Save this file as STATION08.MAX

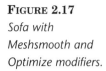

TIP

You should always consider collapsing the modifier stack, especially on objects that have Meshsmooth or Optimize modifiers, because both modifiers require a fair amount of computer resources to evaluate. If you suspect that you may need to make modifications to the object, select the object and save it to disk (File/Save Selected) before collapsing the modifier stack. You can then merge the original into a scene or open the file to edit the object.

Exercise 2.10 illustrated a method of creating rounded, organic objects with a low face and vertex count. The process can be used for "soft-edged" objects like furniture, branching trees, simple characters, and low resolution vehicles, as well.

Using Bevel Profile to Create a Lamppost

A new modifier in 3D Studio MAX R2 is called *Bevel Profile*. If you have ever tried to use Deform Scale or Deform Bevel on a lofted object and wished for more accurate control over the actual profile, Bevel Profile is the answer to your problem. Bevel Profile is a 2D modifier that requires two elements: a 2D profile, (open shapes make more sense but closed will work also) and a 2D cross-section shape. You apply the modifier to the cross-section shape to extrude it into a 3D object with a base the size and shape of the cross-section and a height and profile of the profile shape.

TIP

While using the Bevel Profile modifier is similar to lofting with Deform Bevel, the process differs. With Bevel Profile you can use profile shapes imported from other sources, such as AutoCAD. Bevel Profile is also a good modifier to try when beveling text shapes.

WARNING

If you use Bevel Profile with profile shapes that have had the Fillet/Chamfer modifier applied to fillet corners in the shape, the resulting 3D object can have many faces and vertices.

EXERCISE 2.11: CREATING A STREETLAMP WITH BEVEL PROFILE

1. File/Merge the 2D profile from \LAMPPROF.MAX from the CD-ROM, select streetlamp_prof as the object to merge.

2. In the Top viewport, create a 0'8" radius circle near the front left of the TICKET_BOOTH. Name the object LAMPPOST01.

TIP

When Bevel Profile is applied, the First Vertex on the profile determines the direction of the object.

3. With LAMPPOST selected, choose Bevel Profile from the Modify/More list.

4. Click the Pick Profile button, press H, and choose lamppost_prof from the list. You can adjust the diameter of the object by clicking Sub-Object/Gizmo and moving the profile Gizmo.

5. Finish the streetlamp by merging the LAMP group from LAMPS.MAX on the CD-ROM and aligning the group with the top of the lamppost. The finished lamp should look similar to the one in Figure 2.18.

6. Save this file as STATION09.MAX

You used Bevel Profile in Exercise 2.11 to create a lamppost from a base circle and a profile spline. While Bevel Profile is intended for beveling text for flying logos, it functions very well for creating complex architectural objects. Next, you will use it again to create a hip roof.

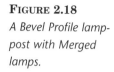

FIGURE 2.18

A Bevel Profile lamp-post with Merged lamps.

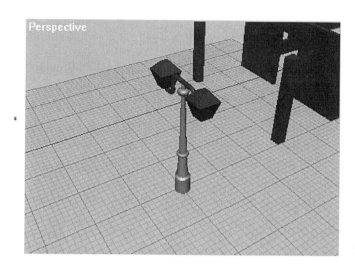

Use the Bevel Profile Modifier to Create a Hip Roof

Another architectural application of the Bevel Profile modifier used in the last exercise is not readily apparent, that of creating a hip roof with fascia trim.

EXERCISE 2.12: BUILDING A HIP ROOF

1. Open the file STATION11.MAX.

2. Click, then right-click on the 3D Snap icon. Check Vertex from the list, and deselect any other settings.

3. In the Perspective viewport, make a rectangle (Create/Shape/Rectangle) that stretches from the top outside corner of a TICKET_BOOTH post to the top diagonal corner at the opposite side of the wall. Name the object hiproof.

4. In the Modify panel, click Edit Stack and convert to an Editable Spline.

5. In Sub-Object/Spline mode, pick the rectangle, type –1'0" in the Outline Width field, deselect Copy if necessary, and click the Outline button.

6. Click Detach (Copy unchecked) and name the object roof.

7. Delete the original hiproof rectangle.

8. In the Modify panel, select the rectangle named roof and choose Bevel Profile from the More list of modifiers.

9. In the Modify panel, click Pick Profile, press H, and choose hipprofile from the list. Name the object HIPROOF.

10. Press H, and choose hipprofile from the list. Click Zoom Extents All Selected to zoom in on hipprofile in all viewports. It is a 2D line describing the profile of the roof and trim. This profile could have been imported from CAD or created in 3D Studio MAX R2

11. Save the file STATION12.MAX The scene should appear similar to Figure 2.19.

FIGURE 2.19

A Bevel Profile Modifier Hip Roof.

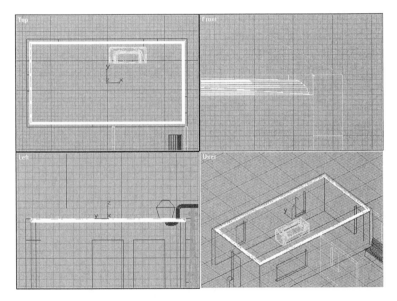

Create a Lofted Cove Molding

In the next exercise, you will use Create/Geometry/Loft Object to create cove molding around the ceiling of the TICKET_BOOTH. This method is essentially the same as it was in 3D Studio MAX R1, except that in R2 the profile size does not need scaling. For example, when you Loft a four-inch trim, it remains four inches on the straight sections and scales accordingly at the miter joints.

EXERCISE 2.13: CREATING A COVE MOLDING BY LOFTING

1. In the Perspective viewport, Zoom Extents All Selected on TICKET_BOOTH.

2. Right-click 3Dsnap and set to Vertex mode.

3. Click Create/Shapes/Rectangle, and pick two corners diagonally across from each other on the TICKET_BOOTH's inside top walls. Name this object covepath.

4. Click File/Merge for COVESHAP.MAX, and select coveshape from the list.

NOTE

Step 4 is to remind you to use File/Merge to retrieve objects that you have already created in other scenes, thus saving time and avoiding duplication of effort.

5. With covepath selected, Select Create/Geometry/Loft Object/Loft/Get Shape, type H, and choose coveshape from the list. Coveshape jumps to the path but still needs some adjustment for orientation.

6. In the Modify panel, click Sub-Object/Shape and click the new shape on the path. It should turn red.

7. In the Align area, click Bottom, then click Left to align the coveshape on covepath.

8. Click Sub-Object to exit Sub-Object mode, and in the Skin Parameters rollout, check Options/Optimize Shapes and Display Skin. The cove molding is now around the top of the wall and retains its proper size all around. Checking the Optimize Shapes option reduced the face count by about 1000 without affecting the appearance of the molding. Uncheck and check the Constant Cross Section checkbox to compare how it now affects the size of the lofted object. Name the object TICKET_COVE. It should appear similar to the one in Figure 2.20.

FIGURE 2.20

*A Lofted Cove
Molding.*

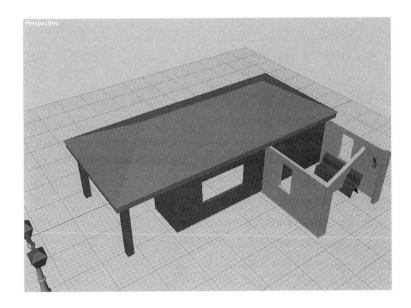

9. Save this file as STATION10.MAX.

TIP

You can build any sort of architectural element with the Create/Geometry/Loft Object method. Both the path and the cross-section shape can be closed or open, straight or curved. Some other uses of this lofting method are:

■ Window and door trim

■ Picture and mirror frames

■ Kitchen cabinets

■ Complete wall systems

■ Roads with gutters and sidewalks

Lathed Cove Molding

Another method for quickly creating square moldings or edging is to use the Lathe modifier. It has the advantage of being more efficient than the lofted cove when used to create square lathings. In this exercise, you will create a lathed molding.

EXERCISE 2.14: LATHED COVE MOLDING

1. If you skipped Exercise 2.13, click File/Merge for COVESHAP.MAX, and select coveshape from the list. Otherwise, press H and select it from the list of objects.

2. In the Modify panel, click Lathe modifier.

3. Type 4 in the Segments field, and click the Align Max button. Name the object COVE.

4. Click Sub-Object/Axis, then select and move the axis in the Front viewport to set the size of the object. If you move the Sub-Object Axis left in the Front viewport, you will create an inside cove. Moving right in the Front viewport will create and outside cove. The distance you move the Axis is the radius of a circle describing the outer edge of the square object. Right-click the Select and Move icon and enter –5′0″ in the Offset:Screen X-axis field. This creates a square cove molding 10 feet across the diagonal. Exit Sub-Object mode.

5. Right-click the new mesh object, and choose Properties from the menu. This molding should have around 144 faces. It is a fairly low density object.

6. Next you will edit and align the object to become a cove molding in the waiting room, using WALL_WAITFRONT and WALL_WAITBACK. In the Top viewport, rotate COVE 45 degrees in the View Z-axis, and move it approximately in the center of the waiting room. Press W to toggle to full display.

7. Click the Align icon and pick WALL_WAITFRONT. Check Z Position and Current Object:Maximum, Target Object:Maximum. This aligns the top of the COVE with the top of the WALL_WAITFRONT.

8. In the Modify panel, click Edit Stack and in the Edit Modifier Stack, click Collapse All. Click Yes in the warning dialog. Click OK. This collapses the lathed object to an editable mesh.

9. In the Modify panel, click Sub-Object to enter Vertex mode. Select all vertices at the two corners on the left side.

10. In the Modify panel, click More and choose XForm from the modifier list. Then click Sub-Object Gizmo.

TIP

If you try to align just the vertex selection set, MAX R2 uses the geometric center of the selected vertices as the alignment point. Using the XForm modifier places the alignment center on the outside edge of COVE.

11. In the Top viewport, click the Align icon, pick WAIT_WALLFRONT, check X Position, and check Target Object:Minimum. The Align Gizmo center should align to the inside of WAIT_WALLFRONT. Click Sub-Object to exit Gizmo mode.

12. In the Modify panel, click Mesh Select and click Sub-Object Vertex mode. Select the vertices at the top two corners of COVE.

NEW TO R2

In previous versions of MAX, you would apply an EditMesh modifier to select new vertices. In MAX R2, however, you can use Mesh Select to select new vertices, faces, or edges to pass up the modifier stack. This is much more efficient than using the Edit Mesh modifier.

The Mesh Select operation allows no transforms, so you must use a XForm modifier above it in the modifier stack.

13. In the Modify panel, click More and choose XForm from the modifier list.

14. Click Align, check Y Position, and check Target Object:Maximum. Click OK. The top edge of COVE aligns with the top end of WALL_WAITFRONT.

15. Repeat steps 12 and 13 to align the other two sides of COVE to WALL_WAITFRONT and WALL_WAITBACK.

TIP

It is good practice to edit the names of a series of Mesh Select operations in the Edit Stack Name field. Select the modifier in the stack that you want to rename and enter something like Mesh Select—COVE left. This makes it easier to edit the selection later on.

Also, at the top of a series of Mesh Select modifiers, apply a final Edit Mesh and exit Sub-Object mode to clear any visible selections. Rename the modifier something like Mesh Select—COVE END.

16. Press W to view all four viewports.

17. Save this file as STATION11.MAX.

Using CAD Models as a Starting Point

You don't always have to start from scratch to build your structures in 3D Studio Max R2. Someone else in your office may have already done the work for you in a CAD program; all you have to do is import it. In this section, you will learn some the issues to be concerned with when modeling from CAD files is a part of your repertoire. Take the time to analyze your office procedures and involve the entire staff in an open discussion on how you might best adapt current practice with new methods that will enhance the transfer from CAD to 3D Studio MAX R2 and back. Every office will have different methods and there is no right or wrong way.

Use Proper CAD Methods

One of the most important aspects of insuring the best possible result from the exchange of data between 3D Studio MAX R2 and AutoCAD is proper training of CAD operators. The age-old saying "Garbage in, garbage out" has never been truer. The following are some issues to pay close attention to:

- Proper use of Osnaps

- Layer management

- Block management

- Facetres and Viewres system variables

If architecture is your profession, you must take the time to analyze your offices' working methods. The following are some issues that you will need to address:

- Define management and modeler/render's expectations of the 3D process.

- Determine how storyboarding is integrated into the design process.

- Determine if MAX is to be used as a conceptual study tool, a project marketing tool, or a combination of the two.

- If your office uses CAD, calculate the level of data you need to exchange between the MAX and the CAD program.

- Determine the level of output quality you require; for example, the level of detail needed in the models for high-resolution still images or conceptual low-resolution animation.

Importing CAD Files into MAX

In this short exercise, you will import an AutoCAD R14 drawing to experience a few of the effects that you will encounter in the real world and to experiment with the DWG import options.

EXERCISE 2.15: IMPORT AN AUTOCAD R.14 DRAWING

1. From the File pulldown menu, click Reset to insure you are starting with a fresh scene.

2. From File again, click Import and choose AutoCAD (*DWG) from Types of Files.

3. Choose acadtest.dwg from the CD-ROM.

4. Check Completely Replace Current Scene from the DWG Import dialog; then click OK.

5. Press H, and choose Correct2D.01 and Incorrect2D.01 from the Named Selection List.

6. In the Modify Panel, click Extrude and type 100 in the Amount field.

7. Study the objects that are imported into 3D Studio MAX. Some of the problems you'll notice include:

   - INCORRECT2D.01 was drawn without Osnaps.

   - SOLID3D.01 is an open object.

   - SOLID3D.01 and SOLID3D.02 are separate objects, not a group.

   - Faces of FLIPPED_NORMAL.01 are unified.

   - MULTI_ON_1_LAYER.01 is all one object.

8. Repeat Steps 1 through 7 several times, changing one option in the Import AutoCAD Drawing File dialog each time, to see the difference in the resulting imported objects. Again, there is no right or wrong way, but you must experiment to get acceptable results for your office. For more information see Appendix A, "AutoCAD and 3D Studio Max R2: Getting Them to Talk."

How Much Detail Is Enough?

The temptation for architects is to completely model a project with all details, both modeling details and lighting. In the real world, you will seldom encounter a client who wants to pay for or needs "too much" information. For 3D modeling and rendering to be a cost-effective tool, you *must* know when "enough is enough." That's not to say you want to skimp on quality, but to enhance quality where it will have the most benefit to you and the client. The advice that follows is not intended as gospel, but as food for thought.

Plan Ahead

Do not start work on the computer until you know the scope of the work and the quality level expected. Planning ahead can save you time and effort during the editing process. For example, if you have walls that intersect and will probably be moved around, do not break the walls at the intersection. Use solid walls that pass through each other. The model will render the same; you will save on the number of faces and vertices and reduce editing time.

Predetermine as much material and color information as possible. If an object is bright red plastic to begin with and then changes to dull black plastic later, you may be in for time-consuming changes in material and lighting when you can least afford the time.

Get a firm commitment from the client to determine what areas and views are most important to be visualized in 3D. Usually a long corridor or a storage room will not be important and you will get better result spending the time on the lobby.

Avoid Complex Models

To reiterate, each face and each vertex in a model require computer resources to store and process. The more complex the model becomes the less RAM is available for rendering. By reducing the face/vertex count, you can often cut the rendering time enough to equal the speed of adding a new computer to the network.

Just as too much information can overload your system's processor, it can overload yours, so work in manageable chunks. Imagine, for instance, you're modeling a new school building to present to the school board on videotape. You want to show the school as it relates to the neighborhood; and you want to highlight the attractive front entry and show off the new chemistry lab and gym.

To see the exterior in the neighborhood, you have to be 2000 yards away from and above the building. At that distance, the resolution of the video-tape used as output will only show details larger than three feet. It is unrealistic to work with a fully detailed model of the school with all the interior furniture and fixtures in place. Instead, make one low detail model of the massing of the building, and add windows and doors using mapped materials instead of geometry. Trees and shrubs at this resolution can also be mapped onto flat planes rather than created as complex mesh objects.

Next, have a more detailed model of the front entry viewed from ground level at a distance of 200 yards. Such details as door handles and window and door trim details may still be too small to show in the tape. Keep the shapes true, but leave fine details out and use higher resolution mapped materials to simulate details like brick grout or shadows.

Next is an interior shot of the lab or classroom with the important details included, especially where the camera will get close. If the client decides later to see a classroom, it is usually easier to create the new model than to have it already in the scene "just in case."

Avoid Walkthroughs

Avoid walkthroughs? What sacrilege! One of the reasons you got involved in 3D modeling in the first place was because you *could do* walkthroughs. Architectural walkthroughs are sometimes necessary, but you will seldom see a good one that was worth the effort and heartache expended producing it. Before your camera starts walking, ask yourself, "What's the point? What's the benefit? What's the cost?"

In the school building example, a slow 20 degree orbit of the exterior, a slow, short approach to the entry, and a camera pan and zoom on a detail might give all the information needed with great impact. A fly-around, a run to and through the entry, and miles of high speed trips down boring corridors and up through atrium space make the audience very uncomfortable and leave you prone to problems with lighting, shadows, and animation glitches.

Watch movies and adopt some of their editing techniques, such as cuts and fades. If you count the seconds any scene is active before a cut or fade, it is seldom more than 10 seconds (300 frames) and often less than three seconds (90 frames).

Test Your Detail Options

In this next exercise, you will view two 3D Studio MAX R2 parametric, six light windows, and create two windows from 2D splines. You will then compare the details from several distances as an example of some options available for saving time and resources.

The file used in the exercise (MULLION.MAX) contains two parametric windows from the Create/Geometry/Windows panel. One has no detailed chamfering, but otherwise they are the same. Also included in the file are two 2D mullions that you will convert to 3D windows.

EXERCISE 2.16: DETAIL EXAMPLES

1. Open the file MULLION.MAX from the CD-ROM.

2. In the Modify panel, select mullion01 and apply an Extrude modifier with 2″ in the Amount field.

3. In the Modify panel, select trim01 and apply an Extrude modifier with 8″ in the Amount field.

4. In the Modify panel, select mullion02, choose Bevel modifier from the More list and use the following settings:

- Level 1: Height=0'1/4", Outline=0'1/4"

- Level 2: Height=0'1 1/2", Outline=0'0"

- Level 3: Height=0'1/4", Outline=0'–1/4"

5. In the Modify panel, select trim02 and apply a Bevel modifier with the following settings.

  - Level 1: Height=0'1/4", Outline=0'1/4"

  - Level 2: Height=0'7 1/2", Outline=0'0"

  - Level 3: Height=0'1/4", Outline=0'–1/4"

6. In the Modify panel, select glass01 and click Edit Stack. Choose Editable Mesh from the menu. This converts the shapes to a mesh with no z-axis dimension.

7. In the Modify panel, select glass02 and click Edit Stack. Choose Editable Mesh from the menu.

8. Render the scene from different camera distances and notice how close you must come to an object before the details start to show up.

9. From the File pulldown menu, pick Summary Info and compare the face and vertex count of each object. Do not forget to add faces for mullion01, trim01, and glass01 for an accurate count.

Production Tools

Several features are built into 3D Studio MAX R2 as great enhancements to productivity, but they are often overlooked or not fully utilized. Some of these productivity tools are:

- Snap Settings

- Grid Helpers

- Tape and Protractor Helpers

- Sections

Snap Settings

3D Studio MAX R2 offers new object snap capabilities that rival some CAD software. Many of these snaps were offered with 3D Studio VIZ but have been improved for MAX R2. The Snap settings menu can be accessed by right-clicking the Snap icon at the bottom of the display.

The Snaps enable you to use existing geometry or Grids to accurately pick specific points or transform other objects. Figure 2.21 shows the object snap options for mesh objects.

FIGURE 2.21.

Snap Settings dialog.

The default Grid and Snap Settings dialog is for Standard Snap options. To access snap options for NURBS objects, pick on the Standard field, and choose NURBS from the list.

If you have several Snap options checked, but find that you need a different Snap option for one pick, you can right-click in any viewport to call up the Snap Overrides menu. Choose the option you want to use for that one pick from the menu, make the pick, and the Snap options return to the original selection.

It is usually more predictable to work in a User or Perspective viewport with the 3D Snap option set. Working in 2D or 2.5D always forces the pick onto the active current grid plane.

T IP

If you want the snaps to respect the Restrict to Axis settings, you must right-click the Snap icon, pick the Options tab, and check the Use Axis Constraints checkbox shown in Figure 2.22.

FIGURE 2.22
Use Axis Constraints checkbox.

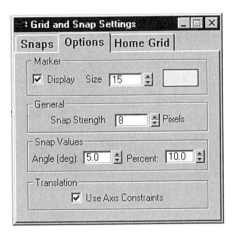

Grid Helpers

In the Create/Helpers panel, you will find the Grid Helpers button. Grid Helper creates a new working Grid plane. You can then align the Grid to any surface with Normal Align, activate it by right-clicking the Grid, and, using the Grid Reference Coordinate System, you can create all new objects on that work plane.

To put a skylight on a roof, for example, you would create the Grid, align it to the surface of the roof, switch to Grid Reference Coordinate system, and create a box. The Grid object can be named and deactivated or reactivated at any time by right-clicking it and choosing appropriately from the menu. You can create an unlimited number of Grid objects in your scene.

TIP

You could create a file with predetermined Grid planes and Merge those into a new file if you have repetitive applications.

NEW TO R2

Using Normal Align to align Grids with curved surfaces now aligns with the mathematical interpolated curved surface. 3D Studio MAX R1.2 aligned with the actual selected face plane, makes the aligned object appear to sink into the curved surface.

Tape and Protractor Helpers

Like Grid Helpers, Tape and Protractor Helpers are also found in the Create/Helper panel.

You can use Tape Helpers to measure a distance between two points and display the X,Y,Z delta distances and X,Y,Z angles. You can have as many Tapes as you like and each can be named. Tapes are easiest to use in User or Perspective viewports in conjunction with Snaps.

The Protractor Helper can be placed in the scene then aligned with an object. In the Protractor panel, you then click the Pick Object 1 button, select an object, click the Pick Object 2 button, and select another object. The angle is measured as the included angle between the pivot of Object 1 and the pivot of Object 2 with the Protractor at the apex. Moving the Protractor in the scene changes the measured angle.

TIP

A real-world application might be to place two dummy objects in a scene and link the camera to a Protractor to read out the Field of View angle between the dummies. This could be useful in health care or theater applications.

Sections

In the Create/Shapes panel, you will find a Section button. Clicking Section enables you to click and drag a plane similar to a Grid, but this plane takes a section through any object in the plane by default, shown by a bright yellow shape. This command is greatly improved from the original Section in 3D Studio VIZ. You can now:

- Create a 2D shape of the section with the Create Shape button.

- Define the section area to infinity or only objects within or touching the Section plane.

- Update the section automatically as you move the Section plane or update manually.

T IP

You can build complex mesh objects in 3D Studio MAX, create sections, and export the sections to a CAD package for dimensioning.

Try applying some of the tools and methods mentioned in this chapter to add doors, windows, and details to customize the STATION12.MAX model. Don't be concerned about the design of the station, but use it as a test bed to familiarize yourself with all the options available. Once you are comfortable with the tools, they will become second nature during those high-production projects.

In Practice: Architectural Modeling

Architectural models tend to be large, that is, contain a high number of faces and vertices. It is imperative that you develop good modeling habits to minimize the complexity of your models.

- Try to avoid becoming obsessive about a high degree of accuracy. 3D Studio MAX R2 is not a CAD program but a visualization tool. Learn the methods of working as accurately as possible—Units Setup, Grid Snap Settings, Snaps, for example—but keep in mind that when objects are seen in perspective size is relative to distance and camera angle.

- Use "simulated" geometry when possible. Instead of creating a 3D chain link fence with all its faces and vertices, see if you can get away with an Opacity map material on a flat plane. Use Bump maps and Opacity maps to create the illusion of 3D geometry when none exists.

- Design your models with efficient presentations in mind. Don't model parts of the building that will never be seen in the final rendering. Don't model details that are too small to show at the final rendered resolution. Instead of long, boring walkthrough animations, try to design a presentation that will be snappy and contain the highlights of the information you are conveying to the client.

Chapter 3

INDUSTRIAL AND MECHANICAL DESIGN MODELING

Many mechanical designers and engineers buy MAX R2 for its powerful Materials Editor, lighting features, and animation tools. However, they plan to do all the modeling in a CAD program and import the finished 3D models into MAX 2. In this chapter, you will discover some of the reasons why you may want to rethink that strategy. As you perform the chapter's exercises, you will easily create objects that are often very difficult to construct in a CAD program. If you like, you can export these MAX R2 objects to your CAD software later.

Remember, most objects can be created in more than one way—extruding, lofting, or lathing—or with more than one program. The more exposure you have to all modeling options, the easier it is to use the right tool for the right job. Some of the issues the chapter will consider are:

- Transferring between MAX R2 and CAD software

- Balancing detail and efficiency

- Creating a threaded bolt

- Providing a flexible connection between two objects

- Lathing and lofting

- Building superstructures with Lattice

- Using NURBS as a smooth surfacing tool

File Transfer Between MAX and CAD Software

No matter where you start the creative process, chances are your models will end up being transferred between MAX R2 and a CAD program at some point. To find the most efficient flow for your project, carefully analyze the reasons you are using each program and some of the pitfalls of object transfer. You will probably have to make compromises to work efficiently, because CAD software for engineering and visualization programs, such as MAX, still suffer from imperfect communication. Information is always lost in the transfer. For example:

- Parametric or Solid CAD objects become "dumb" mesh in MAX 2.

- Parametric MAX R2 objects become surface polygon mesh in CAD.

- MAX R2 NURBS objects become surface polygons in CAD.

- MAX R2 material assignments are lost in some CAD formats.

Starting With CAD Models

Importing 3D models from CAD is an option that all of you should consider. In many cases, it will be the main method of creating your models. A few advantages of using CAD models are:

- They are highly accurate.

- The same models can be used for both visualization and working drawings.

- Complex Boolean operations are possible.

- Compound filleting/blending is possible.

- Often more experienced CAD operators are available.

Some disadvantages of using CAD models are:

- They can create overly dense meshes.

- CAD creates flipped face normals/missing faces.

- CAD operations can create long, thin faces that can cause shadow casting and materials problems.

- Imported objects have no parametric editing capability.

TIP

Many companies have years of 2D CAD information or drawings in the archives that can be used as a basis for many 3D models. The user should process the CAD drawing to remove irrelevant items, such as dimensions and text. Keep only the shapes that comprise the top, side, and end profiles, which 3D Studio MAX can use with Create/Loft and the Deform Fit option to create the model.

Practice File Exchanges

Meet with your CAD department managers and drafters to exchange a few small typical files or portions of files before you start your first project to get a feel for the problems that may arise with each import/export option. MAX R2 can import the following types of files:

- **3DS Mesh (*.3DS, *.PRJ)** Imported and exported by AutoCAD and 3D Studio R3&4. Objects created with plug-ins may not be included in the file specification and will not translate.

- **3DS Shape (*.SHP)** Native 3D Studio R3&4 2D format. No 3D information translated in the file type.

- **AutoCAD (*.DWG)** Excellent 2D and 3D import format for AutoCAD users. Intelligent transfer of block to group information and layer name to object name. Adds modifiers for editing.

TIP

Kinetix is constantly updating and improving the AutoCAD to MAX R2 import/export translators. Check www.ktx.com often to obtain the latest revisions.

- **AutoCAD (*.DXF)** Common generic file format for 2D spline and 3D mesh objects only.

- **Adobe Illustrator (*.AI)** 2D vector file transport from CorelDraw, Adobe Illustrator, and Photoshop, for example. CorelDraw can trace bitmaps and convert to 2D vector .AI files. These traced .AI files are very useful for building logo mesh from images.

- **Stereolithography (*.STL)** Common 3D mesh transfer format for rapid prototyping equipment and is available on many workstation CAD programs.

MAX R2 can export:

- **3DS Mesh (*.3DS, *.PRJ)**

- **AutoCAD (*.DXF)**

- **AutoCAD (*.DWG)**

- **Stereolithography (*.STL)**

- **ASCII Scene Export (*.ASE)** Used by many game developers to transfer to rendering engines.

- **VRML 2.0 (*.WRL)** Used for web animation and real-time effects.

Investigating file transfer methods in and out of MAX R2 should be done early in the scene creation process. Each method of transfer will come with some surprises that can slow production. Start with small files or break larger transfers into smaller parts to insure better results. Also, make sure you are only transferring relevant information, not text and dimensions, for example.

Balance Detail and Efficiency

No one likes to do unnecessary work or produce inappropriate results. Before beginning any project, the 3D design team, the client, and the firm's financial department should brainstorm a bit to put the project in perspective. You may find the best solution is to "fake it," such as creating the illusion of geometry with mapping where none exists.

Clarify the Model's Purpose

When you get your assignment, don't fire up your software immediately. First, reflect on why the project requires animation or rendering. Some of the most likely reasons are:

- Clarification of a concept or process

- Design study

- Ergonometric study

- Education or training

- Marketing

- In-house presentation

The modeling criteria for each of these presentations can vary widely. For example, models used in a concept clarification need not be as detailed and accurate as those used for a design study for mating parts, or an educational presentation on how to pack equipment in a tight space. Models for marketing purposes may not need a great deal of modeling details but will require more impressive materials and lighting. Alternately, models for training or in-house presentations may be more effective using false color material, such as bold primary colors to visually separate parts from one another.

Other issues that must be carefully considered by the client, the production staff, and the financial managers should also carefully answer the following questions before you begin work:

- What end purpose will the animation or images serve?

- Who is the target audience?

- What is the focus of the presentation?

- How much detail is enough?

- What is the most cost-effective method to accomplish the task?

To work cost effectively you must be able to quickly determine what is the minimum detail you can live with for a particular project. A project may entail more than one scene with several versions of the same object at different degrees of accuracy and details for viewing at a distance or close-up. If you are looking at a detail of a mechanical assembly, for example, it will usually be more efficient to work with a model with only the important parts, not the whole complex assembly mesh. Bolt and screw threads should not be included in the model if only the heads are visible in the scene. As a matter of fact, even the bolt holes in the part add unnecessary faces and vertices.

Don't Model, Simulate Geometry

One feature that may tip the scales to working in 3D Studio MAX instead of a CAD program is MAX's use of simulated geometry. In many cases, you can create the illusion of more complex objects from very simple meshes by using MAX's:

- Bump mapping

- Opacity mapping

- Wireframe materials

Bump and Opacity mapping and material types use mathematical algorithms based on the brightness or luminance values in 2D bitmaps to give the illusion of invisible or raised surfaces without adding to the physical complexity of the mesh. The Wireframe option in the Materials Editor uses the visible edges of the mesh object to simulate wire with varying width. The advantage of using these mapping types is that you keep a low vertex and face count while making the objects appear complex at render time. (Materials will be covered in more depth in Part II, "Designing Convincing Materials.") Figures 3.1, 3.2, and 3.3 illustrate some simple mesh objects using materials to simulate geometry.

FIGURE 3.1

Bump mapped flexible light on a leather table.

FIGURE 3.2
Antique pewter candle sconce on a wood table.

FIGURE 3.3
Wire baskets with eggs on a wood table.

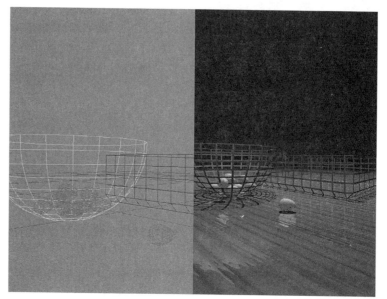

Put Theory into Practice: The Exercises

The best way to understand the benefits MAX brings to the industrial and mechanical modeling process is to see the program in action. In the exercises that follow, you'll learn how to solve some common design problems, such as creating a threaded object, making a flexible connection between a stationary and a moving object, and building a bridge and its roadbed. Along the way, you'll explore such MAX features as lofting, the Bevel Profile modifier, Linked Xform modifiers, lathing, and the Lattice modifier.

Create a Threaded Bolt

Using a combination of MAX's lofting and powerful new Bevel Profile modifier, you can easily create a reasonable accurate threaded object. In Exercise 3.1, you will bring these tools to bear on a typical threaded bolt. The example is simple, but the basic concepts introduced may be expanded to create a more accurate bolt with varying features. For example, you may want to use a shape other than a triangle for the thread profile or the bolt may have a different head style. The body and thread could also be tapered to create a wood or metal screw.

Tip

Keep in mind that if you are designing a part held together by bolts, you would not want to use a bolt with this much complexity. The example bolt is made up of separate objects and the head may be used on an object without the body and the threads, greatly reducing the number of faces and vertices in your scene and speeding the render time. Even the bolt holes in the part are more detail than is necessary.

I once heard of a company that imported a CAD model for a deep dive submarine that had every bolt and screw to the smallest detail. It took a day to import the mesh into 3D Studio MAX and they never could get it to render the mesh object with just default materials and lighting. Within two days, they recreated the submarine in 3D Studio MAX and it not only looked better, but it rendered in minutes.

EXERCISE 3.1.1: CREATING A BOLT

1. Open the file called \CH3_B_OR.MAX on the CD-ROM. Your screen should appear similar to Figure 3.4. The file contains several 2D Shapes: a helix and triangle for the thread, a line and a circle for the body, and a hex and two circles for the head of the bolt. The scene units are set to Decimal Inches with a Grid Snap of 0.1 and Major Lines every 10 Grid lines.

TIP

In Chapter 2, you set Units and Grid and Snap settings and saved the file as MAXSTART.MAX. If your work is primarily mechanical or industrial design, you would want to create a new or overwrite an existing MAXSTART.MAX with the new decimal settings.

FIGURE 3.4

Open

CH3_B_OR.MAX.

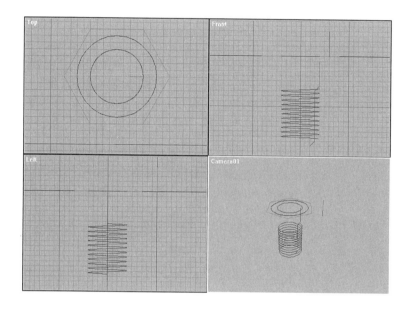

2. You will use a new MAX R2 modifier called Bevel Profile to create the body of the bolt. Bevel Profile requires two 2D Shapes, a side profile shape, and a cross-section shape. Press H on the keyboard, and select bolt_shaft_circle from the list.

3. In the Modify panel, click More and choose the Bevel Profile modifier from the list. The 2D circle becomes a 2D mesh object that is shaded in the Camera viewport.

4. In the Parameters rollout, click Pick Profile and pick the bolt_shaft_bevel_profile shape either in a viewport or by pressing H and selecting from the list. Name the object SHAFT.

NOTE

The circle is extruded with a side profile matching the profile shape. The exercise's file is set up so that the first vertex of the profile and the first vertex on the cross-section are in the correct position. This is accomplished by converting a shape to an Editable Spline and working at the vertex Sub-Object level. The newly created object may also be adjusted by entering Sub-Object Gizmo and transforming the Gizmo.

TIP

The 2D Shapes could have been imported from a CAD program for added accuracy. Importing the 2D information and creating the 3D object in MAX R2 offers both control and efficiency.

In the next section of Exercise 3.1, you create the threads as a separate mesh around the lower bolt body.

EXERCISE 3.1.2: CREATING THE THREADS

1. The bolt threads are created by lofting a triangle along a helical path with a diameter equal to the bolt shaft and a height from the shoulder of the shaft to the chamfer. Select the helix called thread_path.

2. In the Create panel, click Standard Primitives/Loft Object/Loft/Get Shape, and pick the thread_profile 2D Shape. Name the object THREAD.

NOTE

The triangle has its pivot point aligned to the outside apex so it attaches itself to the path at that point.

3. In the Camera viewport, zoom closer to the objects and notice the thread has an odd twist to it similar to the one in Figure 3.5.

TIP

You may see part or all of the scene disappear if you zoom too close. Unhide the Camera01. In the Modify panel, set Clip Manually to On, type 0.1" in the Near Clip field, and type 10" in the Far Clip. Anything outside this range as measured from Camera01.Target will be clipped. Clipping can be used to hide unwanted objects in the scene. Red squares with diagonal lines show the planes in the viewports.

4. In the Modify panel with THREAD selected, rollout the Skin Parameters menu, and check Optimize to reduce vertices from 4770 to 795 and faces from 9536 to 1586. Uncheck Banking to keep the threads from twisting.

FIGURE 3.5

Thread before turning Banking off.

5. Right-click in any blank space on the Modify panel, and choose Deformations from the list of rollouts.

6. Click Scale in the Deformations rollout to launch its dialog. Click the Make Symmetrical icon in the upper-left area of the dialog box to turn it off.

7. Click the Insert Corner Point icon, and click twice on the red scale line near either end.

8. Click the left most black scale point, and, in the text fields at the bottom of the Scale Deformation dialog, enter 0 in the left field and 70 in the right field.

9. Click the next scale point, and enter 8 in the left field and 100 in the right field.

10. Click the third scale point, and enter 92 in the left and 100 in the right field.

11. Click the rightmost scale point, and enter 100 in the left and 70 in the right field. Close the Scale Deformation dialog box. Steps 5 to 11 scaled the thread down in the X-axis at each end to eliminate the abrupt lofted ends. The Scale Grid should appear similar to the one in Figure 3.6.

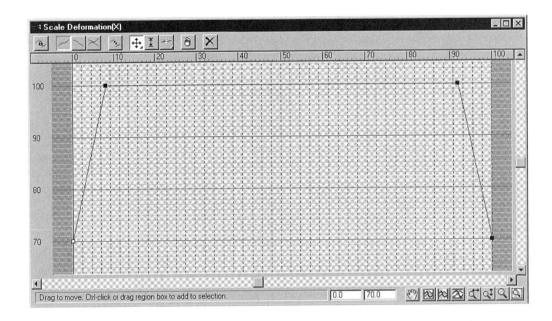

FIGURE 3.6

Thread Scale Deformation Grid.

TIP

You can see the result of the Scale Deformation better if you hide all objects except the thread and use Arc-Rotate in a Perspective viewport. You can also right-click a scale point and adjust the tangency for a smoother transition.

Now that the bolt body and threads are complete, you will add a hex head to the bolt.

EXERCISE 3.1.3: CREATING THE BOLT HEAD

1. Press H, and select head_circle from the list.

2. In the Create panel, click Standard Primitives/Loft Object/Loft/Get Path and pick the head_path shape.

NOTE

Remember, the Get Path option that you are using leaves the cross-section shape in place and uses an instance of the path to loft the object.

3. In the Modify panel/Skin Parameters rollout, set Path Steps to 0. Click Yes in the Warning dialog.

4. In the Path Parameters rollout, check Path Steps and enter 1 in the Path field to move up the path to the next vertex.

5. Click Get Shape, and pick head_hex.

6. Enter 2 in the Path field.

7. Click Get Shape, and pick head_hex again.

8. Enter 3 in the Path field.

9. Click Get Shape, press H, and choose head_circle from the list. Name the object HEAD.

10. In the Surface Parameters rollout, uncheck Smooth Length. The bolt should now look similar to the one in Figure 3.7.

FIGURE 3.7
Completed 3D bolt with threads.

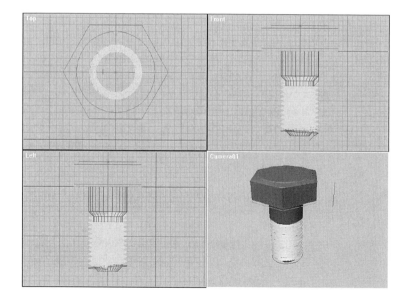

11. Hide all shapes. Select all mesh objects and, in the pull-down menu, use Group/Group to form a unit called Bolt that can be manipulated in your MAX scene as a single object.

12. Use File/Save As to save the file to disk with the name BOLT01.MAX

You can apply variations on the combination of lofting and Bevel Profile modifier techniques used in the Exercise 3.1 series for other shaft objects— Archimedes screws and augers, jig and fixture pins, open ended sleeves (a compound rectangle or circle with Bevel Profile), to name a few.

The bolt shaft could also have been created with the Lathe modifier or by using the Scale Deformation with a lofted bolt_circle. Try using either of those methods for different results and levels of accuracy.

Use your imagination and experiment, the more tools you have at hand the quicker the job will go. For further inspiration, view the file called BOLT.AVI on the CD-ROM for an animated bolt similar to the one just created.

Provide a Flexible Connection Between Two Objects

Sometimes the simplest looking element is the most challenging to model. To prove this point, you'll add a flexible hose to an existing scene, connecting a vacuum cleaner body to its handle and cleaning head assembly. The key is creating the hose so that it remains connected at each end and so that the connections stay flush to the surfaces when you animate the object. An extra control point is added in the middle of the hose to allow more realistic movement. This approach could be used for any type of flexible connection between two rigid bodies. Hydraulic hoses, electrical cabling, or the disc between two vertebra in a medical animation are just a couple of examples.

EXERCISE 3.2.1: CREATING A FLEXIBLE HOSE

1. Open the file called \CH3_F_OR.MAX on the CD-ROM. It should appear similar to Figure 3.8. The file has Units set to Decimal Inches and a Grid Snap of 1″. In the file are: a vacuum cleaner body, a handle, and a cleaning head.

FIGURE 3.8

Open
\CH3_F_OR.MAX.

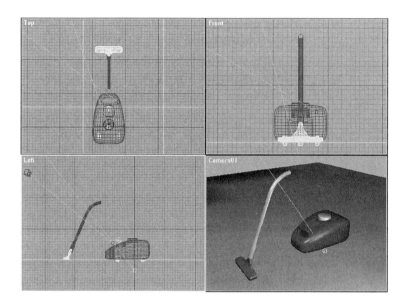

2. Press H for the Select By Name dialog, and check the Display Subtree checkbox at the bottom to see that the WHEELS and HOSE_ATTACH objects are linked to the BODY and the HANDLE is linked to the HEAD.

3. In the Left viewport, press W to fill the display with the viewport.

4. In the Create/Helper panel, click Dummy and click and drag just to the right of the top of the HANDLE to create a small Dummy. Name the Dummy Handle01.

5. From the toolbar, click the Align icon. Align the Dummy to the HANDLE. Set Current Object to Center and Target Object to Center; check the Z Position.

6. Click the Apply button, then choose Center for Current Object and Maximum for Target Object. Check the X Position, and click OK. Handle01 should be centered on the end of the HANDLE.

7. Click the Move icon and the Restrict to X icon. Shift-click on Handle01 and clone copy the dummy about four inches to the right. Accept Handle02 as the name.

8. In the Left viewport, create a Dummy called Attach01 and center it at the top of HOSE_ATTACH.

9. Click the Move icon and the Restrict to Y icon. Shift-click on Attach01, and clone copy the dummy about four inches up in the positive Y direction. Accept Attach02 as the name.

10. Create a Dummy called Hose_mid above and to the right of the existing Dummies. Use File/Save As to save to a file called VACUUM01.MAX. Press W to view all viewports. The scene should look similar to Figure 3.9.

NOTE

Throughout these exercises you should save to a new file often. Also, if you are performing steps you are unsure of, use Fetch and Hold in the Edit pull-down menu.

FIGURE 3.9
Vacuum and Handle with five new Dummy objects.

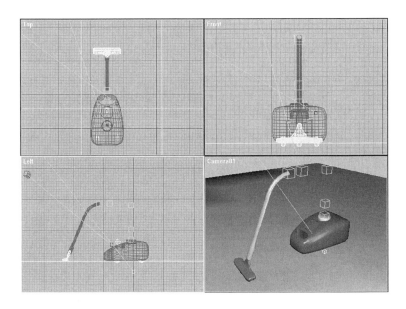

11. Click, then right-click the 3D Snap icon, and set Snap to Pivot Mode Only. You are about to create a line to use as a lofting path for the vacuum hose, and this enables you to snap the line from dummy pivot to dummy pivot. This assures a vertex at the center of the dummy so any subsequent scaling of the dummy is centered at the vertex. Close the Grid and Snap Settings dialog.

12. From the Create/Shapes/Line panel, click to create a line from the pivot of Handle01 to Handle02 to Hose_Mid to Attach02 to Attach01. Name the Object hose_path. Click the 3D Snap icon to turn it off. The display should appear similar to Figure 3.10.

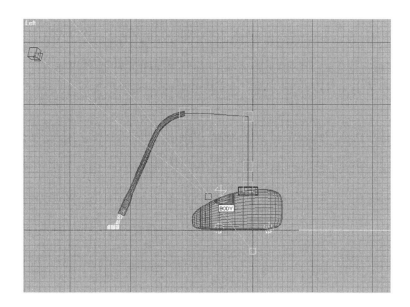

13. In the Modify panel, with hose_path selected, click Sub-Object vertex mode.

14. Pick the path vertex inside Hose_mid dummy. Right-click the vertex and choose Smooth. Right-click again, and choose Bezier. The vertex at Hose_mid should now have green Bezier handles. Click Sub-Object to exit vertex mode.

T IP _____

When you later use Linked Xform, the curvature at this vertex can be adjusted by scaling the Hose_mid dummy.

15. From the toolbar, click Select and Link icon.

16. Pick Handle02, and drag to Handle01; pick Handle01, and drag to HANDLE.

17. Repeat the process, linking Attach02 to Attach01 and Attach01 to HOSE_ATTACH.

18. Press H, check Subtree. The Select Objects dialog should look similar to Figure 3.11.

FIGURE 3.11

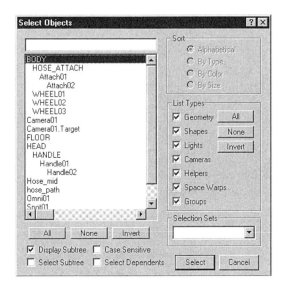

NOTE

You will not link Hose_mid to other dummies as it will be animated by hand later for more "action."

19. Use File/Save As to save the file as VACUUM02.MAX.

In the next segment of the exercise you link the vertices of the path to the dummy objects. The dummies will essentially be large handles to hold the vertices in place and to give you easy editing capability at the middle of the hose.

EXERCISE 3.2.2: LINKING THE PATH VERTICES TO THE DUMMIES

1. You will now use Linked Xform modifier to link each vertex in hose_path to the Dummy around it. In the Left viewport, select hose_path. In the Modify panel, click the Sub-Object button.

2. Select the vertex on the path at the top of HANDLE.

3. In the Modify panel, click More and choose Linked Xform from the list of modifiers.

4. In the Parameters rollout, click Pick Control Object and pick the Handle01 dummy around the vertex.

T IP

While vertices can be directly animated in MAX R2, they cannot be hierarchically linked to each other. Adding a Linked Xform allows the hierarchy and also offers a larger named object to serve as a handle for animating.

5. In the Modify panel, click Spline Select, select the next vertex, apply a Linked Xform, and pick the Dummy as a control object.

6. Repeat Step 23 for each dummy/vertex pair along the hose_path.

7. Click Spline Select modifier again and exit Sub-Object mode. In the Modify panel, click the Edit Stack icon. Press W to view all viewports. The Edit Modifier Stack dialog should look like the one in Figure 3.12.

FIGURE 3.12

Edit Modifier Stack dialog for hose_path.

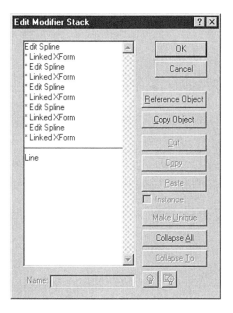

T IP

Adding the last SplineSelect modifier and exiting Sub-Object mode clears the selection set and cleans up the display for less confusion.

8. In the Top viewport, choose Create/Shape/Circle to click and drag a circle, then enter 0.75″ in the Radius field of the Parameters rollout. Name the object hose_prof.

9. In the Left viewport, select hose_path.

10. In the Create/Geometry/Loft Object/Loft panel, click Get Shape and pick the hose_prof object. Name the new object HOSE.

N OTE

If your hose appears made of straight segments the Path Steps could still be 0 from the last exercise. Open the Skin Parameters rollout and set Path Steps to 5 to insure a curved hose.

The hose is complete but needs a convincing material to give the illusion of a real ribbed-plastic hose. In the next segment of the exercise, you apply an existing material and adjust its mapping.

EXERCISE 3.2.3: APPLYING MAPPING AND MATERIAL TO THE HOSE

1. Select the HOSE object in any viewport. In the Modifier panel/Surface Parameters rollout, check Apply Mapping and enter 75 in the Length Repeat field. Click the Skin checkbox in the Display Area of the Skin Parameters rollout to view the hose in all viewports.

2. In the Material Editor, click the sample slot with HOSE material. It should be slot 8 in a 6×4 slot layout. The material has a black and white gradient map type in the bump slot to create the illusion of a ribbed flexible hose. The 75 in the Length Repeat field in Step 1 keeps the ribs close together.

T IP

You can right-click any slot to change the number of sample slots visible.

3. Click and drag the HOSE material to the HOSE object in a shaded viewport. Close or minimize the Material Editor.

4. In the Display panel, choose Unhide By Name, choose head_path and click UNHIDE.

5. In the Top viewport, select the HEAD object.

6. In the Motion panel/Assign Controller rollout, click Position: Bezier Position and click the Assign Controller icon.

7. Double-click Path in the Assign Position Controller list, and click Pick Path in the Path Parameters rollout.

8. Pick head_path in the Top viewport.

9. Scrub the Frame Slider through the 100 frame animation. The cleaning head should move back and forth and the hose stays correctly attached to the handle.

10. Check the Follow checkbox in the Path Parameters rollout and the hose still stays attached although it will kink. The Perspective viewport at frame 0 should look similar to Figure 3.13.

FIGURE 3.13

Shaded Perspective viewport at Frame 0.

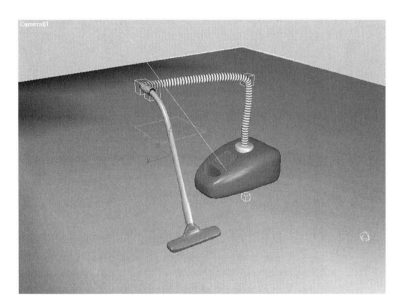

11. On your own, click the Animate button, step through a few frames, such as frames 15, 30, 45, 60, and 75, and Move, Rotate, and Scale the Hose_mid dummy object to keep it in a more realistic position in relation to the handle and vacuum.

12. Render the scene to an AVI file or view VACUUM.AVI included on the CD-ROM.

In Exercise 3.2, you produced a flexible hose object spanning one stationary object and one moving object. By applying a series of Dummy object attached with Linked Xform modifiers to vertices along the Hose loft path, you created a rigid contact with the Hose and Vacuum. This enabled you to animate the Head without keeping track of the attachment at either end of the Hose. You then were able to animate a Linked Xform Dummy at the middle of the Hose with the three transforms—Move, Rotate, and Scale—to keep the Hose from kinking.

This process can be applied to dust sleeves on robot arm joints, view camera bellows, hydraulic hoses, muscle and joint structures, and flexible lamps or medical probes to name a few.

The most important feature is the extra Linked Xform Dummy at each end. This Dummy keeps the flexible object fluFsh with the surface to which it is attached. Without the extra Dummy, the connection opens above and drops into the surface.

Two Routes to the Same Model: Lathing and Lofting

In Exercises 3.3 and 3.4, you will use two methods—lathing and lofting—to create a generic pump housing. The objects you will build are simple, but the concepts may be applied to any mechanical part that has its form derived from a lathed surface or lofted cross-sections.

T IP

Once you no longer need to edit complex objects, you should select the objects along with their 2D shapes and save the selections (File/Save Selected) to a new file on the hard drive. Then, collapse the modifiers and delete the 2D control shapes in the scene to minimize the overhead. If you find that you do need to edit the object again, edit the copy on the hard disk and use the File/Replace option to substitute the old object with the new one.

Creation by Lathing

In addition to lathing, the Exercise 3.3 series introduces the Tape Helper, MAX 2's new Protractor Helper, and the new Measure utility. You will also learn ways to use Align that were not possible in previous releases of MAX.

EXERCISE 3.3.1: LATHING A PUMP HOUSING

1. Open the file called CH3_P_OR.MAX from the CD-ROM. It contains five 2D shapes and has Units set to Decimal Inches with a Grid Snap of the default 10″. Your display should appear similar to the one in Figure 3.14.

FIGURE 3.14

Open CH3_P_OR.MAX from the CD-ROM.

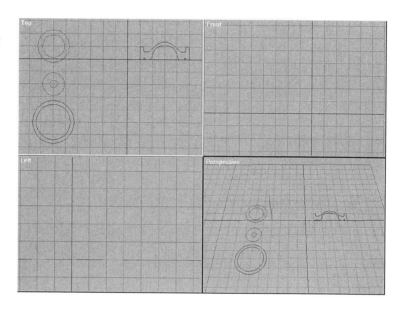

> **T**IP
>
> The next operation, lathing a 2D shape, is a basic process with which you should already be familiar. The more important part of this exercise is the new alignment capabilities in MAX 2, which give you more accurate control over modeling.

2. In the Top viewport, select the pump_hse_section 2D shape.

3. In the Top viewport, click the Restrict to X-axis icon, Shift-Move pump_hse_section to the right, and choose Reference from the Clone Options dialog. Name the new 2D object ph_ref.

4. Pan in the Top viewport to see both pump_hse_section and ph_ref.

NOTE

In Step 3, you chose the Reference option, because it has a one-way link to the original shape. You can modify the Reference without affecting the original, but modifying the original affects the Reference.

5. This 2D pump_hse_section came from a source unfamiliar to you, so you must determine its size before you lathe the 3D object. In the Top viewport, click Create/Geometry/Helpers/Tape, and click and drag a Tape object anywhere in the viewport.

NOTE

The first click sets the pyramid tape itself, and the drag and release sets the "dumb" cube end of the tape.

6. In the Top viewport, with the pyramid tape end selected, click the Align icon, then click the ph_ref object.

TIP

NEW TO R2

MAX R2 allows you to use Gizmos with the Align commands.

7. In the Align Selection dialog, check X Position and Y Position, and set Current Object to Pivot Point and Target Object to Maximum. Click OK. The Tape should align with the upper-right bounding box of ph_ref as seen in Figure 3.15.

8. In the Top viewport, select the cube end of the tape named Tape01.Target. Click the Align icon, and pick ph_ref.

9. Check Y Position and set Current Object to Pivot Point and Target Object to Minimum. Click the OK button.

10. Click the Align icon again, pick the pyramid end of the Tape in the Top viewport, check X Position, and set Current Object to Pivot Point and Target Object to Pivot Point.

NOTE

Aligning Tape01.Target with the Tape01 object insures that the Tape is vertical in the viewport and is measuring a vertical distance between the highest point on the object (Y Position Maximum) to the lowest (Y Position Minimum).

FIGURE 3.15

Pyramid end of Tape aligned with upper-right bounding box of ph_ref.

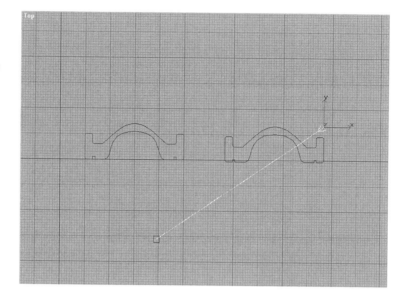

11. Click on Tape01 and, in the Modify panel, note that the height of ph_ref is 14.0″. You will need that number later. Your screen should look similar to Figure 3.16.

FIGURE 3.16

Tape measure aligned to determine height of ph_ref object.

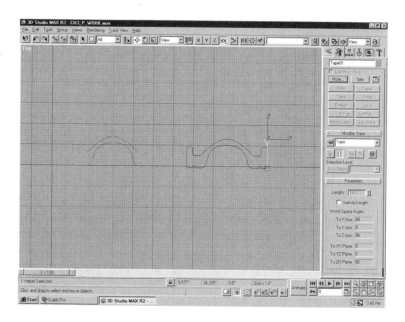

TIP

Take the time to familiarize yourself with the World Space Angles that can be determined with the Tape Helper in MAX 2. The information can be very useful to determine accurate distances and angles in a 3D model.

WARNING

When you are placing a Tape Helper or any object with 3D Snap on, check the result in two or three viewports to insure you haven't forced the object through 3D space resulting in a false reading or a misplaced object.

12. In the Top viewport, select Tape01.Target. Click and right-click the Select and Move icon, and enter -2.0″ in the Y field of the Offset:Screen column. Tape01.Target moves down 2″. Save this file with the name PUMP01.MAX

NOTE

You will use this Tape as a guide to lathe a part that is 16″ (14+2) in overall radius. The size of the part itself has no significance in this exercise.

TIP

After creating a Tape Helper, it would be helpful to click the Push Pin icon to the left of the Tape name in the Modify panel. The Push Pin locks the current modifier display. You could then pick the target end of the tape in the current viewport and still read the updated information in the Tape Parameters rollout. Remember to unpin by clicking the push pin icon after you are finished.

You have used the Tape Helper to determine the size of the 2D shape and to locate an axis of revolution. In the next segment you will lathe the 3D object. You'll use Align to move the lathe axis to the Tape target for accuracy.

EXERCISE 3.3.2: LATHING THE SHAPE

1. In the Top viewport, select the ph_ref object.

2. In the Modify panel, click Lathe. You will observe the object lathing about the Y-axis of the viewport.

TIP

A big advantage of creating parts with the Lathe modifier is the option in the Parameters roll-out to set the number of degrees of lathing. For example, enter 270 in the Degrees field, and the part will have 90 degrees cut out for sectional viewing. You have to rotate your view or the part in this exercise to see the section. By using a Multi/Sub-object material, you could have the sectional face a contrasting material or color.

MAXR2 now allows lathed objects to be output as mesh, path, or NURBS objects.

3. In the Parameters rollout, click the X button in the Direction area. The object lathes about the X-axis but is also lathing about its own geometric mid-point.

4. In the Modify panel, click Sub-object to enter Axis mode.

5. Click the Align icon, check Y Position, and check Pivot Point in the Target Object column. Click OK. In the Parameters rollout, click Sub-Object to exit Axis mode. Name the object PUMP01. Save the file with the name PUMP02.MAX. The display should look similar to Figure 3.17.

FIGURE 3.17

Lathed PUMP01 at 16" overall radius with original 2D shape.

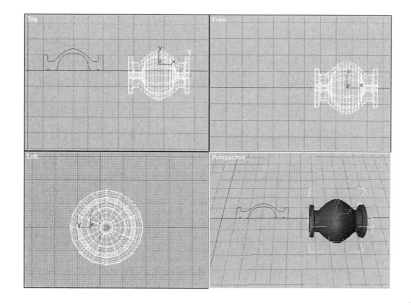

NOTE

The Current Object column is grayed out because there are no alignment choices for the Lathe Axis as it has no dimensions.

In the Exercise 3.3 set, you used the Lathe modifier on a Reference Clone to create a pump housing. During the process, you experimented with a MAX R2 Tape Helper to set the axis of the lathe and learned that the Tape Helper contains more information about angles than it did in previous releases of Max. You also learned that MAX R2 has a new feature to align Gizmos, which enables much higher accuracy when building off existing geometry.

Creation by Lofting

Sometimes you want the security of always being able to edit your original shape. Lofting gives you that security; the advantage of lofting a cross-section on a path is the ability to use Reference Clones of the original shape for ease in editing. The disadvantage is the difficulty of controlling the exact surface form due to interpolation between the shapes. In the next exercise, you'll practice lofting several cross-section shapes along a straight path to build another pump housing. In real life, the creation method you choose is influenced by the information you have to build from and the type of editing you may have to do in the future. Remember to save your work to a new file on the hard drive often.

EXERCISE 3.4.1: LOFTING A PUMP HOUSING

1. From the Tools pull-down menu, use Display Floater to hide Exercise 3.3's PUMP01 and pump_hse_section. You can also hide or delete the Tape01. Click the Zoom Extents All icon. The display should appear similar Figure 3.18.

2. Select the pump_hse_path shape, and, in Modify panel, click the Sub-Object button. The vertices are located at the following distances along the path:

    - 0″ (start of path)
    - 3″
    - 7″
    - 20″
    - 33″
    - 37″
    - 40″ (end of path)

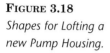

FIGURE 3.18

Shapes for Lofting a new Pump Housing.

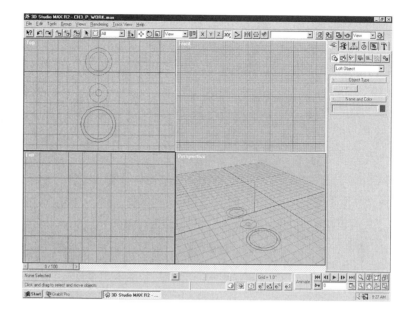

TIP

You will notice there are several vertices along the path. These are points where new cross-section shapes are imported to form the major transitions. While it is possible to import shapes onto a path that has only end vertices, you have much more control with a vertex at each transition.

3. Click Sub-Object to exit Sub-Object mode.

4. In the Create/Geometry/Loft Object/Loft panel, click Get Shape, then press H and choose flange from the list. A straight tube is lofted. Name this object PUMP02.

5. In Path Parameters rollout from the Modify panel, check the Distance option and enter 3″ in the Path field. Press Enter. You will notice a yellow tick move 3″ along the path in any viewport.

6. Click the Get Shape button if it is not already on, press H, and choose flange again. You will notice no change to PUMP02 because the two shapes on the path are exactly the same.

7. Enter 3.01″ in the Path field. Press Enter.

NOTE

The very slight movement along the path for the next shape is because you cannot have two shapes on the same path step.

8. Click Get Shape, press H, and choose body_neck from the list. The flange appears at the top of the tube and should look similar to the one in Figure 3.19.

FIGURE 3.19

Tube with flange.

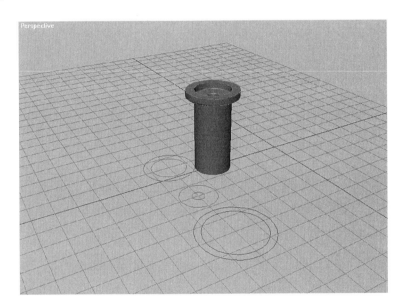

9. In the Modify panel, enter 7″ in the Path field, click the Select icon, click Get Shape, and choose body_neck again. Note that the default option for Get Shape is Instance. This will allow editing later so accept it throughout the exercise.

10. In the Modify panel, enter 20″ in the Path field, click the Select icon, click Get Shape, and choose body_mid.

11. In the Modify panel, enter 33″ in the Path field, click the Select icon, click Get Shape, and choose body_neck.

12. In the Modify panel, enter 36.99″ in the Path field, click the Select icon, click Get Shape, and choose body_neck again.

13. In the Modify panel, enter 37″ in the Path field, click the Select icon, click Get Shape, and choose flange.

14. In the Modify panel, enter 40″ in the Path field, click the Select icon, click Get Shape, and choose flange again. Save the file with the name PUMP03.MAX. You should now have a lofted pump housing that appears similar to Figure 3.20.

FIGURE 3.20

Lofted Pump Housing.

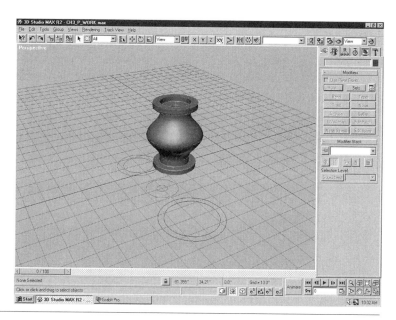

Now that you have created a lofted pump housing, you can edit it by cloning shapes on the path or manipulating the original loft cross-sections.

EXERCISE 3.4.2: EDITING THE PUMP HOUSING

1. Now, try various methods of editing a lofted object. In the Perspective viewport, select PUMP02.

2. In the Modify panel, click Sub-Object to enter Shape mode, and pick the shape on PUMP02 at the middle of the body. The shape turns red, and you should see 20″ in the Path field. It may be easier to select the shape if you right-click the Perspective label and choose Wireframe from the menu.

3. In the Path Level field, enter 15″. The active shape moves up the path to the 15″ level.

4. Press Shift, and set the Path Level spinner to about 25″. Click OK for an Instance in the Copy Shape dialog.

5. Enter 25″ in the Path Level field to place the shape exactly at 25″ along the path.

TIP

Editing and cloning the shape position along the path allows quick changes in the look of the object. If you exit Sub-Object mode and, at any path level, choose Get Shape, you can add new shape or replace existing shapes at any time.

6. Click Sub-Object to exit Sub-Object mode.

7. Press H and choose flange from the list.

8. In the Modify panel, click Sub-Object and choose Spline from the list. Pick the outer spline on the flange compound shape. The outer circle should turn red.

9. Click and hold on the Select and Uniform Scale icon, and choose the Non-Uniform Scale rollout.

10. Right-click Non-Uniform Scale icon, and enter 200 in the X and Y fields of the Offset: World column.

NOTE

When you enter first 200 in the X field the flanges on PUMP02 become elliptical and the field reverts back to 100. That means that the spline is scaled 200 percent of its original size and is now 100 percent of its new size. When you enter 200 in the Y field, the pump housing becomes circular again and all Offset fields read 100. The Absolute fields will reflect the total change in scale. These edit steps can also be animated!

11. Close the Scale dialog, and click Sub-Object to exit the mode.

12. In the Utility panel, click Measure and select the PUMP02 in any viewport. This new MAXR2 utility offers the following information and capabilities:

- Area and Volume calculations

- Center of Mass location

- Ability to create a point at Center of Mass

- Length (if the selected object is a 2D shape)

- Outside dimensions

- Ability to create a display Floater with the information for comparison with other objects in the scene

Save the file named PUMP04.MAX. The new PUMP02 and the Measure utility panel should appear similar to Figure 3.21.

FIGURE 3.21

Edit Pump Housing and Measure utility panel.

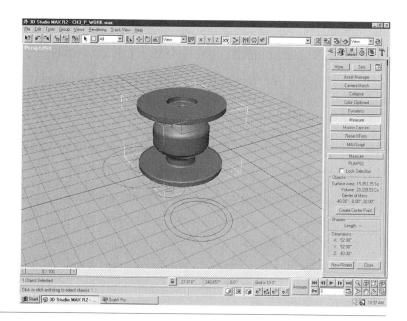

TIP

If you need a cut-away view of a lofted part and find that a Boolean operation is not reliable, you could:

1. Create/Shape/Section to draw a section plane.

2. Align the section plane to the center of the lofted part.

3. In Modify panel/Section Parameters rollout, click Create Shape.

4. Cut the newly created section in half (Trim/Extend modifier) and lathe the shape less than 360 degrees for the cut-away.

In Exercise 3.4, you used lofting to create a pump housing similar to Exercise 3.3's PUMP01. The methods of editing a lofted object were presented along with editing an Instance clone of a shape on the path. You must evaluate both exercise's processes and choose one that is right for a particular project. Again, knowing the tools in MAXR2 enables you to make a choice that will enhance productivity.

You also learned about the new MAXR2 Measure utility to determine spatial information about a mesh object. Measure is also useful for determining the length of a 2D path used in lofting or animation.

Building Superstructures with Lattice

The Lattice modifier is one of the most useful new modifiers added to 3D Studio MAX R2. It turns any mesh object into a lattice of struts and junctions based on the visible edges in the mesh object. In Exercise 3.5, you will create a bridge superstructure and the bridge roadway out of simple lofted 2D shapes and quickly turn it into a detailed 3D structure. You will also edit the mesh at the Sub-Object/Edge level to adjust the visibility of edges. Any object that is built from rounded, triangular, or square members can be easily created with Lattice.

TIP

If the object you are creating with Lattice is viewed from a distance only, it may be much more efficient to use a material with the Wire option turned on. The Wire option uses the visible edges of the mesh to create the illusion of a lattice structure, but if you get close to the object, the illusion is not convincing. On some projects, you might use a distant Wire material object, and cut to a Lattice modified object for close-ups.

EXERCISE 3.5: BUILDING A BRIDGE WITH LATTICE MODIFIER

1. Open the file called CH3_L_OR.MAX on the CD-ROM. It contains three Shapes and has units set to Decimal Feet and Snap Spacing set to 1 foot.

2. Select the straight line shape named roadbed_path.

3. In the Create/Geometry/Loft Objects/Loft panel, click Get Shape and pick the bridge_prof rectangle. Name the new object ROADBED.

Tip

For this exercise, it is best to work in the Perspective viewport in Wireframe mode.

4. In the Skin Parameters rollout, check Display Skin. The lofted wireframe box has five segments along the path and five segments between each corner vertex.

5. In Skin Parameters rollout, enter 2 in the Shape Steps field and 2 in the Path Steps field to reduce the number of segments around the box.

6. Select the super_path 2D shape then choose Loft/Get Shape and pick the bridge_prof rectangle again. Name the object SUPERSTRUCT. The display should now be similar to Figure 3.22.

FIGURE 3.22

Lofted SUPERSTRUCT and ROADBED objects.

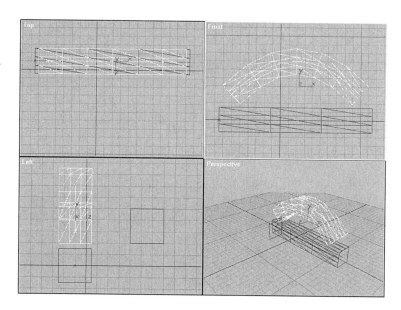

7. Select SUPERSTRUCT and in the Modify panel, access the Deformations rollout, and click Teeter.

8. In the Teeter Deformation (X) dialog, click Insert Corner Point and pick near each end of the red scale line. This add two new points for scaling. Click the Move Control Point icon in the dialog.

9. Pick the new Control point on the right, and enter 90 in the leftmost field at the bottom of the dialog.

10. Pick the new Control point on the left, and enter 10 in the leftmost field.

11. Click the yellow Make Symmetrical button to turn it off, and click the Display Y Axis icon. The Teeter line should be green.

12. Pick the left end Control point and enter 45 in the rightmost field at the bottom of the dialog. Pick the right end Control point and enter −45 for it. The display should look similar to Figure 3.23.

FIGURE 3.23

Y Axis Teeter Deformation grid.

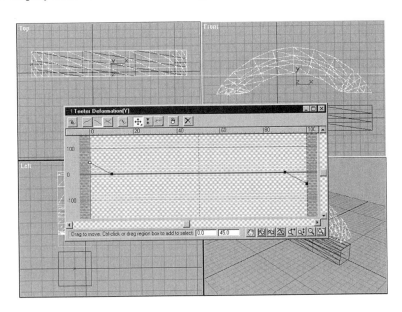

13. Close the Teeter Deformation dialog.

14. In the Front viewport, move ROADBED up in the Y-axis to touch the bottom of SUPERSTRUCT.

NOTE

Align will not work in this case because Minimum/Maximum values are calculated from the bounding box of the mesh before Teeter Deformations.

15. In the Modify panel, select ROADBED, click More, and choose the Lattice modifier from the list.

16. In the Parameters rollout, check Struts Only, set Radius to 1.0′ and set Sides to 4.

17. Select SUPERSTRUCT and apply a Lattice modifier with the same settings as above. Save a file named BRIDGE01.MAX. It should look similar to Figure 3.24.

FIGURE 3.24

Lattice modifier applied to SUPER-STRUCT and ROADBED.

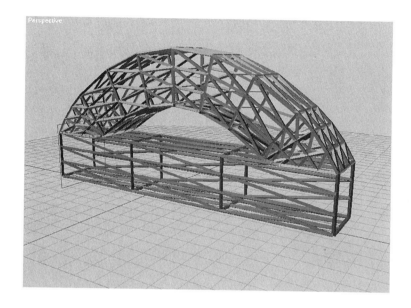

TIP

The Lattice modifier applies struts and junctions to the visible edges of faces in the mesh. By collapsing ROADBED and SUPERSTRUCT to Editable Mesh objects before applying Lattice, you can adjust the visibility, direction, and layout of visible edges to control the beam structure.

In this exercise you lofted simple shapes on simple paths and adjusted the segments with Path and Shape Steps. By modifying the SUPERSTRUCT with Teeter Deformations and adding a Lattice modifier to each object, you assembled a complex beam structure that would have been very difficult in previous versions of MAX. You can use Lattice for any wire or beam space frame and may have triangular, square, or round struts, with or without junctions at the joint of each beam set. Familiarizing yourself with the Sub-Object Edge editing options will enable you to create complex frameworks in a minimum of time.

TIP

A Lattice modifier applied to an open 2D shape will create a series of junctions at each shape step without any connection struts. On a closed 2D shape, Lattice creates struts and junctions. A edited circle with Lattice could be used to create a string of pearls, for example (see Figure 3.25).

FIGURE 3.25

String of Pearls made with Lattice junctions only.

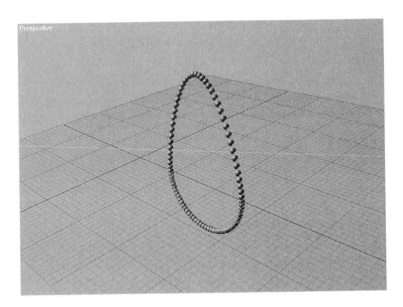

NEW TO R2

If you want the pearls to be evenly spaced on the string, you could:

1. Create a dummy.

2. Assign a path controller to the dummy.

3. Pick the string as a path.

4. Check MAX 2's new Constant Velocity checkbox.

5. In Motion panel/Trajectories, pick Convert To.

    Apply Lattice to the newly created spline.

NURBS as a Smooth Surfacing Tool

In Exercise 3.6, you will create a smooth NURBS surface from three splines and a background image. The splines in the example file were traced over a front image and a side image of a 1950's Citroen. To view two separate images in the background and switch easily between them, the images were renamed ctro0001.bmp and ctro0002.bmp. From the Views pull-down menu, Background Images was chosen and the name of the background file was entered as ctro*.bmp. In MAX this automatically creates an .ifl (Image File List) and enters it as a background animation.

In Time Configuration, the End Frame was set to 1 to create a two frame animation.

In Views/Background image, Animate Background was checked and Match Bitmap aspect was checked. Clicking the Next Frame and Previous Frame icons switch the background from a side photo to a front photo and back. The NURBS splines were traced and adjusted based on the two views.

EXERCISE 3.6: DESIGN A CITROEN FENDER

1. Open a file called CH3_C_OR.MAX from the CD-ROM. It should look similar to Figure 3.26.

FIGURE 3.26
*Open
CH3_C_OR.MAX.*

2. In the Perspective viewport, press H and choose the spline named Outside from the list.

NOTE

All three NURBS splines are separate and must be attached to a single spline before creating a surface.

3. In the Modify panel, click Attach Multiple, and select Inside and Middle from the list. Click Attach.

4. Click the Edit Stack icon and for Convert To specify NURBS Surface. This step prepares the NURBS Splines to accept a surface.

5. If the NURBS Toolbox is not on the screen, click the NURBS Creation Toolbox icon in the Modify panel.

6. Click the U-Loft icon in the Surface area, and pick the outside spline.

7. Move the mouse to the middle spline and pick, then to the inside spline and pick it. A NURBS Surface is created, but if you look at the Top viewport you will see that the surface between middle and inside has a twist. It should look similar to Figure 3.27.

FIGURE 3.27

U-Loft NURBS Surface with a twist.

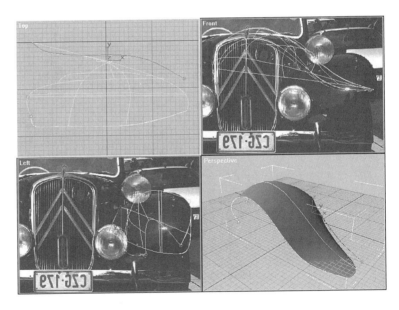

8. In the Modify panel, click Sub-Object Curve and pick the inside Curve. It turns red.

9. Click the Reverse button in the Selection area. The NURBS Surface between will untwist. Exit Sub-Object mode.

NOTE

The NURBS may now be tweaked into place by editing Surface, Point, or Curve Sub-Objects.

In this simple exercise, you saw a complex smooth NURBS Surface created by tracing NURBS Point Splines over one photographic background image of a side view and adjusting them over another front view image. The splines were then attached and converted to a NURBS surface. The final step was to use U-Loft to create a smooth surface over the splines. See Chapter 7, "Character Modeling," for a more in-depth look at NURBS in MAX 2.

WARNING

NURBS surfaces and splines can be very resource-intensive. Use them when no other modeling option is appropriate.

In Practice: Industrial and Mechanical Design Modeling

- Using CAD models. You have learned some pluses and minuses of modeling with CAD and importing the models into MAX R2. To make the process easier, extensive pre-planning between CAD and MAX R2 operators and testing will be helpful. It is critical to keep the models as efficient as possible and only model what will be seen in the final output.

- Simulate geometry when possible. Use the Materials bump, opacity, and wire attributes to create the illusion of complex geometry. Everything is fake, so fake it well.

- Use MAX R2's new Bevel Profile modifier, lofting, and lathing to turn 2D shapes into 3D objects. Become familiar with all the tools available, and it will be easier to choose the right tool at the appropriate time.

- Take advantage of Referenced shapes to loft or lathe into 3D objects. Referenced shapes give you a 2D control structure from which to easily edit the 3D object.

- Dummy objects combined with the Linked Xform modifier are a powerful tool to simplify the editing of path vertices on a lofted object. The dummies act as large handles to speed production.

- For flowing curved objects, MAX R2's new NURBS features offer a flexible, animatable surface creation tool. (For more detail on NURBS modeling, see Chapter 7 and adapt the lessons there to a mechanical scenario.)

Chapter 4

MODELING FOR REAL-TIME 3D GAMES

No area of 3D graphics is garnering as much attention as real-time gaming—and no other area shows as much potential for massive growth in the next few years.

Real-time 3D is only in its infancy in the consumer market. Set-top gaming systems that support real time are in their first generation. Many real-time graphics engines (as opposed to 2D sprite graphics) are only now beginning to be widely used by PC game developers. Renderware, Brender, Multi-Gen, and Microsoft's DirectDraw (a software engine for Windows 95/98 graphics) are among the real-time graphics engines gaining popularity. 2D sprite graphics, however, still dominate the PC gaming market.

The massive influx of Internet games is also fueling the drive to real-time 3D games (the Quake series is currently the most notable). Real-time 3D games using various technologies have been popping up all over the world. Whole companies are being built around the concept of 3D multi-player games available to anyone on the Internet.

The skills of the real-time 3D artist are broad and varied. In addition to in-depth knowledge of the software used to generate source materials (3D meshes, texture maps, animations, and so on), a real-time artist must have a firm grasp of the programmatic principles that make real-time 3D possi-ble. This does not mean that one should be a computer programmer—far from it, in fact. The excitement of real-time games lies in the artist's cre-ations, generated on the spot and in instant response to the user's whims, with a life and personality of their own.

Modeling is the key issue and the most critical part of creating graphics for real-time games. The myriad issues and technical details that go into mak-ing a model efficient (low-polygon count), believable, aesthetically pleasing, and poised to behave and display properly in the real-time world are issues that face the real-time artist alone. Real-time engines, after all, rely on only the most basic elements of 3D graphics to create their illusion.

Fortunately, 3D Studio MAX is a dream tool for creating real-time graphics. 3D Studio MAX not only provides excellent modeling tools to control every facet of creating a model, down to the face and vertex level, but it also pro-vides fast, efficient shaded, and texture-mapped views of the model being created. This enables the user to accurately preview the "look" of the fin-ished product in the game itself.

Although all real-time game engines vary slightly in structure, capabilities, and the paradigms used to create speed, the principles behind each engine remain the same.

This chapter covers the following topics:

- 2D versus real-time 3D graphics

- The basics of real-time 3D

- The differences between real-time and prerendered 3D graphics

- Principles and techniques for using 3D Studio MAX in modeling real-time objects

- The future of real-time 3D graphics

Two-D versus Real-Time 3D Graphics

You may be wondering why real-time 3D didn't appear earlier. Actually, it did. Arcade games using 3D vector graphics, such as *Tempest* and *Star Wars*, appeared in the mid-80s. Military simulations have been using real-time 3D on high-end machines for training for quite some time. Only recently, however, could these graphics be nicely shaded and texture-mapped at a speed that could match 2D animated graphics. To fully appreciate the speed difficulty, you need to understand the difference between 2D and 3D animation at the computational level.

Two-D animation relies on the principles of traditional cel animation. A huge number of pictures are created and then captured in sequence for playback in the chosen medium—in this case, a computer of some kind (including PCs, set-top gaming systems, custom-designed arcade systems, and so forth). The computer pulls the pictures from memory and displays them onscreen as fast as necessary to give the illusion of movement. The factors critical to 2D animation are data storage space (which accounts for the rise of the CD-ROM as the preferred gaming medium), the speed at which that data can be read, and how fast that data can be displayed. The computer does not have to do much "thinking" to display 2D animation.

Three-D graphics require much less storage than their 2D counterparts because the 3D pictures are not pre-drawn (with the exception of texture maps). The "recipe" for the 3D picture (meshes and animation) is stored as a mass of formulas and called up when needed. Because the pictures are being drawn onscreen by the program as they are being seen, and not before, the computer must "think" much more and much faster than it does with 2D images.

Imagine the difference between someone pulling nicely arranged pictures from a stack, and someone else trying to accurately draw, at the same speed as the person who's pulling pictures, a collection of objects that yet *another* person is moving around. Imagining such a scenario should help you easily grasp the difference in what is demanded of a machine running a real-time application. Only the current high-speed processors are capable of meeting these extreme demands. Even then, the geometry being drawn must be simple and have a low polygon count to make the process fast enough to meet acceptable display speeds.

Real-Time 3D Basics

Modeling for real-time graphics is a delicate process. You must have an accurate picture of what the result will be after the object being modeled is exported into the real-time engine. The more you know about how the average real-time engine thinks, the better your initial efforts will be, and the more time and frustration you will save yourself.

Real-time 3D and high-end, pre-rendered 3D graphics have many elements in common. To achieve the speed necessary for presentable game play, however, real-time must use only the most necessary elements—namely, the geometry, the transform, and the surface properties of the mesh. Most of the time, these elements are created by the export program (a third party application that converts the source model into a language the game engine can read) and put into some kind of text file (or a "c" file, before compilation into binary code) so that they can be manually edited, if necessary. Sometimes these elements can be parceled out to a number of separate files (one for geometry, one for surface properties, and one for the transform) that are combined when the file is compiled for the game engine.

Currently, there are plug-ins that enable the user to export directly from 3D Studio MAX into Playstation, Sega Saturn, Nintendo 64, and Direct Draw formats. More plug-ins are always under construction to support the myriad of real-time formats being used in gaming. Most pre-made, real-time 3D Application Programming Interfaces (APIs) provide a proprietary converter that works with the 3DS or DXF format. Freeware converters for exporting OBJ and VRML files are available from several Web sites on the Internet, such as 3dcafe.com and max3d.com.

The geometry is exactly what you would expect: a list of numbered vertex positions in 3D space, followed by a list of how to connect these vertices into coherent polygons. The normal (or visible solid) side of the polygon is determined either by the order in which the vertices that comprise the polygon are chosen, or by a separate list of vertex normals, also attached to the polygon construction list.

Most real-time engines use triangular polygons, just as 3D Studio MAX does. Some systems use quadrilateral polygons. Still other systems let you define quads and other types of polygons but break them down into triangles at rendering time. This can be a computationally expensive and unpredictable process. The best results seem to come from predefined triangular polygons. Although they require more storage than other polygons, predefined triangular polygons tend to render faster and always display as intended. The .3DS file format exports only triangles, which is why it is so widely supported among real-time engines.

A smooth export of the source model into the game engine always proves a bit tricky and often requires a great deal of tweaking. High-powered modeling programs, such as 3D Studio MAX, often add unusable information to the relatively simplistic real-time game engine. Most of this information is *invisible* (it may or may not be apparent when you look at the model in 3D Studio MAX). This information can have drastic effects on the exported real-time model, causing it to be drawn in the wrong orientation or position, or to behave improperly when animated in the game engine. The biggest trouble areas for export are generally the transform and the surface properties.

The Transform

The *transform* is a numerical matrix that describes the orientation, position, and often the scale of an object in 3D space. This number is applied to every vertex in the object and therefore acts as the object's center. In practice, imagine that every object you create is written as though it were centered at the global origin (0,0,0). To create this object farther off in 3D space, you could rewrite every vertex to the new location, or you could add to each vertex the distance (x, y, and z) the object must travel to reach the new position.

Clearly, the latter method is the more efficient. Even though it takes two processes to achieve the new position, only one number is being created on-the-fly. The same process can be used to rotate or scale the object. This matrix may change syntax from program to program, but it is always there because it is critical to controlling objects in 3D space.

When an object is moved in a 3D game, it is the transform that is actually affected. Pre-scripted animations, such as a character walking or the wheels of a car turning, are performed as if the object is standing still. To move the main object through space, the player's input is translated into a series of numbers that is combined with the transform to propel the object in the desired directions. In this way, a simple series of numbers can be generated from whatever input device is used (keyboard, joystick, and so on) to create fast, responsive action.

As mentioned earlier, the transform is usually an invisible number set in the modeling program and a numerical string in the data file(s) created by the export program. In 3D Studio MAX, however, the transform is also a visual tool that shows exactly how the physical geometry of the object is written.

When you select both the object whose transform you want to see and Reset Transform from the drop-down menu of the MAX Utilities panel, a bounding box appears that represents the object. A bounding box representation of your object appears. When an object is created, it is automatically aligned to the orthographic viewports. If you rotate this object, scale it, or move it, the bounding box goes with it and maintains its relative location and orientation. If, however, the object is reoriented away from its orthographic alignment and then has its transform reset, the bounding box moves back into orthographic alignment. This effectively rewrites the object geometry and resets the axis of the object, causing the object to behave differently than expected. The results will be obvious when you animate the object in a real-time game.

Normally, the transform is not something you have to worry about. When you work with primitives, MAX automatically generates them properly aligned. The only time a transform can get misaligned with primitives is when they are cloned or mirrored. When you perform these operations, always check the object's transform immediately after the modification. If a transform is off on an object that is part of a hierarchical model, to correct the transform you must detach the hierarchy, realign the object, and recreate the hierarchy. Figure 4.1 shows an object with a properly aligned transform. Figure 4.2 shows an object whose transform will cause problems when animation is applied to it.

The only other time transforms can be generated differently than what you might want is when you are lofting objects that are naturally skewed. Remember that, by default, MAX automatically sets an object's local coordinates to align with those of the global coordinate system. If a Loft object is created askew to the global system, its local transform matrix will be misaligned. If an object must be created this way, manipulate it after it has been completed so that it comes as close as possible to orthographic alignment. Then reset the transform and proceed with the rest of the model and animation.

FIGURE 4.1

An object with a correctly aligned transform.

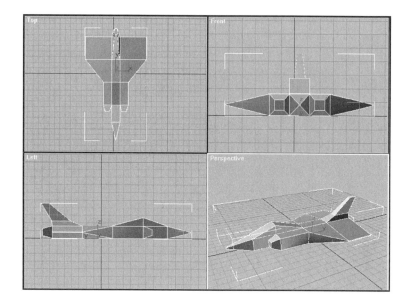

FIGURE 4.2

An object with an incorrectly aligned transform.

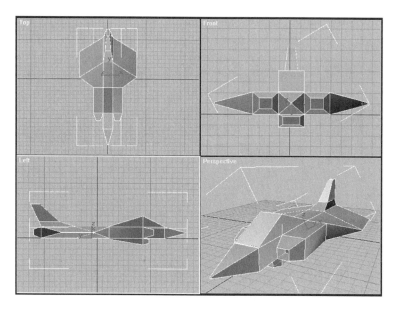

You may be thinking that realigning the object center would accomplish the same thing as resetting the object's transform. That is correct when you are not exporting the object into a real-time engine. Unfortunately, most exporters are not able to use this bit of information, as it does not rewrite the actual geometry of the object as performing a "Reset Transform" does.

In fact, to ensure that an object performs in the real-time engine in the same way it performs in MAX, make certain that the Pivot point is aligned to the object. The Pivot point dictates the origin of the object, but having its alignment correspond to the object ensures that rotational alignment and values are the same in the game engine.

Surface Properties

Surface properties in a real-time engine are almost identical to those in MAX—namely, the smoothing algorithm (flat shading or Gouraud shading only for real time), the color of the polygon, the shininess, opacity, Self-Illumination, and the Texture map applied to the polygon. These properties generally are defined after the vertex list but before the faces they apply to.

In addition, several real-time engines allow colors to be assigned to the vertices themselves, which can create the illusion of the object being lit, without direct lighting being applied to the model. Because most of the surface attributes are translated into numerical data, some strange translations can happen during the exporting process. Colors, for example, are translated from a 0 to 255 scale to a 0 to 1 scale. No hard and fast rules dictate how to minimize problems when exporting source materials from MAX. Generally, these materials must be manually adjusted in the real-time text file, unless a third party visual exporting system is used (such as those used with most set-top gaming systems). The best approach here is to be aware that surface properties may be a trouble area during exporting and to examine the final product closely.

Again, MAX proves to be an excellent real-time tool. It provides flat and Gouraud shaded viewing options, enabling the artist to view an object (before the object is exported) in a manner that closely represents what the object will look like in a real-time gaming engine.

Differences Between Real-Time and Pre-rendered 3D

The way in which real-time games and pre-rendered 3D graphics are created differs in five major areas:

- Z-buffering
- Levels of detail (LODs)

- Shadows

- Texture map size (and color depth)

- Shading modes

The basic difference in these systems is a result of what they are intended to do: Pre-rendered graphics need to look as realistic as possible; real-time graphics need to be as fast as possible.

Z-Buffering

Z-buffering is a computationally intensive process of determining which polygons are behind which (from the active viewpoint), so that a scene is drawn correctly with the proper depth. When you render a scene from MAX, visible portions of objects with correct mapping, shadows, and so on are produced for a near-photorealistic reproduction of the way the physical world is perceived. This process can be much too slow for real-time games, but most game engines have the capability to perform modified z-buffering (a faster but less accurate process than in MAX).

For fastest performance, however, *binary separation planes* (or BSPs) are created to give the processor a simple decision process as to what gets drawn in front of what. These planes divide concave (self-overdrawing) objects into convex pieces. These pieces, combined with the transform of the object, can be quickly evaluated by the computer to determine proper placement of objects.

Most real-time games also have a *far clipping plane*—a predetermined distance from the user's viewpoint, beyond which no objects are rendered, even though they are stored in memory. The far clipping plane allows the designer to greatly increase the number of objects in a game world, because the computer doesn't always have to draw everything simultaneously. Often, far clipping planes are disguised by fog, so objects don't just "pop" into the universe but appear to arrive out of a misty veil.

Levels of Detail

Levels of detail (LODs) also are critical in achieving the speed necessary to create an enjoyable game. In short, they are "stand-in" objects used to represent the real object at a greater distance from the user's viewpoint. When the object is close to the player, the highest-resolution model available is drawn. When the object takes up a small portion of the screen, a lower polygon count model is swapped in. Very often, at the greatest distances when the object can still be seen, a colored box is used to represent the object. The increase in speed is dramatic, because the processor does not have to calculate all the faces of the full object, but it still draws the same number of pixels the object takes up onscreen. Figure 4.3 shows a model with its high, medium, and low LODs.

FIGURE 4.3

A model with high, medium, and low levels of detail (LODs).

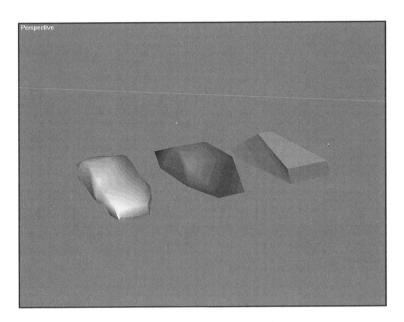

Complex objects (such as trees), which require a large number of polygons even to approximate, can be represented by an x-shaped arrangement of quads. This arrangement can be mapped with a picture of a high-resolution object and an opacity map (or "cookie cutter" map) that makes everything outside the desired object invisible. This technique can also be used effectively with LODs or complex game *sprites* (2D animated objects). In MAX R2, you can use the LOD manager to effectively switch between different levels of detail based on the object's distance from the camera. Figure 4.4 shows a tree model created with this cookie-cutter method for use in a real-time environment.

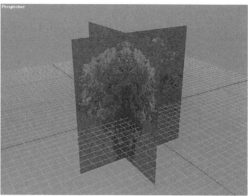

FIGURE 4.4
A real-time tree model.

Shadows

Although shadows add a great deal of realism to any 3D scene, they require far too much calculation time to be feasible in a real-time engine. Instead, shadows are generally created by mapping a silhouette onto a semitransparent polygon positioned parallel to the ground plane of the game world. The same cookie-cutter technique mentioned earlier can be used for simulating shadows. Figure 4.5 shows an object with its real-time shadow plane attached.

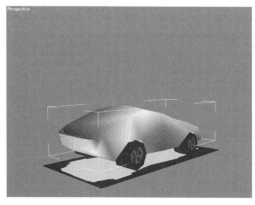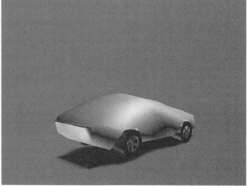

FIGURE 4.5
An object with a shadow plane attached.

Map Size and Color Depth

Because of active memory limitations (RAM) and the processor demands of calculating true color (24-bit) images, most real-time engines utilize smaller texture maps at a smaller color depth (usually 8-bit). Most systems use texture maps sized from 16×16 pixels up to 128×128 pixels. As a result, texture maps can be stored in RAM for quickest access whenever necessary (depending on the platform, up to 60 times a second).

Although some set-top gaming platforms can use 24-bit color maps, most systems use 8-bit color for texture maps. On many PCs, 8-bit color is the average display color depth. Because this is 3D, however, remember that light sampling is still calculated, in some form, and colors will vary. On systems that can display higher color modes, your 8-bit map can reach true color levels when different lighting is applied.

Shading Modes

Real-time engines currently support only two shading modes: Flat shading (which makes an object look faceted) and Gouraud shading (which smoothes out most edges). Phong shading is too processor intensive to be fast enough for real-time games.

Modeling for Real Time

With all the limitations of real-time games, modeling for real time involves a great deal of thought and precision. Real-time models must achieve the right balance of detail and low geometric complexity to make them fast, recognizable, and believable elements of the gaming experience.

Although modeling varies some from platform to platform, several basic principles should always be considered at the start of a gaming project:

- Put the detail in the map, not the mesh.
- Don't build what you don't need.
- Model convex whenever possible.
- High-res for low-res modeling.

Put the Detail in the Map, Not in the Mesh

Every polygon added to a real-time mesh takes a certain amount of time to render. Even if it is less than a 1000th of a second, that time adds up and diminishes the possible frame rate during game play. Texture maps are drawn much faster than the polygons needed to create the details that could be "painted" into the Texture map. To be effective, an object's texture maps must simply be able to fit into RAM. Therefore, any detail that can be effectively simulated by adding it to the texture map should be mapped, not modeled—as should any detail that is too mesh intensive to be effective (such as the "cookie cutter" trees discussed earlier).

A great example of when to map instead of model is the muscle tone in a character. Nice, rounded muscle structure is far too polygon intensive to accomplish in real time. When muscles are added to a texture map, however, a similar effect can be achieved through careful use of simulated highlights and shadows, with almost no cost in frame rate.

A helpful process when you create real-time models is to create a fully detailed, high-face-count model first. Then construct the low-resolution model over the high-res model, using the latter as a template. You can then take individual orthographic renderings from the high-count model, tweak them in a paint program, and then use them as texture maps for the low-res model. This process is discussed in more detail in the "Dealing with Texture Limitations" section later in this chapter.

Another related process is to load two images (preferably scanned pictures) of the object you're creating, seen from the side and the front, as a texture map to be placed on a two-quad "tree" in MAX. This tree can then be displayed as a shaded template to be built over. This technique can be very handy as a reference for building real-time characters.

Don't Build What You Don't Need

Not modeling unnecessary objects may seem obvious, but it should be a principle you return to often to ensure that your objects maintain the lowest possible polygon count.

Real-time game environments are more akin to Hollywood movie sets than they are to real-life environments. Like a movie set, they are seen only from limited viewpoints. Specific knowledge of where your objects and environments are and are not visible by the player is critical to efficient modeling. Figure 4.6 shows a real-time environment from a top-down view (a view the player would never be able to see) that illustrates set-like construction.

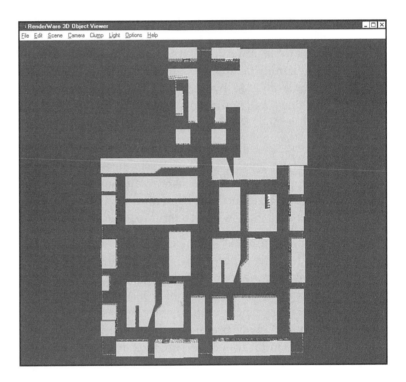

If you were building the cars for a racing game, for example, you would need to know whether the cars would ever flip over, exposing the undercarriage. If not, you could eliminate that part of the mesh and add detail (if necessary) to the parts of the vehicles that would be seen most often.

Segmented real-time characters offer another example. Normally the segments are modeled solid at the joints so that no holes appear in the mesh throughout a full range of motion. In a game setting, your model may not need a full range of motion, or different versions of the model may be swapped in depending on the action, damage to the character, and so forth. By eliminating the "capping" polygons inside the joints (which are never seen), you lower the total face count of the model and make rendering more efficient.

Model Convex (Whenever Possible)

The differences between z-buffering and using BSPs in real-time gaming systems were discussed earlier in this chapter. *BSPs* are a system by which game designers can "pre-make" decisions for the game hardware. This can include which objects (or parts of an object) are drawn onscreen last (over the other screen objects) to create the illusion of depth. The use of BSPs creates a dramatic speed increase over z-buffering, which not only has to keep the movement of the game going but also must determine object placement onscreen based on the position of every polygon in the scene.

For BSPs to be effective, they must divide objects into pieces that can be drawn correctly on their own, without any sort of depth information. This means that you must make convex pieces—where all the face normals of the object face away from the center of the object and do not point into each other. Convex pieces are absolutely critical to real-time game engines because they can be rendered at the maximum speed possible and still display correctly. Figure 4.7 shows a model with its BSPs visible. The data would be invisible in the real-time game engine.

FIGURE 4.7

A model with visible BSPs inserted.

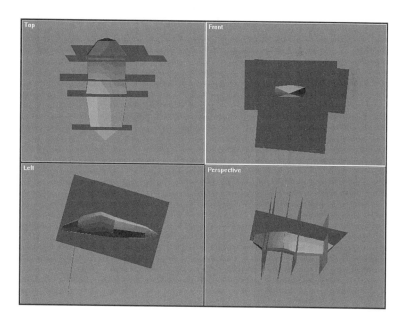

The best test of convexity is to look at the object in a shaded, perspective view (smooth or faceted), hide the faces on opposing sides of the object (top and bottom, left and right, or front and back), and rotate the object in multiple directions. If you can see a solid face through an empty space in the model (where the normals are facing away, making the polygons invisible), the object is not convex and needs modifications (or more dividing) before it can be used effectively in a BSP sorting engine. Repeat the process for each opposing pair of sides. Figure 4.8 shows the visible differences between a convex and a concave object.

FIGURE 4.8

A convex object section and a concave object section.

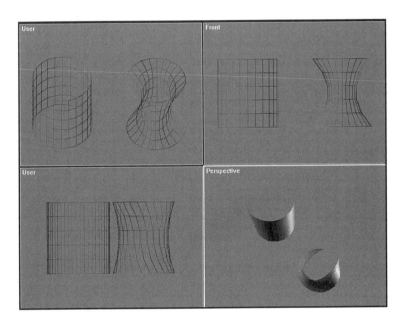

High-Res for Low-Res Modeling

When you're working with low polygon counts, it can be extremely difficult to see whether a proper level of detail has been accomplished to make the object clearly recognizable and distinguishable from other similar objects. It can be extremely helpful, therefore, to build a high poly-count "template" object with as much detail modeled as possible, over which to construct a low-count model. This process clarifies where detail is needed in the low-count object and where it can be omitted and placed in the texture map. And, as mentioned before, the high-detail model can be used to generate intricate texture maps for the low-count model later on.

Note that trying to use the Optimize modifier in MAX to lower the polygon count of the high-detail mesh to acceptable real-time levels is highly inadvisable. The Optimize modifier is an excellent tool for making a complex mesh more efficient and it can even be used on a real-time model if only to make certain that there are no unnecessary polygons. This modifier, however, can easily create unpredictable losses in detail when you're trying to drastically reduce a high-count model.

The Optimize modifier works by eliminating faces that are determined to be coplanar, based on the entered face and edge threshold angles. The Optimize modifier has no intelligence as to which details are important and which are not; it just uses a straight numerical algorithm. When a parameter that is high enough to bring drastic face count reductions is entered, the Optimize modifier also eliminates most of the nice, smooth areas that have been created to round out certain edges.

Real-Time Modeling Techniques

The best way to ensure that your model has appropriate detail where it's needed and the lowest-possible polygon count is to create the model with a low polygon count to begin with, and then to add detail and subtract faces only where necessary. The Sub-Object editing tools of the Editable mesh become your best friends when you finalize a real-time model.

For object creation, however, the best options fall into the following two categories:

- "Conscientious" lofting
- Modifying primitives

Conscientious Lofting

Lofting Mesh objects has long been a mainstay for creating complex shapes in 3D Studio and continues to be a critical MAX tool for the real-time artist. Lofting with Deform-Fit creates beautifully detailed meshes by adding interpolative steps between vertices on both the Fit shapes and the shape(s) being lofted. Unfortunately, this can add a tremendous number of polygons very quickly. By lofting with no added steps and by using multiple shapes on the loft path, however, you can generate extremely detailed models with predictable face counts and detail. Also, lofting objects this way creates clean cross-sections that can then be divided by BSPs, if necessary.

Deform-Fit works by creating a path that derives its shape from the vertices of the two fit shapes. Wherever a vertex is present, a path step is inserted. If the two fit shapes share the same vertices in the same alignment, a minimum number of path steps is created, therefore creating the minimum amount of geometry in the Loft object. To insure the fit shapes contain the same vertex alignment, you just clone the more complex of the two shapes.

Figure 4.9 is a low-res car that closely approximates a more detailed model. Using the detailed model as a template, you can construct a lower-detailed version using the Deform-Fit options within the Loft object. You could add modifications to the original Loft shape and place them on your Loft path to further enhance the detail of the vehicle, without adding more faces. The level of detail can be taken as far as necessary, however, by manipulating the vertices of multiple cross-section shapes and placing them into the existing path steps.

FIGURE 4.9

A low resolution model created using the Deform-Fit method of modeling.

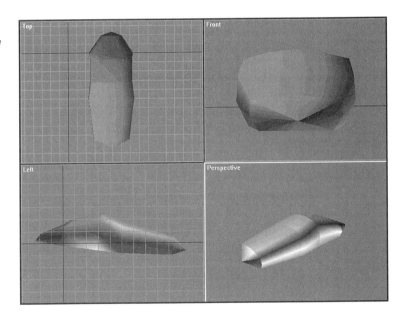

Modifying Primitives for Low-Resolution Models

The other primary way of creating an efficient real-time mesh is to start with a primitive (preferably a multi-segmented cylinder or box) and manipulate the individual vertices to match the Template object. Modeling this way allows you to start with any detail model you want and either reduce or add geometry as needed. For modelers who prefer to model from the "inside-out," using primitives for modeling is ideal.

Exercise 4.1 will demonstrate how to modify primitives to produce low-resolution models. Here you will build an imaginary fighter jet from a box. In the exercise, you'll see how you can model strictly from a box being converted into an Editable Mesh.

EXERCISE 4.1: MODELING A JET FROM A PRIMITIVE

1. Reset 3D Studio MAX.

2. In the top or perspective viewport, create a box that's approximately 180 units in length, 75 units wide, and 20 units high. Set the number of Length and Width segments to 3 (see Figure 4.10.)

TIP

You can turn on the Edged Faces option in the shaded viewports so that you can see the faces of the box you'll need to edit. Otherwise, you'll have to constantly switch between Wireframe and Shaded modes.

FIGURE 4.10

The box in the viewports with Edged Faces turned on.

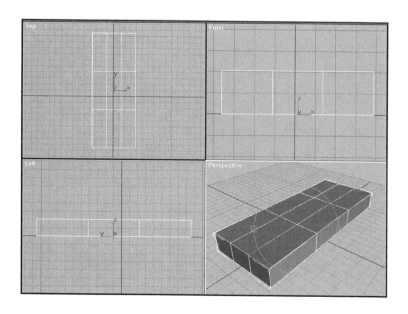

3. Go to the Modify panel, click the Edit Stack button, and convert the box to an Editable Mesh.

4. Click the Sub-Object button to enter Sub-Object mode, then switch the Face Selection level.

5. In the perspective viewport, click the middle segment of the box at the "front" end of the plane to select it.

6. In the Extrude Amount field in the Modify Panel, type 40, hit Enter, then type 40 again, and hit enter. This creates a two-segment "extension" on the plane that will be its nose.

7. Click the Scale button in the toolbar and scale the currently selected face down to a small point to create the tip of the nose. You can use the Lock Selection button to avoid inadvertently selecting another face during the scale (see Figure 4.11).

FIGURE 4.11

The plane is beginning to take shape with the nose being extruded and scaled from the front of the box.

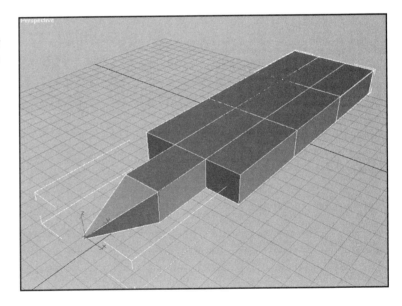

8. Select the other two segments on the box on either side of the nose and extrude them 20 units. (You can do both at the same time by holding down the Ctrl key during the selection process.)

9. Scale the faces down to about 50 percent of their original size.

10. Use the Extrude command again but extrude -15 units. This creates the intake "holes."

11. To Create the Canopy, first select the top face on the nose *and* the face immediately behind it on the "body" of the aircraft and extrude them 20 units.

12. Switch to the Vertex Sub-Object selection mode and select the vertices at the top of the "canopy" but exclude the middle two.

13. To finish, use the Move command to move the selected vertices down so that they're level with the body of the aircraft. Figure 4.12 shows the sequential actions of Steps 11 through 13.

FIGURE 4.12

By extruding the top faces of the box and moving the end vertices down, you can make the canopy portion of the low polygon jet model.

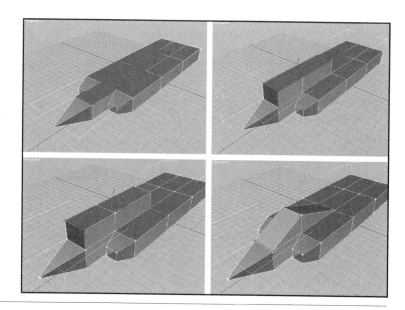

TIP

While modeling this way, it's always a good idea to keep a shaded Perspective viewport active, checking it often to make certain that a vertex has gone where you intended. If it did not, use the Undo feature until it reaches the place where the error occurred. (The more often you check, the less you have to undo in case of an error.)

By using simple extrusions and transforms on a standard primitive, such as a box, you can basically create anything. Remember to first convert the geometry to an editable mesh before working at the Face or Vertex Sub-Object level. This method helps maintain the low polygon counts required for gaming environments. Try using the same techniques to create the wings, tail, and exhaust port. To see a completed version of the jet, see the 04imx01.max file on the CD-ROM.

Dealing with Texture Limitations

As you have already seen, quite a bit of detail can be accomplished with limited meshes. To get the most out of limited geometry, however, you must rely on Texture maps. Maps have their own limitations—either limited size, limited color depth (usually 8-bit), or both. Fortunately, you can work around these limitations and still produce excellent results.

Dealing with Limited Colors

Opinions abound on the subject of how to create a real-time environment by using 256 colors. Many people favor starting with a limited palette (pre-picking the colors that will be used) and making all Texture maps from those colors. Others believe that better results derive from creating the maps with the full 16.7 million colors available, and then using another program to evaluate the Texture maps and remap them into the 256 most-used colors.

Generally, however, when you create texture maps with 16.7 million colors, you don't use them all (or even a significant percentage of them). To achieve a happy medium between the two previously mentioned methods, first decide on a general scheme (based on the scene, time of day, mood, and so on), and then paint in 24-bit color, focusing on the selected color scheme. This method also provides a better distillation to 256 colors when you create the final game palette, while still keeping the scene focused toward the visual goals identified with the color scheme.

If you don't have access to a program capable of distilling a 256-color palette from multiple images (and remapping the colors in those images to the new palette), your best choice is to start with a predetermined 8-bit palette.

Limited Map Size

All gaming platforms today use small texture maps, ranging from 16×16 pixels to 128×128. Although this may be intimidating for those whose smallest maps are 320×240 (one-quarter the size of the average monitor display at low resolution), after a bit of practice you will discover how much detail you can achieve in a very small area. You may even find that texture mapping with small maps opens new techniques for creating larger maps when you're creating prerendered 3D images.

A great temptation is to create a Texture map at a high resolution and then scale it down to the parameters of whatever real-time engine you are working with. This seldom works well. Scaling, in most paint programs, is done by a mathematical elimination of pixels based on the percentage of down-scaling. When you reach real-time limits, where every pixel counts, this process can make quite a mess of an originally great texture map—filling it with scattered, color-cycling pixels and making an otherwise smooth map look rocky or rough.

Your best bet for making certain that the exact detail you want (and nothing else) appears onscreen during game-play is to start with the same size texture map that will be in the game. This technique leaves no room for extraneous information and enables you to be very precise as to what amounts of detail go where. And, you can use multiple maps (or a large map carved into real-time sizes) on an object, with very little impact on the speed of the game.

Adding "Impossible" Detail

As you might have gathered from everything discussed in this chapter so far, real time is mostly a matter of creating the best illusion with what is technologically possible. Most of the model creation process, so far, has been accomplished by using limited versions of what is already available in 3D Studio MAX, and using simple planning and efficiency to achieve results.

Some items, however, cannot be done in real time. Certain mapping types (Bump mapping, Shininess, and Specular mapping), specific lighting design, and many other techniques are beyond the limitations of real-time games at this point, because of the bare-bone shading limitations needed to create speed. These more complex maps require the computationally expensive Phong shading mode and must simply be "faked." Here again, a little planning can go a long way.

Faking a Bump Map

Bump maps, in pre-rendered 3D, are a way to create the illusion of limited surface relief on an object. Artists have been doing this in flat images for thousands of years by creating highlights and shadows in still images. The same techniques work very well for creating "fake" Bump maps. Determine the angle of your light source (high and right always creates a believable, recognizable source), and paint in the highlights and shadows. The only difference is that your shadows do not move in response to the real-time light source and the "bumps" are not visible from the edge of the faces to which they are applied. Figure 4.13 shows a "faked" Bump map.

FIGURE 4.13

A "faked" Bump map.

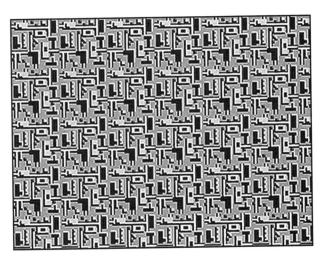

If creating bumps through painting seems a bit intimidating, you can create your bump-mapped material, apply it to a flat plane in 3D Studio MAX, add lighting, and render the image out to a file for use on your real-time mesh. But remember the earlier comment about map sizes: render the image to the size it will be in the game, instead of rendering the image larger and scaling it down later.

Faking "Mood Lighting"

To create spotlight effects (such as under-lighting or light pooling), you can repeat the preceding "create it in MAX" technique or use the lighting filters available in many image-editing packages (such as Adobe Photoshop or MetaCreation's Painter) to get similar results. Moving a MAX light around in 3D space can give you a much more specific effect than using a light fixed to a two-dimensional plane.

Curved Surfaces

Creating a curved surface with geometry is an almost impossible accomplishment in real time because curves require a high number of polygons.

Fortunately, creating the illusion of a curved surface in a Texture map is not difficult. It can be painted into the map—using a highlight for the highest point on the surface and blending that into half-tone at the sides of the curve with shadows reacting to the light source. Again, rendering a fully mapped, highly-detailed curved surface in MAX and then using it as a Texture map for the flat-surfaced real-time object yields great results.

Exercise 4.2 demonstrates most of the previously mentioned concerns when Texture mapping.

EXERCISE 4.2: REAL-TIME TEXTURE MAPPING

1. From the accompanying CD, open the file called 04max02.max. This is a sporty mag-wheel that would add a nice bit of detail to add to your real-time sports car (see Figure 4.14). It was modeled in high detail and is obviously much too complex to be used in real time, especially when you consider that it would have to be multiplied by four. The Chrome Reflection map on the spokes of the wheel would also be impossible in real time but renders very nicely in MAX.

2. Change the left viewport display method to Bounding Box mode. With the Zoom Region tool, go into the left viewport and scale the view very close to the wheel's bounding box, leaving a small space around the outside for cropping later (see Figure 4.18). In the Environment settings, set the background color to a bright yellow (red -255, green -255, blue 0). This makes cropping and manipulation in your paint package much easier later on.

FIGURE 4.14
The high-detail wheel mesh in MAX.

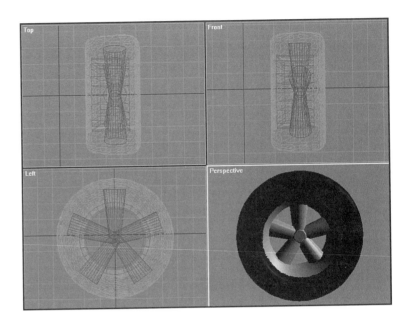

3. Render the left viewport at a size of 64 × 64 pixels (an average real-time texture map size) with anti-aliasing turned off. Save the file as a 32-bit Targa filecolor with alpha channel and name it wheel_src.tga. This is the source file for your texture map.

4. In your favorite image editing program, open wheel_src.tga.

5. First, crop the image down to only the pixels you want, leaving no border around the wheel. With the Cropping tool, create an outline that fits exactly to the outside edge of the tire. Crop the image (see Figure 4.15). Resize the image back to 64 × 64 pixels.

NEW TO R2

In MAX R2, you can use the cropping features of the Bitmap Map type rather than having to crop in a paint program. This exercise, however, requires more than just cropping, so you'll need to use a paint program.

6. Now, with the Magic Wand tool, select the yellow pixels that are left. If you are using Photoshop, select one of the yellow corners around the wheel and under the Select drop-down menu choose Similar. This should select all the yellow pixels, including the ones between the spokes of the wheel.

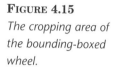

FIGURE 4.15

The cropping area of the bounding-boxed wheel.

NOTE

Rendering the image from MAX with anti-aliasing turned off provides a clean edge around the wheel. By setting the background to an extremely bright color, not found anywhere else in the image, you can create a map in which you can easily replace the background color. Additionally, you can add other colors if your map does not easily fit exactly onto the real-time object (and might leave undesired edges). If you see strange edges when the map is applied, you can go back to the image and tweak it to make certain that you get a clean texture map.

7. Choose pure black as your foreground color and fill the yellow area. If any partly yellow pixels remain at the selection line, stroke the selection line with a two-pixel line of black, centered on the selection line.

8. In the Channels panel, go to the alpha channel (channel 4 in Photoshop), select all the image, and cut it.

9. Go back to the RGB channel and from the filters drop-down menu, select Blur. This adds back the anti-aliasing you removed from the rendered image. Set Color mode to 8-bit (256) and save the image as wheel64.tga. This is your Color Texture map.

10. Under the File menu, select New. The setting should automatically be 64 × 64 pixels because this is the size of the alpha channel you cut to the Clipboard. Paste the alpha channel into the new file and set Color mode to Grayscale. Select white as your foreground color. This time, fill in just the black corners around the edge of the wheel; this ensures that the edges of your wheel are solid all the way around. Save the image as wheel64o.tga (see Figure 4.17). This is your Opacity map.

FIGURE 4.16

The wheel64o.tga image.

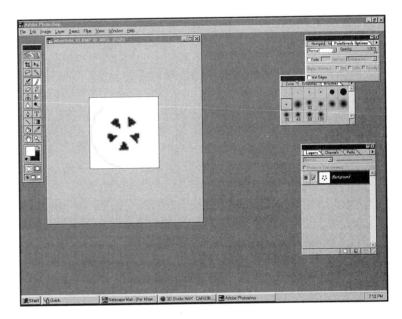

11. Go back into MAX, but this time open the file called 04max04. At one of the wheel-wells, create an eight-sided cylinder with one height segment to be used as a wheel for your car. Make the depth and radius roughly the appropriate size for your vehicle (see Figure 4.18). Keep the new wheel object selected and choose the UVW modifier from the Modify panel. Make certain that the Mapping type is planar and that the top is aligned with the top of your newly created wheel. Then choose the Fit option to fit the Mapping coordinates to the bounding box of your wheel.

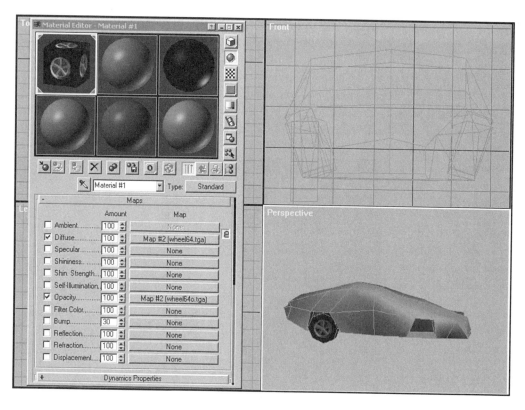

FIGURE 4.17

The real-time car, with one wheel added.

12. Open the Material editor and create a new material that has constant shading, no Shininess, and no Shin.Strength. Apply the material to the wheel.

13. In the maps area of the Material rollout, load wheel64.tga into the Diffuse channel and wheel64o.tga into the Opacity channel. Change the material sample type from a sphere to a cube so that you can see exactly what the map looks like on the wheel. In the Alpha Source section of the Map Parameters panel, set the Alpha Source to None (opaque).

14. Render a clean view of the newly mapped wheel and adjust it until it has a nice rounded feel on the edge of the tire and you can see through the spokes. Clone this object three times and place the copies into the other wheel-wells (see Figure 4.18).

Working with real-time models often requires a balanced use of both low-detail geometry and convincing maps. You'll find that most real-time inter-active titles on the market do this very well. This exercise demonstrates that you don't even have to be a 2D artist to create those convincing maps. Use your 3D skills whenever possible. With the right lighting, materials, and geometry your renderings can serve very well as 2D maps for lower-detail models. The final result of Exercise 4.2 is shown in Figure 4.18.

FIGURE 4.18

The finished wheels on the low-res car.

Using Opacity for "Impossible Detail"

Sometimes an object is far too complex to be modeled convincingly in a low-polygon fashion. When you are using 3D Studio MAX to create models of objects with holes and complex edges—objects so detailed that you cannot make them recognizable—you can use a simple Opacity map to create the effect.

Fortunately, almost all real-time systems have some capacity for using Opacity maps—whether they are 8-bit grayscale maps or just 1-bit black-and-white, cookie-cutter type maps. This capability enables the model maker to add detail that would otherwise be impossible. The effect is not quite as clean as it would be in 3D Studio MAX, but the result is still quite effective. Figures 4.19 and 4.20 show how opacity can be used to create the illusion of hair on a real-time character.

FIGURE 4.19

A head with the hair molded around it.

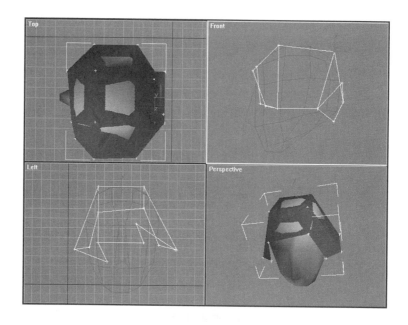

FIGURE 4.20

A rendered version of a head, with the hair molded around it.

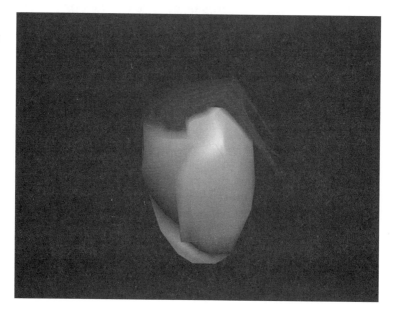

In Practice: Real-Time Modeling

- **Real-time 3D gaming relies on speed and must use only the bare basics of 3D to accommodate the extensive calculations necessary.** These basics include limited geometry, limited texture map sizes and color depths, and often the use of Binary Separation Planes (BSPs) rather than slower z-buffering calculations for depth.

- **Modeling is the most critical process in real-time 3D.** If your models are too detailed, the real-time game engine will simply not be able to process the data fast enough for the players. If it's too simple, then the interactive title doesn't look professional—or worse, the models don't look anything like what they're supposed to represent. Either way, effective modeling can make a title. Poor modeling can break it.

- **Use templates when possible.** Creating a 3D template over which to model is a useful procedure for creating real-time objects with enough detail in the right places. This way, you can construct the lower detail models as close as possible to the originals, yet have enough of a low polygon count to be useable in a real-time environment.

- **Be conscientious and primitive in your modeling**. The basic procedures in creating a real-time model are "conscientious lofting" and the manipulation of primitives. Using lofting, you can build low-detail models based on simple shapes. With primitives, you can push and pull on the faces or vertices of an object to build more interesting models.

- **Texture maps are the key to realism in real-time**. Detail that cannot be accomplished with mesh can be created with texture maps, using Opacity, "faked" Bump maps, and rendered images of high-detail meshes manipulated for real-time use.

Chapter 5

MODELING FOR VR AND THE WEB

The World Wide Web's unexpected emergence and hectic growth have been one of the phenomena near the turn of the millenium. Although exact figures are not available, it's generally believed that the number of people accessing the Web will grow from about 60 million today to about 200 million by the turn of the century. During this same time period, computer processing power is expected to continue to double every 18 months, coupled with an enormous expansion of line bandwidth and modem speed. Barring some disaster, the future of the Web is very bright indeed. It's no wonder, therefore, that so much creative talent—and money—is being invested in it. Virtual Reality Markup Language (VRML, usually pronounced *vermal*) is one of the best ways that 3D artists and animators can take advantage of the tremendous opportunity presented by the Web's growth.

VRML, as conceived by its creators, is much more than a method of displaying 3D models. It's a conceptual system that might ultimately enable you to navigate the Web as one continuous 3D space, in the same way that HTML enables you to navigate the Web as one giant hypertext document. This is the real potential of "cyberspace." In the future, Web addresses will map to the interiors of personal or corporate 3D spaces within the context of a borderless virtual world. This world continuously will be extended but will always be coherent and consistently navigable because it is implemented in a common language—VRML.

This chapter helps you keep up with the fast-paced world of 3D on the Web. It covers the following topics:

- Modeling tools and techniques

- A summary of what is and is not exported by the VRML Exporter

- Creating a virtual world with 3D Studio MAX and the VRML Exporter

- VRML browser reviews

- The best of the Web

NOTE

If you want to find out more about the goals and potential of VRML, go to Mark Pesce's site at www.hyperreal.com/~mpesce/. The latest VRML specification is available at vrml.sgi.com/moving-worlds/spec/index.html.

VRML is an "open" standard—a specification openly published that does not contain code owned by any corporation. VRML was created and is maintained by individuals who have a vision of 3D on the Web and want to make it possible for anyone to use it freely. The outlook today is very positive. The VRML Consortium, formed in December 1996, has taken over responsibility for the development of the language from the VRML Architecture Group.

Hopefully, all those companies that might otherwise have gone their separate ways will now come together and make VRML the single, solid standard it needs to be.

Modeling Tools and Techniques

As with all files destined for display on the World Wide Web, smaller is better with VRML. On a standard 28.8KB modem with average network traffic, a VRML file of 150K downloads in about 120 seconds. To that, you must add extra time for downloading any texture map files. Download performance, then, is the first issue: How long does it take to download the file from the Web server and load it into memory? This is a function of file size. The only time file size might not be an issue is when you are creating VRML worlds for access over an intranet in a particular organization.

The second issue is navigation speed or performance after the file loads into memory, a function of model complexity. This relates to file size, of course, because the more complex the model and the more faces it has, the larger the file. The main bottleneck here, however, is in the video display: How many pixels does the video display card have to process and put out to the screen? When you navigate within a VRML world, the browser interprets the VRML code and passes it to your PC hardware, which actually renders it in real time.

N OTE

The term *browser*, as used here, refers to the VRML-viewer software that plugs into your Web browser (Netscape or Internet Explorer). Available VRML browsers are reviewed later in the chapter.

Keep in mind that performance that depends on file size is a more subjective measure. What seems an unacceptably long download time to one person may seem quite acceptable to another. Download time is the lesser of the two limitations. Generally speaking, you won't want to miss out on the vitality that texture maps bring to your model for the sake of the extra time needed to download them. What you definitely want to avoid is creating models with so many faces that the computer gets bogged down trying to display them.

This section introduces tools and techniques you can use to work with both these limitations to produce VRML files optimized for download and navigation performance on the Web.

Using Tools Built into 3DS MAX

You can reduce file size and increase performance in several ways, one of which is by careful management of the objects you create. Before you begin modeling a scene for the Web, set a face (polygon) "budget" appropriate for the complexity of the scene and then roughly portion out the number of faces for the different objects. The Polygon Counter (a utility that comes with the VRML Exporter for MAX) helps you stay within your budget.

The sample world used throughout this chapter (City.wrl), for example, has about 2750 faces. Its file size is about 150KB, while the compressed size is less than 30KB—still a large file.

Reducing the Number of Segments

The simplest thing you can do to cut your face count is to reduce the number of segments in any primitive you create. The default segment settings for MAX primitives give you more faces than you want for a VRML world. When you create a primitive in a scene destined for export to VRML, go immediately to the Modify panel and use the spinners to reduce the number of segments.

Figure 5.1 shows two rows of primitives rendered in MAX. The upper row shows the primitives with the default number of segments. The lower row shows the same set of primitives after segment reduction. How much you reduce depends on how the primitive will be viewed in the scene. Objects that remain in the background can be reduced much more than objects intended to be viewed up close. This illustration shows how you can easily cut the face count in half (or more) without losing an enormous amount of quality. Table 5.1 summarizes the face savings between these two sets of primitives.

FIGURE 5.1

MAX primitives, before and after reducing the number of segments.

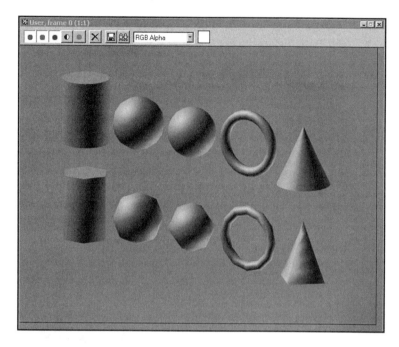

TABLE 5.1

Summary of Face Savings Earned by Segment Reduction

Primitive	Default Segments	Face Count	Reduced Segments	Face Count
Cylinder	24	96	12	48
Sphere	24	528	16	224
Geosphere	4	320	3	180
Torus	24/12 sides	576	16/6	192
Cone	24/5 height	288	12/1	48
TOTAL		1808		692

Deleting and Hiding Faces

Another very simple thing you can do is delete any faces that will never be visible from the objects in your scene. In the scene of an ancient city in this chapter, for example, deleting the faces on the underside of the landscape object cuts the number of faces from 1072 to 709 (see Figure 5.2). This particular object is a box with 14 segments each way, which was molded with the Freeform Deformation modifier to create slopes and hills. If you were happy with a completely flat landscape, you could reduce the face count to 12 by using a simple box.

FIGURE 5.2

Hiding faces that will never be visible.

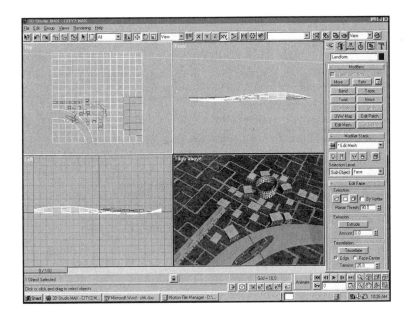

Actually, you don't have to use a base object to create an effect of the ground under your buildings. VRML 2.0 provides a Ground Color option for the Background helper, which enables you to set the color of the viewport below the horizon (this helper is described later in the chapter).

Another option is to hide the faces you don't want instead of deleting them. Because the VRML Exporter doesn't export hidden faces, those faces will not be part of the eventual download file size. MAX still counts the hidden faces, however, and you will not have a completely accurate face count during the modeling process. Whether you delete or hide faces is up to you. You may find it more convenient to delete them if your model is intended solely to be viewed in a VRML browser.

When you upload texture maps, remember that the UNIX system your Web server is most likely running is case sensitive and will not find the map files unless the case is exact. If you specified a map called bridge.gif in the Material editor, for example, but the file you upload to the Web server is called Bridge.gif, the map will not display.

Texture maps look strange, but not unattractive, when you zoom in close enough to see the pattern of the colored pixels. This is becoming part of the "style" of VRML models, as you'll see if you look at some of the Web sites listed later in this chapter. One way to work with this limitation rather than against it is to design texture maps that make no attempt to look realistic, but look as though they were painted on, like stage scenery.

You might have noticed in Figure 5.4 that the buildings appear to have different maps on their different sides. You can apply the same map to all sides of a box by using the Box option of the UVW Map modifier in MAX. To get different maps on different sides, however, you have to use different maps. The mapping in this scene was done using a feature of the 3D Paint program, Fractal Design Detailer (MetaCreations). This feature, called implicit mapping, enables you to use a single texture map to paint on all six sides of a box (see Figure 5.5). You can do the same thing without a 3D Paint program by using a freeware plug-in for MAX called Unwrap (available on the accompanying CD-ROM).

FIGURE 5.5

Box-mapping technique in Fractal Design Detailer.

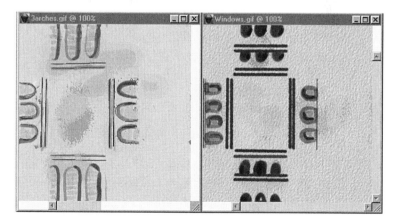

Creating Camera Views

Placing cameras in the scene is not, of course, a modeling technique per se, but it needs to be mentioned here because cameras are so useful in making a successful VRML world. The different cameras you create in your scene are listed by the VRML browser, usually in the menu that pops up when you right-click in the browser's viewport. Users can navigate within the scene by selecting one Camera view after another; be sure to provide plenty of them and name them descriptively. Even very large worlds that navigate painfully slowly in the browser can be viewed pleasurably from a series of Camera views.

Use the cameras you create to show off the best views of the scene—to point out unusual perspectives or to provide close-ups of the parts of the scene over which you lavished the most care. If you leave it to the user to navigate through the scene, you have no control over what he or she will look at. With a good selection of Camera views, on the other hand, you can control this to a large extent. Because selecting cameras is simpler than manually navigating with the mouse, and because the browser makes an elegant transition from one camera to another, if you make an interesting and original sequence of Camera views, they will be used.

Types of Animation

VRML 2.0 provides animation support for the VRML worlds you export from MAX. The following list identifies a fairly wide variety of animation methods that you can use:

- Simple transforms (Move, Rotate, and Scale)

- Animated hierarchies and inverse kinematics

- Coordinate interpolation animation, such as animated modifiers (Bend, Taper, and so on)

- Morphing

- Character Studio animation

You can do any kind of animation that doesn't involve changing the number of vertices. If the animation requires use of the Modifier stack, you need to turn on the Coordinate Interpolation option when you export the scene.

It's easy to exceed your file size budget quickly when you start using animation, especially with coordinate interpolation. With this last type of animation, the VRML Exporter has to track the position of every vertex over time, requiring the generation of a lot of code in the VRML file. Simple transform animation, on the other hand, is not nearly so demanding. Use it whenever possible.

It's useful to think of animation as a moving accent in an otherwise-still VRML world; in the current climate of the Web, a little goes a long way.

Some animation examples follow in the project section, "Creating a Virtual World with MAX and the VRML Exporter."

Using Tools Provided by VRML Exporter

The VRML Exporter provides some special tools for managing your scene. These include the Polygon Counter, the Level of Detail Helper, and the Export dialog box.

Note

In Max 2.0, the command panel dropdown containing the VRML Helpers is called VRML 2.0. In the 2.5 upgrade, in beta at press time, this dropdown is called VRML 97. Throughout this chapter it will be referred to as VRML 2.0.

The Polygon Counter

The Polygon Counter is an excellent little gadget that keeps count of the number of faces in the scene as a whole, as well as in the selected object or objects. You can set a budget for the number of faces in the scene or for each object; the counter displays a colored "thermometer" when you approach the limit or go over the top. This utility is invaluable when modeling for VRML export. You soon get a sense of how many faces should be in various objects, according to their relative importance in the scene, and the Polygon Counter helps keep you on target. Use it in conjunction with the Optimize modifier for a real-time graphic display of the optimization process; as you change the modifier values by using the spinners, the Polygon Counter changes also. Figure 5.6 shows the Polygon Counter in use with the Optimize modifier.

FIGURE 5.6

*Using the Polygon
Counter utility.*

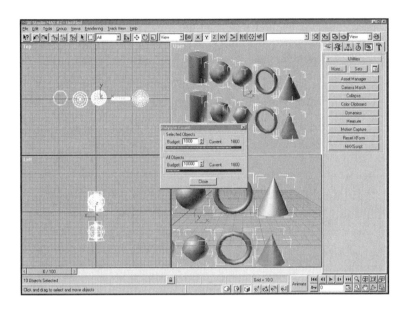

The Level of Detail Helper

The Level of Detail (LOD) is one of the VRML Helper objects you can place in your scene. It speeds up navigation in the viewport by displaying different objects, depending on their distance from the viewer. You can have the browser display a detailed version of a building, for example, when the viewer comes within 100 units. As soon as the viewer moves farther away, the browser can display a less detailed version of the same building with fewer faces.

You don't have to use different versions of the same objects. By substituting completely different objects, you can do a kind of simple morphing. LOD objects are covered in the project section of the chapter, "Creating a Virtual World with MAX and the VRML Exporter."

Settings in the Export Dialog

The VRML Exporter's Export dialog box has a number of settings that affect file size. Always leave the primitives to VRML primitives, which require less code in the VRML file. The MAX scene with the two rows of primitives shown in Figure 5.1, for example, exported to 45KB with this option checked but increased to 85KB when it was unchecked.

If you never need to look at the VRML code generated by the Exporter, you can uncheck the Indentation parameter. Indentation makes the VRML code easier to read. Unchecking this parameter reduced the 45KB file just mentioned to 38KB.

The Digits of Precision option controls the accuracy with which dimensions are calculated. Reducing the Digits of Precision option from the default 4 to 3 is probably acceptable unless you have an architectural model or some other scene in which measurements need to be precise. Decreasing this parameter reduced the size of the test file to just under 36KB.

It's probably not worth reducing the value of the Sample Rate parameter for transform animation. Doing so doesn't save you much in terms of file size, but it does rapidly start to make the animation play back less smoothly. You might want to experiment with the sample rates if you have coordinate-interpolation animation in the scene. Reducing the value in this case can make a significant difference in file size.

Other Techniques

You can use a couple of other techniques to speed things up: one to help control screen-update performance and the other to help reduce download time.

The EMBED HTML Statement

The EMBED statement is a technique for constraining the size of the viewport occupied by the browser on the Web page. By controlling the size of the browser, you can ensure, for example, that the user will not try to display the scene maximized on a 17-inch monitor or otherwise on such a large scale that the computer cannot properly process the number of pixels that must be rendered.

The HTML format for the statement follows:

```
<C1><EMBED SRC=filename.WRL WIDTH=300 HEIGHT=200>
```

Figure 5.7 shows the Cosmo browser constrained to an area of the screen with the EMBED statement.

FIGURE 5.7

Use of the EMBED HTML statement to constrain the size of the browser viewport.

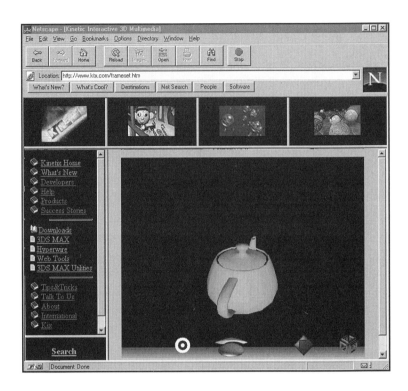

GZIP File Compression

The good news about file compression is that it works well, greatly reducing the size of the VRML (WRL) file. The bad news is that you probably have to use a UNIX command to do it. If your Web site is on a UNIX Web server, as most of them are, you are probably already familiar with the Telnet-type commands needed to create directories, set access rights, and so on. To compress a VRML file, change to the directory where the file resides and type:

gzip filename.wrl

This creates a gzipped (compressed) file with the name:

filename.wrl.gz

When you attempt to view a gzipped file from your Web page, the message "Warning: Unrecognized encoding: x-gzip" appears. This is not a problem because when you click OK, the file opens as usual. Browsers may some day be smart enough not to display pointless messages. Until then, the inconvenience is minor; don't let it stop you from compressing your files.

What the VRML Exporter Can and Cannot Export

Before you create a scene for export to VRML, you should be aware that not everything you can model or animate in MAX is supported by the VRML 2.0 standard. Table 5.2 lists the elements of the MAX scene that can be exported to a VRML 2.0-format file, as well as some notable elements that cannot be. If you're not sure whether something will or will not export, you can always make a simple test scene, export it and load it in your VRML browser.

TABLE 5.2

Summary of Exportable and Non-exportable Elements

Can Be Exported	Cannot Be Exported
Geometry	Smoothing groups
Hidden objects (Export option)	Hidden faces
Transform animation	
Coordinate interpolation animation	
Inverse kinematics	Inherit links
Animated cameras	
Light color	Volumetric lights
Standard materials and multi/sub-object materials (see the following indented list)	Other types of materials
Ambient, diffuse, and specular color	All other aspects of the material not listed in the first column
1 map (in diffuse channel)	
Shininess	
Opacity	
Wire frame	

Creating a Virtual World with MAX and the VRML Exporter

This section explains how to create a virtual world for the Web, using MAX and the VRML Exporter. You can access a Web page that displays a completed world—just use your favorite search engine to find sample VRML sites on the Internet. You can use these samples to get the real-world experience of the way a large VRML file actually performs.

You can load the VRML file, CITY.WRL, included on the accompanying CD-ROM. Open it locally by using your Web browser's Open File menu option. Whether you view the file live on the Web or locally, you need to have a VRML 2.0 browser installed, and, as discussed in the "Browser Review" section of this chapter, Live3D 2.0 is recommended.

The CITY.WRL sample world is designed to demonstrate most of the helpers of the VRML Exporter. This section steps you through the process of adding each helper to a partially complete version of the sample scene. It describes the procedure used and indicates what you then need to do to see that helper in action in the browser (navigation, clicking objects, and so on).

General Procedure for Using the VRML Exporter

The following list summarizes the general procedure for adding the individual helpers. Consulting this before you begin should prove helpful, because the procedure is the same or very similar for all of them.

1. Create your scene in the usual way with lighting, materials, and animation. Pay special attention to creating and naming cameras; they are listed in the VRML browser and are an important means of navigation. (In the MAX file you start with, the cameras are already defined.)

2. Go to the Create panel and choose Helpers. Then select the VRML option from the dropdown list. Select VRML 2.0 for all the features described in this section unless otherwise noted.

3. Click the button for the helper you want (TimeSensor, for example), and then click and drag in the Top viewport to place the Helper icon. (Figure 5.8 shows some of the Helper icons used in the sample file.)

Most of the Helper icons can go anywhere in the scene. Some, such as the Level of Detail helper, must be placed next to the objects they affect.

4. Link the helper to the objects in the scene that it affects. You usually do this by picking the objects, as described in the procedure for each helper.

5. Export the file in WRL format. Select VRML 2.0 for all the features described in this section.

6. Test the file in your VRML browser. To test the file, open it from your hard disk first to make sure that the helper works as expected. Then upload the file to the Web server and test the world live on the Web.

FIGURE 5.8
VRML Exporter helpers in the MAX scene.

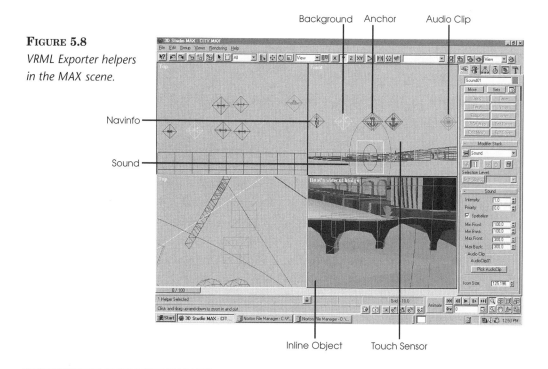

Adding the VRML Exporter Helpers to a Scene

You don't need to add the helpers to the sample scene in any particular order. There's no right order to placing them, although starting with the background seems logical.

This chapter does not attempt to describe all the many parameters for these helpers; that is done adequately in the VRML Exporter section on the online help file and elsewhere. Instead, this chapter focuses on the parameters you should be especially aware of and those that need to be changed from the default values.

Background

The Background helper defines the colors for a sky or ground backdrop to the world. This can be a plain color or a gradation made of two or three colors. If you define both sky and ground, you get a horizon line. The Background helper also provides options to set a bitmap image for the sky and ground (however, no browsers support this feature yet).

You should place a Background helper in your scene whenever you want to control the colors of the Browser viewport. In daylight scenes, for example, you want a sky-colored background. (Cosmo and Sony Community Place both display a black background by default.)

In this procedure, you use a Background helper to create a blue-sky backdrop for the scene:

EXERCISE 5.1: CREATING A VRML SKY

1. Open the 05max01.max file on the accompanying CD-ROM.

2. Select the Background helper from the VRML 2.0 helpers in the MAX Create panel. No linking is required; just place the icon in the Top viewport and adjust the settings. Figure 5.9 shows the settings to use (the blue in the sample file has an RGB value of 40,140,220).

3. From the File menu, choose Export and then choose VRML from the list of export formats.

4. In the Export dialog box, select VRML 2.0 from the list. You can leave the other settings as they are. Save the scene as *myVRML.WRL*.

5. Open the VRML file in your Web browser (in Netscape, choose Open File from the File menu). (If you have never browsed VRML files and you receive an error, then you should proceed to download the Cosmo player from the Silicon Graphics Web site. After installation has completed, continue with the exercise.)

FIGURE 5.9

*Settings for the
Background helper.*

The colored-sky background should be visible as the file loads.

NavInfo

The NavInfo helper enables you to control some of the characteristics of the browser display, such as navigation type and speed, whether a headlight is on, and so on. The default browser settings are generally acceptable, so a NavInfo helper is not essential. You may want to place one to increase the speed setting from 1.0 to about 5.0, however, if navigation seems slow when you test the file on the Web.

In Exercise 5.2, you use a NavInfo helper to speed up the navigation slightly.

EXERCISE 5.2: WORKING WITH NAVINFO

1. Continue with the 05max01.max file.

2. Select the NavInfo helper under VRML 2.0 helpers in the MAX Create panel. No linking is required; just place the icon in the Top viewport and adjust the settings. Figure 5.10 shows the settings to use.

FIGURE 5.10

Settings for the NavInfo helper.

3. From the File menu, choose Export and then choose VRML from the list of export formats.

4. In the Export dialog, select VRML 2.0 from the list. You can leave the other settings as they are. Save the file as myVRML2.WRL.

5. Open the VRML file in your Web browser (in Netscape, choose Open File from the File menu).

The NavInfo settings take effect when you load the file.

TimeSensor

The TimeSensor helper controls animation settings such as Start and End Frames and Looping. By adding a number of TimeSensors to the objects in your scene, you can play segments of the scene's animation out of sequence—something you cannot do in MAX. Suppose, for example, that you have two boats rowing down the river with exactly the same animated stroke of the oars. By using a separate TimeSensor for each boat and selecting a different range of frames, you can have the stroke of the oars different for each.

In Exercise 5.3, you place a TimeSensor to loop an animation and to start the animation when the file is loaded. Figure 5.11 shows the settings to use.

FIGURE 5.11

Settings for the TimeSensor helper.

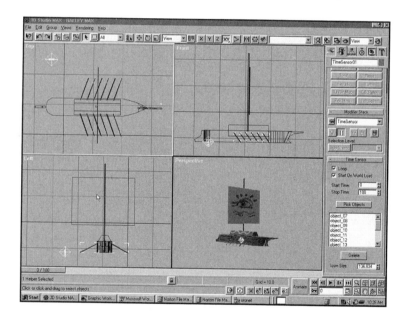

EXERCISE 5.3: USING TIMESENSORS

1. Open the 05max02.max file. This file already has an animation for the movement of the oars.

2. Select the TimeSensor helper under VRML 2.0 helpers in the MAX Create panel.

3. Place the icon in the Top viewport.

4. Click the Pick Objects button and then click each of the oars individually. Make certain that you select all the animated objects to be controlled by the TimeSensor.

5. Turn on the Loop and Start on World Load options.

6. Export and test the file. You'll see the completed galley.

Inline Object

The Inline Object helper inserts another WRL file into the world in place of the Inline helper icon. This is useful for the following reasons:

- Because inline files start to load at the same time as the "host" file, the scene as a whole builds faster.

- By instancing one inline file, you can quickly insert more than one copy of an object.

- You can include objects created by someone else.

When you use an Inline object, always make certain that the helper icon is positioned and rotated correctly relative to the other objects in the scene. The object or objects to be inserted must have been created at the same scale as the host scene. The inline file must be in the same folder as the host file.

NOTE

The two galleys (boats) on the river are the Inline objects (see Figure 5.12). The initial Camera view's setting for the world gives the best view of these objects. Note that the two boats start loading almost immediately when you load the exported file (see Figure 5.13).

FIGURE 5.12

Inline objects as they appear in the MAX scene.

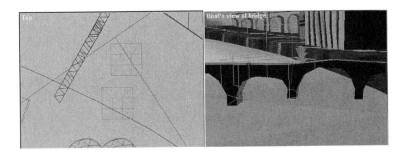

FIGURE 5.13

Inline objects as they appear in the VRML world.

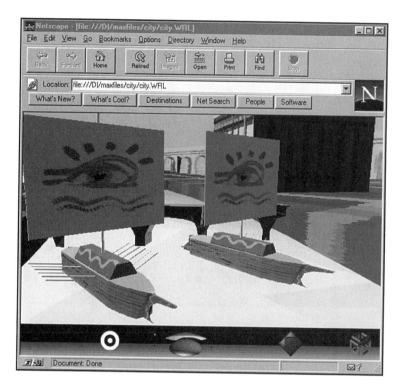

Level of Detail (LOD)

The LOD helper speeds redraw time by substituting different versions of an object. The more detailed, complex object is loaded when the viewer is close; the less detailed, less complex object is loaded as the viewer moves away.

To add a LOD object to a scene, choose VRML 2.0 from the list in the Helpers section of the Create panel to display the LOD helper. Follow the procedure in the VRML Exporter section of the MAX R2 online help file to create the LOD objects. Because you need to place the objects at the same coordinates, you cannot see them all simultaneously. The best way to handle them is to hide and unhide them as necessary. Figure 5.14 shows the settings used for the LOD objects in the sample file.

To see this feature in the sample file, open the Lodcity.wrl file in your browser. The initial Camera view's setting for the world gives you a view of the LOD objects. Navigate forward in the viewport toward the building immediately in front of you. As you draw near, the plain texture-mapped-box building changes to a fully modeled version.

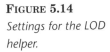

FIGURE 5.14

Settings for the LOD helper.

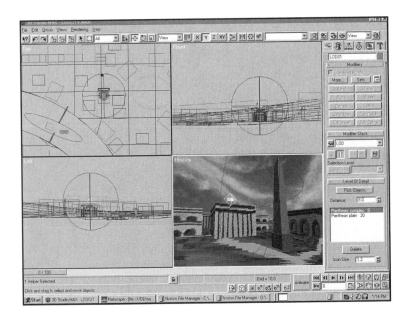

Anchor

The Anchor helper creates a link from an object in the VRML world to another URL (WRL or HTML file) or to another Camera viewpoint in the same world.

In Exercise 5.4, you add several Anchor objects to set up jumps to different cameras in the scene. The viewer can then click four objects to go to close-up Camera views: the Colosseum, the Island, the Aqueduct, and the River.

EXERCISE 5.4: USING THE ANCHOR HELPER

1. Open the 05max01.max file. The different Camera views are already defined.

2. Select the Anchor helper under VRML 2.0 helpers in the MAX Create panel.

3. Place the icon in the Top viewport.

4. Click the Pick Trigger Object button and then click the Colosseum Building object.

5. In the Description field, enter Go to Colosseum camera. Some browsers (such as Live3D 2.0, for example) display this text in the Browser viewport to guide the user.

6. Select Set Camera and then choose the Colosseum camera from the list.

7. Repeat Steps 3 through 6 to add three more Anchors to the scene. The trigger objects are the Island (Go to Island view camera), the Aqueduct Structure (Go to Aqueduct camera), and the River (Go to Downriver camera).

8. Export and test the file.

NOTE

Select the *Map View with Anchors* camera viewpoint from the list in the browser. You should then be able to click the four objects—the Colosseum, the Island, the Aqueduct, and the River—to go to close-up camera views. In Cosmo, the pointer in the Browser viewport changes to a cross to indicate that you are over an object for which an Anchor has been defined (see Figure 5.15).

FIGURE 5.15

Selecting an Anchor link.

TouchSensor

The TouchSensor helper starts an animation or sound file when the user clicks the linked object.

In Exercise 5.5, you add a TouchSensor helper to open the Colosseum door.

EXERCISE 5.5: USING THE TOUCHSENSOR

1. Open the 05max01.max file.

2. Select the TouchSensor helper under VRML 2.0 helpers in the MAX Create panel.

3. Place the icon in the Top viewport.

4. Set one of the MAX viewports to show the Colosseum camera view.

5. Click the Pick Trigger Object button and then click the right door (Door2) to the Colosseum. The name of the object appears in the Control panel.

6. Click the Pick Action Objects button and then on both doors (Door 1).

7. Export and test the file.

When you place a TouchSensor, first pick the trigger object (the object to be clicked). Then pick the Target object or objects (the object(s) animated or the Sound helper activated). Figure 5.16 shows the settings used in the sample file.

NOTE

Select the Colosseum camera viewpoint from the list in the browser and click the right door to open the door.

AudioClip and Sound

The AudioClip and Sound helpers work together to provide 3D, spatialized sound in the world. Spatialized sound is sound that increases in volume as you approach its source.

Figure 5.16

Settings for the TouchSensor helper.

In Exercise 5.6, you add an AudioClip helper and a Sound helper to create the 3D sound of oars splashing in the water.

Exercise 5.6: Working with AudioClips

1. Open the 05max01.max file.

2. Select the AudioClip helper under VRML 2.0 Helpers in the MAX Create panel.

3. Place the icon in the Top viewport.

4. For URL, enter splash.wav.

5. Add a text description (optional); this text does not appear in the browser.

6. Check the Loop box and the Start on World load box.

7. Select the Sound helper under VRML 2.0 Helpers in the MAX Create panel.

8. Place the Sound helper in the Top viewport, near the bridges on the river.

9. Click the Pick AudioClip button and then click the AudioClip helper you just added. The name of the AudioClip01 appears in the Control panel.

10. Use the Min/Max spinners to adjust the blue and red ellipsoids. These two ellipsoids show the distances within which the sound is at full volume and still audible, respectively. Figure 5.17 shows the settings to use.

11. Export and test the file.

FIGURE 5.17
Settings for the Sound helper.

NOTE

Navigate toward the ships on the river. As you get closer, you should hear the oars splashing in the water. As you go farther away, the sound fades out.

This completes the construction of the ancient city world. If you've followed the steps in this section, you now know how to use all the helpers provided by the VRML Exporter, except for Fog and Billboard. Fog colors objects based on their distance from the camera and Billboard helpers set objects so that they face your camera at all times.

Browser Review

Several VRML browsers are available that do a fine job of implementing the VRML specification. As this book is being written, VRML means VRML 2.0. The VRML 2.0 spec was approved in mid-1996 and the best browsers support it. Not all VRML 2.0 browsers are equal, however. This section looks at some of them, comparing them specifically in terms of how well they handle VRML files exported from MAX with the VRML Exporter.

WARNING

URLs discussed in this section can and often do change. If you find that a link is no longer correct, it's best to use your favorite search engine, such as Yahoo!, to find the most current location of the Web page. You can also visit the VRML respository at: **www.sdsc.edu/vrml/** for the most up-to-date information on VRML.

A Note on VRML 1.0 Browsers

Things change very quickly on the Web and what is true today may not be true—or be only relatively true—tomorrow. Other browsers may appear that are superior to the ones discussed here, but these browsers are the best available today, however. They are likely to continue to evolve along with the VRML specification itself.

On the other hand, some browsers have not evolved fast enough to be included in this review. The most notable of these is the Topper browser from Kinetix, which still supports only VRML 1.0. Topper adds some extra functionality (called VRBL) that is not in the VRML 1.0 specification, but these extra functions (which are for basic animation) have been superseded by the new functionality in VRML 2.0. However, Topper has been discontinued in favor of more recent products by other vendors.

NOTE

Changing VRML browsers is a simple task: download the new browser and run the setup program. In most cases, this automatically installs the new browser over the old one. The next time you access a VRML world, the new browser should run (exceptions are noted in the following browser description sections).

World View 2.1 from Intervista

Intervista's World View is a handsome browser with excellent navigation tools—a genuine and very fast VRML 2.0-compliant browser. Intervista does not display the lights and texture maps of the MAX model very well, however, having obviously sacrificed some display quality to speed. Figure 5.18 shows the sample WRL file in the World View browser. Even though the sample is in black and white, you should be able to see the pixelation of the textures and the absence of shadows (compare this with Figures 5.19 and 5.20 in the next two sections). World View is recommended as a primary browser only if navigation speed is much more important to you than appearance.

FIGURE 5.18

A sample VRML file in Intervista's World View.

T IP

World View has a Pointer tool that enables you to click an object to zoom in on it. Another tool, Stand-Up Straight, puts you in an upright position relative to the horizon.

Download the browser at **www.intervista.com**. World View automatically installs itself over Live3D in Netscape without stopping to inform you that it has renamed the Live3D DLL. It has an uninstall program in case you want to get Live3D or another browser back again.

Community Place, from Sony

Community Place, a browser from Sony, is promising but has some peculiarities. In particular, the navigation tools are difficult to use and don't seem to do what you expect (not easily zooming directly forward in the viewport, for example). This browser supports Gravity, a feature also found in the Cosmo player. With collision detection on, it provides a suitably unpleasant thudding sound effect when you walk into something. As for the display of lights and textures, Community Place generally is somewhat better than Intervista's browser (compare Figure 5.19 with Figure 5.18), and Community Place loads and navigates a file almost as quickly as the Intervista browser.

Cosmo Player 2.0, from Silicon Graphics

The VRML Exporter was originally developed and tested with the Cosmo browser in mind. Cosmo's capability to display MAX lights and textures is much better than that of the other browsers reviewed here. The drawbacks to Cosmo are its speed—it can be extremely slow. You can navigate either by manipulating the navigation control in the dashboard or by moving the mouse in the viewport itself. Lastly, the display quality is also much more faithful to the original.

Download the browser at cosmo.sgi.com. Cosmo automatically installs itself over Live3D in Netscape.

FIGURE 5.19
*Sample VRML file in
Sony's Community
Place.*

FIGURE 5.20
*Sample VRML file in
Silicon Graphics'
Cosmo Player.*

Live3D 2.0 from Netscape

Netscape produces a VRML browsing plug-in for Web browsers called Live3D. Live3D is a very attractive, very fast browser with good light- and texture-display capabilities (see Figure 5.21). This is really the browser to use for general-purpose Web surfing, although you might want to try Cosmo to see whether you prefer it. You can give Live3D a test drive as well as seeing what's possible by visiting the Netscape Web site and searching the keywords "Cool Worlds."

FIGURE 5.21

Sample VRML file in Netscape's Live 3D 2.0.

The Best of the Web

What makes a great VRML world, given the limitations of today's technology? This section points you to some of today's best VRML Web sites and discusses some general characteristics of these top-flight VRML implementations.

The Genesis Project
(www.3d-design.com/livespace/genesis)

The Genesis Project, an ongoing demonstration site for VRML features, operates under the auspices of *3D Design* magazine. It provides a good example of a world created with MAX and the VRML Exporter, showing simple but effective use of animation and texture mapping.

Intervista's VRML Circus
(http://www.intervista.com/3D/Circus/circus.wrl)

FIGURE 5.22

Animated juggler from Intervista's site.

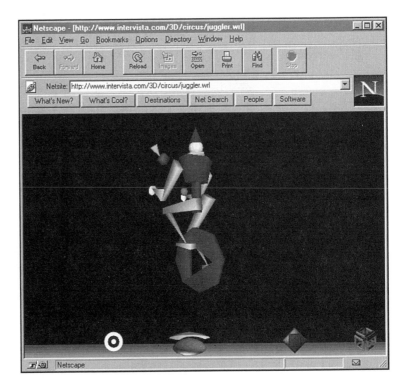

Steel Studio Landscape
(www.marketcentral.com/vrml/gallery.wrl)

This VRML world provides a great example of the use of scale. Try zooming back from the initial camera view to see the real extent of the objects that make up the scene (see Figure 5.24).

FIGURE 5.23

The Steel Studio land-scape.

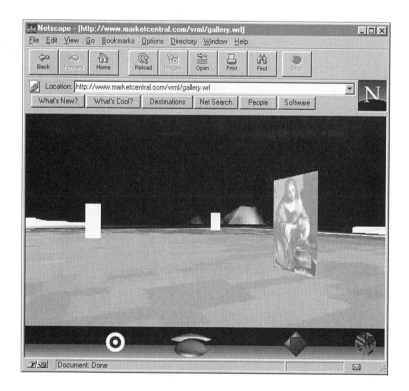

Construct's Stratus Gallery
(www.construct.net/stratus/)

The Stratus gallery is an elegant way of displaying 2D artwork in a 3D world (see Figure 5.25). The gallery shows good use of many different camera viewpoints (one for each canvas hung in the gallery).

FIGURE 5.24

*Artwork hanging in
the Stratus gallery.*

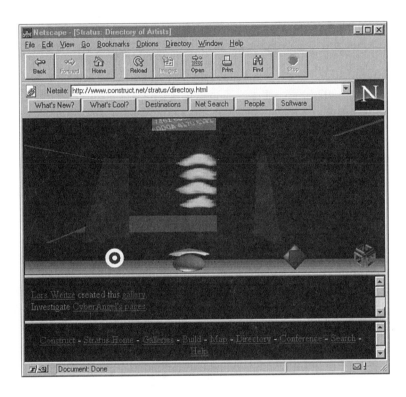

In Practice: Modeling for VR and the Web

- **VRML's bright future.** VRML is an open standard that provides an evolving framework for 3D artists. The combination of MAX, the VRML Exporter, and VRML 2.0 browsers such as Cosmo and Live3D makes it possible for you to create truly interactive environments you can share with others through the medium of the World Wide Web. If you are an architect, for example, you can point potential clients to models they can walk through. If you are a game designer, you can set up spaces where users can play against one another online. VRML has tremendous potential for many applications.

- **Modeling techniques.** You can use many simple techniques to keep down the size of your scenes so that when you export them to VRML format, they load quickly and perform well. These techniques include reducing the number of segments in primitives, deleting unnecessary faces, optimizing objects, and using instances.

- **The VRML Exporter.** The VRML Exporter enables you to export VRML 2.0-compatible worlds from MAX scenes. Using the VRML Exporter helpers is a simple process, but you can create some powerful effects with them (multiple, clickable trigger objects and 3D sound, for example).

- **Think VRML.** Creating scenes for display and interaction on the World Wide Web is essentially different from creating scenes for film and video or CD-ROM. You always have to think about the limitations of the medium and how to make the most of them. "Thinking VRML" also means trying to visualize how people will relate to the worlds you create, as well as how they will experience and navigate through them. All of this implies cooperation and sharing—and that's what the Web is all about.

Chapter 6

CINEMATICS AND HIGH-DETAIL MODELING

If there's one thing that almost every person is familiar with, it's cinematic 3D graphics. These days we are completely surrounded by all kinds of computer-generated items—digital actors, props, even complete films. Furthermore, the game industry has brought Hollywood to the monitor. You can now experience games as if you were watching a movie. Many games have already been produced with budgets that surpass those of many films! Where is all of this money and effort being spent? The producers are buying computer technology and artists to go along with it.

Whether you are already an animator in the "biz" or are thinking about it, there's one thing that you must have—impatient patience. This means knowing when something is feasible and when something is completely beyond the scope of what a computer can do—and figuring a way around it. Anyone can shove a project through with brute force, but this often leads to excessive spending on both people and resources. A skillful animator knows when a project, as it's currently defined, is simply beyond the scope of the software and how to adjust the approach to get the same result through different means.

Although the preceding paragraphs aren't necessarily unique to the film or game industry, you'll tend to find much more of this impatient patience behavior in these industries. Why? Tight deadlines. As an animator in these industries, you're always given a heap of projects to complete and not enough time to complete them.

The trick of being an animator in this business is knowing how to streamline your projects *before* you get into them. This mentality is what you'll find outlined here. You'll start not so much by learning the modeling process but rather what to avoid *before* you start to model. You'll be more efficient in the long run and you might even be able to finish a project in time. To that end, you'll explore the following topics in this chapter:

- Hardware considerations
- Texture mapping for detail
- Starting with primitives or lofts
- Scene optimization

Although there's quite a bit of cinematic and film modeling information contained within the chapter, you'll find that there's information for just about anyone who needs to know more about high-detail modeling. Let's first start with the bad news.

High-Resolution Modeling Pitfalls

Many novice animators wonder, "Why do those animators need all that expensive workstation hardware to get the job done? Everyone says that MAX can do it on a well-equipped PC." Well, if you've ever tried to work with a high-detail scene, you know what the answer is processing power.

Whenever you throw a bunch of triangles at your system's processor (CPU) and say, "Chew on these and give me a model," it taxes the system's power. The more highly detailed a scene is, the more power you need. This is perhaps the most serious pitfall of doing high-resolution work. Even the fastest computer isn't fast enough for richly detailed scenes.

Although the PC has come of age in terms of its status in being a workstation-quality computer, it still faces the same problems that more expensive workstations face: processing power. As an animator, you need to know where the bottlenecks are so that you can minimize the "slow-CPU syndrome" as much as possible.

Hardware Limitations

When you talk about a workstation—in the case of MAX, a PC workstation—you're actually talking about several components. Even though they are independent of each other, they must all work together to give you the best performance possible. These components include the

- CPU

- RAM

- 3D accelerator (display)

Although this book isn't an advertisement for hardware manufacturers, hardware is king in this business. If you don't have the top of the line in all three categories, you're in the wrong business. The time you sell yourself short on hardware is the time that you lose a bid for a job because you can't complete it on time. Like a Boy Scout, "Always be prepared."

The question is how. If you have to upgrade, what should you upgrade first? To find the answer, first evaluate what it is about your computer that seems slow. Is it the display, the rendering time, or just a general "slowness" that you can't quite isolate to one component? Whatever the case is, you'll find that there are really three steps to upgrading (or buying a new computer) and they should be followed religiously. These steps are upgrading the

1. RAM

2. CPU

3. Display

RAM

No matter what anyone tells you, consider RAM first when buying or upgrading a computer, especially if you work with high-resolution models. You see, MAX R2 has no concept of external reference modeling to help streamline the process. External referencing objects, or *XREF*s, are proxy components within your scene that point to, or reference, another file. Using XREFs enable you to see an entire scene for reference but save RAM by loading only the part of the scene you need to work on.

Take a character, for example. While working on its torso, you would probably like to see the arms and legs, but you wouldn't need to edit them. By making the arms and legs XREFs, you can conserve RAM and improve system performance. Because MAX does not have this capability, you'll eventually need to load the entire scene into MAX. Even if you work on it in small parts, you'll have to bring the whole scene together at some time. Loading in high-detail models takes a good amount of RAM.

The absolute *last* thing you want to have happen is for your computer to start using your hard drive as virtual RAM. As you may already know, your high-end workstation can turn into a high-end "pig" that moves about as fast as you do when you wake up in the morning. To avoid this, get as much RAM as you can afford, or that your computer can take. Realistically, you'll need a minimum of 128 MB of RAM to do most cinematic projects, but don't be surprised if you end up needing more. It's not uncommon for workstation PCs to have 256 to 512 MB of RAM these days. If there's one thing you should remember about the importance of RAM, it's this: Even the fastest CPU becomes unimaginably slow if it doesn't have enough *physical* RAM to work with.

CPU

The next consideration is the CPU, or processor. The CPU is almost as important as RAM, so you shouldn't skimp here either. The first thing to consider is a single or multiple CPU solution. For most cinematic work, you'll want to have a dual CPU system. Notice that we didn't say more than dual—this is due to the way MAX works with the CPUs in your computer:

- MAX performs nearly twice as fast when running a dual-CPU computer versus a single-processor model with respect to interactivity— that is, your interaction with the MAX interface. Adding more than two CPUs does not benefit you as much in the interface.

- MAX benefits from more than two CPUs in rendering speed. Complex scenes using environmental effects and high-detail geometry exercise the CPUs more than a simpler scene does.

So if you're going to be doing the modeling/animation *and* rendering on one computer, load up on CPUs. If you're going to be modeling on the computer and sending the rendering off to a rendering farm (a network of rendering-only computers), two CPUs will be fine. Because speeds change so quickly, it's pointless to mention a specific speed to get. The easiest thing to remember is that if you can afford the fastest, get it.

3D Acceleration

There's been a ton of progression in the 3D acceleration market since NT has become more prominent in the 3D animation industry. PC users used to be restricted to fast 2D acceleration video cards. It wasn't until about 1993 that 3D acceleration manufacturers began to produce for the PC. Since then, many technologies have come. In fact, some are already gone.

When you're modeling for cinematics or anything high-resolution, a 3D acceleration card is a must. The primary reason for this is that an accelerator card can relieve the CPU somewhat from having to make the calculations to display geometry in the viewports. If the CPU has to worry less about what to display and more about what to do with the geometry, you'll be working much more efficiently. The key to accelerators is that they take some or all of these processing tasks to their own processor and free up the CPU to work on other tasks. The more they are designed to take on, the faster the display will be.

MAX R2 supports three technologies for 3D acceleration. They are

- HDI or Heidi
- OpenGL
- Direct3D

All three technologies are faster than just using a standard VGA card—even a 2D accelerated one. Many cards on the market support at least one of the three technologies—many support all three.

Heidi Versus OpenGL

When MAX R2 shipped, there was much debate as to which would be best: Autodesk's new Heidi technology or the already established OpenGL technology. Since then, it has become obvious which seems to be winning. The most prominent technology currently is OpenGL.

The interesting thing is that OpenGL came from Silicon Graphics. OpenGL actually began as an acceleration technology for workstations. Today, it is the fastest way to accelerate your 3D display. If you're looking into a card that will accelerate your display, make sure that it supports OpenGL.

Heidi is still a very viable solution, however; but because Heidi is an Autodesk-developed technology, it isn't as prominent in much of the industry. Heidi is supported in Windows 95/98 and NT 4/5.

NOTE

Windows NT provides OpenGL emulation that works with most cards, accelerated or not. If you select the OpenGL option, you might think you have 3D acceleration when in fact you don't. Likewise, Heidi with specific hardware drivers provides 3D acceleration for R1 (but no manufacturer is presently developing R2 Heidi drivers.) Software Z-Buffer is also part of Heidi and is strictly software-based.

Direct3D

Direct 3D is an acceleration technology developed by Microsoft for Windows 95/98 and NT 5.0. Although it's still in its infancy for the workstation market, many game developers are already supporting it for their real-time 3D interactive games in Windows 95. Because Microsoft is the owner of both OpenGL (a licensed technology) and Direct3D (their own), it will eventually come down to choosing one of the two technologies to support in upcoming versions of Windows. To be safe, get a card that supports at least OpenGL, and then check to see if the manufacturer supports Direct3D. Most will in the future—even if they don't currently. It's important to note that many cards support all three acceleration technologies.

Editing Issues

So why all this talk about hardware? Simply put, it comes down to how fast you can work on the PC. If your computer is slower than you can think, you're not at your peak productivity level, especially for editing. If you want to change the look of a model or an entire scene, you'll need a high-powered machine. However, you can take other steps to make modeling on high-detail scenes a little easier.

Hide Geometry

The most obvious method of speeding up the editing process is to hide objects that you aren't working on. This can be done two ways. The first is to use the Display panel, which is where you control which objects or object types are displayed and how they're displayed. The other method, new to MAX R2, is to use the Display floater.

Using the Display Floater

Rather than having to access a panel, you can call up the Display floater and keep it up, regardless of what you're doing to an object in a viewport. This can save a great deal of time by eliminating switching back and forth between panels. The Display floater comes in extremely handy in full-screen or Expert mode. Figure 6.1 shows MAX R2 in Expert mode with the Display floater active.

You can launch the Display floater from the Tools pulldown menu, but not, however, in Expert mode. You can alleviate this problem by assigning a keyboard alternate to call the Display floater. This is especially crucial because you'll often find yourself closing the Display floater. Unlike most floaters, the Display floater cannot be minimized. Figure 6.2 shows the Tools pulldown menu displaying a good keyboard alternate for the Display floater.

FIGURE 6.1

A shot of the Titanic model in Expert mode. The Display floater helps control which elements are being displayed without having to go to the Display panel.

FIGURE 6.2

The Display floater option in the Tools pulldown menu with a keyboard alternate assigned to it. A keyboard alternate helps speed access to this critical function.

Setting Up Display Groups

Hiding geometry can be the easiest way to speed the editing process, but it can also be tedious if you don't organize your scene properly. One of the easiest things you can do is to arrange your objects into "display groups." These groups can consist of objects that you hide or unhide collectively. Because you can instruct MAX to display and hide objects by name, the "display group" technique can be very effective. The only downside is that you cannot *hide* objects in Expert mode using this method, only restore them. Otherwise, this method works great for just about any high-detail scene you might be working on.

Using Proxies

One method for working with high-detail scenes is to use proxies—or stand-in objects. Instead of having every piece of the original geometry in the scene, you replace them with simple geometric primitives. This way, you have an idea of the shape, size, orientation, and animation of an object without the complete object's overhead. Hiding or unhiding objects does not have this benefit. Once you're ready to replace a proxy mesh with the real object, you can use the Replace command, new to MAX R2.

 Replace lets you work in your scene with stand-in geometry and then replace the geometry with the working model later on. The geometry must be named the exact same thing as the proxy and must be loadable from a .max file. Figure 6.3 shows the Replace dialog.

FIGURE 6.3

The Replace dialog allows you to select geometry from a .max file and replace the objects of the same name in your scene.

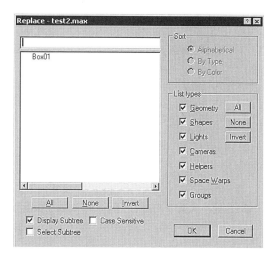

T IP

A benefit of using replacement objects is that your transform animations (Move, Rotate, and Scale) are based on the object being replaced. The replacement object, however, imports all other animated parameters, such as Material and Modifier properties.

Streamlining Texture Mapping

Textures are an essential part of any scene, especially high-resolution models. As of MAX R1, you've been able to display those textures in your viewports. This invaluable feature makes placing decals and the like on objects extremely easy. As an animator, it becomes a critical component of the scene design process.

The benefits of being able to display maps in a viewport far outweigh the downsides, but they do exist. When working with high-detail scenes, you'll find that it isn't difficult to push the limits of your computer or video card by displaying many textures in the viewports. In MAX R2, some features are designed to help you out in the texture display department.

Displaying Maps

By clicking the Material Editor's Display Maps button, you can display the most common Map types, such as Bitmap, in viewports. If you're using Heidi through the standard Software Z-Buffer option, you'll use the computer's memory to display textures. Although this is a great thing if you have a good amount of RAM, it also means that there's less RAM for other MAX operations.

If you're using some type of hardware acceleration in the viewports, the hardware usually has some sort of texture memory onboard. This form of texture memory is often much quicker than the computer's generic RAM, but it is limited. In high-detail scenes, it's not uncommon to reach your card's upper limit of texture memory. When you do reach that limit, the card now takes on the process of both loading and clearing its memory in order to display the textures. This swapping process is analogous to your computer using its hard drive to swap RAM data. It also results in similar but not equal performance degradation.

So the golden rule should be display only what you need. Let's face it, the only *real* reason you need to display textures in the viewports is for placement on a 3D mesh. After that, you're usually done. If you are done, turn off the Display Map option in the Material editor. This speeds up performance all around.

Deactivating All Maps and Disable Textures

Switching off maps in your viewports can be done in two other ways. One is more permanent while the other is designed to be temporary. The Deactivate All Maps option, new to MAX R2, turns off the Display Maps button for every material that is currently displaying a map in the viewport. The key thing to remember about this option is that it is not a toggle. It's a one-way trip. The only way to reactivate the maps is to turn them all on again one by one. Use this feature only when you need to turn off all the maps in the viewports. MAX will confirm the operation as seen in Figure 6.4.

FIGURE 6.4

The Deactivate All Maps option in the Views pulldown menu. Use this feature to turn off the Display Maps option for every material being used in the scene.

A less permanent option for turning off maps is Disable Textures, located in the Viewport Configuration dialog. To get there, right-click any viewport label and choose Configure. You'll find Disable Textures in the Viewport Configuration dialog's Rendering Method tab. The default is off. Turn this feature on to temporarily disable textures in your viewports. Turning on Disable Textures enables you to keep the Display Maps option on for your materials, while still being able to turn off the display of the map in the viewports. Figure 6.5 shows this dialog.

FIGURE 6.5

FIGURE 6.5

The Viewport Configuration dialog where the Disable Textures option is located. Use this feature to temporarily turn off texture displays in your viewports.

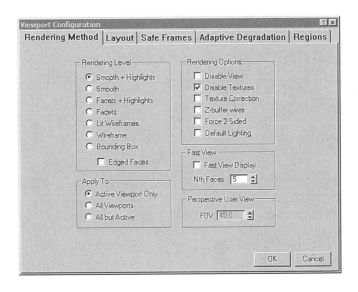

Building the Basic Model

Models that you build for cinematic sequences will more than likely start from simpler objects. As a matter of fact, this is often easiest to do. Depending on your background, you may find "building" a model from a simple object or "sculpting" a more complex model from a simple piece of geometry easier. In either case, with MAX you have the luxury of starting simple and getting complex only when and where you need it.

In this section, you'll explore some of the more common ways to model in MAX. Later on, you'll see how you can apply some of these techniques to more complex modeling techniques.

Starting with Primitives

Modeling with primitive objects is, by far, the easiest way to model. The trick is to think ahead a bit to determine what you want to end up with. When you're modeling for high-detail models, don't rely on just one primitive object to complete your model. Instead, you might want to think of your model in terms of smaller pieces that you can put together later to produce the final result. This is especially true if the camera is going to closely examine a particular surface.

Knowing which primitive to start with and what detail level is appropriate is the challenge. Let's first talk about which primitive works best for a given situation.

The Box Primitive

It can be said that almost anything can be modeled from a box. For the most part, it's true. You can push, pull, or rotate a box of just about any detail level to produce a more complex model. Using the MeshSmooth modifier produced the smoothness of the model.

The biggest benefit of using a box model is that the faces extrude at right angles. This means that shaping a model into some more complex geometry is much easier to do. Instead of faces extruding in every direction, as it often happens with rounded primitives, the faces of a box extrude in the direction you intend.

Non-Box Primitives

You'll often find yourself using primitives other than a box for a more rounded look. For instance, a very common model to build from a sphere is a head. Figure 6.6 shows what's possible using the Displace modifier to push and pull on the vertices of a GeoSphere.

FIGURE 6.6

A GeoSphere shaped by the Displace modifier. Using this method, however, requires that the model be somewhat detailed in order to deform properly.

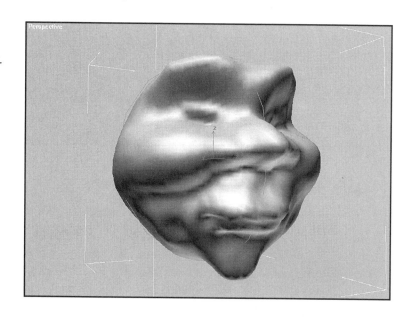

Loft Objects

Building from Loft objects can sometimes be a better way to design a model. First off, you have more control over the way an object is surfaced. Secondly, you can custom design the style and shape of your model by using different cross-sections along the extrusion path. For instance, if you were to design the exhaust pipe of a truck, you might want to use lofting. Figure 6.7 shows what this might look like. Producing the complex twists, scaling, and turns of the pipe would not be as easy if you used a primitive.

FIGURE 6.7

Complex exhaust pipes produced through the lofting process.

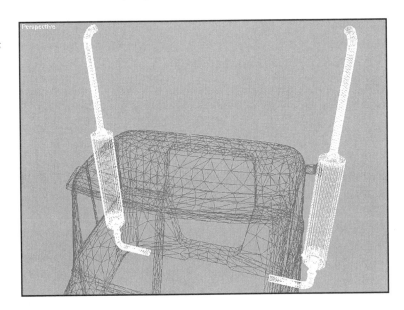

MeshSmooth

Now that you've seen the basics, let's get into how to actually *use* MAX for high-detail scene design. The first feature that you'll look into is MeshSmooth.

MeshSmooth has turned out to be the sleeper hit for MAX. Since the later days of MAX R1, people have discovered its usefulness as a tool for turning low-detail models into high-detail ones. Whether you're building a character or designing a spaceship, it's fair to say that MeshSmooth should be part of your modeling arsenal. If you're not familiar with MeshSmooth already, it does two basic things. It adds faces to the mesh like Tessellate does and softens the edges like Relax. In effect, it smoothes the topology of the mesh.

In MAX R2, MeshSmooth has been enhanced in a few ways. One of the enhancements is the toggle buttons that indicate whether MeshSmooth operates on triangular faces or N-sided polygons. (This feature is identical to the Eliminate Hidden Edges feature of MeshSmooth in MAX 1.2.)

Essentially, working on faces produces a result that is tessellated based on all edges of your mesh—even the invisible ones. The result is that you'll have a mesh that looks like a bunch of interconnecting triangles. It also means that your polygon count increases dramatically. Use this option when you're working with very smooth, rounded geometry. Otherwise, use the second option—Operate on Polygons.

Operate on Polygons forces MeshSmooth to work only on the visible edges of your mesh. The result works really well for shapes such as box and cube-like objects. This option also keeps your face count down. You can usually get away with using Operate on Polygons most of the time.

The third new MeshSmooth option, Quad Output, actually produces a mesh that is built from quadrilateral facets. Although the mesh itself is still made from triangles, you'll see what appears to be quadrilateral faces. Figure 6.8 shows this feature with Operate on Quads on as well. Notice how uniform the mesh looks. This is because the mesh is built from a Box primitive. The MeshSmooth modifier is restricted to operate only on visible edges and produce quadrilateral faces only. The end result is what you see in Figure 6.8. It almost looks as if the mesh was scanned in using a 3D scanner versus being built from a Box primitive.

FIGURE 6.8

A model built from a Box primitive. The quadrilateral mesh produced is a result of using MeshSmooth using Operate on Polygons and Quad Output.

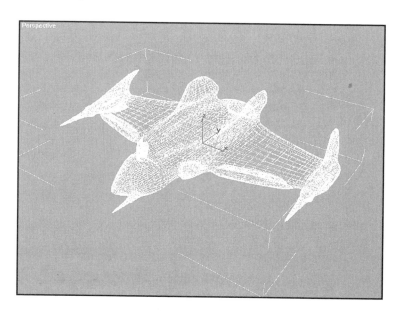

When building high-detail models for cinematics, you'll find MeshSmooth a great tool. Later on in this chapter, you'll explore some of the ways to use MeshSmooth in your day-to-day modeling techniques.

Applying MeshSmooth to Your Model

You can use MeshSmooth on your model in a few different ways. The first is to apply the MeshSmooth to the whole mesh. The other option is to apply MeshSmooth to a specific section of your model. Using one versus the other completely depends on your intended final result. Exercises 6.1 and 6.2 will explore the usage of each option on the same model. The model, first shown in Figure 6.8, began from a box and was rounded out using MeshSmooth.

Using Apply to Whole Mesh

MeshSmooth's new Apply to Whole Mesh option allows you to apply the modifier to the whole model regardless of what sub-object elements you may have selected on the geometry. This means that you can work on any area of the model without having to worry about the wrong selection getting passed up the modifier stack to the MeshSmooth modifier.

To illustrate this, take a look at a how to model using MeshSmooth and Apply to Whole Mesh. Exercise 6.1 demonstrates using MeshSmooth on an entire model, while working on only one area of the model at a time.

EXERCISE 6.1: MESHSMOOTH ON AN ENTIRE MODEL

1. Load 6max01.max from the CD-ROM. This contains a scene with a simple Box primitive that has been converted to an editable mesh.

2. Select the Box. From the Edit pulldown menu, select Clone.

3. At the Clone options dialog, choose Reference and name the object Reference. Then click OK.

4. Go to the Modify Panel and click the More button. Choose MeshSmooth.

5. In the MeshSmooth Parameters rollout, change the strength to 0.2, select the Operate on Polygons button, turn on the Apply to Whole Mesh option, and set Iterations to 2. This produces a slightly smoothed box.

6. The original Box primitive, called ship, should not be smoothed at this point. Select the Ship primitive.

7. Switch to Sub-Object mode at the Face Level.

 8. Select the Long Faces-named selection set from the Named Selection Set pulldown list. Press the Spacebar to lock the selection.

9. Use the Extrude Amount spinner to extrude the side faces six units. Note that at this point, the reference copy shows the MeshSmoothed version. It is being fully affected despite the Sub-Object selection being passed up the stack.

10. Right-click over either of the selected faces and choose Scale.

11. Scale the selected faces to about 75 percent of their original size.

12. Use the Extrude command again to extrude the selected faces 25 units.

13. Again, use the Scale command to scale the faces to about 50 percent of their original size.

14. Choose the Move command and select Restrict to Y. Move the selected faces back so that their nearly parallel to the back of the craft.

15. Click the Material Editor button in your toolbar and choose the Wireframe material in the lower-left slot.

16. Click the Assign Material to Selection button to assign a Wireframe material to your "framework" mesh.

17. Render the viewport.

This example shows the value of having the Apply to Whole Mesh option. Without it, you would have seen the smoothing on only the selected faces you were pulling on, rather than the entire model. This would have made using this particular modeling method useless. The completed result is in Figure 6.9.

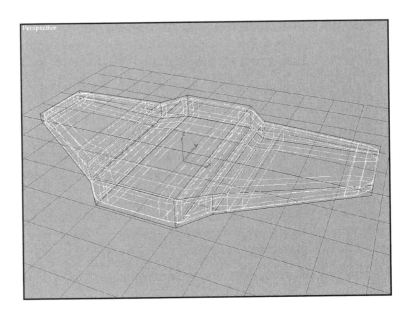

MeshSmooth for Sections

Sometimes you'll want to control the smoothness of a specific area of your model. For instance, you may want to select the wing tips of the ship model and smooth them less or more than the rest of the model. MeshSmooth works the exact same way on a selected area of a model as it does on the entire model. Using MeshSmooth in combination with the MeshSelect modifier can do this fairly easily.

Using MeshSelect

MeshSelect, a new modifier for MAX R2, contains the same capability as VolumeSelect to select the faces, edges, and vertices of a 3D mesh. Unlike VolumeSelect, MeshSelect allows you to select non-contiguous areas of a model. MeshSelect does *not* allow you, however, to animate your selection—unlike the VolumeSelect modifier. MeshSelect is also dependent upon mesh topology. This means that if you alter the number of faces in the model somewhere in the stack before the MeshSelect modifier, you destroy your selection.

A big feature that's gained with the MeshSelect modifier is the ability to grab sub-object selections from other selection levels. For instance, if you have vertices selected on a mesh and then switch to the Face selection level, you can use the Get Vertex Selection button to select those faces that are based on the selection of vertices.

In Exercise 6.2, you'll come back to the ship that's been modeled a bit more. At this point, you'll use the MeshSelect modifier to select the wing tips to smooth them at different levels than the rest of the body.

EXERCISE 6.2: MESH SELECT AND MESHSMOOTH ON THE WING TIPS

1. Open 16max02.max from the CD-ROM. This scene contains two views of the same ship. You'll start by working in the Front viewport.

2. Select the Ship model and go to the Modify panel.

3. Apply the MeshSelect modifier. At this point you can select the wing tips one of two ways. You can either use the Select Invert command or you can manually select the wing tips. Which one do you think is easier?

4. From the Edit pulldown menu, choose Select Invert.

5. Click the More button in the Modify panel. Choose MeshSmooth.

6. Set the Strength of the MeshSmooth to 0.4, Quad Output to On, and Iterations to 2.

7. Click the MeshSelect button.

8. From the Edit pulldown menu, choose Select All to select not only the wing tips but the rest of the mesh as well. Note that you can also exit Sub-Object level to instruct MeshSelect to select the whole object.

9. Click the More button in the Modify panel and choose Smooth.

10. In the Smooth Parameters rollout, turn Auto Smooth on to apply smoothing the entire model.

11. Choose Zoom Extents in the Perspective viewport and render the scene.

As you can see, by using a combination of MeshSelect and MeshSmooth on specific sections of the model, you can vary the levels of smoothing on a model fairly easily. Both the authors and Kinetix recommend that you collapse the model from time to time to save on computer resource usage. Figure 6.10 shows the completed result from Exercise 6.2.

FIGURE 6.10

The completed result from Exercise 6.2. The varying levels of mesh smoothing are a result using multiple MeshSelect and MeshSmooth modifiers on the model.

Using the Clone System

When it comes to modeling, cloning multiple-repeating geometry—such as a swarm of bees—can often be the quickest way to edit your scene. As a matter of fact, it's sometimes the only way to model efficiently enough to get a project done by deadline time.

Cloning an object refers to making some sort of duplication. This duplication can result in a straight copy of the object, a Reference of the object, or an Instance. All three types have their own benefits, but the Instance is proving itself to be a very valuable clone object. Figure 6.11 shows both stair and column objects that are Instances.

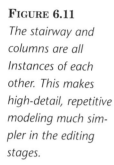

FIGURE 6.11

The stairway and columns are all Instances of each other. This makes high-detail, repetitive modeling much simpler in the editing stages.

An Instance is an *exact* duplicate of the original object. They both behave the same way and they look the same. The only things that can be different are the material they use and their position, rotation, and scaling data. Figure 6.11 is a good example of a typical scene needing Instances. Here are some tips for dealing with Instances:

- **Use the Array operation when necessary.** Use the Array tool whenever possible. Array can make multiple clones—as Copies, Instances, or References—at calculated distances in both 2D and 3D directions.

- **Use named selection sets when possible.** The example in Figure 6.11 would be well suited for this. You could create one named selection containing the columns and another for the stairs. That makes applying materials and hiding objects for editing purposes very efficient.

Lofting for Detail

Most of your modeling can be done without lofting these days. Instead of lofting being one of the few ways to model, it's now one of many. Because careless lofting of shapes can result in a great amount of detail in the model, most animators avoid it. Take Figure 6.11 for example. The columns could have been easily lofted, but without careful planning, the resultant objects would have been far more detailed than was needed. As it stands, one of the columns, created with the Lathe method, is just shy of 1,500 faces. A lofted object, using default settings, would have nearly double the faces.

There are times, however, when lofting can be quite beneficial. Using the columns again as an example, you may need to add finer detail to the column itself than a Lathe operation can do. The only way to build an object like a column with more detail than the Lathe modifier provides is with lofting.

Exercise 6.3 enhances the columns in this scene. You'll use a Loft object to build a new column and then replace the columns in the scene with new Instances.

EXERCISE 6.3.1: BUILDING A COMPLEX COLUMN USING LOFTS

1. Open 06max03.max from the CD-ROM and render the scene. You'll see an image very similar to Figure 6.11.

2. From the Floater pulldown menu, choose Display Floater.

3. Select Unhide All to reveal the hidden Loft object.

4. From the Named Selection Sets pulldown menu, choose Instances.

5. In the Display Floater dialog Hide section, click Hide Selected. Then click the Object Level tab.

6. Uncheck the Shapes category and then close the Display floater.

7. Go to the Modify Panel and select the Loft Object.

8. In the Path Parameters section, type 5 in the Path field. Then in the Creation Method section, click Get Shape and select the circle shape in the viewport. By repeating this technique, you will get shapes for several path levels and define the contour of the loft.

9. Type in 8 and select the circle shape again.

10. Type in 10 and select the rounded star shape. Select the star again at Path level 85.

11. Type in 90 and select the circle shape again to complete the column.

12. Change the name of the object from Loft01 to c and press W to return to a four viewport configuration.

13. From the File pulldown menu, choose Save Selected. Call the file c.max.

14. Render the scene to see the completed column (see Figure 6.12.)

FIGURE 6.12

The completed, more complex-looking column created using Loft objects versus a Lathe.

The completed rendering in Figure 6.12 demonstrates that lofting a column can produce a much more realistic result. In the next exercise, you'll use a little trick to replace all the existing columns with the new one.

EXERCISE 6.3.2: REPLACING THE SIMPLE GEOMETRY

1. Open 06max03.max, the original column scene. Open the Select by Name dialog and select any one of the objects beginning with "Line."

2. Rename this object to c. (These columns are all Instances, so in the next step replacing any one replaces them all.)

3. Select Replace from the File pulldown menu. Load the file you saved earlier called c.max. If you do not have it, you can load the one from the CD-ROM.

4. When the Replace dialog appears, choose the object named c and click the OK button.

5. When prompted to Replace materials, choose Yes.

6. The old columns will be replaced, but they are slightly higher than the old ones. To correct this, start selecting one of the columns.

7. Go to the Modify panel and click the More button.

8. Choose Xform from the list and then click OK to apply the modifier. Because all the columns are Instances, they all have Xform applied.

9. Right-click the Move button in the top toolbar. (Make sure Move is active as well.)

10. In the Offset column, enter –3.0 for the Z value.

11. Close the Move Transform Type-In dialog and render the scene. You now have a new set of columns!

This method is a clever way to replace multiple objects in a scene with one incoming object easily. By working with just one of the columns, you are able to affect all in the scene, because they are all Instances. When working with complex, repeating geometry, this can be a big time-saver. Figure 6.13 shows the completed rendering from Exercise 6.3.2.

FIGURE 6.13

The completed rendering from Exercise 6.3.2. The old columns are replaced with the new ones using the Replace command and the benefits of Instances.

NURBS U-Lofts and UV-Lofts

The object created with the loft process described in the previous section is a polygonal mesh. As a result, you must primarily perform Sub-Object level operations on the geometry to edit it. As of MAX R2, you can now create similar types of NURBS-based surfaces, called U Lofts and UV Lofts. Both surfaces rely on NURBS curves to work properly.

The process for creating U and UV lofts is very similar to creating a Loft object. The primary difference, however, is that there is no path, only cross-sections. You can use U and UV lofts to build all sorts of geometry, but for cinematics you'll often find yourself using NURBS to create characters and complex organic-looking surfaces. You can find more information on U and UV lofts in Chapter 1, "Modeling Concepts."

Cinematics can benefit greatly by using NURBS surfaces. The primary reason for this is that the level of complexity in the viewports is far less than what is actually rendered. Consider Figure 6.14. The engine was modeled from a photograph of a real jet engine. The curves are accurate as well as the cross-sections. The viewport model, however, is relatively low detail as compared to the model that is rendered.

FIGURE 6.14

*A 737 engine modeled
from photographs of
an actual engine using
NURBS U Lofts.*

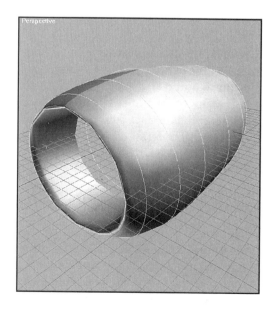

For most uses, you'll need to work with the Surface Approximation values for the surface to render smoothly. There are three options for the way the surfaces approximate either in the viewports or the renderer. Typically, you can leave the viewport settings to their defaults, but the defaults for rendering rarely work well for highly-detailed models. Figure 6.15 shows the Surface Approximation section in a NURBS surface object level edit parameter.

FIGURE 6.15

The Surface Approximation rollout of a NURBS surface. You'll often need to set the Rendering values lower to produce a smooth mesh.

Curvature-based approximation works the best for smoothly contoured models. The default values for Distance and Angle should be more along the lines of 0.5 and 5 respectively. Note this produces a *much* more detailed mesh at lower settings. If your rendering time is already long, you might consider reducing face counts in other areas of your scene before proceeding to increase the detail of your model. For more information on the various settings for the NURBS surfaces within MAX R2, consult the online help.

Optimizing the Model for Animation

When you're building high-detail geometry, chances are you'll be viewing it from different angles as well as for different lengths of time in your animation. Because high-detail models can get a bit unwieldy during complex sequences, you might try to evaluate what is absolutely critical for the scene to pass without the viewers noticing. For instance, there's no need to model people in a stadium if you're not going to get close to every one of them. Even if you are, you can swap low-detail versus high-detail as you get closer or farther away.

These aren't really cheats, but rather optimizations. There's no need to overload the computer with a highly detailed model if you're viewing only one section of it for a particular shot. Studios don't build entire buildings just so they can shoot one room on one floor. To do such a thing would be just plain impractical. Even though a computer can theoretically handle an entire high-detail model, there's no practical reason to do it. When you're working with an animated shot, you'll find yourself being able to take advantage of some of these optimizations.

Determining Animated Entities

The first step in working with high-detail animated scenes is determining which parts of it are actually animated. For instance, is there an asteroid somewhere in the scene that comes hurtling past the camera? Is there a character that is in the scene for a second or two? Run through the shot to see which parts of it are animated in the camera's view. This will help you figure out which areas of the scene you can optimize. Let's take a look at some possibilities for optimizing your scene:

- To go back to the asteroid example, think about the asteroids themselves. Are they all individual objects? If so, think about using a Particle system instead. Not only can you control an asteroid field more easily this way, you can also randomize the animation much better. Less individual objects means less transform data that MAX has to keep track of and, consequently, less resource usage.

- If you are animating several of the same pieces of geometry, are you using the Scatter compound object? This is a much more efficient way to model and animate if your scene contains several of the same object. The Scatter compound object even has the capability to display proxy geometry instead of the actual mesh. This can be a huge time-saver. For more information on the features of the Scatter Object, refer to the MAX R2 online documentation.

NOTE

The Scatter compound object is great for randomly distributing multiple iterations of the same object across the surface of some other object. Each Instance of the scattered object, however, will not have its own Transformation matrix. This means it cannot be moved, rotated, or scaled independent of the distribution object.

By figuring out which areas you can cut down with respect to objects, you'll find that both your scene editing process and the rendering times are greatly reduced. The principle of "less is more" holds true for high-detail scenes and animation.

Removing Non-essential Animated Components

There will be times when you realize that a particular element within your scene can be eliminated—at least as geometry—from the rendered shot. Determining this takes rendering a few previews of your animation or perhaps even a thumbnail 320×200 rendering of the shot. Those elements that pass by the camera too quickly for the viewer to notice should be eliminated or replaced by lower detail components.

For instance, many less-experienced animators tend to model every small element of a detailed model. Although this is fine for still and close-up shots, there's no need to have some of the minor elements present for an animated shot. There's no need to have a high-detail model of a pilot in a fighter ship that's passing by quickly. You can often get away with a small bitmap representation of the pilot instead.

Camera Angle Optimization

How can you optimize the camera angle? By including those elements in the scene that are *critical* to the shot and eliminating everything else. (Of course, if you're not the director of the piece, you may not have any control over this.) Some beginning animators worry about every component that *might* be present in a shot rather than what *is* in the shot. By reducing the area that the camera sees and focusing on the subject more, you can get rid of elements outside of the camera and therefore increase rendering performance.

Removing Elements Not Seen by the Camera

In Figure 6.16, you can see a few objects. The engines of this starship are in the shot, but the camera is positioned in such a way that it cannot see the rest of the ship. Your immediate reaction should be to eliminate the rest of the starship model.

FIGURE 6.16

The starship has been reduced to just its engines because that's all the camera sees. This helps both editing and rendering performance.

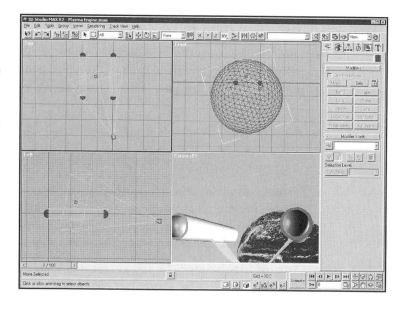

Warning

Sometimes elements in the scene out of sight may still influence the rendering. Be careful not to remove objects that cast shadows or are reflected in other visible objects.

Texture Map Considerations

Most animators learn early on that if you can do it with a Texture map, then don't model it. For animators who do high-resolution film cinematic work, this can often be impossible to do. Texture maps tend to fall apart visually as you get closer. The only workaround is to model it.

As a cinematic animator, however, you're also able to take advantage of the fact that the camera, the objects, or both are often moving. Where possible, substitute Texture maps for your geometry—especially for models that are far off in the distance or moving rapidly. Again, think of Particle systems, which are capable of emitting texture-mapped flat planes. These planes render very quickly and provide a level of realism that you would normally achieve only through models.

In Practice: High-Detail Modeling

- **Don't sell yourself short on hardware**. Clients don't care that your PC wasn't fast enough to render the project on time. It's up to you to make sure that the hardware you have can meet the deadlines you take on.

- **RAM is king.** Before all other components, you should invest in RAM. A high-end workstation computer without sufficient RAM for cinematic modeling is like a Porsche without gas.

- **Hide geometry when possible**. Even with the most sophisticated hardware, your computer will eventually slow down in more detailed scenes. A great way around this is to hide extra geometry. You'll find that MAX is much more responsive that way.

- **Apply MeshSmooth to geometry for smoother surfaces.** Although not the same as applying smoothing groups, the MeshSmooth modifier actually adds faces to the edges of your object to produce a smoother model. Rendering times are longer but often worth it.

- **Cull down your scene for animations.** Whether it be reducing geometry count in a model, hiding non-essential objects, or liberal use of Texture maps, you can always find ways to optimize your animations before rendering.

Chapter 7

CHARACTER MODELING

You might refer to the task of modeling characters as the ultimate challenge. With so many different yet critical factors playing a part in making a character what it is, it's no wonder that people stress out at the thought of having to assemble a character. Fortunately, if you're new to modeling characters, many other animators have gone before you. As a result, several styles and techniques have surfaced that can help you along in your quest. On the other hand, if you're tried modeling a character or two in the past, you may find that there are some features hidden within MAX that can make your character modeling life easier.

With the addition of NURBS and some polygonal tools, modeling characters in MAX has never been easier. It's just a matter of knowing where everything is and where to begin. Although this chapter explores character modeling in MAX R2, you'll also get a chance to explore:

- Character modeling basics

- Building characters using NURBS

- Building characters using patches

- Building characters using polygons

The discussion will focus not so much on techniques for how to build character components but rather on the various modeling technologies that are available in MAX R2 and how you might use them to build characters. For a more in-depth discussion on character modeling and animation, you should look at *Inside 3D Studio MAX 2, Volume III: Animation*.

Character Modeling Basics

No matter what type of character you build, all characters have the same foundation: basic shapes. By beginning with 2D shapes or 3D primitives, you start from a very simple object that will eventually turn into a more complex character. Where you start on your character, however, depends on what your end result must be.

Common Starting Points

Characters can be built from several starting points. The most common is to begin with the body and model outward. In the case of a character modeled from a human, this is the hip and torso area. By starting from the body, you can then add on arms, legs, and a head. For many animators, this method proves to be the easiest.

Figure 7.1 shows an example of a character modeled with the body-outward approach. The hips and torso are part of one object. The arms, legs, and head are all separate objects that are added on later. The only major downfall of this method is that when the character animates, the seams where the limbs meet the body might become evident. You can, however, work around this problem. For Polygonal models, you can use the new Connect compound object to join shapes. Exercise 7.5 demonstrates how to use the Connect object along with ShapeMerge to correct this problem.

FIGURE 7.1

Modeling a character using the body-outward method.

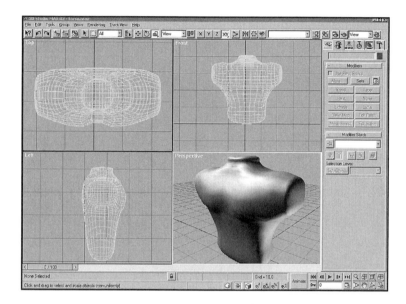

Another method for building characters is by breaking the body into a upper and lower half. If your character has an obvious waist, then this type of modeling might work best. Essentially, you'd use one or two objects for the top half and a similar method for the bottom half. Then, using either Boolean Union or just attaching via Editable Mesh, you can connect the character at the waistline. Figure 7.2 shows how a character could be built using this method. The best feature about using this method is that you'll find it animates the best, especially if you can hide the waistline through clothing or a belt or something similar.

Lastly, you can build a character one side at a time—basically splitting it right up the middle. Some animators find this method easier because it means that you can simply mirror over the entire model and you have a complete character. The primary fault with this type of modeling is that it restricts your character to being symmetrical. Of course, you can always edit one side of the body afterwards, but that can be extremely time-consuming, especially if you spent a great deal of time already modeling the first side. The second problem is that because the seam runs right down the middle of the character, it may become noticeable when the character is animated.

FIGURE 7.2

A character modeled with separate top and bottom halves. The seam at the waist can be easily hidden with some other object such as a belt.

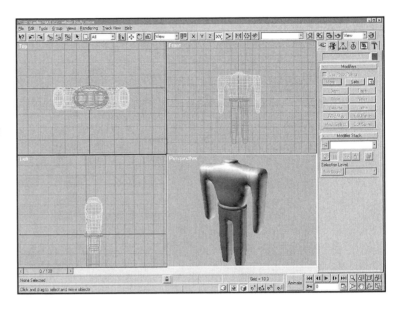

Finding which technique works best is a matter of trial and error. After some time, you'll discover which technique is better for the type of character you usually model and you'll stick with it.

Modeling Various Forms

You can create all kinds of characters. Don't limit yourself to just people or animals. You can turn a microwave into a character just by giving it a bit a personality. If the folks at Budweiser can turn a few bottles into a football team, then anything is possible! The key is the animation component. This chapter focuses mainly on modeling a character, but you're almost always going to want to animate the character in one form or another. If that's the case, then you should model with animation in mind. How will the character move? Where will it bend? From what angle will it be viewed? Answering these questions can help you determine exactly where you'll need to concentrate your modeling efforts.

Characters can be classified as either typical or unusual. A typical character is something that you'd expect to see animated like a character, such as a person. An unusual character is something that you wouldn't normally think of as having a personality, such as a microwave. Although we're not going to focus on giving either one an animated personality in this chapter, you can certainly set a "tone" for your character through just its static appearance. As a matter of fact, characters are often viewed in their "still" form more than animated. How many times have you seen a character from a show that's on a billboard, at a bus stop advertisement, a web site, or just about anywhere else animation is not possible? The way the characters pose, their facial expression at the time, all play a part in the message they convey to the audience. As a modeler, you can convey all sorts of feelings through your character just by the way they look on a "freeze frame."

Typical Characters

Typical characters, whether they be human or otherwise, are something that we can all relate to. For instance, if you look at a cartoon, the facial features and movements of the characters are usually very human-like. In that sense, we can relate to the character. If nothing else, the movements are familiar to us. Creating a typical character is actually the most difficult for this very reason. Reality is one of those elements that is still very difficult for computers to recreate. For the best in realism, you'll need to use a combination of modeling and mapping. Through effective materials, you can create a realistic skin and even folds in the skin through bump mapping. There's often not a need to model every component.

Unusual Characters

Unusual characters represent something that we wouldn't normally think of as being animated or having a personality. Although they're equally challenging to bring to life, you're not limited to what the audience "expects" to see because your model is not based on real life.

When modeling these types of characters, you need to take into account how you might build their components. For instance, take a look at Figure 7.3. If you wanted to animate the stapler, you'd probably want to have it opening and closing much like the mouth of an alligator. Therefore, you'd have to make sure that you modeled the components in such a way that when the stapler opened and closed, both the model and the movement looked correct. We all know what a stapler looks like and even how it operates, but no one knows how it would "live" because it's not possible—except in the world of MAX. From a modeling standpoint, it's just a matter of building the stapler from a real-world prop. From there, all you need to do is to make the model animate correctly by placing pivot points in the proper location.

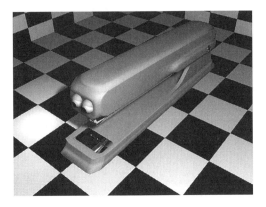

Let's suppose you wanted to have the "head" of the stapler twist and turn so that it's less like a hard plastic and more of a clay stapler. You would need to add enough detail so that the stapler could bend properly. Figure 7.4 shows how this might be done via the MeshSmooth modifier.

FIGURE 7.4

The stapler with more of a "clay-like" composition. This makes objects like a stapler appear to be more organic.

Character Modeling with NURBS

The most appropriate technology for modeling most characters is NURBS. NURBS models work well because they can be very smooth and organic without much detail in the geometry—something that is a major limitation for Polygonal models. This can be easily demonstrated with a Sphere primitive. Looking at Figure 7.5, you can see that the sphere on the left, which is made of polygons, must be of much higher detail to achieve the same level of smoothness as the NURBS sphere on the right.

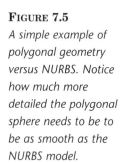

FIGURE 7.5

A simple example of polygonal geometry versus NURBS. Notice how much more detailed the polygonal sphere needs to be to be as smooth as the NURBS model.

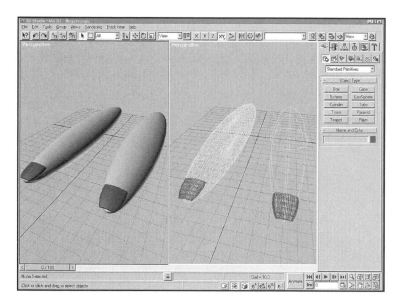

NURBS modeling provides you with several options for building character geometry. From the head all the way down to individual toes, NURBS models can work best. MAX R2 gives you several options for creating your characters. In the coming sections, you'll see how to use the various modeling technologies to construct different components of a character.

U-Lofts and Ruled Surfaces

U-Lofts are created by "draping" a surface over a series of NURBS curves. The surface itself is interpolated across several curves so as to produce a "flowing" look. This means that you'll never see where the cross-sections exist. They act more as framework for the surface to loosely adhere to.

U-Lofts work best when you're trying to create a complex shape from a series of similarly shaped curves, such as an arm, for instance. The arm is essentially a circular shape created down a long axis. Figure 7.6 shows an arm created with U-Lofts. You can build incredibly complex surfaces this way. The primary limitation is that the loft cannot split. This means that when you get to the end of the arm, you'll need to stop at the palm and then join the fingers.

FIGURE 7.6

An arm created from a series of NURBS curves used together to form a U-Loft surface. You'll create this arm in a later exercise.

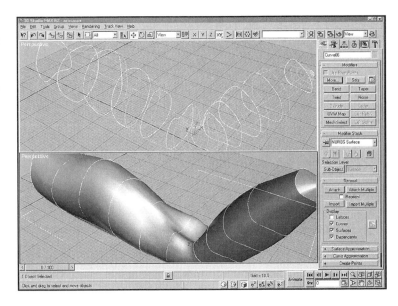

Building Cross-Sections

In order for the example in Figure 7.6 to work properly, you need to build cross-sections that will make up the overall shape of the arm. This is best achieved by using one shape and then copying it multiple times until you have enough cross-sections to build the object you want. For NURBS surfaces to be built from cross-sections, you'll also need to attach them so that they're treated as one object. Lastly, you'll need to convert the entire set of curves into a NURBS surface. From there, you can use the U-Loft command to loft across the cross-sections to create the object.

In the next exercise, you'll create cross-sections from a simple NURBS curve. Using the processes described in this section, you'll create the upper arm of a character.

EXERCISE 7.1: CREATING AN ARM USING CROSS-SECTIONS

1. Open 07max01.max from the CD-ROM. This scene consists of one NURBS curve that serves as the starting point for your cross-sections.

2. Click the Move button in your top toolbar and constrain the movement to the X axis.

3. In the Left viewport, while holding down the Shift key on your keyboard, click the curve and drag about 100 units to the right (about the equivalent of one grid square).

4. When the Clone Options dialog appears, set the number of clones to 5. Make sure Copy is the clone type selected and then click OK.

5. Using the Scale command, scale the middle curves so that they are about 150 percent larger than the end curves. You're creating the bicep/tricep shape. (This works best in the Left viewport.)

6. Click any curve and go to the Modify panel, then select Attach Multiple.

7. In the Attach Multiple dialog, select all the curves, and then click OK.

8. Now that the curves are all one object, click the Edit Stack button and choose Convert to: NURBS Surface.

9. Click the NURBS Creation Toolbox button if the dialog isn't already onscreen.

10. Click the U-Loft button and then click from one end of the cross-sections to the other. (If the normals are flipped, undo the U-Loft creation and repeat the process from the opposite end.)

11. You now have a surfaced arm, but you need to shape the muscles, by editing Control points. Switch to Sub-Object at the Point selection level.

12. Using the Move command, select and move various points on the upper arm until you have something that looks like Figure 7.7.

13. Render the Upper Arm object.

Using the U-Loft surfaces, you can easily create smooth, contoured objects through the use of cross-sections. Although a similar result could have been generated using the polygonal Loft object, the NURBS equivalent requires less geometric detail and it's much easier to animate.

FIGURE 7.7

The completed result from Exercise 7.1. The upper arm was created using cross-sectional NURBS curves and a U-Loft surface.

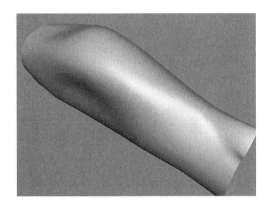

Ruled Surfaces

Ruled surfaces work, in many ways, similarly to a U-Loft. The primary difference is what happens at the cross-sections. Rather than smoothly interpolating in and out of a cross-section, the Ruled surface creates a noticeable seam. The resultant surface looks much more like a series of sections rather than one continuous surface. For smooth flowing surfaces, a Ruled surface is not as ideal as a U-Loft surface, but you can used Ruled surfaces for items such as clothes. In Figure 7.8, you can see how MAX's cape can be built very easily using a Ruled surface from two curves.

FIGURE 7.8

A simple cape object created from a two NURBS curves and a Ruled surface.

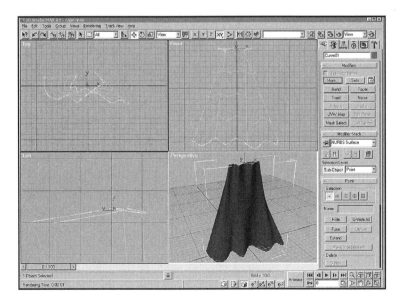

Creating Ruled surfaces works much like creating a U-Loft. You start by clicking your first cross-section and follow by selecting the remaining cross-sections. Again the main difference is that the surface appears to have a noticeable "edge" to it at the cross-sections.

Blend Surfaces

Blend surfaces allow you to join two existing surfaces together. The Blend surface is a dependent surface, meaning that it relies on the position and orientation of the two surfaces used to create it. The surface created also has no apparent seams. This means that the connection of the two surfaces is not only physical but apparent in your rendering as well. Because the Blend is dependent, if you alter the two surfaces in any way, the Blend will update.

You can use Blend surfaces all over a character. Any time you need to connect two surfaces together but cannot connect them via a U-Loft or Ruled surface, you can use Blend surface to connect them. For instance, in Figure 7.9, you can use Blend to connect the forearm and upper arm. Contained within the Blend are parameters for adjusting the tension between the two surfaces. This allows you to adjust the overall "tightness" of the Blend.

In Exercise 7.2, you'll return to the arm example. Using the Blend surface, you'll connect the two arm components. From there, you can adjust the tension of the Blend to create a better-looking elbow joint.

EXERCISE 7.2: CREATING AN ELBOW WITH BLEND

1. Open 07max02.max from the CD-ROM.

2. Click the Upper Arm object, go to the Modify panel, and then choose Attach.

3. Click the Forearm object. This attaches the two together. The forearm should switch colors to the upper arm's color.

4. Click the NURBS Creation Toolbox button to activate the dialog if it isn't already onscreen.

5. Click the Create Blend Surface button.

6. Move your cursor over the last cross-section curve of the upper arm (closest to the forearm). It should turn blue.

7. While the curve is blue, click and drag your cursor to the first curve of the forearm (closest to the upper arm) and when that curve turns blue, release the mouse button. A surface should appear now.

8. Click the Sub-Object button and set to the Surface selection level.

9. Click the new Blend surface that you just created. Switch to Wireframe mode if you're having trouble selecting the surface.

10. Scroll down to the bottom of the Modify panel until you see the values for Tension 1 and Tension 2.

11. Set Tension 1 to 1.3 and Tension 2 to 0.9.

12. Render the scene.

FIGURE 7.9

These two arm segments represent an ideal candidate for using the Blend surface. Not only are they separate surfaces, but they can also help "shape" the Blend surface through their own contours.

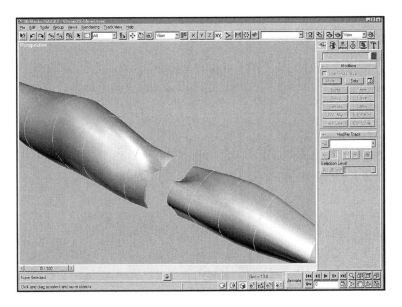

By using the Blend surface, you can create a smooth and flexible transition surface between the upper arm and forearm. The end result is something that animates very well—and you don't have to worry about it staying connected. It deforms as necessary to remain connected to the two arm components. The final result is shown in Figure 7.10.

FIGURE 7.10

The arm pieces sewn together through the use of the Blend object. Notice how the surface properly deforms to create the divot at the elbow joint.

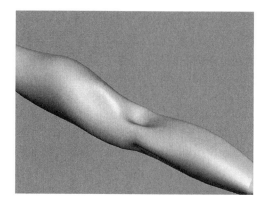

Blend surfaces can be used in other ways as well, such as if you wanted to connect the arm to the torso. Blends also work very well when you want to connect fingers to a palm. Simply trim away the areas on the palm and fingers that you want to eliminate and then connect them using the Blend command.

As with any dependent surface, both Blend and Ruled surfaces can be made independent. This disassociates the Blend or Ruled surface from the other two surfaces or curves that originally created it.

Character Modeling with Patches

Before NURBS modeling was available within MAX, the only way to get smooth, complex surfaces without too much polygonal detail was via the Patch surface. Patches come from a similar background as NURBS and they behave much like a NURBS surface. NURBS surfaces have evolved in MAX, however, to be much more complex than patches. In MAX R2, patches cannot be lofted, trimmed, or constructed from cross-sections. Instead, patches, as their name implies, are built-in sections that connect together to produce a smooth surface. Patches do require a somewhat different modeling thought process. (For a more detailed comparison of NURBS and patches, see Chapter 1, "Modeling Concepts.")

Building patches in MAX can be done in one of two ways: through Patch surfaces or primitives. Primitives give you the ability to start with a more complex shape from which to build. For instance, building an arm from a patch cylinder is much easier than building from a series of Quad Patch objects. Figure 7.11 is taken from an example in Chapter 1. This ski boot was constructed from a cylinder with the Edit Patch modifier applied.

WARNING

Although it is possible to turn any type of geometry into a Patch surface using Edit Patch, this technique is highly unadvisable. Doing so creates an enormous amount of Control points that will either be extremely difficult to edit or may crash MAX entirely. The best way to build patches is either from Patch surfaces or via the MAX primitives.

FIGURE 7.11
A simple ski boot created from a Cylinder primitive. The cylinder has Edit Patch applied to it.

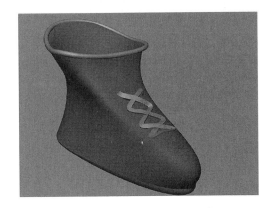

Quad Versus Tri

If you decide to use Patch surfaces as your foundation for patches, you have two choices: *Quad* or *Tri* Patches. Both types of patches create the same geometry initially. Looking at Figure 7.12, you can see what happens when you create a Quad or Tri Patch: they look very similar. The visual difference is that you can see the Tri Patch is made up of triangles, whereas the Quad Patch is made up of four-sided shapes. The main geometric difference between using either one is what happens when you add to an existing patch. When you add a Quad Patch, you're adding another square-like patch. When you add a Tri Patch, you are adding a three-sided Patch object—that is, a patch that comes to a point. When you're adding massive sections to an overall object, you should probably use Quad Patches. When you're adding in a patch to cover a small area for detail, you should use a Tri Patch. The results of using Add Tri and Add Quad are shown in Figure 7.13.

FIGURE 7.12

A Quad patch (left) and a Tri patch (right). Note that the base objects are essentially the same shape. When you add patches, as shown in Figure 7.13, the types of patches added on are quite different.

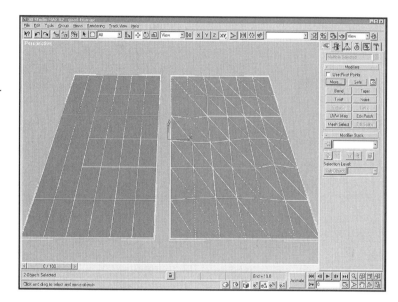

N OTE

You can add either type of patch to existing Quad and Tri Patches. This means that if you prefer to use Quad Patches most of the time, you can always add a Tri Patch where you need it.

Choosing Quad Patches

Quad Patches are best for large sections of geometry. When you're building the cheeks of a face or the forehead, you can usually get away with Quad Patches. As a matter of fact, it's better to start with Quad Patches and *add*

Tri Patches where you need them. This is primarily due to what happens when you use a patch as a flat surface. Quad Patches have less geometric detail information to bend with and produce more faces in order to bend properly. Therefore, if your surface requires little curvature, stick with Quad Patches. They'll work better when it comes to editing.

FIGURE 7.13

The same patches with added edges.

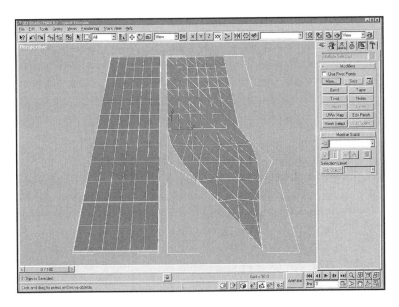

Choosing Tri Patches

Tri Patches already have enough built-in detail information to bend more efficiently. Therefore, flatter surfaces should use Quad Patches and more intricate surfaces should rely on Tri Patches. Figure 7.14 shows the combined use of Quad and Tri Patches to produce a forehead with the eye sockets. The eyes are Polygonal objects.

Building in Sections

The model in Figure 7.14 was built in sections, that is, one piece at a time. Because patches limit you to either building with flat surfaces or primitives, you'll find that you'll often need to build in small sections one at a time. This also allows you to focus in on detailed areas much more easily because there's less "extraneous" geometry to deal with. With this method, however, you eventually have to put the pieces together.

FIGURE 7.14

A forehead created using Quad and Tri Patches. The Quad Patches work well for surfaces requiring less curvature. The Tri Patches used around the eye sockets work better in areas needing more curvature.

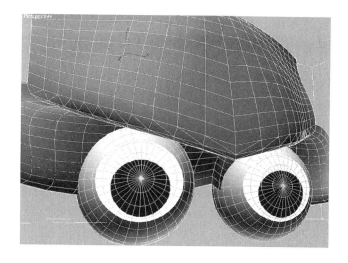

Stitching via Weld Operations

You can combine pieces of your patches with the Weld operation. This process of welding vertices together is sometimes called *stitching*. When you weld vertices together, the seam between two patches virtually disappears from the model. By combining two co-located vertices into one, you're not only joining the surfaces, you're also reducing the number of Beziér handles that are present. In a way, this helps to better control the geometry. Figure 7.15 shows what happens when the vertices along the edges of one patch are welded to an adjoining patch.

N OTE

When you add a Tri or Quad Patch to an edge of an existing patch, there's no need to weld vertices because MAX does this automatically. The main difference is that Add Tri and Add Quad just add a default patch. Manually welding vertices of patches together allows you to connect patches that you've already shaped and formed for the character.

FIGURE 7.15

The result of two patches (left) that had adjoining vertices welded together (right). Note that one patch is a Quad Patch and the other is a Tri Patch.

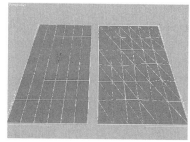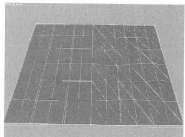

In Exercise 7.3, you'll explore how to weld two independent Patch objects together using the Edit Patch modifier. The objects started out as two cylinder primitives and were then collapsed to Patch objects. Unlike with polygonal or NURBS surfaces, MAX does not have an Editable Patch level. To be able to edit the vertices or edges of a patch, you'll need to apply an Edit Patch modifier.

EXERCISE 7.3: STITCHING TWO PATCHES TOGETHER

1. Open 07max03.max from the CD-ROM. This scene contains two independent Patch objects.

2. Select the larger (beige) Patch object and go to the Modify panel.

3. Apply the Edit Patch modifier and then click the Sub-Object button to turn Sub-Object mode off.

4. Click the Attach button and select the other patch in the Current viewport. The attached patch should change to the color of the original patch.

5. Turn on Sub-Object mode and switch to the Patch Sub-Object selection level.

6. Change to Window Selection mode.

7. In the Top or Front viewport, use the Window Selection mode to draw a window around the "gap" area that exists between the two patches. (Make sure that you select the ends of the patches that are facing each other.)

8. The end cap patches should be highlighted in red. Press the Delete key to remove the selected patches.

9. Using the same Window Selection method, select either entire patch.

10. Move the selected patch closer to the other patch so that they're almost touching.

11. Switch to the Vertex Sub-Object selection level and select all the vertices on the ends that you just moved closer to each other.

12. In the Topology section, set the Weld Threshold value to 2.0 and then click the Weld button. The vertices should connect. If they do not, raise the Weld Threshold value and click Weld. Repeat until they do.

13. Render the Perspective viewport.

This is a rather simple example of how to weld patches together, but it does show that the patches can be joined together to eliminate the seam. Unlike drawing a Blend surface between two existing NURBS surfaces, you must physically join patches together via the Weld command. The final rendering of Exercise 7.3 is shown in Figure 7.16.

FIGURE 7.16

The resultant rendering from Exercise 7.3. This figure shows how two independent patches can be welded together to not only join them but to also remove the seams.

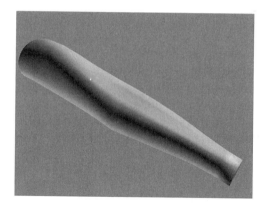

Polygonal Character Modeling

Until MAX R2, character modelers could only really rely on patches and polygons to develop their models. As a result, quite a few tools are designed to make character modeling both easier and more powerful. The Editable Mesh object is a prime example. Designed to replace the EditMesh modifier, Editable Mesh requires less memory to use and also incorporates better Sub-Object selection tools. The configurable Free Form Deformation modifiers (FFDs) are also new and improved, allowing you to wrap a lattice around a mesh for easier, more organic vertex manipulation. Lastly, a few improvements have been made to the MeshSmooth modifier to make it easier to round off the corners of a blocky model.

With all these improvements, you might wonder why polygonal modeling isn't the best way to go when modeling characters. After all, if you're already familiar with creating and manipulating polygons, why re-invent the wheel? It all boils down to how much detail you need on your model. If you're looking for high-resolution, high-detail models, you should try to work with NURBS as much as possible. NURBS models are by far the best way to model complex, organic surfaces. However, if you're looking to build a character that either requires less detail or has components on it that aren't NURBS friendly (such as hard edges), then Polygonal models will more than likely work best.

Using Editable Mesh and MeshSmooth

The Editable Mesh object allows you to work on just about any piece of geometry as a Polygonal object. You can even convert NURBS and Patch surfaces to an editable mesh. The primary benefit of using Editable Mesh is that is requires little memory and it's probably the most natural way to model with Polygonal objects. When this object is used in combination with MeshSmooth, the results can be quite amazing.

In the Exercise 7.4 series, you'll use Editable Mesh and MeshSmooth to create the right half of a character's torso. Not only will you model the torso, but you'll also organize it so that you can properly edit the model later on when you want to deform sections of the mesh.

EXERCISE 7.4.1: CREATING A TORSO WITH EDITABLE MESH

1. Reset MAX. Create a Box primitive in the Top or Perspective viewport with the dimensions of Length: 25, Width: 20, and Height: 33. Give the box two height segments as well.

2. Go to the Modify panel and click the Edit Stack button. Choose Convert to Editable Mesh.

3. Click the Sub-Object button.

4. Select the middle row of vertices in the Front viewport.

5. Move the vertices so that they're about ⅔ of the way up the box. (You may want to constrain to the Y axis so that you don't move the vertices out of their X axis orientation.) This step is basically dividing the chest from the abdomen.

6. Switch to the Face selection level and select the bottom face (the waist) of the box. Press the Spacebar to lock the selection.

7. Use the Uniform Scale command in the top toolbar to scale the face to 65 percent. Then use the Move command, constrained to the X axis and reposition the selected faces so that the left side of the box is straight in the Front viewport. Press the Spacebar to unlock the selection.

8. Turn on Edged Faces display mode in the Perspective viewport and rotate the viewport so that you can see the left side of the body.

9. Select the top-half side face (the faces just about the obliques) along the tapered side of the box. This is the beginning of the arm's socket.

10. Use the Extrude command in Editable Mesh to extrude the selected face four units. Extrude again 15 units.

11. Scale the selected face down to 80 percent and extrude another four units.

12. Lastly, extrude another 15 units and scale the end of the arm down to 75 percent. Deselect the face.

13. Select the faces on the non-tapered side of the torso. You can do this easily by dragging a window along the left edge of the torso in the front view. Press the Delete key to remove the faces.

14. Save the model, which should look similar to Figure 7.17. You can use the saved model in the next exercise if you wish.

FIGURE 7.17

The result of Exercise 7.4.1. This box-looking torso was created just by using the Editable Mesh object on a Box primitive.

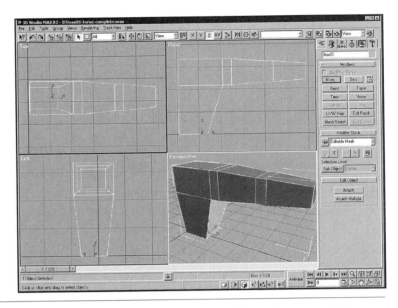

Although the result isn't all that impressive at this point, you do have a good model that will serve as a foundation for more editing in the next exercise. This is also where you'll add named Sub-Object selection sets to the model.

EXERCISE 7.4.2: ADDING DETAIL TO THE TORSO WITH MESHSMOOTH

1. Open the file 07max04.max from the CD-ROM. This is the model that you built in the last part of this exercise. (You can also use the file you saved, if you wish.)

2. Select the model and go to the Modify panel.

3. Click the More button. Select MeshSmooth.

4. Set the MeshSmooth values to Strength: 0.35, Quad Output: On, Iterations: 2, and Smooth Result: On.

5. The object is smooth at this point. Begin adding selection sets by applying the MeshSelect modifier.

6. Select the forearm portion of the model first and name it Forearm in the Named Selection Sets pulldown list in the top toolbar.

7. Repeat the process for the upper arm, the upper torso, and lower torso.

8. Save the model, which should look like Figure 7.18. You'll need it later in this chapter for another exercise.

FIGURE 7.18

The result of Exercise 7.4.2. Notice the named selection sets at the top of the figure.

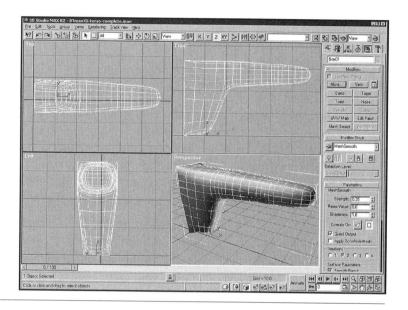

By using MeshSmooth and Editable Mesh together, you can easily create any component for a character. Although the model looks fairly simple at this point, it does serve as a good foundation for modeling more complex geometry later on. The only hitch about Exercise 7.4.2 is that you may want to add or remove detail to the torso later on in the MeshSmooth modifier. This destroys your Sub-Object selection sets. To avoid this in the future, use the Vol Select modifier instead. Because Vol Select selects geometry based on what's inside it, you can add or remove detail as needed.

Using FFDs on Polygonal Objects

The easiest way to alter polygonal geometry is to use any of the FFD modifiers. This works much like using NURBS Control points. MAX R2 contains two new FFD modifiers that help you alter the surface of a model. In all, you now have five FFD modifiers to apply to your geometry. All are located in the More button by default. They are:

- FFD 2×2×2

- FFD 3×3×3

- FFD 4×4×4

- FFD Cylinder

- FFD Box

The two new FFD modifiers—FFD Cylinder and FFD Box—have configurable points, that is, you can set the number of points that you can use to alter the shape of the underlying geometry. As you may know, the concept behind FFD modifiers is simple. Upon applying the FFD modifier to an object, MAX places a Lattice around the object. The Lattice is connected by a series of points, called Control points. As you move the location of one or more points, the model reacts as if the points are magnets pushing and pulling on the surface of the geometry. It's much like shaping a lump of clay.

FFD modifiers can be applied at the object or Sub-Object level. In either case, the Control points affect the faces that they are applied to only. The points also store their own position, rotation, and scaling data so that you can animate them. They cannot, however, be assigned to named selection sets.

For character modeling, FFDs work great for shaping basic models, much like the one you've been working with in the past few exercises. By applying FFDs to Sub-Object selections on basic characters, you can shape just the areas you want at a time. This means that you can have varying levels of detail in different portions of the model, getting more control where you need it and less where you don't.

Exercise 7.4.3 continues with the torso and arm that you created earlier. You'll apply the FFD modifier to the forearm first and then to the upper arm. This way, you can shape the arm so that it looks more muscular and less like Gumby's arm.

EXERCISE 7.4.3: SHAPING THE ARM WITH THE FFD MODIFIER

1. Open 07max05.max from the CD-ROM or use your saved file.

2. Select the object and go to the Modify panel. Choose the Face Sub-Object level.

3. Select Forearm from the Named Selections pulldown list in the top toolbar.

4. In the MeshSelect parameters in the Modify panel, click the Copy button for Named Selection sets. Choose Upper arm. You'll use this later.

5. Click the More button in the Modify panel and choose FFD (box). This applies a $4 \times 4 \times 4$ lattice around the Forearm Selection set.

6. Click the Sub-Object button to enter the Control Point Selection Level.

7. Using Move and Scale, shape the forearm so that it looks more like a human forearm. Use your own arm as a guide.

8. After you've shaped the forearm, apply another MeshSelect modifier to your object.

9. In the Named Selection Sets section of the MeshSelect modifier, click Paste.

10. Open the Named Selection pulldown list and observe that Upperarm has been successfully pasted. If it is not presently selected, select Upperarm now.

12. Click the More button in the Modify panel and choose FFD (box).

13. Click the Sub-Object button to enter the Control Point Editing mode.

14. Using Move and Scale, shape the upper arm so that it looks more like a human bicep/tricep. Again, you can use your own arm as a guide.

15. Render the Perspective viewport.

After you've shaped the arm, you can repeat the process on the upper and lower torso. Lastly, you can apply the MeshSmooth modifier to the entire model to further round out the geometry. The result can be very believable. The end result of your model might look like Figure 7.19.

Although Polygonal models don't represent the most efficient way to model characters, they can prove to be very useful for building richly detailed models that look great close up. Using a combination of Editable Mesh, MeshSmooth, and FFDs, you can build just about anything out of Polygonal primitives.

FIGURE 7.19

*A Box primitive con-
verted to an editable
mesh with
MeshSmooth and FFD
modifiers applied to
produce the right half
of a character's torso.*

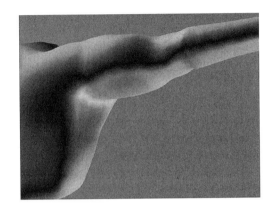

Putting It All Together

In Exercise 7.5, you will connect an arm and a torso in a way that ensures a fairly smooth blended connection. You will use the new MAX R2 feature called Section to define the openings in the arm and torso. You'll also use the new Compound object feature called ShapeMerge to cut the openings. The two objects will then be connected with the new Connect Compound object. Because ShapeMerge determines its result based on the negative Z axis of the shape used, you will learn how to cut holes on the reverse side of an object.

EXERCISE 7.5: CONNECTING AN ARM AND TORSO

1. Open 7max06.max. It contains two meshes: TORSO and ARM. Each was created from a simple box and a Meshsmooth modifier. ARM also uses several FFD modifiers. The objects were adjusted with MeshSmooth so that each has roughly the same size faces in the areas to be joined. Having the same face size makes the Shape Merge operation more predictable. The display should look similar to Figure 7.20.

2. In the Left viewport, click the Create/Shapes panel and click the Section button. Click near the upper middle portion of the arm and drag a small Section plane object. It should look like Figure 7.21.

FIGURE 7.20

ARM and TORSO mesh objects.

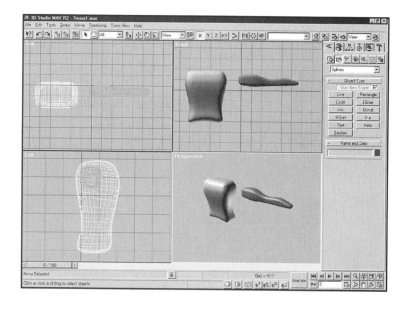

FIGURE 7.21

Section plane.

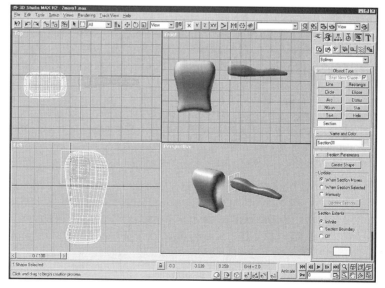

TIP

The size of the Section plane you drag doesn't matter in this case; it just describes an infinite plane in space. You can use the Section Boundary checkbox in the Section Extents area of the Create or Modify panel to restrict the section to only objects in physical contact with the Section plane.

3. With the Section plane selected, click the Zoom Extents All Selected icon. In the Front viewport, move the Section plane to the right until it looks similar to Figure 7.22. The yellow shape is defined by the plane passing through the arm mesh.

FIGURE 7.22

Section plane moved and rotated into place.

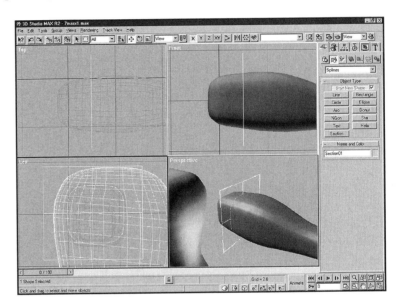

TIP

You want to take the section far enough down the arm to approach the tangent points as seen in the front and top viewports. For example, if you took a section at the tip of the arm you would only be connecting a small portion of the arm to the torso, not the full size of the arm.

4. Zoom out a little in all viewports. In the Modify panel, click the Create Shape button in the Section Parameters rollout. Name the shape arm-hole in the Name Section Shape dialog. You now have a 2D shape the same size and shape as the yellow section.

5. Press H, double-click Armhole in the Select Objects dialog, and press the Spacebar to lock the selection. In the Front viewport, click the Select and Move icon, click the Restrict to X icon, and hold the Shift key while clicking and dragging to move the armhole shape to the left into the torso. In the Clone Options dialog, check Copy and click OK to accept the name armhole01. Right-click the Front label and set the viewport to Wireframe if it isn't already. Press the Spacebar to unlock the selection. The display should look like Figure 7.23.

FIGURE 7.23

armhole01 copy inside the torso.

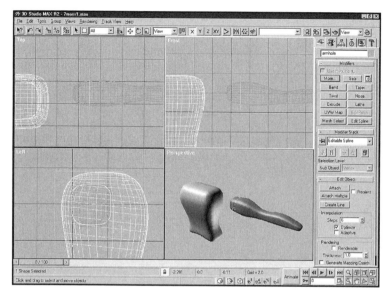

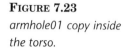OTE

The negative Z direction of this shape is pointed toward the far side of the torso, if you use it as is, it cuts a hole in the far side only. Simply rotating the Pivot Point in the Hierarchy panel does not help in this situation. You need the more complex solution outlined in Steps 6 and 7.

6. In the Top viewport, select armhole01. Click the Select and Rotate icon, then right-click the Select and Rotate icon to access the Rotate Transform Type-In dialog. Enter 180 in the Offset:Screen Z: axis field. Close the Rotate Transform Type-In dialog. The Z axis of the shape now points in the correct direction, but the shape is reversed as seen in the Left viewport.

7. In the Modify panel, click the Sub-Object button and choose Spline from the list. Pick armhole01. It should turn red. In the Edit Spline rollout, click the Mirror button to flip the shape back to its prior orientation. Click the Sub-Object button to exit Sub-Object mode.

TIP

You don't want the shape to extend outside the torso at any point because it cuts into the back portion of the torso. Move armhole01 in the Left viewport if necessary to keep it inside the torso.

8. In the Left viewport, select TORSO. In the Create/Geometry panel, click Standard Primitives and choose Compound Objects from the list. Click the ShapeMerge button.

9. In the Pick Operand rollout, click the Pick Shape button, press H, and double-click armhole01 in the Pick Objects dialog list. This merges armhole01 with TORSO and creates a new set of faces and edges.

10. In the Parameters rollout/Operation area, check Cookie Cutter. This cuts a hole of the shape instead of merging the shape. The display should look like Figure 7.24.

FIGURE 7.24

armhole01 shape cut from TORSO.

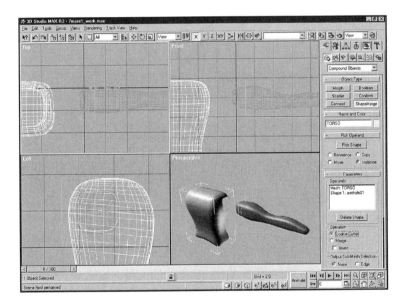

NOTE

You will see through the TORSO object because the face normals on the inside are facing away from you.

11. In the Front viewport, select ARM. In the Create Geometry/Compound Objects panel, click the ShapeMerge button. Click the Pick Shape button, press H, and double-click Armhole in the list. In the Parameters rollout/Operation area, check Cookie Cutter. This cuts the same

opening in the ARM object. The negative Z axis of the original shape is already facing the correct direction for the ARM object.

12. In the Front viewport, move ARM in the X axis until it almost touches TORSO.

13. In the Create Geometry/Compound Objects panel, click the Connect button. Click the Pick Operand button, press H, and double-click TORSO in the list. In the Smoothing area, check on Bridge to smooth the new faces. ARM is now connected to TORSO with new faces closing the two opposing holes created by the ShapeMerge operation. It should look similar to Figure 7.25.

FIGURE 7.25

ARM connected to TORSO.

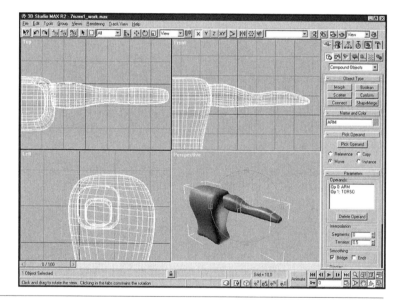

In Exercise 7.5, you learned three new features of MAX R2. You used Section to create a 2D shape that was then used by the ShapeMerge Compound object to cut holes in the arm and torso. To use a copy of the section shape in the torso, you first had to rotate it in the World Z axis, then mirror the spline at Sub-Object level to cause the negative Z axis of the shape to point in the correct direction. After you combined the holes in the arm and torso with ShapeMerge, you used the new Compound object called Connect to close the facing holes.

In Practice: Character Modeling

- **NURBS produce the best animated characters.** Pound for pound, NURBS models work the best for characters. Because they can produce relatively high-detail models with the least amount of geometry, you'll find that NURBS models are the ideal way to build a character.

- **Use Lofts and Blends to build NURBS characters.** By building characters in sections, you can use MAX's NURBS editing tools to piece everything together. NURBS Loft and Blend surfaces are the optimal surfaces with which to model when using this technique.

- **Polygonal models are easy to make but require more detail.** MAX's polygonal modeling tools are superb. You can build just about anything that you want using the Editable Mesh, MeshSmooth, and FFD modifiers.

- **Use Compound objects for Polygonal models.** You can blend two polygonal surfaces together, much like you can a NURBS surface, by using the Connect compound object. The geometry that Connect builds acts much like a dependent NURBS Blend surface.

Part II

DESIGNING CONVINCING MATERIALS

Chapter 8

MATERIAL CONCEPTS

Perhaps the most critical element of any scene, realistic or otherwise, is the type of material applied to the geometry. Surfaces can be shiny, dull, reflective, transparent, translucent, and just about any other surface property you can think of. If you've built materials in previous versions of 3D Studio or any other product, you know that creating your own materials can be both challenging and even frustrating. The flip side is that when you get the material right, the rendered image can look incredible.

When building materials from scratch, you need to understand and apply three somewhat obvious rules:

- Know the tools you have at your disposal for material creation.

- Understand how those tools work.

- Practice, practice, practice with those tools to find the settings and techniques that work best for you.

Fortunately, this chapter will help take some of the guesswork out of Rule 3, explaining how MAX R2's material creation tools work and the optimum settings to provide the best results—for most cases. You'll get a chance to see both the pros and cons of the various tools in the Material editor, such as:

- What are materials and shaders

- Procedural maps versus Raster maps

- Raytracing—the good and the bad

- Organizing your materials

There is one caveat, though. Working with and designing materials is purely subjective and you should almost certainly expect that what might work for one scene will not work for another. That being said, the examples in this chapter provide general but solid foundations for understanding the Material Creation tools in MAX R2.

Shaders

For several years, most animation software has referred to the definition of how a rendered surface should look as a *shader*. Shaders are essentially mathematical algorithms that, through various parameters, can make surfaces on geometry appear as water, wood, or even fur. You, the user, adjust the settings to produce the right look. Depending on the software, your interaction in the user interface could be visual or even strictly through numbers!

If you've used the 3D Studio product line for several years, you've always known shaders as *materials and maps*. Materials are defined by properties such as shininess, opacity, and reflectivity. This is essentially another way to work with shaders. With MAX and MAX R2, you've also seen the way a material is defined grow significantly. With the addition of the Raytrace material, there are now many new possibilities—and potential traps as well.

Types of Shaders (Materials)

Shaders in MAX appear at both the Material level and the Lower Map level. Seven default materials ship with MAX R2. Some function as *Rendering materials* that actually produce the color information that you see when you render. Other materials, *Root materials*, act as a foundation for other materials to be embedded within. They render nothing unless they contain Rendering sub-materials. The materials that ship with MAX (and their functions) are

- Blend—Root

- Double Sided—Root

- Matte/Shadow—Rendering

- Multi/Sub-Object—Root

- Raytrace—Rendering

- Standard—Rendering

- Top/Bottom—Root

This chapter focuses on the inner workings of the Standard and Raytrace materials. Although the other materials are important, the only way they can function is through the Standard or Raytrace materials being embedded within them (with the exception of the special purpose Matte/Shadow material).

Procedural Shaders and Maps

In the digital imagery field, the term "procedural" has come to mean the "automatic" or "computer-generated" way of producing renderings. Rather than being defined by bitmaps, *Procedural shaders* work by the user adjusting various numerical settings. The renderer calls the shader, which in turn processes those settings and turns them into a correctly colored image.

For instance, you could have a wooden plank shader with the sole purpose of procedurally rendering wooden planks. As the user, you could adjust the base color of the planks, maybe a default spacing for the planks, and then the average size. The renderer would then render a series of wooden planks (usually randomly generated) on the geometry where you applied the shader. Although it is possible to just convert shaders from other products into full MAX materials, it's far more flexible to convert them to maps instead.

In MAX, many shaders have already been converted into maps. Maps can be used in any Map type such as Bump, Diffuse, or Opacity. An example of a Procedural map is Perlin Marble. Rather than having to create a bitmap image of marble, you can specify two colors and the size variable; the Perlin algorithm then automatically creates a marble surface.

Another nice benefit of Procedural maps and shaders is that you don't have to assign Mapping coordinates. Because you're not using bitmaps to define how the material will look, there's no need to tell MAX how to apply it. Instead, the Procedural map knows how to evenly distribute itself across the surface or, in the case of 3D Procedural maps, through the volume of an object. MAX R2 offers several other Procedural maps for you to take a look at, such as Noise, Dent, and Wood. Refer to the MAX manuals for more information on the Procedural maps that ship with the product.

FIGURE 8.1

The result of using Procedural maps instead of bitmapped images. No Mapping coordinates are required to produce this image.

Mapped Shaders

In MAX, the two default renderable materials are the Standard and Raytrace materials. Rather than being completely procedural, these two materials are Mapped shaders that allow you to use digital images, such as bitmaps, to represent various attributes of the surface. The main benefit of using Mapped shaders is that you usually get exactly what you're looking for. Take the wood plank example from before. If you used an image of wood planks versus a procedurally defined surface, you'd get exactly the rendering of planks that you wanted.

Using Mapped shaders requires that you usually use mapping coordinates, but note that you need Mapping coordinates only when you're using a Non-Procedural map, such as Bitmap.

Using MAX's Two Main Shaders (Materials)

When you design scenes in MAX, you're almost always going to apply one of the two main Mapped shaders—the Standard material or the Raytrace material. Both provide you with the ability to apply surface characteristics to your geometry. In some ways, the Standard and Raytrace materials are the same, but in many they are different. Deciding which material works best for you can only be determined by understanding which features each one does or does not have.

The Standard Material

The Standard material is made up of several sections—Basic Parameters, Extended Parameters, Maps, and Dynamic Properties—all of which play a role in how the material performs in the MAX scene. This book focuses on all but one of the sections—Dynamic Properties. For more information on Dynamics and animation within MAX, please consult *Inside 3D Studio MAX R2: Volume III, Animation* from New Riders Publishing.

Rather than doing a feature-by-feature rundown of the Standard material, this next section will discuss the way the material works instead. After all, that's what really matters. It's not so much how high a spinner value can go but rather what effect changing that value has on the look of your material.

Basic Parameters

The *Basic parameters* of the Standard material are essentially the "core" of the material. By altering the settings in the Standard material's Basic Parameters rollout (see Figure 8.2), you are changing the basic look of the material when it's rendered. The effect of changing these values is global for the material—meaning the changes affect every part of the rendered surface. The Maps rollout, discussed later, allows you to specifically control many of the values in Basic Parameters through maps. So remember, Basic parameters equal Global Control and Maps equal Precise Control. For more complex and interesting materials, you can use a mixture of the two as well (more on this later).

FIGURE 8.2

The Basic Parameters rollout in the Standard material.

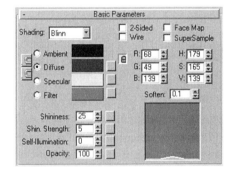

Shading

Take a look at the Shading options in the top-left corner of the Basic Parameters rollout. As you can see, four Shading methods are available in MAX R2—Constant, Phong, Blinn, and Metal. Veteran users will notice that the Flat Shading option has been removed. There was no real need for it because you can always duplicate the Flat Shading method by just setting the Shin.Strength of a Constant Shaded material to zero.

The Constant Shading method gives you the ability to render a surface without any smoothing—using only facets. If you turn up the Shin.Strength, you'll be able to add in specular highlights. So why use this feature instead of reassigning smoothing groups in Editable mesh or the Smooth modifier? Well, it's not really an "instead of" situation but rather an "either-or." In some cases, you may want facets to appear on only certain parts of your geometry depending on the material applied. In this case, you'd use the Constant Shading option of a material—probably in a Multi/Sub-Object material. If the same material is applied across the entire surface, however, you can use the Smooth modifier (or Editable mesh) to dictate where the surface renders smooth and where it renders faceted.

NOTE

Smoothing groups eliminate facets between adjoining polygons at rendering time. On geometry without smoothing applied, all materials render with facets, regardless of the Shading setting.

The next two shading methods, Phong and Blinn, appear to be very similar. In many ways, they are. If you look at the same material in the Material editor, one using Phong and the other using Blinn, it might be difficult to distinguish the difference. The real difference lies in how the two Shading methods work with specular highlights.

Try this simple test with your identical materials using different Shading methods. Expand both their windows by double-clicking them. Then set Shininess and Shin.Strength to 50 for both materials. Still don't see it? Look at the specular highlight on the back side of the material (the lower right-hand side). Notice how much more broad the specular highlight is on the material with Phong shading? That's the difference. It's much more apparent at lower Shininess settings. Why would you use one over the other? Typically, the Phong shading method produces rendered surfaces that look more plastic-like. Blinn shaded surfaces have much softer highlights. Note that both render in the same amount of time, so there is no rendering speed hit using one versus the other.

NOTE

Using Blinn shading is one way to soften glancing highlights of backlit objects. The Soften field in the Material Editor Basic Parameters rollout also has an obvious effect on the backlit portion of a material. It has little effect on the specular highlight directly facing the camera.

Lastly, there's the Metal Shading method. When you use this method, you'll notice that the Specular Color swatch disables. The reason for this is that the Metal shader uses the Diffuse Color property (map or color) to dictate the color of the specular highlight. Another difference is that when you increase the Shininess value for a metal-shaded material, you're also increasing the intensity of the specular highlight. Conversely, when you increase Shin.Strength, you're decreasing the intensity of the Diffuse color. So what's going on here? Well, the assumption is that if a metallic surface is incredibly shiny, then it reflects more of its environment rather than its inherent Diffuse color. That's the assumption, however—not the rule. In fact, the material won't reflect *anything* unless you apply some sort of reflective characteristic to the material. Metal materials actually produce a very nice shiny glass-like surface. Although metal surfaces look good using Metal shading, the fact is that the Raytrace material does a much better job of reproducing metal with *Blinn* shading.

SuperSample

Among the checkboxes in the upper-right side of Basic Parameters is a new option called SuperSample (refer to Figure 8.3). If you've ever had the misfortune of using high contrast Bump maps that have radical grayscale changes within a few pixels, SuperSample will help you immensely. In the past, such a scenario would have caused the resultant rendered surface to have a great amount of aliasing along the areas of the bumpy surface where the great changes occured. SuperSample eliminates this problem by resampling the material at Rendering time, four times to be exact. This means— you guessed it—longer rendering times. As a consequence, use this feature only when you need it. This is especially true of Raytraced materials and maps because they already do SuperSampling.

FIGURE 8.3

The effect of using SuperSampling. The left image shows a tile floor rendered in one minute, six seconds without SuperSampling. The right-hand side shows the same image with SuperSampling on and had a rendering time of four minutes, 23 seconds. The improved bump edges may well justify the added rendering time.

Color Swatches

The color swatches in the Material editor represent the color of light reflected back to the eye (camera) off the object's surface. Although we won't go into detail as to what the various color swatches mean (that's in the MAX manuals and just about every other fundamental book on MAX), you should consider their role with respect to lighting and maps.

Each of the four color swatches—Ambient, Diffuse, Specular, and Filter—determines the color of the surface as it is illuminated and sent to the eye. By using both material and light combinations, rendered scenes take on much more depth. Seasoned animators rarely use pure white lights in their scenes. For more information on lighting setups refer to Chapter 14, "Cameras, Camera Effects, and Lighting."

The Filter color is something of an exception to the reflection rule. It acts more like the colored film, called a *gel,* placed in front of a stage light. The only time you'll see the Filter color is if the object is mostly transparent. Higher Opacity values (less transparent) are less obvious.

The Filter color is the color that is perceived by the viewer when looking through a mostly transparent surface. In older versions of 3D Studio (prior to MAX), the Filter color was the same as the Diffuse color. This was not only inflexible for the user but also wrong. Many materials exist in the world that reflect one color on the surface while tinting objects behind them a different color.

For instance, consider an F-16's canopy. The canopy's surface has a thin, gold film designed to reflect the sun. However, the film covers the canopy glass, which is a smoked color. Therefore, looking at the surface of the canopy, especially in direct sunlight, you'd see a golden surface. But if you look through the canopy to the other side, everything appears darker because of the smoked glass. This rather lengthy example is designed to demonstrate why Diffuse and Filter colors are separate in MAX. Using the two *independent* of each other gives you more realistic-looking rendered surfaces.

T_{IP}

If you shine lights using Raytraced shadows on mostly transparent surfaces, the Filter color is transmitted with the light onto the surface receiving the shadow. Hence, you can tint your shadows with this method.

Shininess and Shin.Strength

Both the Shininess and Shin.Strength fields in the Standard material work together to produce the specular highlight on the surface of a object using the material. Shininess controls the broadness of the highlight, while Shin.Strength controls the highlight's intensity. The Shininess Bell Curve display is an excellent tool for determining the size and intensity of the highlight itself.

If you've used earlier versions of MAX, you may have noticed something different about the six sample materials in the Material editor (see Figure 8.4). First, they all use Blinn shading. Second, the Shininess and Shin.Strength settings are much lower, resulting in default materials that are much more "dull" in their look (refer to Figure 8.4). The primary reason for this is that most animators aren't adjusting the sample materials' Shininess settings and, consequently, everyone's renderings have that plastic look. With MAX R2, you now have to "dial in" Shininess if you want it. The key with Shininess is control. Surfaces that are too shiny not only look bad in a rendering, they'll also distract attention from your subject—not a good thing.

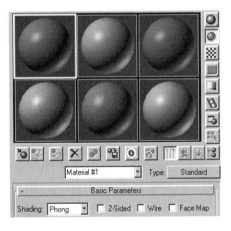 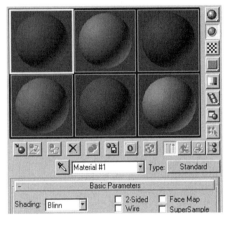

FIGURE 8.4

The Material editor samples in MAX R1 (left) and MAX R2 (right). Notice the default shading is Blinn and the Shininess settings have been reduced for R2.

TIP

An interesting technique for creating highlights on an object without over-illuminating it is to add an extra light using its Affect Specular feature, found in the Modify Panel/General Parameters rollout, while not using Affect Diffuse. This adds highlights to your object without blowing out the Diffuse colors in your scene.

Self-Illumination

When you're creating materials that represent an object that is illuminated from within, you can use the Self-Illumination option. It's a fact that a self-illuminated object does not actually cast light—it just appears to be lit. A point about Self-Illumination is that it essentially removes the Ambient color component of a material while making the Diffuse component disregard light sources. Basically light does not affect the intensity of the Diffuse color and there is no Ambient component. The effect can be convincing for many uses, such as neon tubing. If you're trying to simulate the effect of a light source illuminated from within, however, you might consider using the new Raytrace material instead. See the section "The Raytrace Material" for more information on its features.

Opacity

Opacity in Basic Parameters gives you global control over the opacity of a material. Lower values make an object more transparent and higher values make it more opaque. It does not, however, attempt to simulate refractive effects when looking through many transparent surfaces. For those effects, you'll need to use a Refraction map or, better yet, use the Raytrace material instead. If you have a flat plane of glass, there is no real perceived refraction, so using the Opacity value would be prudent here. In the section on maps, we'll discuss examples for using Opacity maps.

WARNING

If you are using a Refraction map to simulate refraction, you should not drop the Opacity below 100 percent because it ruins the Refraction effect. Refraction mapping is an illusion and not an actual refraction of a scene through a transparent object.

Extended Parameters

The Extended Parameters rollout (see Figure 8.5) gives you more precise control over many of the settings contained within both Basic Parameters and Maps. For instance, using the Out setting for Opacity Falloff produces a great looking light bulb or any self-illuminated source where the light emanates from the center out.

FIGURE 8.5

The Extended Parameters rollout in the Standard material. Notice that a new section, Reflection Dimming, has been added for MAX R2.

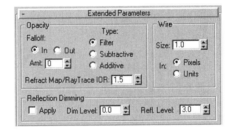

Using the various Transparency methods—Filter, Subtractive, or Additive—can help the realism of a Transparent material. For instance, light bulbs and light beams that are geometrical are great candidates for Additive transparency. Subtractive transparency can work well for neon tubing against lighter backgrounds. Filter transparency, by the way, is the default. Rather than adding or subtracting pixel whiteness values behind the transparent object, it simply tints them the Filter color.

Wire (the upper-right section of the rollout) is a method of simulating open Mesh objects, such as wire baskets, radio transmission towers, open Web beams, and so on. When the Wire option is checked, MAX uses the visible edges of a Mesh object to represent wires and the faces become invisible. The apparent thickness of the wire edge can be adjusted in the Wire section of the Extended Parameters rollout. The wire thickness can be based on pixels, in which case the wire always appears the same size no matter how close or far from the viewer. Wires can also be set as unit sizes, so that the closer you are to the object, the larger the wire appears. Wire Material attributes are an efficient method of simulating complex open Mesh objects.

NOTE

You should generally check the 2-Sided option above the Wire option so the back side of an open Mesh object becomes visible.

The newest addition to the Extended Parameters section (and a very welcome one at that) is Reflection Dimming. One of the biggest problems with Reflection mapping is that the maps don't respect light sources all that well. If you've every tried to render a Chrome object in darkness or darker scenes, you know the problem. Essentially, the Reflection Mapped material appears to be somewhat illuminated. Reflection Dimming corrects this problem.

As a rule of thumb, it's a good idea to turn Reflection Dimming on for just about every material using a Reflection map. This instantly improves the rendering quality of your scenes, but you can also use Reflection Dimming to your advantage in other ways as well. Exercise 8.1 shows how you might use Reflection Dimming to accentuate the sun illuminating the surface of the Earth.

EXERCISE 8.1: SUNRISE WITH REFLECTION DIMMING

1. Open the file 08max01.max and render the scene. Notice that the Earth looks okay, but the clouds could be much brighter where the sun is hitting the planet.

2. Click the Material Editor button in the toolbar.

3. Choose the Earth material in the lower, right-hand Material slot.

4. Expand the Maps rollout.

5. To add a Reflection map, click and drag earthy.jpg to the Reflection Map slot. When prompted, select Copy Map.

6. Set the Reflection amount to 50.

7. Render the scene. Here you can see the problem associated with using Reflection mapping. The dark side of the Earth is now completely gone—the lighting hasn't changed.

8. Go back to the Material editor and expand the Extended Parameters section.

9. Check the Apply checkbox on for Reflection Dimming.

10. Set the Reflection Level to 2.0. Dim Level should be 0.0.

11. Rerender the scene.

FIGURE 8.6

The sun illuminating the surface of the Earth. The intense clouds are a result of using a Reflection map in conjunction with the new Reflection Dimming feature of MAX R2.

You now have a much more believable planet by adding a Reflection map and using the Reflection Dimming feature. Although this feature can be used in other ways, this example clearly shows how the problem of using Reflection mapping might creep up and how you can solve it.

Maps

The Maps rollout contains slots where maps can be used to control many of the Standard material's parameters. On a basic level, some slots provide color information to the material, such as Ambient, Diffuse, Specular, Filter Color, Reflection, and Refraction. The others—Shininess, Shin.Strength, Self-Illumination, Opacity, and Bump—use the intensity of a map to alter surface characteristics of the material. By adding a map, you gain precise control over various areas of the material surface. Note that if you use a bitmap in any slot, you will need to apply UVW Mapping to your object.

Summary

The Standard material provides you with several options for creating outstanding materials. The fundamental concept that every animator must first master is control. It's both tempting and easy to alter several parameters at once. If you're just getting the hang of the Material editor, this probably isn't a good idea. Instead, adjust one parameter at a time to analyze its effect. Granted, production schedules don't often allow for close analysis of every little thing you may do; however, you may find that by just taking the time to "stop and smell the roses," you might discover a subtle function of the Standard material that you never knew existed.

The Raytrace Material

The Raytrace material, now part of MAX R2, gives you even more control over the look of your rendered surfaces—almost to an excessive level. This is the second form of "renderable" material mentioned earlier in "Mapped Shaders." Although many interface similarities exist between the Raytrace material and the Standard material, their underlying code and functionality are very different.

If you haven't spent much time with the Standard material, you should do so before taking on the Raytrace material. Take some time to learn the interface and how the various Map channels work. When you feel comfortable with the Standard material, come back to this section to get up to speed on the Raytrace material.

Basic Parameters

The Raytrace material is an extension or enhancement of the Standard material. At first glance, you might think the Raytrace interface is just Standard's shuffled around a bit with certain items renamed (see Figure 8.7). Fortunately (and unfortunately) this is not the case—not at all the case, as a matter of fact.

The Raytrace material requires that you think beyond just normal color theory to the physics of how light is transmitted, absorbed, and reflected in your rendered scene. In actuality, the Raytrace material is more accurate and realistic than the Standard material. As with learning the Standard material, learning and understanding the Raytrace material means adjusting one parameter at a time to see its effect. There are easily twice the number of features in the Raytrace material that there are Standard material. This means that you'll probably spend some time just exploring the new parameters.

FIGURE 8.7

The Raytrace material's Basic Parameters.

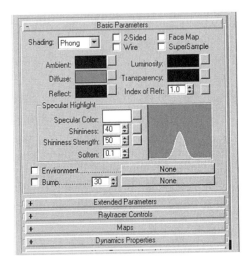

Ambient and Diffuse

Under the Raytrace material, Ambient and Diffuse have different relationships to each other than in the Standard material. Rather than Ambient just being known as the "dark side" of a material, it now becomes the amount of Ambient light that the material absorbs. Black means the material is absorbing all the Ambient light, whereas pure white means that it reflects all Ambient light (and the Ambient color is now the same as the Diffuse). Changing the hue of the Ambient color means that you'll tint the reflection of the Ambient light.

Reflection

Reflection, rather than being just a spinner and a map, is now a color too. By increasing the Whiteness value of the Reflect color, you are increasing the amount of the environment being reflected around your object. At full intensity, you will not see *any* of the Diffuse color properties in the material. If you are using any color above R0, G0, and B0, you are using the Raytracing engine and, therefore, renderings will take more time.

NOTE

Assigning Raytrace materials to all objects in a scene doesn't necessarily result in a "Raytraced scene." The Render algorithms are selectively applied during rendering to give a balance of speed and quality. More raytrace detail will be included in the following sections.

NOTE

When not using reflection or refraction features of a Raytrace material, rendering times will be nearly identical to the same surface using a Standard material.

Luminosity

A nice feature about Luminosity is that it doesn't depend on the Diffuse color as the Standard material's Self-Illumination does. You can tint the Luminosity color to anything you want to simulate Self-Illuminated effects. Although this sounds great, it has limited use because most objects, when illuminated from within, use the Diffuse color. Luminosity enables you to tweak that Self-Illuminated color to a *variation* of the Diffuse color. For instance, you may want the Luminosity color to be a brighter color of the Diffuse. Just copy the Diffuse color to the Luminosity color swatch and increase its Whiteness value. Then, if you want to animate luminosity, use the Value slider.

Transparency

Transparency has much of the same control as the Reflect color; black means no transparency and white means full transparency (and any amount of transparency invokes raytracing). However, if you want true Refraction values, you must alter the index of refraction by entering a value in the Basic Parameters rollout, Index of Refraction field. (For a complete discussion of Indices of Refraction, see the "Transparency and Refractive Surfaces" section.)

WARNING

Again, as with Standard materials, if you are using a Refraction map to simulate refraction you should not drop the Opacity below 100 percent because it ruins the Refraction effect. Refraction mapping is an illusion and not an actual refraction of a scene through a transparent object.

continues

In contrast, for a Raytracing renderer to calculate refraction, the material *must* be transparent. This is a difference of simulated refraction versus calculated refraction.

Specular Highlights

Notice that specular highlights have been put into their own section for the Raytrace material. Although not much different than their Standard material counterparts, some minor differences make the Raytrace material worth using. Many of the spinners can go well beyond the "clamped" settings of the Standard material. This means you can have incredibly shiny surfaces now. Instead of using the Metal Shading method of the Standard material, you can now use the Raytrace material's Shininess settings to produce shiny glass or metal. Soften now goes as high as 10. This can really diffuse your highlights—to the point where you can't even see them.

Environment Map

A new Map type that appears in the Basic Parameters section (and not in Maps) is the Environment map. This allows you to use some maps, other than the scene's environment, to reflect and refract. Why would you use this? Well, both the Raytrace material and the Raytrace map require that you have some sort of environment to reflect. If you don't have one, as in a case where you're using a Screen Mapped background, you need to fake it. Often, you can just use the same map as your environment.

Extended Parameters

The Raytrace material's Extended Parameters rollout opens up a whole new can of worms. First of all, notice that the Standard material's Opacity and Reflection Dimming sections have been removed, including the Transparency Filtering method. This is mainly because you don't need it. Transparency can be tinted any color now with the Transparency Color swatch or map.

What you do have are the new Special Effects and Advanced Transparency sections. Within the first section are three new Color swatches. Within the latter are several controls for fine-tuning Transparency settings. Take a look at how you might use these Extended parameters in real-world situations.

Extra Lighting

Extra lighting actually adds light from whatever color you choose to the Ambient color area of a material. The result is an effect that closely *simulates* radiosity. To get the proper control to simulate radiosity, however, you should use a map. In the following exercise, you'll see how you can use this feature.

EXERCISE 8.2: USING EXTRA LIGHTING FOR RADIOSITY EFFECTS

1. Open 08max02.max and render the scene. This is a small room with white stucco walls and a blue carpet. Click the Clone Framebuffer button in the Rendered Window. You'll want to compare differences later on.

2. Click the Material Editor button and select the lower-right Material slot, called Wall Material. Then click any one of the Walls' sub-material.

3. Expand the Extended Parameters rollout.

4. Click the blank, square button to the right of the Extra Lighting color swatch.

5. When the Material/Map browser appears, double-click Gradient to put the Gradient map into the Extra Lighting Map swatch.

6. The material is too bright. Change Colors 1, 2, and 3 to dark blue hues—from a lighter shade at Color 1 to the darkest shade by Color 3. Make the hues similar to the color of the carpet in your first rendering.

7. Set the Color 2 position to 0.8 and then click the Return to Parent button in the Material editor to go back to the main Raytrace Material interface.

8. Expand the Maps section and set the Intensity amount of the Extra Lighting map to 50.

9. Rerender the scene.

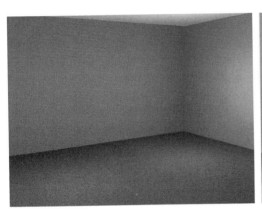 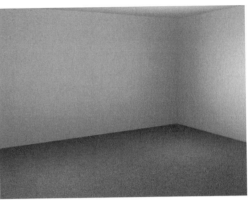

FIGURE 8.8
A Gradient map being applied to the Extra Lighting Map channel of the Raytrace material (right). In this situation, the Gradient map helps create the illusion that the color of the carpet is being reflected on the walls.

As you can see from the results of the rendering, the image gets a bit lighter, but there's much more blue now on the walls. The upshot is that it appears as if the color of the carpet is tinting the color of the walls—but more along the bottom of the wall versus the top. If you need a better idea of the color scheme for the Gradient map, see the file called Extra Lighting.max in the CD-ROM's Tutorial directory.

Translucency

Perhaps one of the best features of the Raytrace material is its capability to simulate the transmission of light through translucent surfaces. If you're not familiar with the concept of translucency, it's actually pretty easy. Think of a lampshade. When you turn on the lamp, the shade itself is illuminated from the light inside. The degree of illumination is dependent on both the light's intensity, the thickness of the shade, and the shade's proximity to the light bulb. With the Translucency feature of the Raytrace material, you can duplicate this effect. Simulating candle wax being illuminated by a lit candle is quite easy with Translucency. For finer control, use a map instead of just a global color.

NOTE

It's important to point out that you don't need bright colors for good translucency. As a matter of fact, brighter colors look less realistic. If a color is too bright, just use the Value slider to decrease its brightness.

Fluorescence

The Fluorescence parameter allows you to create rather cool, black-light effects, albeit of limited usage. To produce something akin to a black-light effect, you'll need to use both the Fluorescence color and Bias settings. Values of 0.5 and higher create black-light effects. However, you'll need to get pretty close to 1.0 for this to happen. The best effects happen when you go below 1.0. As an experiment, try setting the Fluorescence color to pure black. The rendered surface looks amazing.

Advanced Transparency

The Advanced Transparency section allows you to fine-tune a transparent material. Here's how both Color and Fog work: The Start value is the starting distance of a ray leaving a surface, the End distance is the distance that the ray must travel to fully achieve the Color or Fog effect. Think of them as environmental range settings for a camera or, better yet, like a hotspot and a falloff setting. The distance between Start and End is how long a ray must travel (in MAX units) before the pixel it affects is fully tinted or made opaque (through Fog). You could use this for a thick piece of glass, for instance.

Raytracer Controls

The Raytracer Controls section is designed to give you access to almost all the functionality of the Raytrace Map type. The main feature that's missing is attenuation control. You have falloff capabilities but not explicit controls like you do in the Raytrace map. If you need that level of control, you'll need to use the map for reflections or refractions.

A more in-depth look at some of the parameters of the Raytracer Controls section is covered later in this chapter.

Other Material Types

As mentioned previously, several other Material types ship with MAX R2. They are

- Blend

- Double Sided

- Matte/Shadow

- Multi/Sub-Object

- Top/Bottom

The main difference between these materials and both the Standard and the Raytrace materials is that they require Standard material, Raytrace material, or an equivalent to function. Although going into the functionality of the other Material types is not in the scope of this book, you can find more information on them by consulting the MAX manuals or *Inside 3D Studio MAX R2, Volume I* (New Riders Publishing).

Reflection and Refraction Concepts

As you began to see in your travels through the materials above, one of the most intriguing features of MAX R2 is its Raytracing capabilities. Raytracing adds a new level of realism that wasn't previously available in the base package. However, this realism comes at a price of both speed and ramp-up time for mastery, as you've recently experienced in the introductory sections. You can literally spend weeks working with and tweaking the Raytracing settings for just one scene.

One of the most common difficulties for people just learning about raytracing is the fundamental concept of how it works. Raytracing is based largely upon simple angular math. There are, however, many fine-tuning variables associated with angular math that make learning the Raytracer a bit daunting at first. To better understand what's going on internally with the Raytracer, let's first look at some basic, foundation-building concepts.

Light Rays and Illumination

For you to see anything, whether it be in real life or on the computer, you need light. Light travels through *rays*, infinitely small trajectories from the source. Rays travel in a constant direction until they encounter another atmospheric condition or a surface. In real life, rays not only alter their trajectory when encountering another atmospheric condition, but they also might change their grouping.

For instance, imagine light entering your favorite outdoor swimming pool. As the rays enter the water, they change direction and grouping, altering the way the light falls on the floor of the pool. That effect is known as *caustics*.

Although MAX is capable of altering the direction of a ray based on the Index of Refraction of a transparent surface, it has no way of doing caustics. Fortunately, caustics can be simulated through Projection maps.

Reflection and Reflective Surfaces

Light, except when hitting a pure black surface, is always reflected, in some way, back to the eye. Reflective surfaces can be thought of as reflective in two ways:

- *Reflecting Color.* Any surface other than matte black reflects light in some way back to the eye. The colors perceived by the eye are the color of the light spectrum not absorbed by the surface of the object.

- *Reflecting the Environment.* Surfaces can also reflect the environment depending on their surface characteristics—normally very shiny. Fully reflective surfaces are black. Other than that, there's always some sort of a mixed diffuse color in the reflection.

Transparency and Refractive Surfaces

When a surface allows light to pass through it (and you can see through it), it is referred to as *transparent*. A easy real-world example is glass. If you look at glass, you can, of course, see right through it. In MAX, this is equivalent to setting the Opacity to near 0 in the Standard material or the Transparency to pure white in the Raytrace material.

As the light ray enters a transparent surface, its course can alter depending on the difference of the density between where the ray came from and where it's entering. The angle at which the light ray strikes the surface also can alter its trajectory as it enters the surface (see Figure 8.9).

FIGURE 8.9

A light ray being refracted as it hits the glass's surface. Notice how the beam is bent as it enters and leaves the glass object. This bending of light is due to the Index of Refraction (IOR) for a given material.

The Index of Refraction is the ability of a medium to alter the trajectory of a ray as it enters the surface. The number is actually a coefficient. Common Indices of Refraction are 1.5 for glass and 1.33 for water. There are several other Indices of Refraction that you can use in MAX besides these two. Table 8.1 lists several other Indices of Refraction that you can use in MAX.

TABLE 8.1

Indices of Refraction

Material	Index
Vacuum	1.00000 (exactly)
Air (STP)	1.00029
Acetone	1.36
Alcohol	1.329
Amber	1.54
Amorphous Selenium	2.92

Material	Index
Barium Borosilicate	1.554
Calspar1	1.66
Calspar2	1.486
Carbon Disulfide	1.63
Chromium Oxide	2.705
Copper Oxide	2.705
Crown Glass	1.52
Crystal	2.00
Cubic Zirconia	2.15
Diamond	2.417
Emerald	1.57
Ethyl Alcohol	1.36
Fluorapatite, synthetic	1.633
Fluorite	1.434
Fused Quartz	1.46
Garnet	1.73–1.89
Glass	1.5
Heaviest Flint Glass	1.89
Heavy Flint Glass	1.65
Hydroxyapatite, synthetic	1.649
Ice	1.309
Iodine Crystal	3.34
Lapis Lazuli	1.61
Light Flint Glass	1.575
Liquid Carbon Dioxide	1.20
Lucite or Plexiglass	1.51

continues

TABLE 8.1, CONTINUED

Indices of Refraction

Material	Index
Opal	1.44–1.46
Polystyrene	1.55
Porcelain, feldspathic	1.504
Quartz 1	1.644
Quartz 2	1.553
Ruby	1.77
Salt	1.644
Sapphire	1.77
Sodium Chloride (Salt) 1	1.544
Sodium Chloride (Salt) 2	1.644
Strontium glass	1.550
Sugar Solution (30%)	1.38
Sugar Solution (80%)	1.49
Tooth structure, enamel	1.655
Topaz	1.61
Triethyleneglycol dimethacylate	1.457
Urethane dimethacrylate	1.481
Water (20° C)	1.333
Ytterbium trifluoride	1.530
Zinc Crown Glass	1.517
Zirconium glass	1.520

(All items except Vacuum are in alphabetical order.)
(STP=Standard Temperature and Pressure)

Note that many animators disregard these values and simply go by what looks right. If you're just getting started with refraction, start with Table 8.1 and then make adjustments to the values to get your "right look."

What Is Raytracing?

Generally speaking, raytracing is the calculation of a light ray from the point of view or camera to the light source. The reverse (from the light to the camera/point of view) is known as *Backward raytracing*. Raytracing technology is typically noted for its capability to generate super-realistic reflections and refractions in renderings. However, the concept of raytracing can be taken much further to include effects such as soft shadows and caustics (light refraction in water).

In the next few sections, we'll explore some concepts surrounding raytracing and, more specifically, raytracing in MAX R2.

Recursive Raytracing

The method of backward raytracing closely emulates the physics of light in the real world. Essentially, infinitely thin light rays are emitted from all light sources in all directions. Of the millions of rays cast, the ones that bounce or intersect surfaces eventually end up hitting the camera. The result is that each rendered pixel on the screen is made up of several rays traced from one or more light sources, each ray having interacted with one or more objects in your scene. More importantly, millions of rays are cast in directions that never approach the camera. As you can imagine, computational times would be outlandishly high if you tried to trace the rays from the light source to the camera because rays are cast in *all* directions.

Since we're only concerned with the rays that actually hit the screen, MAX works from the camera out and only figures out the rays that determine each pixel. More specifically, MAX uses the most popular raytracing technique called *recursive raytracing*. In recursive raytracing, each time a ray bounces or intersects some surface, it spawns a new ray—usually traveling in another direction. Each bounce or intersection is called a recursion. In MAX, you can control the number of recursions by setting the Ray Depth variable. The default is nine, but you may need more depending on the complexity of your scene.

There is a quick way to see if you have a high enough setting for Ray Depth. To the right of the Maximum Depth setting is an option for what the Raytracer should do if a ray reaches its maximum depth and never gets to a light source. Under Color to Use at Max Depth, you can choose to render the background or you can specify a certain color. The only time you'd ever need to use this feature is to test if your Ray Depth setting is too low. MAX's Raytracing engine is adaptive so there's no need to specify a minimum value—the Raytracer automatically finds the lowest possible number of ray bounces each pixel needs. Believe it or not, most surfaces need only one or two bounces.

FIGURE 8.10

The Ray Depth controls in the Raytrace Global Options button. You can access this feature in the Raytrace Map or Material.

NOTE

You can "clamp" the number of ray bounces to a very low setting. However, there's no real need to do this for speed purposes since the MAX Raytracer automatically determines the minimum number of bounces needed.

Lighting and Raytracing

Raytracing is dependent on lighting to work properly. Remember, rays are traced from the camera or point of view to the light source. Good placement of lights always makes renderings using raytracing look better.

MAX's Raytracing engine is not capable of tracing light color through a transparent surface. This means that colors are not projected in shadows—only the shadow itself. Also, take care when using Raytraced shadows. They do not properly cast shadows on surfaces that use the Raytrace material. However, surfaces using the Standard material with a Raytrace map cast shadows fine.

WARNING

MAX's Raytrace material apparently has a bug that prevents it from casting shadows with the Use Raytraced Shadows option checked in the lights' Shadow Parameters rollout.

Scanline Rendering versus Raytraced Rendering

MAX R2 ships with a Scanline Rendering engine. However, MAX R2 also allows for raytracing using the Raytrace map or Raytrace material. For the purposes of this book, we'll discuss the primary differences of how a Raytrace Rendering engine works versus how a Scanline Rendering engine works with respect to reflections and refractions.

In a Scanline Rendering engine, the renderer prepares the entire scene prior to the actual rendering process. It calculates all light sources, their shadows, and reflective surfaces, as well as texturing. While the preparing of the rendering can take less than a second to sometimes more than a minute, the rendering process itself is very quick. During the rendering process, a Scanline Renderer works its way down an image line-by-line. If you watch the process, it's much like a watching a scanner scan down a photograph—hence the name.

A Raytrace Rendering engine works a bit differently. Depending on the implementation, there is usually some up-front processing by the Raytracer prior to the rendering process. However, the main difference is that items such as reflections and refractions are calculated when the renderer reaches the pixel containing a reflection or refraction. If the whole scene is being raytraced, as in many programs, this can take an enormous amount of time.

MAX R2's implementation of raytracing is a bit different. MAX R2 uses what's known as a *Hybrid raytracer* that plugs itself into the Scanline Renderer. This means that the scene is raytraced only where a surface using the Raytrace map or Raytrace Material is used. This can greatly speed rendering times.

There is one caveat: Because the Raytracing engine is now working with the Scanline Renderer, the initial scene processing times tend to take a bit longer on top of the rendering time itself. First, the Scanline Renderer must prepare the scene for rendering, loading all maps, and calculating other scene properties. The Raytrace renderer then kicks in with what's known as *scene division* (discussed later in the chapter). Finally, the rendering process takes place. It is important to note that this method is still much faster than rendering engines that employ raytrace methods only—and it's just as accurate.

Anti-Aliasing

Anti-aliasing has been around since the early days of graphics. Ever since you could see the "stairstepping" effect of thin diagonal lines on a computer screen, there have been ways to smooth them out. The "stairstep" effect is called *aliasing*. To counter the effect, programs use *anti-aliasing*. Anti-aliasing employs an averaging method around a given pixel. In MAX, the anti-aliasing component of the rendering engine first analyzes a pixel, its color, and the color of the pixels around it. It then averages the colors of surrounding pixels to produce a softer edge. Figure 8.11 demonstrates the example of an aliased versus non-anti-aliased geometry in an image.

FIGURE 8.11

The anti-aliasing of the edges of a teapot. Notice that the Checker map is not aliased—this is due to the map's own Blur setting, which is independent of anti-aliasing. To alias the map, just set its Blur to 0.

N OTE

Generally, anti-aliasing is designed to work with geometry. It usually does not affect texture mapping. Most texture maps have a *Blur* setting that allows you to smooth the rendering of a texture map on the geometry. However, when the SuperSample is checked in Standard or Raytrace materials (see SuperSample in the Standard Materials section of this chapter) MAX anti-aliases everything in the scene.

Raytracing and Anti-Aliasing

Suprisingly enough, Raytraced reflections and refractions are not part of the scanline renderer's anti-aliasing calculations. This is due to the implementation of Scanline Rendering with a Hybrid raytracer. In a full Raytracing engine, the entire scene is anti-aliased using the Raytrace method. This technique is often called *oversampling,* where the Raytracer passes over the rendered image many times. Each time, it analyzes the image and determines what areas need further anti-aliasing (blurring). If you thought the rendering process was long for Raytracers, just wait around for the anti-aliasing!

Fortunately, MAX R2's Rendering engines, both Scanline and Raytracing, are more intelligent. The scanline renderer is fully analytical. It requires only one pass over the rendered image to provide the necessary anti-aliasing. The Raytrace renderer uses a method similar to oversampling, but it is *adaptive.* This basically means that instead of making several passes over an raytraced portion of a rendering, it makes only the necessary amounts needed to effectively anti-alias the image. Figure 8.12 shows the Raytracer's Adaptive Anti-aliasing controls.

TIP

If your Scanline Rendering's anti-aliasing is looking less than perfect, try increasing the pixel size of your rendering. This actually increases the size of the averaged pixels. With MAX R2, you can now increase this value to 2.0. (Increasing pixel size increases rendering times slightly.)

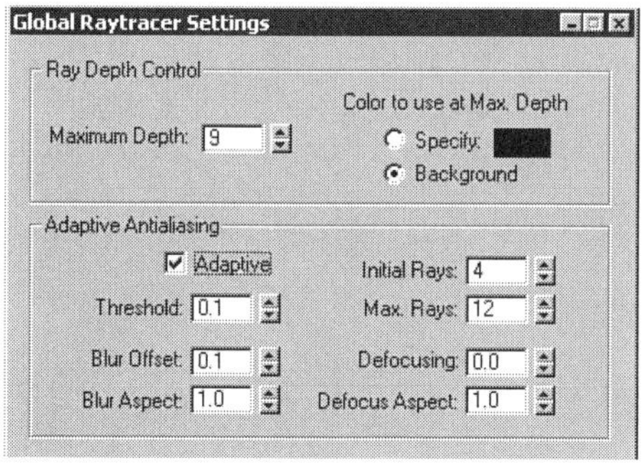

FIGURE 8.12

The Adaptive anti-aliasing controls of the Raytrace engine. This feature is located in the Global Settings button of both the Raytrace map and material.

Anti-Aliasing within an Anti-Aliased Image?

If you haven't noticed yet, when you use raytracing, there are actually two different settings for anti-aliasing—one for the Scanline Renderer and one for the Raytrace Renderer. This means that you must work with two settings now. Fortunately, you can usually leave the Scanline Renderer's settings alone and just tweak the anti-aliasing of the Raytracer.

Why and When to Use Anti-Aliasing

Anti-aliasing can greatly improve image quality in your scenes. When using anti-aliasing with reflections and refractions, this is even more true. If you render a scene with scanline, but not raytraced anti-aliasing, areas where reflections and refractions occur are aliased and usually very noticeable. If you turn both anti-aliasing options on, however, your reflections and refractions look much better. Of course, it is here where you see the major problem with raytraced anti-aliasing—speed. As soon as you enable anti-aliasing in your Raytraced map or material, your rendering performance takes a nose dive.

The best suggestion for using anti-aliasing with raytracing is to use it only when and where you need it. We'll discuss the "where" later on. For now, lets take a look at the "when."

Still-Life Imagery

A still-life is perhaps the most critical time when you'd want to use anti-aliasing. Still-life images are subject to very close scrutiny and, therefore, must be anti-aliased at all times. Fortunately, you usually do not have to worry about turning anti-aliasing on until you're near the final rendering stages. Make it a point to use anti-aliasing on objects only where you need it. See the Optimizations section for advice on how to control where anti-aliasing happens and to what degree.

T IP

You can minimize the need for anti-aliasing in a scene by employing depth-of-field blurring. See Chapter 17, "Focal Effects," for techniques on how to use the Lens Effect Focus module.

Detailed Geometry

Detailed geometry often requires anti-aliasing. The primary reason is the amount of reflection or refraction that takes place on geometry with higher face counts. Raytraced reflections and refractions rely on faces to work. (Refer to the section on voxel trees for more information.)

The more faces a Raytraced Renderer has to work with, the better the reflections and refractions are. Consequently, rendering times are much longer. There is no real way around this because you want reflections to be accurate. You can, however, alter the adaptive settings on the materials applied only to the detailed geometry that are independent of the rest of the scene. That way, you can optimize the anti-aliasing just for the surface.

Animations

Using anti-aliasing for animations is often a divided issue among animators. On one hand, there is the side that says everything should be anti-aliased—especially if you're going out to video. The reason why video is so special is the amount of scintillation you already get by going from RGB to NTSC. There's no need to compound that with aliased reflections and refractions. In many ways, this is a logical and frequently practiced option.

Now consider the other side. The other side argues that anti-aliasing must be used when you're outputting to film or video. What happens if you don't plan to do either? Can you then skimp on not using anti-aliasing in your animation—such as an AVI file or animated GIF on the Web? The answer is sometimes yes and sometimes no. Although the answer is not all that definitive, the quality of a rendered image is always subjective. This means that if it looks good enough for you or your customer, then it's the right option to choose. If you think not using anti-aliasing might work, then render a small segment of *sequential* frames. Render a portion of the animation that has the most reflections and refractions. If the pixels aren't too jagged for you, then you've probably got a good candidate for forgoing anti-aliasing.

T IP

You can use image motion blurring on objects that are moving in an animation to mask the fact that you're not using anti-aliasing. Although this doesn't work for every case, it can definitely help most scenes.

Raytracing Optimizations

At this point, you're probably thinking that you'll never finish another project on time if you use raytracing—doomed to using Reflection and Refraction maps. Although it's true that raytracing can dramatically slow down rendering speeds, there are also some ways that you can maximize the usage of built-in optimizations of the Raytracing engine itself.

You see, out of the gate, the Raytracer is designed to work optimally for every scene that you throw at it. This means that the default settings are general enough so that no one scene is all that much faster than another— or slower for that matter. Just as you have to set up your own preferences in MAX, however, you'll probably need to alter various settings of the Raytracer to get the best possible performance out of each and every scene.

Although it's not absolutely critical that you know every setting for optimizing the Raytracer, the next few sections will give you an idea of when you might use them.

Voxel Trees

When a Raytracer processes the scene before rendering, it breaks the scene into small, cubical areas called *voxels*. Pixel is short for pixel element; voxel is short for volume area.

As mentioned before, the Raytracer relies on faces to determine where the rays will hit. The problem is that if every ray were tested against every face in the scene, processing times would go through the roof. Instead, the Raytracer breaks down the scene into smaller areas, the voxels.

A voxel first starts out by encasing an object—much like a bounding box. Next, depending on where the detail is on an object, the voxel can be broken down further to isolate small, concentrated packs of faces (refer to Figure 8.13). The result is something that's much like a tree of addresses. The easiest comparison to think of is a state-city-street-street number relationship. An object is the state. Areas of concentrations of faces are broken down into cities. If there is enough detail to break a city down into streets, the city will be subdivided, and so on.

FIGURE 8.13

A graphical example of what a voxel tree might look like. This example on the teapot shows how one tree might be broken down from the scene to the teapot (left) to the teapot's spout (right).

This elaborate system of breaking down a scene by objects and faces helps the Raytracer isolate where a ray travels during the course of its life. This in turn eliminates unnecessary hit testing where the ray does not travel. It's much easier to say that the ray will travel through these cities and hit these streets rather than just saying it'll travel somewhere in the world. Tracking it down would just be a pain. Voxel trees help eliminate this problem.

Many Raytracers use what's known as *octrees*. As its name implies, the tree is divided eight times. Although this works for some scenes, it can often lead to voxels that vary in size a great deal. If a small object is left in a large voxel, there's quite a bit of hit testing to do by the Raytracer to see where the object lies within the voxel.

In MAX R2, voxels are adaptive. This means that *you* can determine how far the voxel trees are divided by setting up limits—much like the Ray Depth control discussed earlier. In the next section, you'll see how to control the usage of voxel trees.

Single versus Dual Pipe Acceleration

In the Global Parameters section of the Raytrace material or map, there is a grayed-out section towards the bottom of the dialog box. If you check the Manual Acceleration checkbox, the whole area becomes active—you've just tapped into the Voxel Tree controls of the Raytracer. Normally, you're leaving it up to the Raytracer to decide things. Sometimes, it's better that you take the controls and determine where acceleration will take place. See Figure 8.14.

FIGURE 8.14

The Manual Acceleration area of the Global Raytracer Settings dialog.

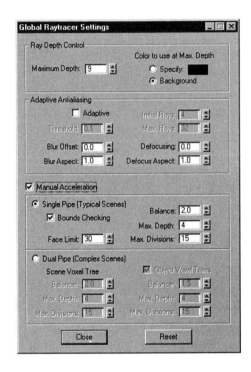

Manual Acceleration is divided into two sections. The first is called Single Pipe, which breaks down your scene by faces. The end result is that most scenes with low face and object counts can benefit from this acceleration. What happens is that your scene is broken down at the face level into a structured voxel tree. The division of the tree is determined by the Max Depth setting (a setting of 4 creates a $4 \times 4 \times 4$ tree). The Max Divisions setting sets how far the tree can be subdivided. Face limit sets how many faces can occupy a voxel before the voxel must be divided again. The higher you set this number, the fewer subdivisions there are. However, this also results in more hit tests per voxel in order for the Raytracer to determine what face it's actually hitting in the voxel.

Balance allows you to control how evenly the subdivision is calculated for the scene. Because most scenes are not evenly distributed (object-wise), a low Balance setting might result in a large voxel that contains only one small object. If you think this might be the case for you, try increasing the balance. Your scene will be divided a bit better. Just remember that it also uses more RAM as you increase the number. You'll find that Single Pipe acceleration works for most scenes because it's primarily designed to handle scenes of less than about 300 objects.

If your scene is a bit meatier, you might want to try using Dual Pipe. Dual Pipe forces the Raytracer to break down a scene first into one big voxel tree and then, if checked, each object into its own voxel tree. Rather than relying solely on where faces are concentrated in the scene, Dual Pipe first looks at the objects. It then subdivides those voxels based on object complexity. The end result is potentially a very complex tree but is very efficient for ray hit testing. All the settings work the same as Single Pipe. The primary thing to remember with Dual Pipe is that it works much better on larger scenes because it breaks them down by scene first and then objects.

Global Exclusion

Global exclusion is designed for you to eliminate an object or objects from being calculated in any raytracing. Use this feature when you don't want any of the materials rendering a certain object through Raytraced reflections or refractions. This works well when you exclude large, complex objects or many small objects.

Think of a Blue Angel F-18 flying low over the desert terrain. The highly polished underside of the jet would tend to reflect every feature of the desert floor. By using Global Exclude, you can eliminate small features of the terrain from being factored in to the raytracing calculations.

Local Exclusion

Local Exclusion allows you to isolate an object or objects from being raytraced just for the particular map or material you're using. This means that other materials using raytracing may still reflect/refract the excluded object; the locally excluded material will not.

Local Exclusion works well when you want to isolate small or complex objects from being raytraced by a particular material. For instance, if you had a small, ornate wine glass next to a chrome wine chiller, you might consider eliminating the chiller from the refraction and/or the reflection calculations of the glass. Whenever you have small, intricate detail in an object, you should evaluate the practicality of using Raytraced reflections and refractions. The golden rule is this: The more detail there is, the longer it takes to raytrace—no matter what.

Adaptive Anti-Aliasing

Adaptive anti-aliasing, in and of itself, is not an optimization for Raytraced renderings. It does, however, provide you with explicit control over how an image is anti-aliased. You can find the settings for Adaptive anti-aliasing from the Global Parameters button located in the Raytrace material or map. With Adaptive off, the Anti-aliasing engine calculates a pixel's color value anywhere between four and 12 times. The result is typically good for most renderings, but with Adaptive off, you don't get precise control of the various settings for anti-aliasing.

As mentioned before, with Adaptive turned off, the Anti-aliasing algorithm calculates a pixel's Color value anywhere between four and 12 times. The problem is that you can often get away with the minimum of four. With Adaptive, you can specify the minimum and maximum amount of calculations to be four—or even less if you like. By doing this, you can often reduce the rendering time by as much as half.

Figure 8.15 shows how similar two images can look. The left side uses default, non-controllable anti-aliasing. The right side is rendered with Adaptive on with Initial and Maximum rays set to four. As you can see, the difference is minimal. The rendering time on a Dual Pentium Pro for the left image was 4:19 while the right image took 2:41.

T IP

By setting both the Initial and Maximum ray values to the same number, you are reducing the amount of calculations that the Raytracer has to make.

FIGURE 8.15

This shows what little difference there can be between regular raytraced anti-aliasing (left) versus Adaptive raytracing with Initial and Maximum Ray values set to Low (right).

Using Blurs and Attenuation

You can use Blur, Defocusing, and Attenuation to your advantage to improve anti-aliasing quality. The Raytracer, out of the gate, has a decent Raytracing engine. Sometimes, however, it needs a little kick in the pants for some scenes. This kick can be done by manipulating the Blur, Defocusing, and Attenuation settings.

Blur and Defocus basically blur an anti-aliased material more than it already is. Blur adds a general blur across the entire Raytraced material/map. Defocusing blurs a reflection or refraction more and more as the reflected surface's distance is further and further away from the material. The end result is that Raytraced reflections and refractions do not appear as sharp. The Raytracer, however, tends to produce crisp, hyper-real images anyway. By using Blur and Defocus, you'll "dirty" up the reflections and refractions. Be careful, however, not to add too much blurring or defocusing. At higher settings, the blurring is overwhelming for most scenes. Lower offset values, anywhere between 0.1 and 0.3, often work fine.

Attenuation helps to control the amount of reflections or refractions taking place on your material by limiting the distance that it can reflect or refract the environment. Because there is less of the environment to reflect, there is less to anti-alias. This also means that rendering times are shorter when a material is more and more attenuated. Attenuation has its own section within the Raytrace map (see Figure 8.16). The material has only checkboxes for attenuation. If you desire a great deal of control over the attenuation of your Raytraced reflections or refractions, you'll need to use the map versus the material.

TIP

A good Attenuation type to use is Exponential. Set the Start and End Ranges to values that reflect objects and the environment in the immediate vicinity of the reflective/refractive surface. The Exponent value acts as a multiplier. The higher the value is, the more attenuation will occur.

FIGURE 8.16

The attenuation controls of the map (left) versus the material (right).

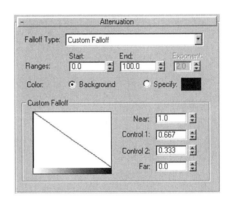

Rendering Limitations and Problem Areas

Every great feature always has a downside. With anti-aliasing, we already know that slow rendering speeds can be a major downside. As an animator and 3D artist, you'll have to determine when and where you should take advantage of this feature.

Knowing when you should and should not use a feature takes a little trial and error—no matter what type of scene you're working with. However, there are some items you should be aware of when rendering scenes with Raytraced materials and maps. By knowing what's good and what's bad for the Raytracer, you can take pre-emptive measures to control longer-than-normal rendering times.

Anti-Aliasing Speed Hits

Anti-aliasing is at its worst, speed-wise, when it encounters complex geometry or surfaces that are both reflective and refractive. Unfortunately, the best reflections and refractions are produced on geometry that is of high detail. An easy way to test this is to render a default polygonal teapot next to a teapot that's been converted into a NURBS surface. The NURBS surface looks much better but can take over twice as long to render.

Because geometry detail is critical for close-up shots, there's not much you can do to avoid long rendering times. However, you can do a couple of things to minimize potential problem areas:

- **Animate anti-aliasing settings.** It's not widely known that you are able to not only animate the anti-aliasing On/Off settings but also any of the Adaptive settings. This means that if your shot starts up close and backs out, you can lower the anti-aliasing calculations as the camera gets further away.

- **When possible, avoid both reflective and refractive surfaces.** There are alternatives, however. If the material is glass, use a Raytrace map in the Refraction slot and an bitmap or automatic Reflection map in the Reflection channel. This isolates the Raytrace calculations to only focus on the refractive qualities of a material.

Organizing Your Materials

No matter what Rendering engine they require, one of the absolute most critical techniques to master early on—or to start mastering now if you're a seasoned animator—is organizing your Material libraries. As you build more and more scenes, you'll often find that you spent hours building a material some time back that you'd like to use on a current project. The problem is that you don't know what scene you used it in or, possibly worse, where the scene is now stored.

The 3D Studio product line, even since the DOS days, has been able to organize materials into libraries. With MAX R2, browsing Material libraries and assigning materials to objects has been greatly improved. You no longer have to use the Material editor to assign materials. You can also browse materials as they're constructed—meaning which maps the material is comprised of—in a tree-like fashion. Figure 8.17 shows the Material/Map browser with the 3dsmax.mat Material library file broken down into Material/Map trees.

FIGURE 8.17

The Material/Map Browser window with the 3dsmax.mat Material library displayed.

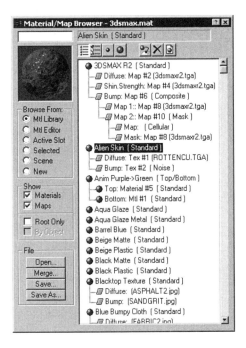

Since building and assigning materials have gotten so much better in MAX, why not take advantage of being able to organize them as well? Organization can involve many aspects, which are outlined below. Depending on how many custom materials you have, you may have a large project ahead of you if you plan to organize them. However, this can be a good way to "condition" yourself in the future when building scenes. Granted, organizing materials may go against the very grain of the person you are. However, when you're under a critical deadline and you want to find a great material that you built a while back, a little organization can go a long way.

Building Libraries

Building libraries is the first, and most tedious, step in organizing your materials. Libraries are nothing more than binary files with the .MAT extension that contain named materials, their settings, and the names of the maps they use—not the actual maps themselves. Material libraries are saved, by default, in the Matlibs directory (this is as of MAX R2; MAX 1.x didn't have a Matlibs directory).

NOTE

You can save thumbnail images of your materials and their maps. Thumbnails are saved automatically with the library if you save the Material library after viewing the thumbnail images in the Material/Map browser.

How you build a library is dependent on how you remember your materials. Some artists/animators prefer categories, some prefer by Material type (Standard, Multi/Sub-Object, and so on), and yet others by project. Which system works best is best determined by the user—you. Here are three ideas for how you might organize material libraries:

- **By Category.** This is the simplest way to think about putting your materials together. All metals go in one library, all animated materials go into another library, and so on. The benefit of this method is that if you know you need a specific Material type, you can easily identify where it might be by looking at the categories you've built. The downside is that you have to open a new Material library each time you need a material from a different category.

- **By Type.** If you've built many Multi/Sub-Object materials, it would be nice to be able to go to a library of only Multi/Sub-Object materials to find what you're looking for. Same with the new Raytrace material. If you know you want some kind of reflective metal but are not sure what kind of Raytrace material you want to use, this method works great. The downside, as opposed to the category method, is that all types of materials—woods, glasses, metals—could potentially all be in the same library. This could make browsing a library rather time-consuming.

■ **By Project.** This method works well if you know what types of materials you used on a project. If you can remember that, "Hey, I created a great textured alien skin for that Project X game," then looking up that material by project would be a snap. Since many projects are documented down to this level during production, it shouldn't be a problem finding a material from a project that you did several years ago. However, this method suffers from one fatal flaw—projects often involve hundreds of materials. If you don't have or remember that material's name or where it is used in a project, you've probably got at least a few hours of searching for the material.

Although each of these methods can be used individually, you might find that a combination of two or all three works well for you. The whole point is that it's much easier to have materials in a place where you at least know where you can go find them. Having materials scattered across *.MAX* files is just not efficient 3D design.

Naming Materials

Perhaps one of the most common mistakes of many novices is to accept the default material name that MAX gives you. How many Material #1s have you built before? This can be painfully obvious if you have multiple Material #1s in your Material editor and you try to assign them to two different objects. MAX likes to have unique material names in a scene. This means that you'll need to spend a little time creating material names as you use them in your scene. Fortunately, if you get in the habit of at least giving the whole material a unique name, you can avoid a major amount of the confusion.

However, did you know that MAX allows you to not only name materials but also sub-materials and even Map names? Most animators don't realize these facts, so their materials are littered with Map #1s and the like. How easy is it to recognize a map named like that when browsing using the Material/Map browser?

Figure 8.18 shows a properly named material with a map versus a material/map combination that uses the defaults. Which one would you rather use when browsing several materials looking for the right "Stucco Wall"?

FIGURE 8.18

The Material/Map browser view of two materials. The top material and map use the MAX Default naming scheme. The lower material uses more descriptive names to indicate what the material looks like and what it's made of. (The lower material takes a few more seconds to create by adding in the names.)

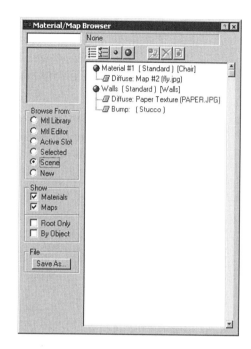

How you name materials is entirely up to you. The only guideline that you should follow is to name the material something descriptive enough that you'll be able to come back to it several months later an recognize what it is. Other than that, you can use any naming scheme you want. When you're browsing materials from the library, they're always listed alphabetically. So if you use certain materials frequently, you could give them names that would put them at the top of the list. Using the number "1" puts any material at the top of the list.

In Practice: Material Concepts

- **MAX's materials are shaders.** Many other products use the name shader to denote the equivalent of a material in MAX. Materials contain all the same type of properties, if not more, as a shader.

- **Use the Standard material for most situations.** The Standard material contains most of the elements you need to design convincing materials. With the addition of the Raytrace feature as a map, you can still employ accurate reflections and refractions.

- **Use the Raytrace material for realism.** The Raytrace material contains features that the Standard material doesn't, such as Translucency and Fluorescence. These features, along with the way the material behaves, can make objects using this material render very realistically.

- **Raytracing is great for hyper-realism.** One of the best qualities of a raytraced image is that if looks extremely convincing. Reflections and refractions are believable. Specular highlights can make metals and glass look more realistic than ever.

- **Raytracing is bad for speed.** Although raytracing produces great imagery, it comes at a price—slower rendering times. However, there are many optimizations for both rendering quality and anti-aliasing that can help reduce your rendering bottom line.

Chapter 9

DESIGNING NATURALLY OCCURRING MATERIALS

Natural, organic materials are among the most difficult to represent with computer graphics. The physics behind generating convincing natural materials is a daunting task because of the way light simultaneously interacts with the surface texture, color pigments, and molecules of objects. The light in nature comes from many sources—the sun, particles in the air, artificial sources, reflections, and radiosity from surrounding objects—all at the same instant. The surface attributes of the natural objects themselves add another level of complexity, with variations in shininess and reflectivity, firmness or softness, mineral content, dirt, and coatings.

What we computer artists must do is use the tools available to create the illusion of these natural phenomena in an efficient and cost-effective manner. "Illusion" is a key word here. If someone asks you, "What color are the leaves on trees?" your most likely response will be "green." Well, yes, you pass the quiz, but...

If you take the time to carefully look at a stand of trees on a sunny day you will generally notice a high percentage of white and blue. Leaves tend to be very shiny in summer and reflect intense specular highlights and more a broad, subtle reflection of the blue sky. Our brains have a tendency to compensate because we "know" leaves are green, and we take the secondary coloration for granted without perceiving it.

An essential element of natural materials is an inherent sense of randomness. This is caused in nature by irregular surfaces, pigment distribution, and coatings of dirt, dust, and moisture. In this chapter, you will simulate these natural occurrences using MAX R2's Materials and Map types. Some of the categories of natural materials you will explore include:

- Sky and earth

- Water

- Trees and shrubs

- Fruits and flowers

- Ice and snow

- Stone and rock

Sky and Earth

A sky background is, of course, essential for any outdoor scenes. There are two basic methods for representing the sky in a scene. They are:

- Environmental background

- Image mapping onto a sphere or cylinder

Environmental Background Sky

You can use any valid 3D Studio MAX R2 bitmap, still or animated, as an environmental background. An environmental background is one that is not mapped to a specific mesh object, rather one that is projected as a background using one of the following mapping options:

- **Spherical:** Stretches the image completely around the scene. Non-tileable images display a seam from their "north pole" to "south pole."

- **Cylindrical:** Maps the image vertically around the sides of the scene; can also display a top-to-bottom seam.

- **Shrink-wrapped:** Stretches the image around the scene like a sheet of rubber around a sphere. Displays only a singular point of distortion.

- **Screen:** Projects the image as a flat backdrop, always perpendicular to the line of view.

NOTE

A sky background can also be included as an entry in the Video Post queue.

Screen Map a Background

In Exercise 9.1, you will use the MAX R2 Asset Manager to load a scene into MAX, then use the Asset Manager again to create an environmental background. Unless you have very high-resolution bitmaps, a good method for sky background is Screen mapping. Cylindrical, Spherical, and Shrink-wrapped mapping stretch the image, often causing unwanted distortion or pixelization.

EXERCISE 9.1: ENVIRONMENTAL SKY BACKGROUND

1. Click File/Reset to clear the MAX scene.

2. In the Utility panel, click Asset Manager and open \Chapter9 on the CD-ROM. Change the File Types filter to Display Only .max Files, and click the Display Medium Thumbnails icon. The screen should appear similar to Figure 9.1.

3. Drag and Drop the thumbnail 09max01.MAX onto the Perspective viewport, and click in the viewport to set its position.

4. Press C to bring up Camera01 viewport, and click in an empty area to clear the selection set.

5. In the Asset Manager, change the File Types filter to Display All Images. Open the Material Editor and Drag and Drop SKY02.BMP onto the first sample sphere.

FIGURE 9.1

*The new MAX R2
Asset Manager.*

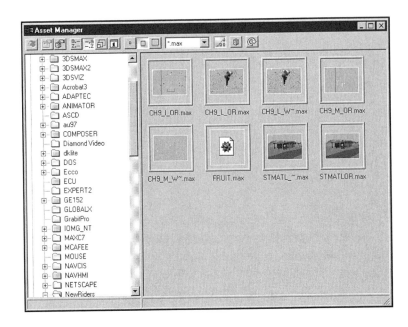

6. In the Material Editor, check Environ in the Coordinates rollout.

7. In the Rendering pull-down menu, click Environment. Drag and Drop the first sample sphere from the Material Editor onto Environment Map: None and check Instance in the Instance (Copy) Map dialog. Click OK. Name the material SKY01 in the Enter Material Name dialog. Click OK. Close the Environment dialog. Close the Asset Manager.

N OTE

At this point, the sky image is not visible in the active viewport. It will only appear when the scene is rendered.

8. In the Views pull-menu, click Background Image. In the Viewport Background dialog, check Use Environmental Background, check Display Background, and set Camera01 in the Viewport name listbox. The Camera01 viewport should turn dark or you should see a hint of image. The sky image is being stretched around a spherical background and is not recognizable as your SKY01.BMP.

NOTE

Note that you are not using SKY01.BMP as a typical material map as in Diffuse mapping, for example. You are loading it directly in the top material level.

9. In the Material Editor Coordinates rollout, click Spherical Environment. Choose Screen from the list. The display should appear similar to Figure 9.2.

FIGURE 9.2

Material Editor set to Screen Environ Mapping.

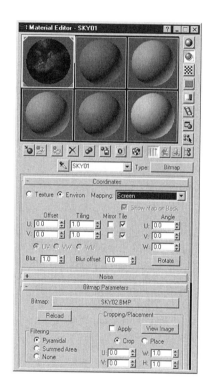

10. Render the Camera01 viewport with the default render settings. The sky background appears more clearly, but is still dark and very flat. The background now is like backdrop that fills the viewport, even the display area below the horizon.

In Exercise 9.1, you loaded a photograph of clouds as a background to the train station scene. You also loaded the file separately as a Display Background Image to help visualize how the background fits into your scene without constantly rendering. Finally, you used the new MAX R2 Asset Manager to view thumbnail images of files on disk and used the Drag and Drop feature to enhance productivity.

Tweak the Bitmap, Not the Original File

It is not always necessary to have Photoshop or another image editor to make adjustments to bitmaps. MAX R2 has the tools to change the appearance of bitmaps without affecting the original file. In Exercise 9.2, you will adjust the coverage of the bitmap in Coordinates rollout and adjust its brightness with the tools provided in the Material Editor Output rollout.

EXERCISE 9.2: ADJUSTING THE BACKGROUND IMAGE

1. In the Material Editor Coordinates rollout, uncheck Tile in the U (horizontal) and V (vertical) coordinate rows. This keeps the bitmap from repeating vertically or horizontally in the scene when you adjust the Tiling amount and makes visualizing easier in the viewport and on the sample sphere.

2. Enter 2.0 in the V:Tiling field. Notice that the sky image only covers half the sphere with black bands above and below the image.

TIP

If Tile were still checked, you would see two vertical repeats of your background image. With Tile unchecked, the image "squashes" to half its height.

This squashing of the image is a vital part in making cloud backgrounds look realistic. It heightens the illusion of "convergence." As you look at the sky on a partly cloudy day, the clouds overhead appear to have space between them, but as you look toward the horizon the angle of view closes the apparent distance between the clouds. Cloud cover on the horizon seems to be complete with no gaps.

The convergence effect is a important clue of distance, especially if the cloud photograph was taken looking up.

3. Enter 0.25 in the V:Offset field. The image moves up the sample sphere to cover the upper half only.

TIP

The numbers entered in the Offset field represent one repetition of the bitmap. At 0.25, you have moved the image a quarter of its distance in a positive vertical distance.

4. In the Output rollout, enter 2.0 in the RGB Level field. Your image should brighten noticeably. The RGB Level amount increases the saturation of the colors by multiplying the RGB pixel values by the number in the field.

WARNING

The higher the RGB Level setting, the more "self-illuminated" the background image appears. Check Clamp in the Output rollout to reduce this effect.

5. Adjust the RGB Level to produce a bold blue sky and adjust the V:Offset amount to position the bottom of the bitmap just below the horizon in the scene. A V:Offset of about 0.32 and a RGB Level of about 5.0 might work on your system, but use your judgment.

6. The image should now fit well vertically and be bright, but it will be too harsh and you may have white stripes on each side. If you see white stripes at the sides of the clouds in the Camera01 viewport, enter 0.9 in the H:Tiling field to expand the white edges beyond the visible range.

7. In the Output rollout, enter 0.02 in the RGB Offset field. RGB Offset "whitens" the image, eventually moving to pure white—self-illuminating. Negative numbers darken the image. The sample sphere in the Material Editor and a rendered image should look similar to Figure 9.3.

FIGURE 9.3

Material Editor sample sphere and rendered image.

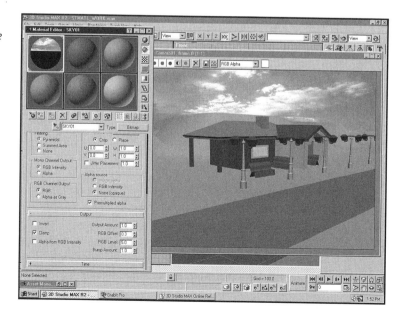

8. In the Virtual Frame Buffer, click the Clone Virtual Frame Buffer choice to replicate the rendered image as Clone of Camera01. This creates a clone of the rendered image to compare with the result of the next rendering, making it much easier to fine-tune renderings.

9. In the Material Editor, click Bitmap in the Type area, and double-click RGB Tint from the Browser. Choose Keep Old Map as Sub Map and click OK.

10. In the Tint Parameters rollout, click the blue color swatch and drag the Value slider to about 150 in the Color Selector dialog. Click Close to exit the Color Selector and click Render Last to render the Perspective viewport. The display should look similar to Figure 9.4. You have reduced the amount of blue in the sky background by reducing the blue tint swatch. You may color correct images with RGB Tint without affecting the original image or without leaving MAX R2.

FIGURE 9.4

RGB Tint Parameters rollout and Color Selector.

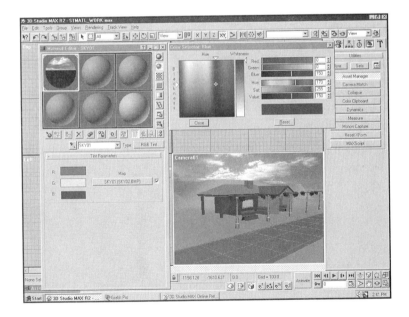

11. Save the file as NEWSTA01.MAX

In Exercise 9.2, you modified the original background image in several ways while still in 3D Studio MAX R2—no additional software required. Some of key operations were:

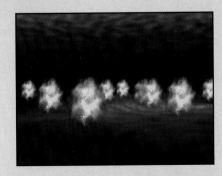

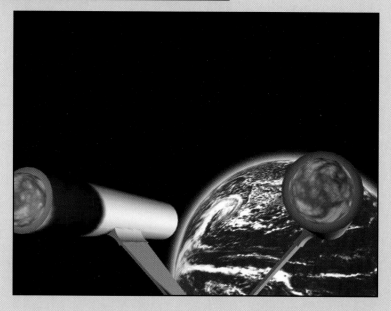

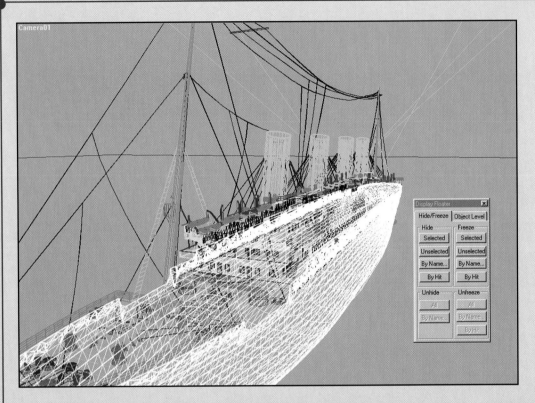

- Unchecked U and V Tile to prevent repetition of the background while resizing and repositioning it.

- Squashed the image with V:Tile to create the illusion of more convergence.

- Repositioned the background with the Offset spinner.

- Boosted the brightness and saturation with the RGB Level spinner.

- Whitened the image with the RGB Offset spinner.

- Color corrected the image by combining the bitmap with a RGB Tint mapping type

- Compared two renderings by cloning the Virtual Frame Buffer.

Mapped Sky Background

In Exercise 9.3 you will continue to use the existing file, but you will take a different approach to creating a sky—mapping. In the process, you'll learn about some new tools for mapping a bitmap on a hemisphere in the scene and adjusting the bitmaps appearance. You will use:

- Mix mapping

- Gradient mapping

- Animated Offsets

The hemisphere that you will unhide in Exercise 9.3 was created from the sphere primitive. The Hemisphere field was set to 0.5, and the Squash option was checked to keep the number of vertical segments at 16 for smoother mapping. A Normal modifier was applied and the normals flipped to be visible from inside the hemisphere. The object was then collapsed to an editable mesh and the bottom faces were deleted to make the object more efficient.

EXERCISE 9.3: MAPPING A BACKGROUND ON A SPHERE

1. In the Display panel, click Unhide By Name and choose SKY from the list. Click Unhide. A green shaded mesh replaces the sky background in the Camera01 viewport.

NOTE

Normally in a project you would use either an environmental background or a mapped background. Using both uses computer resources unnecessarily.

2. Select SKY, and in the Modify panel, click UVW Mapping modifier. Choose the Spherical mapping type. Click Sub-Object Gizmo, and in the Front viewport, click the Align icon and check Y;Position and Minimum under Target Object. Click OK. Click Sub-Object to exit the mode. The display should look similar to Figure 9.5.

TIP

The size of the Spherical Gizmo has no effect because the map is projected in all directions from the center.

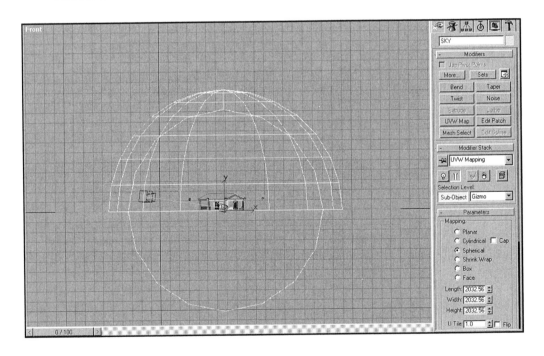

FIGURE 9.5

Spherical Mapping Gizmo centered in front viewport.

3. Open the Asset Manager and Material Editor, and position them side by side in the display.

4. Click an empty sample sphere to activate it, and enter SKY02 in the name field.

5. From the Asset Manager, Drag and Drop SKY02.BMP directly onto the square to the right of the Diffuse color swatch. Close the Asset Manager. This automatically sets the bitmap as the diffuse texture map. Click the square, which now has the letter M, to get to the Bitmap Parameters rollout. Enter sky diff in the name field.

6. Drag and Drop the sample sphere to the SKY mesh object in the scene, and click the Show Map in Viewport icon.

7. In the Coordinates rollout, uncheck the U and V Tile boxes. Enter 2.0 in V:Tiling and 0.25 in V:Offset. This squashes the image to enhance convergence and moves it to the top of the SKY mesh object in the scene and on the sample sphere.

8. In the Coordinates rollout, enter 1.5 in U:Tiling and 0.5 in U:Offset. The image almost disappears around the back of the sample sphere.

9. In the Output rollout, set RGB Level to 5.0.

10. Right-click the sample sphere, and choose Drag and Rotate from the menu. Click and drag in the sample sphere to rotate the sphere and see it from all angles. Double-click the sample sphere, and you have a magnified tear-off sample sphere. You can also right-click the sample sphere and choose Magnify from the menu. You can resize this tear-off sphere by dragging a corner of it. The tear-off will update when you rotate the sample sphere in the Material Editor. It should appear similar to Figure 9.6.

WARNING

On a slow machine, manipulating a large tear-off sample can bog operations down quite a bit.

11. Right-click the sample sphere; choose Reset Rotation. Right-click again, and choose Drag and Copy. Close the magnified sample.

12. In the Top viewport, create an Omni light to light the SKY. Name it SkyOmni.

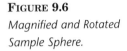

FIGURE 9.6

*Magnified and Rotated
Sample Sphere.*

13. In the Modify panel, set the Lights value to 255. Click Exclude, choose SKY in the left list, and send it to the right list. Check the Include option. This creates an Omni that is just for the SKY object. You will set lighting for the scene later.

14. Select the SKY object, and right-click it. Choose Properties from the menu, and uncheck Cast Shadows and Receive Shadows to keep the object from doing either and making the scene more efficient to render.

15. In the Material Editor, select the SKY02 sample sphere and go to the Diffuse Map sub-level. This is easy to do by clicking the Material/Map Navigator icon, then clicking the Diffuse Map level in the Navigator dialog.

16. Click Type:Bitmap, and double-click Mix in the list. Check Keep Old Map as Sub Map in the Replace Map dialog. Click OK.

17. Click None to the right of Color #2. Double-click Gradient in the list.

18. In the Coordinates rollout, uncheck Tile for U and V and set the Offset and Tiling settings the same as for Color 1:sky diff. Name this Level mix gradient.

TIP

You can jump from Color 1 to Color 2 and back with the Go to Sibling icon or by picking the appropriate level in the Navigator and then type in the settings as in previous releases of MAX. In MAX R2, you can also highlight the field, right-click, choose Copy from the menu, select Go Forward to Sibling, highlight the field, right-click, and choose Paste from the menu. The new copy and paste reduces the chances of mistakes.

19. In the mix gradient map's Gradient Parameters, set Color 1 to a light yellow, Color 2 to a light blue, and Color 3 to a bright orange-red. Set the Color 2 Position to 0.2 to shift the Color 2 down the image. The display should look similar to Figure 9.7.

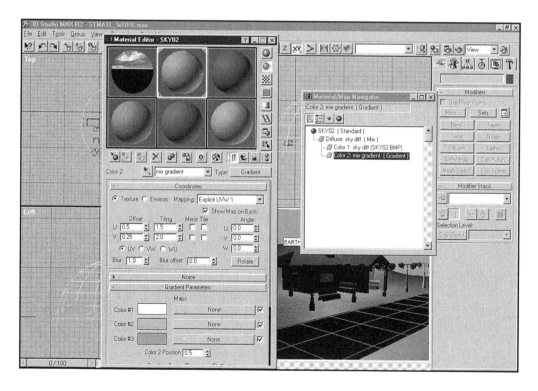

FIGURE 9.7

Mix Gradient settings and Material/Map Navigator.

20. In Material/Map Navigator, click Diffuse sky diff (Mix), or click the Go to Parent icon in the Material Editor and set the Mix Amount to 0.3.

21. Close all dialogs, and render the Camera01 viewport. Save the scene as NEWSTA02.MAX. You should have a partly cloudy sky with a strong reddish tint on the horizon. Experiment with different colors and changing the Color 2 Position amount.

In Exercise 9.3 you:

■ Created a Sky diffuse mapped material and assigned it to a hemisphere.

■ Used the Asset Manager to Drag and Drop maps.

■ Right-clicked a sample sphere to access the new Material Editor options.

■ Adjusted Tiling and Offset to enhance convergence and limit horizontal stretch.

■ Adjusted RGB Level to boost saturation.

■ Added a Mix mapping type to create two material levels.

■ Made the second level a Gradient map with sunset colors and adjusted the mix amount. Higher amounts show more Color 2. Amount 0.5 shows equal amounts of Color 1 and Color 2.

More Realism

In Exercise 9.4 you will add an element of realism that is often missing from animations and images. Very often the clouds in the background are very convincing, but there are no cloud shadows on the ground. Here you will set up a sunlight system with a Noise Projector map to simulate cloud shadows on the ground.

EXERCISE 9.4: ADDING CLOUD SHADOWS ON THE GROUND

1. Activate the Top viewport, and in the Create/Systems panel, click Sunlight.

2. In the middle of the scene, click and drag slowly to show a compass rose radius and click to set it.

3. Release the mouse button, and move the mouse to set an Orbital Scale amount.

You should see a yellow Directional light move in and out from the compass rose center as you move the mouse.

4. Enter 2000.0 in the Site Orbital Scale field.

5. The light position is set for the current date and time (on your computer) at San Francisco, CA. Enter a time in Hours:Minutes to about 12:00 noon.

6. Click the Get Location button, check Nearest Big City, and pick near your current location on the map, or scroll down the City list and choose a city.

If you are not in North America, select from the Map list to choose a different area of the world.

7. In the Modify panel (the Sun01 light should still be selected), enter 1000 in the Hot Spot field of Directional Parameters rollout. This should be enough to cover your entire scene, if not increase it until it covers the entire scene. You can check the Hot Spot coverage by pressing Shift-4 in any viewport. This creates a view as if a Spot or Directional were a camera. Render the scene and you will notice that Sunlight automatically turns shadow casting on. Close the Virtual Frame Buffer.

The render time on some machines could slow considerably because the Sun01 uses raytraced shadows that take longer to calculate.

8. In the Material Editor, click a new sample sphere, and name the material SHADOW PROJ. This material will not be a mapped material but an Environmental material, much like the environmental sky background.

9. Click the Get Material icon, and double-click Noise map type. In the Noise Parameters rollout, check Turbulence. Enter 0.8 in the High field and 0.2 in the Low field. Then enter 300.0 in the Size field, and click the Swap button to swap black for white in the color swatches. This step gives you a mostly white sample sphere. What is white will pass light; the black will project onto the landscape.

10. Drag and Drop the SHADOW PROJ sample sphere onto the Map:None button in Directional Parameters rollout in the Modify panel. Check Instance in the Instance (Copy) Map dialog.

11. In the Modify panel, for Sun01, click the Exclude button, and move SKY from the left column to the right column to exclude it from Sun01. The display should appear similar to Figure 9.8.

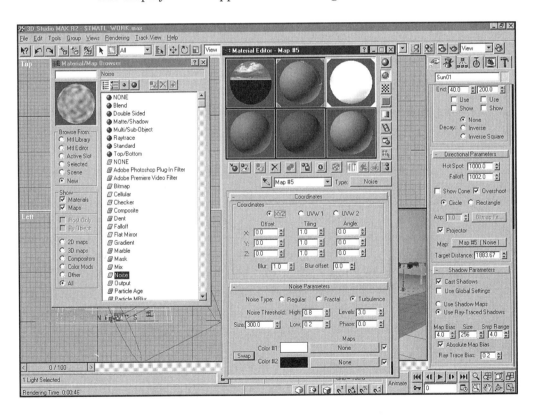

FIGURE 9.8

Dialogs for Shadow Projector Sun01.

NOTE

The effect you get is not a shadow, but a projected image appearing to be a shadow, so setting SKY object properties to not cast or receive shadows in Exercise 9.3 doesn't have any effect. Turning off Cast and Receive Shadows only affects actual calculated shadows. The projected map image shows on SKY if you don't exclude it from the light.

12. Render the Camera01 viewport and adjust the Material Editor Noise parameters to change the cloud effect. Finally, save the file as NEWSTA03.MAX.

TIP

You can animate moving clouds by animating the Phase amount or by animating the W Angle field in the Material Editor.

In Exercise 9.4 you used the new Sunlight System to place a sun. You then created a Noise Environmental map in the Material Editor and dropped it in the Projector section of the Directional spot called Sun01 to simulate cloud shadows.

Clouds with Dimension

Just to finish off the sky, you will add some 3D clouds to the scene using an Atmospheric Apparatus with a Volume Fog environmental effect in Exercise 9.5. Adding physical 3D clouds will do a lot to give the illusion of depth and "tangibility" to your sky.

EXERCISE 9.5: ADDING 3D CLOUDS

1. In the Create panel/Helpers/Atmospheric Apparatus, click on BoxGizmo. In the Top viewport, click and drag a BoxGizmo that is as large as the SKY hemisphere and as tall as the buildings. Move the BoxGizmo up in the Front viewport so it is hovering over the buildings. It should look similar to Figure 9.9.

FIGURE 9.9

BoxGizmo Above Buildings in Front Viewport.

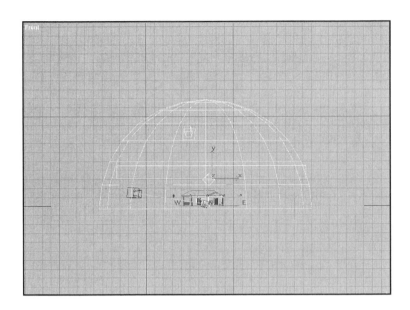

2. In Rendering pull-down/Environment, click Add and double-click Volume Fog.

3. Click Pick Gizmo, and pick the BoxGizmo in a viewport.

4. In the Volume area, enter 3.5 in the Density field, and in Noise area, enter 200 in the Size field. Close the Environment dialog. Volume Fog can now be contained in one BoxGizmo, CylGizmo, or SphereGizmo.

5. Render Camera01 viewport, and you should have 3D clouds above your scene that blend in reasonably well with the cloud bitmap.

6. Save the scene as NEWSTA04.MAX.

In Exercise 9.5 you added 3D clouds to the scene. These clouds can have animated parameters, and the BoxGizmo apparatus can be animated in the scene. Experiment with different variables for Volume Fog to create different types of clouds and adjust the height of the BoxGizmo for fuller or flatter cloud formations.

Top Mapped Earth

In Exercise 9.6 you will apply an earth material mapped to EARTH in the Top viewport. The material is a Multi/Sub-Object material type using a Blend material for dirt/grass areas and a bitmapped material for areas of stone paving. In addition, Exercise 9.6 focuses on the stone paving and you will also learn a method of calculating real-world mapping coordinates.

EXERCISE 9.6: SETTING THE STONE

1. In the Top viewport, select the EARTH mesh object. In the Modify panel, click Sub-Object Face, and click Select by ID in the Edit Surface rollout. Enter 2 in the Select Material by ID dialog, and click OK. You should see the faces around the station and down the face of the track pit turn red. These faces have already had Material ID #2 assigned to them. All other faces in EARTH have Material ID #1. Click Sub-Object to exit the mode.

2. Open the Material Editor, and click an unused sample sphere. Name the material EARTH01.

3. Click the Standard button, and double-click Multi/Sub-Object as the new material type. Click OK to Discard Old Material in Replace Material dialog. Click Set Number, and enter 2 in the Number of Materials field.

4. Click the first material button to access its parameters, and name it GRASS/DIRT. Click Standard and double-click Blend material type from the list. Click OK in the Replace Material dialog.

5. Click Material 1, and name it GRASS. Click the Go Forward to Sibling icon, and name Material 2 DIRT.

6. Click the Material/Map Navigator icon. The Navigator should look like Figure 9.10.

7. In the Navigator, click the last item in the list, material (2):Material#xx of the Multi/Sub-Object to move to that level of EARTH01 material. Name this material level STONE PAVER.

TIP

The Navigator is an invaluable asset to finding your way around complex materials. It is best to keep it open at all times while working on materials.

8. Click the square to the right of the Diffuse color swatch, and double-click Bitmap in the list to get to the Bitmap Parameters rollout level.

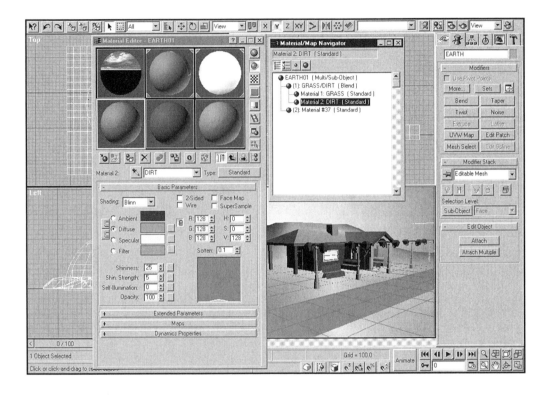

FIGURE 9.10

The Material Editor and Material/Map Navigator.

9. Open the Asset Manager, and from your 3DSMAX2\Maps directory drag and drop ISTONE2.CEL onto the Bitmap button. Name this level stone diff. Click the Show Map in Viewport icon. ISTONE2.CEL won't show yet, however, because you haven't assigned the material to an object with mapping coordinates.

10. Click the Go to Parent icon, click the Maps rollout, and drag and drop ISTONE2.CEL from the Diffuse slot to the Bump map slot. Enter 60 in the Bump Amount field. The Material/Map Navigator should look like Figure 9.11. Now minimize Asset Manager.

TIP

The red parallelogram left of stone diff indicates that that map has the Show in Viewport icon turned on. It is green for maps without Show in Viewport turned on.

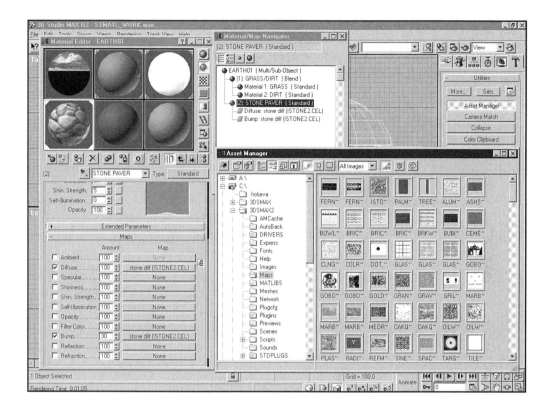

FIGURE 9.11

Material/Map Navigator showing bitmap level.

11. From the Material/Map Navigator, drag and drop the EARTH01 material onto the EARTH mesh object in Camera01 viewport. The object should turn gray with a white area around the station. The white faces are those with Material ID#2 that get the STONE PAVER material. STONE PAVER still does not show because the faces have no mapping coordinates. Minimize the Material Editor and the Navigator.

12. In the Camera01 viewport, select EARTH. Go to Modify Sub-Object Face, and in the Edit Surface rollout, click Select by ID, enter 2 in the ID field of the dialog, and click OK. The faces with Material ID#2 should appear red in the wireframe viewports.

13. In the Modifiers rollout, click UVW Map modifier. The stone diff bitmap shows stretched and streaked in the Camera01 viewport.

NOTE

You are still in Sub-Object Face mode and have applied the UVW Map modifier only to the Material ID#2 faces. The Modifier Stack lists this modifier as *UVW Mapping, the asterisk indication that applied at Sub-Object level.

14. In Parameters rollout, check Box Mapping and the stones appear on the front wall of the track pit, although still too large.

15. In the Asset Manager, double-click the ISTONE2.CEL thumbnail to display it full screen. It is a small image of a river stone. If you make an assumption that the largest stone is about eight inches on a side, then you can assume that the entire bitmap covers a real-world area of about 30 inches wide by 30 inches high. Remember those dimensions. Close the viewer, and minimize the Asset Manager.

16. In the Camera01 viewport, create a Box primitive that is 30 by 30 by 30 units. (Remember those numbers from the previous step—minds like steel traps...)

17. In the Modify panel, apply the UVW Map modifier, check Box mapping, and click the Fit button. You now have a map Gizmo 30 by 30 by 30 units.

18. In the Camera01 viewport, select EARTH. In Modify panel/Alignment rollout, click the Acquire button and pick the new box object in the scene. Click OK in the Acquire UVW Mapping dialog to accept Acquire Relative. Delete the Box01 object. Render Camera01 viewport. Save the file as NEWSTA05.MAX

NOTE

The Map Acquire options enable you to retrieve mapping coordinates from any other object with a UVW Map modifier.

An alternative would be to have entered the 30 by 30 by 30 directly in the height, width, and length fields of the original UVW Map modifier.

TIP

Relative Acquire moves the new mapping Gizmo in center of the face selection set, while Absolute Acquire leaves the Gizmo in its present location around Box01.

In Exercise 9.6, you created one sub-material of a Multi/Sub-Object material type and applied the new STONE PAVER material to a specific selection set of faces. You also applied accurate real-world mapping coordinates calculated by analyzing the bitmap image, creating a box primitive of those dimensions, and acquiring the boxes' coordinates onto the EARTH faces.

It's a Dirty Job

In Exercise 9.7, you will complete the Grass/Dirt sub-material of EARTH. You will use the masking in the Blend material to randomize the pattern of Grass and Dirt on the faces of EARTH with Material ID#1.

EXERCISE 9.7: MAPPING GRASS AND DIRT

1. Open the Material Editor and Material/Map Navigator. In the Navigator, select Material 1:GRASS. In the Maps rollout, click Diffuse map slot. Name this level grass.

2. Click the Type:Standard button, and double-click Noise from the list.

3. Now, make the grass green and yellow: In the Noise Parameters rollout, change Color 1 to a dark green and Color 2 to a pale yellow. Check Turbulence on, enter 2.0 in Levels field, and enter 75.0 in Size field.

TIP

Colors with low saturation amounts are usually more believable in earth tones.

NOTE

Note that the Show Map in Viewport button is grayed out for this level. Procedural maps such as Noise, Cellular, and Dents cannot be viewed in a shaded viewport.

4. In the Navigator, select Material 1:GRASS to jump to that level. Click the Bump Slot None button and double-click Noise in the list. This will be the GRASS bump map. Name this level grass bump. Enter 0.7 in the Noise Threshhold:High field and 0.2 in the Low field to give a sharper edge to the bumps. Enter 20.0 in the Size field. Render the Camera01 viewport to see a green/yellow rolling material on all faces with Material ID#1.

5. In the Navigator, go to Material 2:Dirt level and expand the Maps rollout.

6. In the Diffuse map slot, choose the Noise map type and set the colors to a medium gray and dark brown. In Noise Parameters rollout, enter 0.6 in Threshhold:High and 0.4 in Low. Name this level dirt.

Tip

On the sample sphere, in the Material Editor you should still see the grass material. Click the Show End Result icon below the sample spheres to show only as far as the current level.

7. Click the Go to Parent icon, then click the Bump None button. Click Bump Type:Standard and double-click Cellular from the list. Name this level cellular bump.

8. In the Navigator, click (1) GRASS/DIRT level and in Basic Parameter rollout, click Mask:None, and double-click Noise in the list. Check Turbulence, enter 10 in Levels field, enter 0.8 in Threshhold:High and 0.4 in Low. The Material Editor and Navigator should look like Figure 9.12.

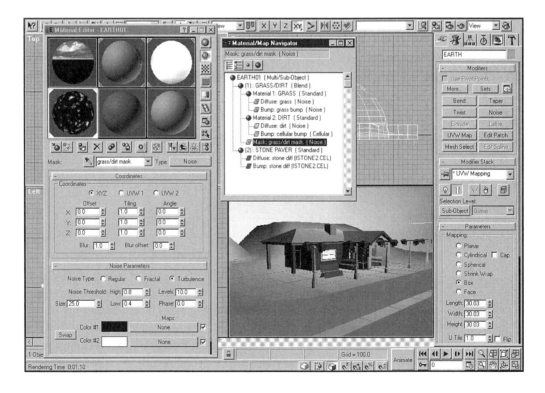

FIGURE 9.12

Material/Map Navigator showing GRASS/DIRT mask level.

9. Render the Camera01 viewport and you should have a green/yellow landscape with patches of brown/gray dirt area. Save this file as NEWSTA06.MAX. You will need it in Exercise 9.9.

In Exercise 9.7 you created a Blend material of GRASS/DIRT with a Mask. Both grass and dirt have their own coloration and noise bump pattern.

Experiment with various settings, especially in the mask and noise bump maps for different coverage of the coloration and bumps. You could change a bump noise to a Mask material type and use another noise as the mask to alter the bumpiness in a more random manner. Use this material only as a starting point for your own inventions.

Quick and Dirty

Exercise 9.8 is a quick method of getting a material assigned and mapped onto hilly landscapes that show the contour of a land mass.

EXERCISE 9.8: CONTOUR MAPPING A HILLY LANDSCAPE

1. Open 09max07 from the CD-ROM.

2. Open the Material Editor, and name the first sample sphere LANDSCAPE. Click the square to the right of Diffuse color swatch, and double-click Gradient in the list. Name this level gradient diff.

3. Set Color #3 to a deep blue. Close the Color Selector.

4. Click None to the right of Color #2, and double-click Smoke in the list. Name this level smoke diff #2. Change Smoke Color #1 to dark green and Color #2 to grayish tan. The Material Editor and Navigator should look like Figure 9.13.

5. Click the Show Map in Viewport icon to turn it on. Drag and drop the sample sphere onto LANDSCAPE in the Perspective viewport.

6. In the Modify panel, click UVW Map. The LANDSCAPE material is applied and mapped to LANDSCAPE so that the mesh object is dark blue in the foreground, gray in the middle, and white at the back.

NOTE

If you render the viewport, you will see the effect of the smoke map on the material. Procedural materials do not show in a shaded viewport.

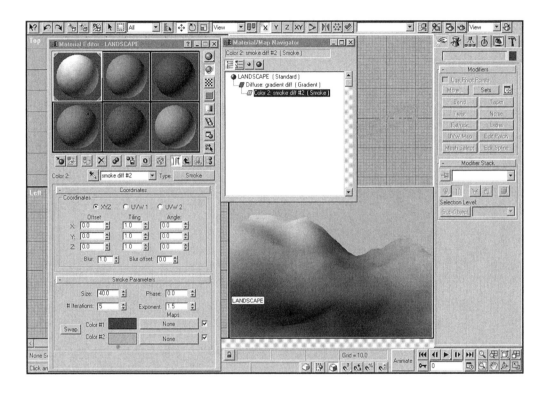

FIGURE 9.13

Material/Map Navigator showing smoke diff #2 level.

7. In the Front viewport, select LANDSCAPE and, in the Modify panel, click Sub-Object Gizmo.

8. In the Alignment area, click the View Align button to flip the map Gizmo planar to the Front viewport.

9. In the Alignment area, click the Fit button. The Gizmo now fits the bounding box of LANDSCAPE creating white hilltops, green hillsides, and blue low areas.

10. In the gradient diff Gradient Parameter rollout, enter 0.2 in the Color 2 Position field to show more snow capped peaks and less water area.

11. Right-click the Top viewport label, and choose Smooth and Highlight to see the colors forming to the contour of the land. Render the Top viewport to see the full effect of the material.

12. Save the file as LANDSCAP.MAX. The rendered image should look similar to Figure 9.14.

FIGURE 9.14

Rendering of Quick and Dirty Landscape.

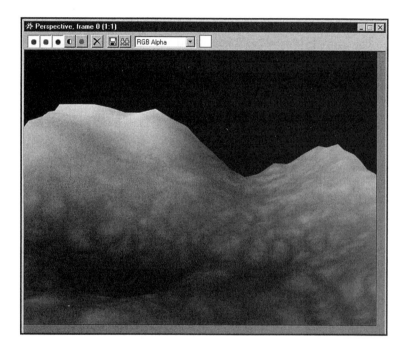

Exercise 9.8 is an example of a quick and easy material to use on object with elevation changes. You have used it here on a hilly landscape, but the concept could also be applied to rough seas or a camouflaged warplane or ship.

Water

An infinite number of variables are possible when representing water in a scene. For instance, you could have:

■ Calm water in bright sun.

■ Softly rippling water on a cloudy day.

■ Rough choppy water on a partly sunny day.

■ Stormy water at night.

Well, you get the idea. Each scenario presents its own unique problems, and very often the deciding factor is not the material itself, but the manner in which it is lighted.

3D Studio MAX R2's raytracing material and mapping types can help enormously in getting a convincing reflection from calm or rippling water, but raytracing has the disadvantage of increasing render time noticeably. Use raytracing when you have to, but try to "fake" it when you can. One distinct advantage of 3D Studio MAX R2 is that raytracing is implemented at the material or the map level and is not applied to the whole scene as in other software programs. Material and map level raytracing requires only those objects with the material needs to be calculated, speeding the process considerably.

You will look at a calm rippling water scenario and an open ocean in winter effect in the next two exercises, first using Raytracing and then without it.

Calm Water

Exercise 9.9 will lead you through the basic steps of creating water in the STATION scene, treating the track pit as if it were a canal with slow running water. The day is sunny and there is a soft breeze blowing down the canal. A bump map will ruffle the surface and you will use a raytrace mapping type to get accurate reflections, something that is difficult to get on a flat object with bitmap or flat mirror reflections.

EXERCISE 9.9: CANAL WATER ON A BREEZY DAY

1. Open NEWSTA06.MAX.

2. In the Display panel or Display floater, unhide the Patch Grid called CANAL WATER.

Tip

The CANAL WATER mesh could have been created with a rectangle that was collapsed to an editable mesh. However, we have found that large flat faces are not as reliable for reflections and shadows as mesh objects with smaller faces. This is one of those situations where the result can often warrant the extra face/vertex count.

3. In the Camera01 viewport, press C and choose Camera02 from the list. This is a low camera closer to the edge of the canal.

4. In the Material Editor, select an unused sample sphere and name it CANAL WATER.

5. In the Basic Parameters rollout, set Ambient and Diffuse colors to a blue/gray; RGB values around 50,50,75 might be a good starting point. Set Specular Color to pure white.

6. Set Shininess to 40, Shin.Strength to 60, and Opacity to 80.

TIP

We think of water as being very shiny, which it is, of course, but if you set Shininess and Shin.Strength to 100, the specular highlights are very bright and tight. This can make them diminish to insignificant or disappear completely. Because the highlights are usually coming from a large expanse of bright sky or clouds, a fairly high Shin.Strength (to keep the specular white) and a moderately low Shininess produces better results.

7. In the Maps rollout, click None in the Bump slot and choose Mask from the list. Name this material level noise/bump mask.

TIP

The bump map is used to create wind wavelets on the surface and they are seldom consistent over the entire body of water. The mask enables you to reduce the effect of the bump map in some areas.

8. In the Mask Parameters rollout, click None in the Map slot to drop to the map branch level and double-click Noise in the list. Call this level noise bump. In the Coordinates rollout, set X:Tiling to 4.0. In the Noise Parameters rollout, check Fractal, and set Size to 15.0.

TIP

A noise map tends to be made of fairly equally sized black-and-white splotches. Ripples on water, however, are usually much longer than they are high or wide. Setting the X:Tiling to three or four times the Y:Tiling elongates the wavelet for a more natural look.

9. To get to the Mask level, click the Go to Parent icon and click the Mask slot. Name this level splat mask. Click Type:None and choose Splat from the list. Splat is a new blotchy map that looks like splattered paint.

10. In the Coordinates rollout, enter 2.0 in the X:Tiling field. In the Splatter Parameters rollout, Size to 100.0, #Iterations to 1, and Threshold to 0.3.

11. In the Navigator, go to the CANAL WATER level, Maps rollout. Enter 10 in Bumps Amount and 30 in Reflection Amount. Click None in the Reflection slot to drop to Reflection map level. Name this level raytrace. The Navigator and Material Editor should look like Figure 9.15.

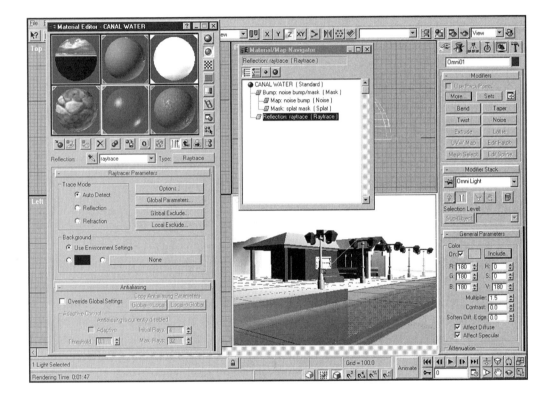

FIGURE 9.15

Navigator and Material Editor for CANAL WATER.

12. Click the Global Parameters button in Raytracer Parameters rollout, and enter 2 in the Maximum Depth field.

TIP

Maximum Depth is the maximum number of reflections within reflections MAX R2 will try to calculate. Always reduce this setting to the lowest you can get away with to save calculation and rendering time.

13. In the Attenuation rollout, click Falloff Type and choose Exponential from the list. Enter 0 in the Start range field and 2000 in the End range.

TIP

Raytrace reflection attenuation diminishes the reflection from objects the more distant they are from the reflecting object. Exponential seems to offer a good balance between realism and system overhead.

14. Click Go to Parent or select CANAL WATER in the Navigator. Drag and drop CANAL WATER sample sphere onto CANAL WATER mesh object in the scene. Close the Material Editor and Material/Map Navigator.

15. Render Camera02 viewport.

You can see the wind wavelets and a few glassy areas on the water, the reflections look good, and the exponential reflection falloff causes the last lamppost to reflect much less than the closest. But something is still missing.

The sky, even though it is overcast, should be quite bright and should be causing specular highlights on the surface of the water. The sky, however, does not cast any light of its own. You will add that effect next.

EXERCISE 9.10: ADDING A LIGHTED SKY

1. Create an Omni light in the Top viewport, move it behind the STATION in line with the Camera02 line of sight, and move it up in the World Z-axis so it is visible at the top middle of the Camera02 view. Name the light WaterOmni01. It should look similar to Figure 9.16.

2. In the Modifier panel, click Exclude in General Parameters rollout. Choose CANAL WATER in the left list and send it into the right list. Check Include at the top right of the Include/Exclude dialog. Click OK and close the dialog.

3. Save the file as NEWSTA07.MAX, and render Camera02 viewport.

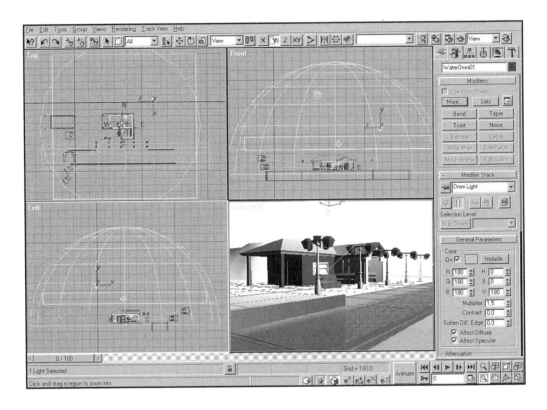

FIGURE 9.16

WaterOmni01 in Top Center of Camera01 Viewport.

Exercises 9.9 and 9.10 lead you through the steps of creating water in a canal on an overcast day with a light breeze. You created wavelets that were much longer than they are wide and masked the surface to give the occasional calm spot. You used raytraced mapping to give accurate reflections and set reflection attenuation to make the scene more realistic. You also reduced the Reflection Depth to decrease render times. And, perhaps most importantly, you added a dedicated back-light to represent the brightness of the open sky and clouds. Almost all water scenes will benefit from Exercise 9.10's back-lighting technique.

Rough Seas

In Exercise 9.11 you create water conditions more like what you would find at sea after winds from a quick squall have died. The whitecaps and spray have ended, but there are still the dynamics of the sea and the surface winds. The WATER01 object is a Quad Patch converted to an editable mesh with a Ripple and Noise modifier. The scene is set up with a sky background mapped to a quarter cylinder.

EXERCISE 9.11: SEAS AFTER THE STORM

1. Open the file 09max11.MAX from the CD-ROM.

2. Open the Material Editor, and select an unused sample sphere. Name this material OCEAN WATER.

3. Click Type:Standard, and double-click the Blend material from the list. Click OK in the Replace Material dialog to discard the old material. In the Basic Parameters rollout, enter 40.0 in the Mix Amount field.

4. Click Standard next to Material 1 and name this BLUE/GREEN. Click the square to the right of the Diffuse color swatch, and double-click Noise from the map list. Name this level blue/green diff.

5. In the Noise Parameters rollout, set Color #1 to a dark blue with moderate saturation. Set Color #2 to a dark green with moderate saturation. Enter 40.0 in the Size field. Drag and drop the sample sphere onto the WATER01 object.

6. In the Coordinates rollout, check UVW 1.

NEW TO R2

You are setting this material to use UVW 1 mapping coordinates. This is a new feature that allows two mapping coordinates to be applied to the same faces. The second material in the Blend will use UVW 2, and you will then be able to place two UVW Map modifiers each using a separate UVW Channel.

7. In the Material/Map Navigator, click Material 2 and name this material BLUE GRADIENT. Click the square to the right of the Diffuse color swatch, and name this map level gradient diff. In the Coordinates rollout, select Explicit UVW 2 from the Mapping list. Leave Color #1 white, make Color #2 a medium green, and make Color #3 a dark blue. Enter 0.6 in the Color 2 Position field.

TIP

Remember that you can click the Show End Result icon to turn it off and make the material at the current level visible on the sample sphere.

8. In the Navigator, click Material 2 BLUE GRADIENT to go to that level. Enter 40.0 in the Shininess field and 60.0 in the Shin.Strength field.

9. In the Navigator, click Material 1 BLUE/GREEN to go to that level. Enter 40.0 in the Shininess field and 60.0 in the Shin.Strength field.

10. Expand the Maps rollout, and put Noise map type in the Bumps slot. Name the level wind bump, and enter 4.0 in the Y;Tiling field and 10.0 in the Size field. Click Go to Parent, and enter 25 in the Bump Amount field.

11. Click in the Reflect slot, and get Reflect/Refract map type. Name this level auto reflect. Click the Go to Parent icon, and set Reflection Amount to 25. The Material Editor and Navigator should look similar to Figure 9.17.

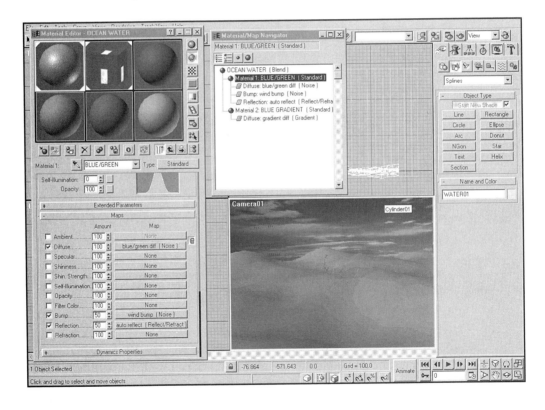

FIGURE 9.17

Material Editor and Navigator for OCEAN WATER.

12. You have the material created and assigned to the mesh object. You must now apply mapping coordinates. BLUE/GREEN material is mapped from the top and you previously set it to use UVW1 mapping. You set BLUE GRADIENT to use Explicit UVW 2 mapping. Select WATER01, and in the Modifier panel, click UVW Map. This step applies a Planar map type to the entire object as seen in the Top viewport. You will notice in the Parameters rollout the Channel is set to 1. This corresponds to UVW1 for BLUE/GREEN.

13. In the Front viewport, select WATER01. In the Modifier panel, click UVW Map and, in the Alignment area, click the View Align button and the Fit button. The Map gizmo is now mapping the gradient material to the side of the mesh, causing the high areas to be white, the middle green, and the lower blue. Check 2 in the Channel area to map coordinates only for BLUE/GREEN.

14. Close the Material Editor and Navigator.

15. Render Camera01 viewport. The rendering is probably not too bad but is still missing one thing—the back-light similar to Exercise 9.10.

16. In the Top viewport, create a Omni light at the back edge of WATER01 and, in the Left viewport, move it up about halfway up the sky cylinder. Enter 255 in the Value field. Click Exclude and exclude cylinder01 from the light.

NOTE

There is already an Omni light for the Sky, but it excludes the water.

17. Save the file as OCEAN01.MAX and render the Camera01 viewport.

In Exercise 9.11 you created a material that takes advantage of the new MAX R2 feature that allows two mapping coordinates, called UVW1 and UVW2, to be mapped to a set of faces. With this feature, you mapped a blue/green noise material to the top of the sea mesh and another gradient material to the side of the mesh, using the Blend material type. This gives a patchy mottled look to the surface and a gradient to make the wave troughs dark and the wave peaks lighter.

Trees and Shrubs

Trees and shrubs are necessary for a realistic scene but even the simplest of 3D mesh trees can grow to incredible face/vertex count. When you copy the tree several hundred times around a scene, the whole file becomes unmanageable and adding shadows to a scene full of trees compounds the problem. This section addresses a simple, yet effective method of adding trees and shrubs to a scene.

Making a Tree

A good method for creating Trees and Shrubs in a scene has always been to map texture and opacity maps to a flat plane with the two-sided option. That is still a very good option with MAX R2 because of the efficiency. In Exercise 9.12 you will create a material to be mapped onto a flat plane, but then you will take it a step farther and use a projector spot to simulate a shadow. You will also set the flat plane up to always look at a moving camera to keep the plane perpendicular to the line of site.

EXERCISE 9.12: CREATING A EFFICIENT TREE

1. Open the file 09max12.max from the CD-ROM. It is a file with a camera, a flat plane made from a rectangle collapsed to an editable mesh, and a Quad Patch ground plane. There is one Omni light in the scene lighting the tree and one spotlight that you turn on later in the exercise. The ground and sky objects have materials associated with them.

2. Open the Material Editor, click an unused sample sphere and name the material TREE. Check 2-sided in the Basic Parameters rollout. Click the square to the right of Diffuse color swatch, and double-click Bitmap in the list. In the Basic Parameters rollout, click the Bitmap button and get TREE_1.CEL from the CD-ROM. Name this level tree diff. In the Coordinates rollout, uncheck the U and V Tile checkboxes.3. Click and hold on the Sample Type icon, and choose the box sample from the flyout.

3. Click the Go to Parent icon, and expand the Maps rollout. Click the Opacity slot, and double-click Bitmap in the list. Get a bitmap called TREE_1OP from the CD-ROM. This map is a black-and-white image of the diffuse map. What is white will be opaque; black areas will be

transparent. Click Show End Result to see the tree mapped to all sides of the sample cube. In the Basic Parameters rollout, check 2-sided to show the material regardless of face normals.

4. In the Maps rollout, drag and drop the Opacity slot map onto the Shininess slot. Check Instance from the dialog, and click OK.

5. Drag and drop the Opacity map onto Shin.Strength and make it an Instance, as well. The Material Editor and Material/Map Navigator should look like Figure 9.18.

TIP

Using the same map to control Shininess and Shin.Strength keeps the flat plane from shining in strong light.

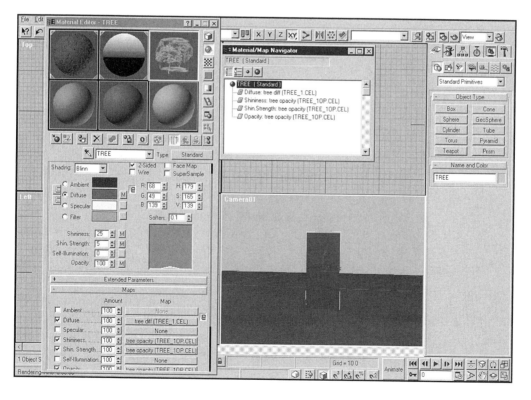

FIGURE 9.18

Material Editor and Navigator for TREE.

6. Drag and drop the sample cube from the Material Editor onto the TREE object. In the Modifier panel, click UVW Map to apply mapping coordinates to the TREE. Close the Material Editor and Navigator.

TIP

While you are at a Map level in the material you can click the Show Map in Viewport to see the map in the shaded viewport.

If you render the scene now there appears to be a tree in the scene. However, if you move the camera around to one side, the tree disappears because it has no depth. To enhance the realism, you need to give the tree depth and add some shadows to the scene.

EXERCISE 9.13: ADDING DEPTH AND SHADOWS TO THE TREE

1. In the Top viewport, create a dummy object near the tree and about the same size in width.

2. In the Front viewport, select the TREE and zoom in to fill the viewport. In the Hierarchy panel, click Affect Pivot Only. Click the Align icon and pick the TREE in the Front viewport. Check Y Position and Current Object:Pivot Point; Target Object:Minimum. Click OK, and click Affect Pivot Only to turn it off. This moves the pivot to the bottom center of TREE.

3. In the Front viewport, select the Dummy01, click Align, and check X, Y, Z Position, Current Object:Pivot Point and Target Object:Pivot Point.

4. Click Select and Link, click and drag from TREE to Dummy01 to link the TREE as a child of Dummy01.

5. Select TREE, and in Hierarchy panel, click Link Info. In the Locks roll-out, *check* everything except Rotate;Z, and in Inherit rollout, *uncheck* everything except Rotate:Z. This ensures that the TREE will follow only the Z rotation of the parent Dummy01.

6. Select Dummy01, and in Motion panel, expand Assign Controller roll-out and pick Transform:Position/Rotate/Scale in the list. Click the Assign Controller icon, and double-click Look At in the list.

7. In the Look At Parameters rollout, click the Pick Target button, press H, and double-click Camera01 in the list.

8. Move the camera around in the Top and Front viewport, and observe that the tree always stays perpendicular to the line of site, but also stays upright in the scene. If you assigned a Look At controller directly to the TREE it would lay down as the camera got higher.

9. Press H, select Spot01 from the list and, in the Modify panel/General Parameters rollout, check the On check box. This is a spotlight projecting a tree "shadow" material to complete the scene.

10. Render the Camer01 viewport, and save the file as TREE.MAX. The rendered display should look similar to Figure 9.19.

FIGURE 9.19

Rendered "Postcard" Tree with Projected "Shadows."

In Exercises 9.12 and 9.13, you created a convincing tree that is about as simple and efficient as a tree can get. You set up a Dummy object and restricted the Inherited Links to keep the tree upright but facing a camera as the camera moves around the scene. You also activated a spotlight to project an image of a tree to replicate a shadow.

Fruits and Flowers

Fruits have a surface quality that has always been a source of inspiration to artists over the centuries. There is a luminescent quality to the skin of fruit that makes it appealing to the eye.

You can create fruits and flower materials with the same basic methods you applied to ground and water—combinations of Blend materials with masks to reveal blemishes and changes of color.

A Fruit-Filled Still-Life

In Exercise 9.14 you will create the materials in a still-life scene with grapes, bananas, and Black-Eyed Susans and try some tips on putting life into these materials. These same tips are useful for any living flora.

EXERCISE 9.14: FRUITS AND FLOWERS

1. Open the file 09max14.MAX from the CD-ROM. The file is set up as a still-life with the objects in place, the lighting set, and materials assigned. The materials, however, are all flat gray. If you render Camera01 viewport, it appears quite dull, so your job is to bring it to life.

2. Open the Material Editor, and notice that some sample spheres are already named and that the right-most on the top row, BANANA, is already set as a Blend material.

3. Select the left upper-most sample sphere. It is named GRAPE PURP. Set the Diffuse color to a dark dusky purple, something around RGB:85,40,65 might be a starting point. Set Ambient color to RGB:75,80,30, a dark olive green. Set Specular color to pure white.

4. Set Shininess to 11 and Shin.Strength to 27. Click the square to the right of Shininess to access the Shininess map, and double-click Noise in the map list. Set Noise Parameters; High 0.8, Low 0.3, and Size 50. Name this level noise shin. Click the Go to Parent icon.

5. In Map rollout, click None in Reflection slot, and double-click Bitmap in the list. Click the Bitmap button in Bitmap Parameters rollout, and from the 3DSMAX2/MAPS sub-directory on your hard drive, double-click RUSTYOID.JPG. This is an image of a rusty steel plate. Name this level rusty reflect.

6. Click Go to Parent icon, and enter 20 in the Reflection Amount field.

T IP

This material wouldn't be a bad looking grape, but to give it a little extra punch, set the self-illumination amount up to 10. Because fruit is living and because of the way its skin reacts to light, the self-illumination adds depth and "presence" rather than just the look of plastic fruit. Don't overdo the self-illumination though; it diminishes the depth and contrast of the scene and ruins the effect.

7. Render the Camera01 viewport. Save the file as FRUIT.MAX. The Material Editor and Material/Map Navigator should look like Figure 9.20.

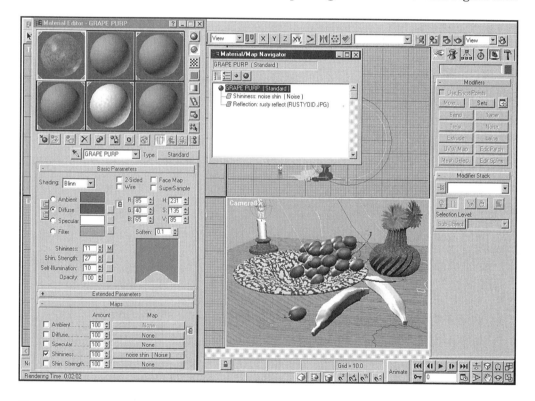

FIGURE 9.20

Material Editor and Material/Map Navigator for GRAPE PURP.

8. In the Material Editor, click the lower-left sample sphere called PETAL. This is the material assigned to the petals of the Black-Eyed Susans in the scene.

9. Check on the 2-sided checkbox as the petals are made from collapsed 2D ellipses.

10. Click the square to the right of the Diffuse color swatch to get to Diffuse map level. Double-click Gradient in the list. Set Color #1 to light yellow (RGB:240,220,75), set Color #2 to darker yellow (RGB:200,160,35), and set Color #3 to a dusty red (RGB:175,70,70). Enter 0.6 in Color 2 Position field. Name this level gradient diff. Click Go to Parent icon.

11. In Maps rollout, click None in the Bumps slot. Double-click Speckle, and set Color #1 to black, Color #2 to white, and Size to 20.0. This gives the petals a slight amount of texture. Name this level speckle bump.

12. Click Go to Parent, and enter 10 in the Self-illumination field for this material to also give it some life. Leave the Shininess and Shin.Strength at default levels, because most flower petals are quite matte.

13. Render the Camera01 viewport, and save the file as FRUIT01.MAX. The Material Editor and Navigator should look like Figure 9.21.

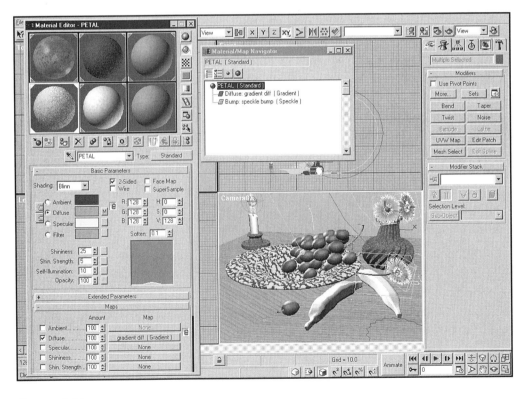

FIGURE 9.21

Material Editor and Material/Map Navigator for PETAL.

14. In the Material Editor, click the upper-right sample sphere called BANANA. It is a Blend material type so that you can create a banana that is partially ripe with yellow and brown mixed and just a tinge of green as if it had ripened in the refrigerator.

15. Click Material 1: slot. Name this level Yellow/Brown. Enter 10 in the Self-Illumination field, then click the square to the right of Diffuse, and double-click Noise. Name this level noise diff. Make Color #1 to a medium yellow and Color #2 to dark brown. Set the X;Tiling to 2.0, High Threshold to 0.8, Low to 0.4, and Size to 40. Click twice on Go to Parent to get to the BANANA level or use Navigator.

16. Click the Material 2: slot. Name this level Green Ends. Click the square to the right of Diffuse, and double-click Gradient in the list. Name the gradient level gradient diff, set Colors #1 and #3 to a dark green and Color #2 to a deep yellow. Click Go to Parent, and enter 40 in the Mix Amount field. This causes the ends of the bananas to have a greenish tinge.

17. Save the file as FRUIT02.MAX, and render the Camera01 viewport. The Material Editor and Navigator should look like Figure 9.22.

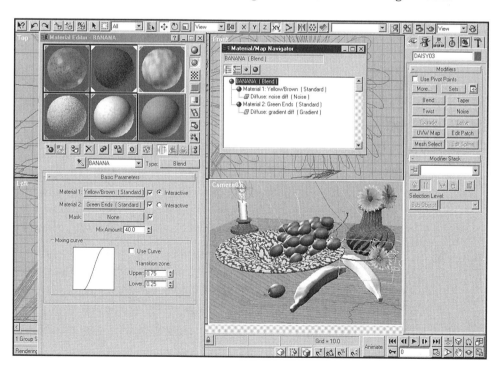

FIGURE 9.22

Material Editor and Material/Map Navigator for BANANA.

In Exercise 9.14 you created materials that have a slight amount of self-illumination added to give the depth and luminance that is the essence of what artists try to capture in all media.

Ice and Snow

Because ice and snow are both made of water, they share some of the same properties as water. However, the crystalline nature of snow and ice reflects and refracts light differently.

The ambient quality of both the material and the lighting becomes more important. If you walk on glaciers and ice fields, you would see an incredible amount of blue and green light in the shaded areas. When you create snow and ice, watch that the specular areas do not burn out to lose all detail.

Open and study the files on the CD-ROM called 09max14a.MAX and 09max14b.MAX to see some examples of ice in the form of a melting cube and snow at the North Pole. Analyze the Material Editor and the lighting in the scene. It is very difficult to get a material to look right without complementing it with good lighting.

Stone and Rock

Stone and rock are to earth as ice and snow are to water. Both are derived from the same material in nature with differing surface attributes.

The key elements in stone and rock are surface reflection and bump mapping. Rocks vary widely in composition and each mineral has different reflectivity. It is also important to change the reflectivity to represent dry or wet stone.

Bitmaps in the diffuse mapping can be a good starting point, but relying on the bitmap image totally for texture makes the stone look like a photo wrapped on a potato—not what you are looking for.

Open 09max14c.MAX and experiment with the three materials set on rocks at the North Pole.

In Practice: Designing Materials

- Creating convincing naturally occurring materials requires randomness in surface texture, bumpiness, shininess, and lighting to give the materials a feel of depth and tactility. Sky should convey the feeling of distance and convergence at the horizon and water needs a "wet" feel, usually associated with shininess, for example.

- In this chapter, you created sky backgrounds as a projected background image and as a bitmapped image on a cylinder. Both methods are interchangeable, but background projection is often better for little camera motion and bitmapping on a mesh allows animation of the map as well as the sky object to create more believable motion. You learned to use Blend material type and RGB Tinting to alter the bitmaps used in skies without having to change the original image. You also rescued a dark sky image by raising Output levels in the Material Editor.

- You learned a method of using a blended gradient to accentuate height in ground and water materials and used MAX R2's new Material Channel 1 and 2 to apply different mapping coordinates one selection.

- By applying a small amount of self-illumination to fruits and flowers, you learned that you can give them a slight inner glow to make them more life-like. You also created a material that highlighted the natural aging process by making a banana that ranged from green to yellow to brown.

- Ice and snow interact with light differently than other materials because of the internal refraction of light that occurs. You saw examples of how to adjust the amount of blue/green color in the ambient portion of materials to simulate that effect.

Chapter 10

DESIGNING MAN-MADE MATERIALS

In the Material Editor, many visualization professionals primarily create man-made materials. The materials mimic the surface information of the everyday objects that you can see looking around the room or glancing out the window. Even materials you can only imagine in a fantasy world are based on materials you know. The best part about creating these materials is that, often, you have ready references at hand. You can look at a nearby object or call up an image on the Internet for a quick example of what you need to create. Image scanning or digital photography can be employed to capture files of materials for later reference. In this chapter, you learn about the following subjects:

- Creating material imperfections
- The role of geometry on man-made materials
- Adding "grunge" to materials

Creating Material Imperfections

Look more closely at your immediate surroundings. Your keyboard is probably made of simple beige or gray plastic, but the closer you look, the more you see. Notice those black areas around the frequently struck keys and where your wrists make contact. How about those little splatters of coffee and the soft layer of dust between the number keys and the function keys? Looking farther on your desk, there are Post-Its with scribbled notes and phone numbers. And don't forget those old 3D Studio Max R1.0 boxes that are falling apart on the bookshelf beside the dog-eared manuals because of a bad glue batch.

Although these objects are man-made, they exist in nature and have been affected by the forces of nature with the randomness of natural organic objects. In computer imagery, this natural phenomenon is often referred to as *grunge* and is as important to quality materials as the bitmaps used. If you don't mimic the flaws and imperfections on the surface of real-world objects in your MAX creations, your scene is sure to look too clean and "plasticy."

The Role of Geometry on Man-Made Materials

A number of physical features in the geometry can contribute to this grunge, among them are:

- Surface dents and bulges
- Chips and cracks
- Wear and tear on edges and corners
- Folds and wrinkles

While it is a good idea to use bump and opacity maps to create the illusion of geometry as often as possible, it is sometimes necessary to build these imperfections into the mesh geometry. You can use mesh modifiers such as Noise and Meshsmooth to distort the edges of objects, or use Boolean operations to create major cracks and crevices, for example. Such major features are just too large to be handled well by the bump and opacity maps.

3D Studio MAX R2 offers some great tools to get you on your way to roughing up your mesh objects, such as:

- Extended Primitives for chamfering and filleting edges

- Meshsmooth modifier for rounding edges

- Relax and Spherify modifier for rounding objects

- Ripple and Wave modifiers and Spacewarps for rippling surfaces

- Noise modifier for random surface perturbations

- Displace modifier for perturbations based on image luminance

- Affect Region modifier for dents and bulges

- FFD modifiers and Spacewarps for molding surfaces

Not all material manipulations have to be on the negative side. You can greatly enhance the look of highly reflective materials by adding objects in the scene—not to be seen directly, but to be reflected. Simply keep them out of the line of sight.

Adding Grunge to Materials

Once you have your mesh object roughed up at the geometry level, you need to add the fine detail that makes the surface look real. Some of the grunge might be bold whereas some other might be subtle. It is very important to add at least one of the effects listed here to all materials, however, to avoid the homogenous plastic look. Several possibilities for grunge are:

- Smudges and discoloration

- Scratches and weathering

- Puddles and variations in reflectivity

- Dust and grime

At the material level, MAX R2 offers several material types that are great tools for creating complex materials. They include:

- **Blend**   Enables unlimited levels of blended and masked materials to be on top of materials on top of materials.

- **Top/Bottom** Materials that are different at the top of an object than at the bottom, such as a boat that has sat in the water for a while, or an object that has sat in strong sunlight and faded on the top but not on the bottom. In MAX R2, top can be defined in terms of World or Local axis.

- **Double Sided** Reduce complexity of mesh objects by applying two materials, one on the side with face normals, the other on the back side. This is good for creating pages of a book from a QuadPatch or a floor/ceiling for an architectural project. You can set the back material to "bleed" through to the front, simulating translucency.

- **Multi/Sub-Object** A combination of materials each assigned to faces with a corresponding Material ID number. Each Sub-Object material can be as simple or as complex as you need. You might, for example, create a ballpoint pen as one mesh object and then assign Material ID numbers to the cap, the body, and the bezel. You then create a Multi/Sub-Object material with three colors and textures to correspond to the IDs.

When you have the material defined, you can add the grunge details by using the various mapping types. Don't be afraid to experiment, and don't become blinded by the map name. Noise can easily be defined as smudge or blotch. Some of the MAX R2 map type possibilities are:

- **Cellular** Use this map type to simulate a growing cell pattern in a petrie dish or a "cracked earth" type pattern. It is useful for bump and diffuse color textures.

- **Falloff** This new map type causes a falloff effect based on distance. The direction of falloff can be according to World or Local axis, viewing direction, or a particular object. You can use it to enhance depth in a scene; it performs best as a mask or modifier to diffuse, bump, or opacity maps.

- **Output, RGB Multiply, RGB Tint** Mimic the controls of the same names found in the rollouts of bitmaps and are useful to add their namesake effects to map types that don't have them built in. For instance, you can use an Output map in the Diffuse slot and then add a Dent map as an Output sub-map to add the Output controls to a Dent map type.

- **Smoke, Speckle, Splat**   Procedural maps such as Noise, but with different patterns. They are excellent for random bump or opacity effects and can be powerful grunge tools when used as masks and Mix or Composite maps. Smoke can be effective as a Shininess or Shin.Strength map to break or boost the surface shininess subtly.

- **Thin Wall Refraction**   Gives the illusion of the jog visible when you put a pencil in a glass of water. MAX R1.2 refraction, however, made only bitmaps appear refracted, not objects.

Material Corruption Techniques

In Exercise 10.1, you will take a clean, plastic-looking teapot and turn it into an old, weathered pot by applying several layers of patina or aging stress. A simple, familiar object such as the teapot shows off the changes you make more readily than a complex object would. Two basic materials are in the exercise file. One is a wood material with flat mirror reflection on the tabletop, and the other is a reddish-brown plastic material on the teapot. To the teapot material, you add:

- Discoloration

- Smudges

- Dents

- Dust

- Weathering

EXERCISE 10.1: AGING A TEAPOT

1. Open 10MAX01.MAX from the CD-ROM. The scene is a teapot on a wood tabletop. Render the Camera01 viewport to get an idea of what the scene looks like.

2. Open the Material Editor and click in the first sample sphere to see the material named TEAPOT01.

3. A Standard material type is very limiting for all but the simplest materials. Blend is a good material type for general use because it can use masking to let underlying color bleed through. You will use the current reddish-brown material as a rust layer in a Blend material type. Click on the Standard button and double-click Blend in the Material/Map Browser list. Check Keep Old Material as Sub-material. Click OK. You now have a Blend material named TEAPOT01 and a sub-material named TEAPOT01. Change the name in the top name slot to TEAPOT.

NOTE

To the right of the Material #1 button, you see Interactive checked. This means you see TEAPOT01 in the shaded viewport. Check Interactive next to Material #2 and the teapot in the Perspective viewport turns gray to show Material #2. Check Material #1's Interactive check box.

4. Click on the Material #2 button and name Material 2 TEAPOT02. Click on the Diffuse color swatch and set the RGB values to 65,100,100. Increase the Shininess to 25 and the Shin.Strength to 60. To see the current material level on the sample sphere, click the Show End Result icon to turn it off. Click Show End Result again to turn it on. There is no blend effect yet because the Mix Amount is set to 0.

5. Click the Material/Map Navigator icon, and click on TEAPOT(Blend) at the top of the hierarchy. In the Basic Parameters rollout, enter 50 in the Mix Amount field. The sample sphere turns a purple-gray because you are blending 50 percent reddish with 50 percent bluish. Click on the Render Last icon, and the teapot appears with this new color.

6. Use a mask to mix the two materials based on the luminance values of a bitmap or procedural image. Click on the Mask;None button and double-click on Smoke in the list. Name the mask smoke mask. Click on Show End result to see what the smoke mask looks like. Black in the mask reveals the reddish material, and white in the mask reveals the blue/green material.

7. In the Smoke Parameters rollout, click on the Swap button. This swaps black for white and reverses the effect of the mask. Render the Perspective viewport, and observe that you have a blue/green teapot with subtle reddish discoloration.

8. In Smoke Parameters rollout, enter 10 in the Size field and 2 in # Iterations field. Click the Render Last icon to see the result on the teapot. The Material Editor and Navigator should look similar to Figure 10.1.

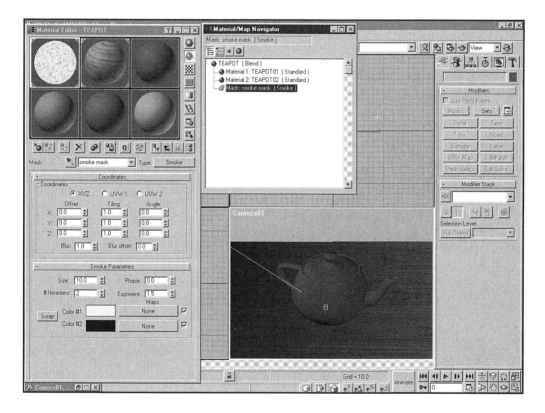

Figure 10.1

Material Editor and Material/Map Navigator.

Tip

When using a blend mask, you can fine-tune the mix strength by checking Use Curve in the Mixing Curve area of TEAPOT level. Try several settings and notice that if the Upper and Lower values are the same, the edge of the mask is sharp, and the farther apart the values are, the softer the edge transition. Enter 1.0 in the Upper field and 0.25 in the Lower field.

9. In the Material/Map Navigator, click on Material 1:TEAPOT01 to jump quickly to that level; then in the Material Editor, open the Maps rollout. Pan the rollout up to see all map slots if necessary.

10. In the Material/Map Navigator, drag and drop Mask;smoke mask onto the Bump slot in Material Editor Maps rollout. Check Instance in the Instance(Copy)Map dialog box, and click OK. Click the Render Last icon, and notice the reddish areas are now slightly dented.

11. In the Maps Parameter rollout, click on the None in Shininess slot and double-click Cellular in the list. Name this level shininess chips. In the Cell Characteristics rollout, check Chips and enter 3.0 in the Size field. Click the Render Last icon. The chips shininess map gives the illusion of a slightly cracked surface. The Shin.Strength spinner in TEAPOT01 effects the strength of the "cracks." Click Go to Parent and in the Basic Parameters rollout, set Shin.Strength to 50.0.

12. The major material problem at this point is the regular specular highlight of the blue/green TEAPOT02. In the Navigator, click Material 2:TEAPOT02 and open the Maps rollout. Click None in the Specular slot, and double-click Noise in the list. Name this level specular noise.

13. In the Noise Parameters rollout, enter 0.5 in the High field and 0.499 in the Low field. Notice the sample sphere turns a hard-edged black and white. This is often a good starting point when applying noise as it is easy to see the result. You can soften it later. Enter 5.0 in the Size field, and click on the Render Last icon. You should see very distinct areas of specular highlights.

NOTE

You might need to click the Show End Result icon in the Material Editor to see the effect. With Show End Result on, you see the whole material; with it off, you see only the material up to and including the current active level.

14. In Noise Parameters rollout, enter 0.6 in the High field and 0.3 in the Low field to soften the edges of the noise. Check Fractal for a more ragged edge to the noise. The Material Editor, Navigator, and rendered image should look similar to Figure 10.2.

FIGURE 10.2

Material Editor sample sphere, Navigator, and rendered teapot.

In Exercise 10.1, you corrupted a plain plastic material by combining it in a Blend material with another plastic material and a smoke mask. The original material shows through only in smaller areas to discolor and smudge the predominant blue/green color. With a smoke bump map and shininess and specular maps, you "dented" the teapot and gave it the illusion of a cracked, oily surface. There is no technical limit to the depth of complexity you can have in a material, but very complex materials increase render times noticeably.

Creating Man-Made Materials

The key to creating convincing man-made materials in 3D Studio MAX R2 is to increase your ability to "see." Many people go through life looking but not seeing. As a modeler, you must sharpen your power of observation and study the world around you. Try to envision an object in your hand as a 2D object made to look 3D. What attributes keep it from appearing 2D, and what attributes give clues as to what the material is? Even among objects of the same basic material, you can have a wide variation in the look. Plastics, for example, can range from soft to almost glass-like. Specular highlights and shininess are often the most visible clues that give the illusion of this material or that. The shinier an object is, the more obvious the reflective qualities will be, so if you have very shiny objects, make sure you also have something for them to reflect. In Exercise 10.2, 10.3, and 10.4, you will open files with several different man-made materials and analyze the construction of the material. Feel free to make changes and experiment with the various settings.

A Compound-Textured Object

In Exercise 10.2, you look at several compound materials on objects in a scene representing a tank lifted from the ground by a crane. The tank has been recently painted, but only the portion that was above ground. The bottom of the tank shows signs of pitting and corrosion. The rendered image is shown in Figure 10.3.

FIGURE 10.3
Rendered tank lifted from hole in the ground.

EXERCISE 10.2: A PAINTED TANK EXTRACTED FROM THE GROUND

1. Open 10max02.MAX from the CD-ROM. Render the Camera01 viewport and compare your rendered image with Figure 10.3. They should appear similar.

2. Open the Material Editor and click on Material/Map Navigator. Click on the first sample sphere to view the construction of OIL TANK material. The screen should look like Figure 10.4.

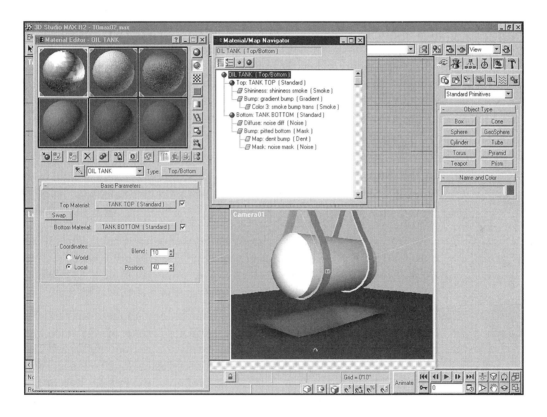

FIGURE 10.4

Material Editor, Navigator, shaded Camera01 viewport.

3. Observe that OIL TANK is a Top/Bottom material type. This allows the top portion to be TANK TOP, a painted material, and the bottom to be TANK BOTTOM, a corroded material. Top and Bottom, in this case, are defined by the check next to Local in the Basic Parameters rollout's Coordinates area. If World were checked, Top would be defined by the World Z-axis, and if the tank were rolled, the painted surface would always be up. With Local Z-axis checked, the painted surface rolls with the tank. The Blend setting of 10 makes a 10 percent overlap transition between the Top and Bottom material. A setting of 0 makes a sharp transition. The Position setting of 40 positions the transition area 40 percent of the way from the bottom of the tank to the top of the tank.

4. In the Material/Map Navigator, notice that TANK TOP has a Smoke map in the Shininess slot. This randomizes the shininess in the painted area to give it a look of having been hastily painted, perhaps with moisture present before the paint had dried. A Gradient map is in the Bump slot, but this in itself doesn't do much. The key is a Smoke map in the Color #3 slot of the gradient. This causes the lower part of TANK TOP to appear rough and blistered as if the corrosion from the bottom is working up under the paint.

5. In the Navigator, click on Bottom;TANK BOTTOM to move to that material level. TANK BOTTOM's Diffuse color is created by a Noise map with a greenish Color #1 and a brownish Color #2. In the Noise Parameters rollout, the settings of 0.5 in High Threshold and 0.3 in Low Threshold create fairly clearly defined patches of color. The Bump map for TANK BOTTOM is a Mask map. The pits are created with a Dents procedural map. The effect of the pits is masked with a Noise map so the pits aren't the same across the entire surface.

6. In the Material Editor, click on the second sample sphere to view the STRAPS material. STRAPS Diffuse color is a Mix map. Mix is much like Blend except that it works at the map level, not the material level. The Mix Amount of the Mix map uses a new map type called Falloff. In this case, Falloff mixes more of Color #2 at the top of the straps than at the bottom giving the illusion of water in the straps settling to the bottom.

7. Click on the third sample sphere to view GROUND. The GROUND material uses Mask mapping in the Diffuse and Bump slots. In the Navigator, click on either of the Mask;gradient masks. They are instances so when one is changed, the other changes also. This Gradient uses the Radial Gradient Type instead of Linear. This causes the brownish color and the bumps to be more prominent in the center of the ground object. The bumps diminish and the color becomes more greenish away from the hole.

In Exercise 10.2, you analyzed materials ranging from a complex Blend material type in OIL TANK, to Standard materials with Mix and Mask map types to randomize color and bumpiness. Use these materials as starting points, and make adjustments to the settings to fine-tune the effects.

Variations on Similar Materials

In Exercise 10.3, you look at some of the materials in a scene of sawhorses with two boards and a pile of sawdust in a basement. A nail box sits on the boards to provide a reflection for comparison. The walls and the floor show two variations on cement-based materials—a concrete floor and cracking stucco walls. The materials of the two boards are practically the same with some changes to make one board appear much older and more distressed. The rendered image should look like Figure 10.5.

FIGURE 10.5

A Basement work-space.

EXERCISE 10.3: A BASEMENT WORKSPACE

1. Open 10max03.max on the CD-ROM. Render the Camera01 viewport and compare your rendered image with Figure 10.5.

2. Open the Material Editor, and click on Material/Map Navigator. Click on the first sample sphere to view the construction of the NEW BOARD material. The screen should look like Figure 10.6. NEW BOARD is a

simple material made of a wood grain bitmap image and a raytrace reflection map. The NEW BOARD object is a simple box. The board is rather boring in the scene, highly reflective and polished, and could just as well be made of plastic.

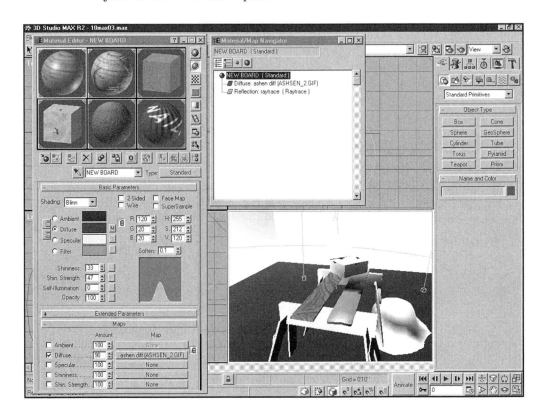

FIGURE 10.6

Material Editor, Material/Map Navigator, shaded Camera01 viewport.

3. Click on the second sample sphere to view the OLD BOARD material; it is a copy of NEW BOARD with further enhancements. The OLD BOARD mesh in the scene is also more complex with a Noise Modifier to "warp" the board. OLD BOARD uses the same wood grain image but adds a Mask map called NICKS.BMP to add cracks and blemishes to the wood grain. The Mask is blurred to soften the hard edges. NICKS.BMP is used again in the Bump slot with different tiling and rotation. The raytrace reflections were eliminated because unfinished wood is less reflective.

NOTE

NICKS.BMP was created in 3D Studio MAX R2 from several 2D shapes collapsed to mesh objects and a white self-illuminated material applied to render as pure black and white, as shown in Figure 10.7. For more information on creating 2D bitmaps in Max, see Chapter 13, "Using MAX R2 as a 2D Paint Tool."

FIGURE 10.7

NICKS.BMP Created in MAX R2.

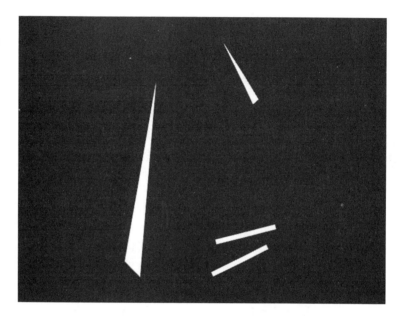

4. Click in the third sample sphere, and notice that the TAN material that is applied to the sawhorses is a very simple color with bumps.

5. Click in the first sample sphere in the second row for a look at the material called ROOM. ROOM is a Multi/Sub-object material. Material 1, WALLS, is applied to all faces with Material ID#1, and FLOOR is applied to faces with Materials ID#2.

6. In the Navigator, click on (1):WALLS(Blend). WALLS is a Blend material with a mask. Material #1 of the blend is a gray stucco with a Smoke shininess map to give the illusion of damp stucco. Underlying the stucco is a brick wall that shows through where the stucco has cracked and fallen away. A rendered image called CRACK.BMP was created much like NICKS.BMP mentioned in step 3 of this exercise. The FLOOR material has only a Mask map in the Diffuse slot with a concrete bitmap being masked by a Splat map to show dark spots.

7. In the Navigator, click on (2):FLOOR(Standard). In the Maps rollout, click on None in Shin.Strength, and double-click on Smoke map type. Render the Camera01 viewport. Smoke in the Shin.Strength varies the "whiteness" of the floor. Smoke in the Shininess slot wouldn't have had much affect because the Shininess and Shin.Strength settings are low. The Smoke map overrides the Shin.Strength setting, using the luminance value of Smoke instead.

TIP

The floor appears bluish closer to the walls. This is the effect of a colored light in the scene. Try to create all materials in "white" light before adding any colored lights or the sample sphere will not be representative of material in the rendered scene.

8. Click on the second sample sphere in the second row for a look at SAWDUST. It is a Top/Bottom material with a tan color and a brown color, each with different bumpiness to simulate a pile of sawdust with old, moist sawdust and a small amount of newer sawdust on top.

9. Click on the last sample sphere. BOX is a material that uses a mask created in MAX R2 to print the word NAILS on the box. It also uses a Gradient map in the Bump slot with V;Tiling set to 20.0 to create the illusion of corrugated cardboard.

In Exercise 10.3, you analyzed typical materials in a damp basement and two variations of wood. Experiment with the shininess and the bumpiness of materials to create a cleaner, drier environment. Also adjust the lighting in the scene to see how it affects the mood.

The Wet Look

Exercise 10.4 depicts a scene of a straight stretch of road after a summer rainstorm. Puddles have formed over the entire road reflecting the cloudy sky in the background as well as the sign structures spanning the road and the light fog. The rendered scene is shown in Figure 10.8.

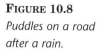

FIGURE 10.8

Puddles on a road after a rain.

EXERCISE 10.4: PUDDLES ON A ROAD AFTER A RAIN

1. Open 10max04.max from the CD-ROM. Render the Camera01 viewport and compare your rendered image with Figure 10.8.

2. Open the Material Editor and click on Material/Map Navigator. Click on the first sample sphere to view the construction of ROADWAY material. The screen should look like Figure 10.9.

3. Click on the second sample sphere in the top row to view a material called ROADWAY. It is a Multi/Sub-object material type made of four sub-materials. The LAND mesh object in the scene has been modified to assign Material ID#1–4 to correspond to the four materials in ROADWAY: ROAD SURFACE, LAND, BERM, and CURB. BERM, LAND, and CURB materials are similar to materials created in other exercises. Look them over to see how Blend material and Mask map types have been used to give the illusion of dirt and grass and granite.

4. In the Navigator, click on (1)ROAD SURFACE(Standard). ROAD SURFACE has no diffuse texture. The color is dark gray and all apparent texture on the road comes from the bump maps. Both the Bump and Reflection slots are Mask map types with the same Splat map used as an instanced mask. Using the same Splat map to mask both insures that the puddle surfaces will always be reflective and flat. You want to avoid puddles with the same bump as the asphalt.

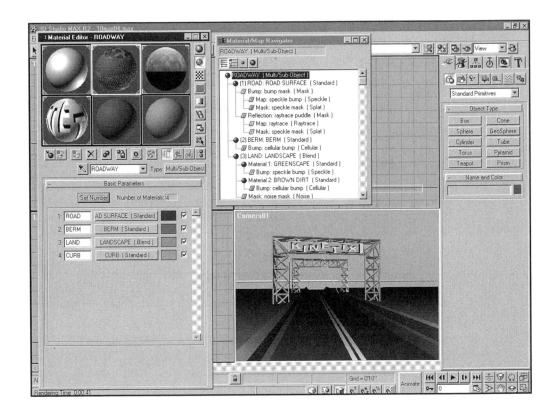

FIGURE 10.9

Material Editor, Material/Map Navigator, shaded Camera01 viewport.

5. In the Navigator, click on (1)ROAD SURFACE again. Click on the Shin.Strength slot, and double-click Dent in the map list. Render the Camera01 viewport. A Dent map in Shin.Strength radically changes the shininess of both the asphalt areas and the puddles because it is applied to the whole ROAD SURFACE material. Remove the Dent map in the Shin.Strength to return the ROAD SURFACE to its previous state.

6. Click on the third sample sphere to see that SKY BACKGROUND is a simple Gradient Diffuse color with the built-in Noise used to create rolling dark clouds.

NOTE

Two forms of Atmospheric Affects, a Volume Fog and a layered Fog, were added to make the scene "muggier" and to hide the hard edge where the land meets the sky.

7. In the Material Editor, click on the second sample sphere to see ROADWAY material. Click on the Material/Map Navigator icon; then click on Map raytrace (Raytrace). In the Material Editor/Raytracer Parameters, click on the Options button and check Antialiasing in the Global column. Click the Close button to close the dialog box. Click the Global Parameters button, check Adaptive in the Adaptive Antialiasing area, enter 10.0 in the Blur Offset field, and render the Camera01 viewport. The reflections in the puddles will be much softer but the render time will be a lot longer.

T IP

In the Global Raytracer Settings dialog box, note that the Maximum Depth field is set to 2. The Max R2 default setting is 9, meaning that a maximum of 9 reflections within reflections is possible. Reducing this number speeds raytrace renderings.

Exercise 10.4 outlined the steps to create the illusion of puddles in a road. The same mask was used to reveal the puddles on the asphalt and to mask the asphalt bumps in the area of the puddles. You could have used Flat Mirror reflection mapping in place of Raytrace reflections with good results and lower render times.

Dress for Success: Mapping a Material

In Exercise 10.5, you apply a bitmap to a simple character in the form of a Raggedy Ann-type doll. The exercise focuses on using a new Modifier called Unwrap UVW, which gives you access to the mapping coordinates assigned to each vertex in the mesh. You can move, rotate, and scale the mapping coordinates to make the assigned material fit the object without affecting either the mesh or the original bitmap.

EXERCISE 10.5: DRESSING A CHARACTER

1. Open 10max05.max from the CD-ROM. Open the Material Editor and click on the Material/Map Navigator icon to open it.

2. Drag and drop the material called RAGANN onto the character in the Perspective viewport.

3. Select the RAGDOLL object in the Perspective viewport. In the Material Editor, click on the Show Map in Viewport icon for the doll diff map. The shaded character has a suit of clothes and a face and hair applied to the front in random fashion. The display should look similar to Figure 10.10.

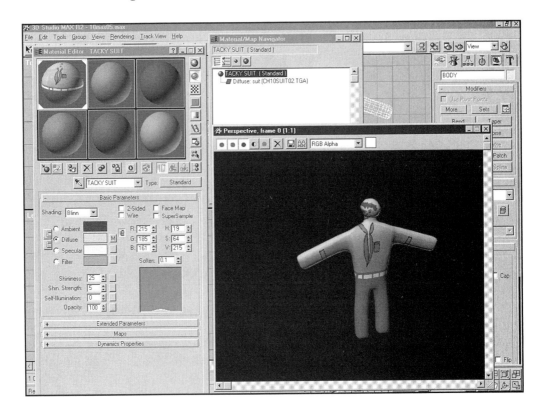

FIGURE 10.10

Material Editor, Material/Map Navigator, shaded Perspective Viewport.

4. You can modify the mesh to fit the bitmap or repaint the bitmap to fit the mesh, but both options are complex. Instead, add the new Unwrap UVW modifier and adjust the mapping coordinate points to fit on the bitmap. Select RAGDOLL if it isn't still selected and, in the Modify panel, click More and double-click Unwrap UVW in the list of modifiers.

5. In the Modify panel's Parameter rollout, click the Edit button. The Edit UVWs dialog box should look like Figure 10.11.

FIGURE 10.11

*Edit UVWs dialog box
for Unwrap UVW
Modifier.*

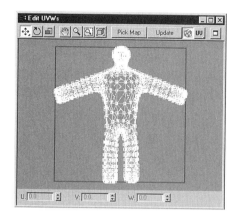

6. Each vertex's UVW map coordinate is represented by a white box connected by white lines. To view a background image of the bitmap applied to RAGANN, click on the Pick Map button, check Scene in the Browse From area if it isn't already checked, and double-click on the entry in the list called Diffuse doll diff. You should see the image appear in the Edit UVWs dialog box. Click OK in the Browser. The dialog box should look like Figure 10.12.

FIGURE 10.12

*Edit UVWs dialog box
with Background
Bitmap.*

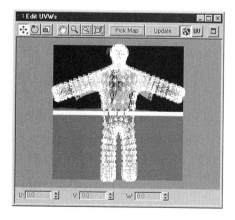

7. Position the Edit UVWs dialog box to give a clear view or the Perspective viewport. In the Edit UVWs dialog box, drag a selection window around all the coordinate points. They all turn red. Click the Move icon and move the selection set to line up the dress collar with the character's neck. You see the map move in the Perspective viewport when you release the mouse button. It is difficult to make the bitmap fit correctly because the mesh is too large. With all coordinate points still selected, click the Scale icon and scale the points down for a better fit. The display should appear similar to Figure 10.13.

TIP

If you have a fast display card, you can click the Unwrap Options icon and check Constant Update in Viewports to get instant feedback on the new coordinate point position in the shaded viewport.

You can also change the Line Color in Colors area of the Unwrap Options dialog box to a light gray to make the lines and coordinate points stand out against the white dress in the bitmap.

FIGURE 10.13

Coordinate points scaled and moved.

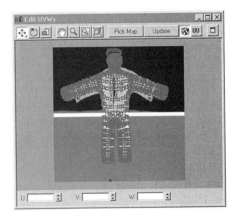

8. In the Edit UVWs dialog box, click the Zoom Window icon and zoom in on the doll's right arm. Select the points for the hand, and scale, rotate, and move the points until the sleeve fits. It might look similar to Figure 10.14.

FIGURE 10.14

Adjusting the points for an arm.

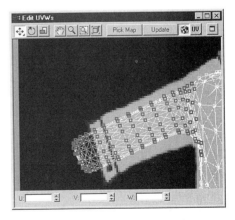

9. Repeat step 8 for the other arm and the head.

T IP

You can change the Selection Color in the Colors area of the Unwrap Options dialog box to a bright green to make the selected coordinate points stand out against the red socks in the bitmap.

10. Select the points from the knees down and move the feet to pull the character's socks up where they belong. She's still not a great-looking character, perhaps, but you get the idea of how Unwrap UVW works.

In Exercise 10.5, you used the Unwrap UVW modifier to transform the UVW mapping coordinate points on a background image of the map applied to the object in the scene. This procedure can be used to adjust simple mapping coordinates to fit complex bitmaps without the need to alter the mesh or the original bitmap.

Reflections for Realism

In Exercise 10.6, you open a file with an automobile and analyze the paint material. Reflections play a large role in how painted metal is perceived. If you look closely at an automobile, you see that it's not the curves and details themselves that you notice, but the way light is reflected from these surfaces. A few years back, most automobile television ads used black cars. If you had observed closely, you would have seen the cars actually appeared to be mostly white. The TV crews used to position large Mylar reflectors lit by powerful spotlights so that the right curves and details were highlighted. Without the reflected white area, the car would seem to be a black hole in the scene.

T IP

Remember that on an automobile the material is paint, not metal. You should not use Metal shading mode for a painted surface; use Blinn or Phong for more realistic results. Try Metal only as a special effect.

W ARNING

Before you begin this exercise, make sure you download the NURBS patch file called *GAPTESS.DLL* from HYPERLINK http://www.ktx.com or from CompuServe's Kinetix forum libraries. It fixes a bug that would cause some machines to lock in files with two or more NURBS models.

The file should be put in the /Stdplugs subdirectory.

EXERCISE 10.6: PAINT ON METAL

1. Open 10max06.max from the CD-ROM. The scene is a fantasy sport coupe on a side street in Warsaw. In the scene, the car sits on a surface with a Matte/Shadow material to catch the "sun's" shadow. This gives the car weight and makes it appear to be on the street surface when rendered. Open the Material Editor and click on the Material/Map Navigator icon. Render Camera01 viewport at animation frame 70. The display should look similar to Figure 10.15.

NOTE

Several objects have auto reflect materials and slower computers might take a few minutes to render the scene. Rendering at 320 by 240 will be quicker.

FIGURE 10.15

Rendered coupe in Warsaw street.

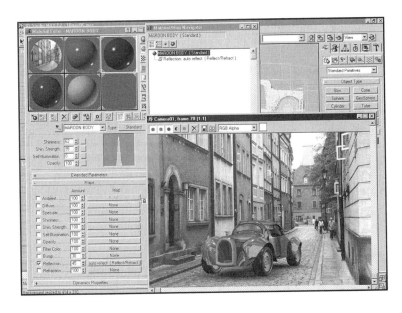

2. In the Material Editor, click on the third sample sphere, called MAROON BODY. Notice the Shininess value is 62 and Shin.Strength is 95. This wide range, with Shin.Strength being higher, keeps the highlights broad and bright.

3. In Material/Map Navigator, click on Reflection;auto reflect to drop to the reflection map level. The reflection source is Automatic and Use Environmental Map is checked, causing the street scene to be reflected in the material. Uncheck Use Environmental Map, and click on GREEN BODY in the Material Editor. Click Reflection:auto reflect in the Navigator, and uncheck Use Environmental Map for GREEN BODY. Click the Render Last icon. The car now shows some specular highlights but is very dark and heavy in the scene. Reflecting the Environmental Map certainly gave you reflection, but they were very "busy" reflections and detracted from the car. However, with no objects in the scene for auto reflect to reflect, the scene has become lifeless.

4. In the Display panel's Hide rollout, click the Unhide By Name button and double-click reflector in the list. The reflector is a large flat mesh object high above the car in the scene. The car has a fully self-illuminated white material assigned to it so it is not affected by scene lighting.

5. Click the Render Last icon. The car should now reflect broad areas of white, defining the curvature nicely.

6. Close the Material Editor, the Navigator, and the Virtual Frame Buffer. Press H, and double-click reflector in the list. Click the Zoom Extents All Selected icon. This will zoom way out in the scene and show the large reflector mesh.

7. In the Top viewport, click the Select and Move icon and move the reflector around the scene. Right-click to cancel the move. The reflector always points at the car because it has a Look-At controller assigned with the car as the Look-At Target.

8. Try repositioning the reflector and rerendering the scene for different reflective qualities. You now have full control of the reflections and they are bold but not as confusing as the environmental background reflections.

WARNING

The reflector material is two sided, and you want to avoid having the reflector show in the rendered scene. So, always test render and check the edges of the rendering to see that it is not in the camera's field of view.

9. To enhance the feeling of depth in the paint, enter 5–10 in the Self-Illumination field for MAROON BODY and GREEN BODY.

In Exercise 10.6, you looked at materials representing shiny, painted metal objects. The key to realistic paint is in the reflections. Automatic reflections of the background detracted from the paint, so you used a flat plane with self-illuminated material as a reflector.

In Practice: Designing Man-Made Materials

- **Rough things up.** Very few objects in the world are perfectly smooth and clean. Taking the time to rough up each object or its material will go a long way to adding realism to your scenes. Use the procedural maps such as Noise, Smoke, Cellular, and Dents to add subtle and not-so-subtle surface perturbations for a more worn look.

- **Shininess and Shin.Strength values.** Take time to look closely at objects around you in the real world. Determine how you would adjust the shininess settings to simulate the different materials you see everyday. Often small changes in shininess are all you need to turn a material from rubber to painted metal.

- **Reflections.** Bring out the best in your scenes by employing time-proven photo and film methods for highlighting your objects. Use reflectors to control the reflections and specular highlights of glossy objects. The method is also especially useful for glass materials.

Chapter 11

DESIGNING FICTIONAL AND SPECIAL EFFECTS MATERIALS

Whether you've been working with MAX for a few weeks or since the early days of 3D Studio DOS, you've already created at least one fictional material—or at least tried to. Fictional and special effects materials are the most taxing to create for one simple reason—they stretch our creative thinking to the limits. Time after time, we need to come up with materials that are both creative and fresh.

Although this chapter won't solve your creative thinking problems, you may find that it'll help you push the envelope of what you think is possible in MAX. With MAX, creating fictional materials is not all that difficult. Knowing the tools that you have available and how they operate can greatly help the creation process. In this chapter, you'll explore fictional and special effects material techniques through several key items:

- Grounding yourself in the real world

- Fictional planet building

- Fictional skin

- Simulating real-world light

- Special effects using Noise

- Working with mirrors

There's quite a bit to explore in both fictional and special effects materials. Let's first start out by taking a look at building two different fictional materials—one for an alien and one for the planet it lives on.

Building a Fictional Material

Fictional materials can be anything that your mind dreams up—even if it's based on something that exists in the real world. Whatever the case, we often find ourselves facing a task that may seem a bit daunting—building a material from scratch. Fortunately, there are many techniques for building fictional materials that can help you in almost every situation.

Use the Real World as a Starting Point

The real world is chock full of great ideas for fictional materials. How many times have you stared at a cloud's shape and thought about what it resembled? Look around you. Unless you're in solitary confinement, you'll see many different ideas for materials. For instance, take a look at some wood. Look at the grain closely. Now imagine the dark areas of the grain receding into the wood and the lighter areas raising. Throw a highly shiny, slimy coating on top of that and you have a nice organic alien muscle.

By looking at the real world, you can come up with an unlimited number of ideas for building materials. The key trick is to know what tools you have at your disposal so that you can easily re-create them. When building organic, fictional materials, for example, it's often a good idea to start with Procedural maps such as Noise or Cellular.

Start from a Concept

Sometimes the real world just won't do. There's just nothing to look at to provide an inspiration or foundation for building a fictional material. If that's the case, you're going to have to rely as much as possible on your creativity. Unfortunately, that's not always an easy thing to do. If you've never been to an alien planet or have never personally met an alien, your experience in designing a material based on either might be a bit frustrating.

Fortunately, people have been going through many of these mental exercises already. Some have produced works on it, books, movies, tabloid articles, and so on. If you're strapped for material, the best solution is to base your work on something already done. This is not to say that you should copy someone else's work. Not only is this unethical, it's illegal. You can, however, look at someone else's work and come up with *your own* ideas for your work. Why reinvent the wheel, right?

Use Procedural Maps

Procedural maps, as mentioned earlier, are great for building organic surfaces. Why? Procedural maps are, by nature, random in their effect. This means that you can design a great, complex, organic surface without having even a remotely repeating pattern. Rather than you worrying about a map that tiles across the surface of an object, a procedural map takes care of evenly distributing itself—without Mapping coordinates.

Using Procedural maps, however, does take away some of the control that you like having when using Mapped materials. Because there are no Mapping coordinates, you can't specify that you want a clump of smoke from the Smoke map to appear in an exact location. Animating Procedural maps can also be a challenge. For instance, if you want the water in a Water map to crest at a certain time, the only way to achieve this is through trial and error. The water's movement is controlled by its phase and offset values, not by some user-specified value for crest timing. Although these limitations may seem a little too difficult to work with, the reality is that they're not all that bad. As a matter of fact, most people don't even think about them since they're so minor. It's only at those certain times when you wish you had explicit control that you actually notice the limitations.

Procedural maps will be the best armament in your fictional material arsenal. Let's take a look at a few of the more prominent maps.

Noise

What do you call perhaps the most popular map of all time in the 3D Studio MAX user community? Noise! Noise is, perhaps, the most used (and sometimes overused) map within the MAX material arsenal. Noise is pretty uninteresting just looking at it bare, when it's not being used as a map anywhere. Essentially, Noise uses two colors—any colors—and blends them together using one of three different algorithms. Don't let the term "algorithm" scare you off. You don't have to know any math, much less how they work. Noise is a very visual map. This means that you'll find yourself looking very closely at the rather random mixing pattern it produces. It is this very randomization that gives Noise its well-deserved status as the most popular map.

NOTE

You see, in earlier days when 3D Studio DOS users produced renderings, they had little to work with in the way of Random maps. Sure, there were many plug-ins (called IPAS) that attempted to simulate various Random effects; but there never was a "catch-all" map that could perform well in almost any Map type within a material. When MAX was introduced to the public in May of 1996, there was a general feeling of relief as many animators now saw the possibilities of doing great, random-looking materials within their renderings.

You can use Noise for just about anything. In this chapter, you'll see how to use it to create a complex-looking alien planet surface. However, you can use Noise for other purposes, too—blotchy transparency, muddled refractions, or even star fields. Noise truly is the multi-purpose map. Figure 11.1 shows how Noise can produce a nice water surface when used as a Bump map. In Chapter 12, "Animated Materials," you'll re-create this very scene.

FIGURE 11.1

A rolling sea surface created with the help of the Noise map used in the Bump Map channel of a material.

Noise has several parameters that allow you to control how it performs. Some of the terminology is a bit strange, but you can use this section to get more of a "real-world" idea of how the various settings might work in production. Figure 11.2 shows the Noise map's parameters.

FIGURE 11.2

The Noise map parameters.

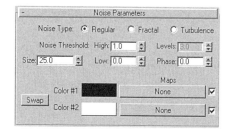

Across the top of the Noise Parameters section are checkboxes for the three types of Noise that you can use. They are

- Regular

- Fractal

- Turbulence

Before you get hung up on the names, there is an easy way to remember which type of noise is good for what occasion. The easiest way to see how Noise might affect a material is to use it as a Bump map. With that in mind, here's how you might look at the three Noise types:

- Regular produces a nice, rolling hills look.

- Fractal looks much like a mountain range.

- Turbulence creates a great moonscape-like surface.

Even though these are geological references, you can clearly see how the three types would work. In case you're having a bit of trouble visualizing the three examples, Figure 11.3 demonstrates the same material using the Noise map with all three types.

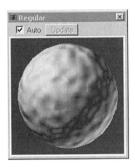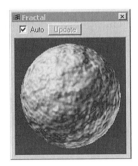

FIGURE 11.3

This figure shows how the three types of Noise work on the same material. They are Regular (left), Fractal (middle), and Turbulence (right).

Once you've chosen the style of randomization you're going to use (Regular, Fractal, or Turbulence), you can then begin to alter some of the other settings. The most common setting to adjust is Size. The Size field controls the overall size of the Noise effect based on MAX-world units. This means that the size of the object does not matter.

High and Low for the Noise Threshold allow you to control the predominance of either color by "ramping" between Color #1 and Color #2 (shown at the bottom of the panel). Ramping is easiest to use when working with black and white. To transition from black to white smoothly, you need a grayscale gradient. That gradient is called the ramp and equates to the difference between the High and Low values. Longer ramps mean more gradient colors exist; shorter ramps mean that fewer colors are used in the gradient.

The Thresholds not only allow you to control the size of the ramp but also to which color it's more weighted. This means that by reducing the High Threshold, you're shortening the length of the ramp, but you're also shortening it in favor of the Low Threshold's color (because it's remaining at 0). When you alter the Threshold values, you're basically just telling Noise you want to use less of one color and more of the other.

Technically, Noise is similar to a mathematical wave, which varies in a random manner between values of 0 and 1. The lower the number goes, the more Color #1 is shown. The closer it gets to 1, the more Color #2 is shown. The High threshold is the point above which Color #2 is shown. Decrease the High and more of the mid-range values on the curve turn to Color #2. Increase the Low and more mid-range values turn to Color #1. Once those colors are filled in, the area between them is filled with a ramp of Color #1 to #2. It helps if you think of Color #1 as the low color and Color #2 as the high color. Draw a zigzag scribble on a piece of paper. Across the page at the bottom peak, draw a line marked 0 = Low Color, and across the top draw a line with 1 = High Color. As the high line moves down, more of the zigzag gets the high color. The same is true of the low color and moving the low line up.

The Swap button allows you to easily switch Color #1 and #2 with each other. This way, you won't have to worry about copying colors between swatches or having to write down the values—a timesaver to say the least.

Lastly, you can alter the Phase of the Noise. Phase controls the shifting of the positions of Color #1 and Color #2 within the map itself. By animating phase, you can make the Noise map appear to undulate on the material.

Notice that you can also substitute Maps for Color #1 or #2. This means that you can use multiple colors from a map instead of a solid color. Using maps in Noise is great for textures like freckles on skin or similar items.

Cellular

Cellular is the first runner-up in the map popularity contest. Rather than randomly mixing two colors to produce an effect, Cellular works by producing small, cell-like patterns. The distribution of the pattern is completely procedural, meaning that it's also random. As a result, Cellular works great for creating organic surfaces. As a Diffuse map, it can create a great skin-like texture. As a Bump map, it is great for creating a scaly surface. Figure 11.4 shows how you might use Cellular. The image comes from the Alien Skin exercise later in this chapter.

FIGURE 11.4
*Using Cellular to pro-
duce the small scaly
bumps you see on this
alien's arm.*

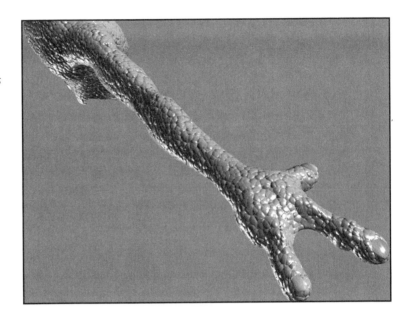

The Cellular interface resembles nothing of the Noise map's interface. As with the Noise map, however, the primary way to manipulate Cellular is by visual reference and not getting hung up on all the technical terms. Some nomenclature has been carried over from the Noise map. Figure 11.5 shows the Cellular map's interface.

FIGURE 11.5
*The Cellular map's
parameters.*

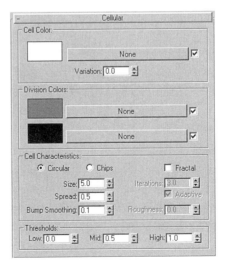

The three colors allow you to control the colors of the cells (Cell Color) and the colors that exist between the cells, which are called *divisions* (Division Colors). The default colors work well for most bump map usage, but you'll more than likely need to change the colors or add a color map—such as a bitmap—for using Cellular as a Diffuse map.

The Cell Characteristics section alters the overall shape and size of the cells and the amount of space between them. Circular works great for scaly, bumpy surfaces while Chips works great for dry, cracked surfaces, such as dry lake beds. By increasing or decreasing Spread, you can increase or decrease the spacing between the cells, respectively.

The cells have no variation of the color within themselves. The Fractal checkbox allows you to introduce a Noise-like pattern into the cells and their divisions. This produces a more splotchy pattern that you might use to distribute something across a surface, such as rashes across skin.

The only hitch to the Cellular map is the rendering speed. Rendering a material that uses a Cellular map can often take as much as four times longer than the same material that uses a bitmap instead. For that reason, you might consider using the Material Editor's Render Map feature. That way, you can render the Cellular map to a bitmap and use the Bitmap map versus the Cellular map. Because MAX doesn't need to do any underlying calculations during rendering time, your rendering speed improves significantly. For more information on the Render Map command, see MAX's online help.

Splat

Imagine a bored painter. One day, the painter just dips the paintbrush into the can and shakes it violently around the room. The end result (besides a mess) is little paint splats all around the room. This is exactly what the Splat map does—except you're the painter. Figure 11.6 shows what the Splat map is capable of when used as a texture map.

The Splat interface is relatively simple. Again, it's not designed for the artist (or painter in this case) so a little deciphering is necessary.

FIGURE 11.6

The Splat map being used to create a nice, reptilian look on the alien's arm.

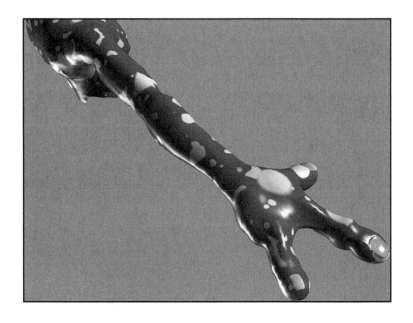

FIGURE 11.7

The Splat map's interface. Notice that the controls, while technically named, are few—and even easy to use!

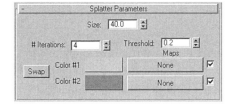

The Size function controls the maximum size of the splats. Some splats will be smaller, but none will be larger than the Size value. Iterations controls how much paint is on the brush. The more iterations you have, the more splats you'll see. However, you'll see more tiny splats. Threshold, like in other maps, specifies which color is more predominant, #1 or #2. At 0, Color #1 is predominant; while at 1, Color #2 is more predominant.

NOTE

Color #2 controls the color of the splats. Color #1 controls the "other" color used to fill in the areas where the splats do not exist. You can think of Color #1 as the wall color before the painter started waving the brush around.

You can use Splat for all kinds of wacky tricks. A great thing to try is to use the same Splat map in both the Diffuse and Bump map channels. This produces raised splats—a nice effect if you're trying for nice, thick splats!

Water

The Water map comes to us from the days of 3D Studio DOS where it first started as an IPAS plug-in. You can use it to create the obvious—such as water—but it also works very well for effects like Opacity and Bump. For clarity, however, we'll refer to the map as if it were being used as a water material within the scene. You can apply any of the concepts or techniques discussed here to just about any situation that calls for the Water map.

The map has several adjustable parameters. The strength of the Water map is not so much the static version of the map—actually Noise produces a much better "still" water—but rather how it animates. Just by animating the Phase value over time, you can produce some pretty incredible organic motion. Figure 11.8 shows the interface of the Water map.

FIGURE 11.8

The Water map's
interface.

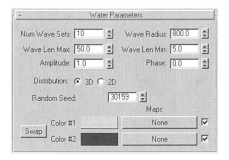

If you've ever observed the way ripples move on the surface of the water, you might see that there are actually many sets of ripples crossing—sometimes they're even crossing each other or moving in the opposite direction. The reasons for this are many—wind and interaction with still objects—but you can simulate this by increasing Water's Num Wave Sets value. The default of 10 works well for many situations but may prove to be too much clutter for calmer effects. The distribution of the waves is completely random.

The Wave Length fields (Wave Len Min and Wave Len Max) control the biggest and smallest sizes of the Wave sets. Wave sets, themselves, can be many sizes. By specifying a different Min and Max value, you're giving the Water map some leeway in randomizing the sizes of the sets. If these two values are the same, the sizes of the sets would be the same and might look a bit unrealistic. For the best random effect, put at least a 20 percent unit difference between these Wave Len Min and Wave Len Max.

Amplitude is a sneaky value—you're controlling a single threshold value. Believe it or not, it's actually controlling the predominance between Colors #1 and #2. At 0, Color #1 is predominant. As you increase the Amplitude, Color #2 becomes more predominant. The default setting of 1.0 should work for most situations.

Wave Radius allows you to control the overall size of the water ripples. Setting the radius to 0 sets the Water map's waves to the smallest size possible. Increasing this value enlarges the size of the effect across the surface of your object. You can see this most easily if you set the number of Wave sets to 1.

Animating Phase is the most powerful part of the Water map. The Phase value moves the wave sets around the material over time. For most animations, you only need to use *small values* when animating Phase. For instance, a 100-frame animation should have about only a five-unit change in phase. This produces nice, brisk water. Anything higher and you're approaching a rapids-like speed. Slower results can produce more bayou-like, slow-moving water.

Wood

Wood in itself does not produce a fictional or special effect material. When you use the Wood map outside of its intended context, however, you begin to see its possibilities. For instance, you can use the Wood map in the Bump Map channel to produce grainy scales for a snake-like skin. If you use Wood as a Diffuse map, you can simulate geological layers on the surface of a planet. Figure 11.9 shows a rendering from Exercise 11.1 later in this chapter. The rendering depicts a fictional planet with geological layers etched into the surface that are very visible along the sides of the canyon walls. These layers are created by the Wood map.

FIGURE 11.9

The Wood map is being used in this rendering as a texture map for the surface of the planet. The grain-like nature of the Wood map gives the planet's surface nice geological layers.

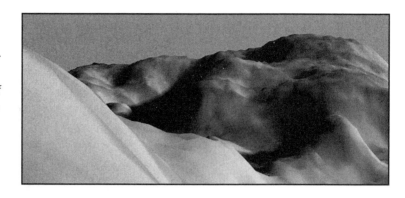

The Wood map's parameters are fairly straightforward, at least a little more so than some of the other maps. Instead of a "Size" parameter, there is a Grain Thickness field. It essentially controls the size of the Wood map. Where the confusion often comes in is what the difference is between Radial and Axial Noise. Before you break those down, take a look at how the Wood map works. In Figure 11.10, you can see the Wood map applied to a block of, well, wood. Notice the circular ripple pattern on one size of the box. The Radial axis travels in the same direction of that ripple. Wood is, however, a 3D effect. The wood grain gets projected all the way through the object. That axis of projection is the Axial value. Therefore, the following is true:

- Radial Noise controls the distortion of the wood grain along the rings of the grain.

- Axial Noise controls the distortion of the grain as it is projected through the wood.

It's highly recommended that you *do not* rely on the Wood map for making realistic Wood materials. The Map parameters are just too limited to make this possible. You should really use a bitmap image of Wood instead, but you can use the Wood map in many other ways to produce complex, concentric, material effects.

FIGURE 11.10

A cross-section view of the Wood map. The circular pattern is the Radial Axis. The grains traveling through the block comprise the Axial axis.

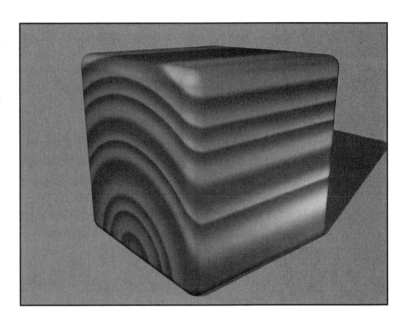

Smoke

Smoke, like Water, comes from the old IPAS collection of the 3D Studio DOS days. Its intended function is to create the appearance of a smoky-like surface on whatever object you've applied it to. However, the smoke map can serve as other great effects, such as clouds or other gaseous anomalies.

The interface of Smoke is very simple. You can see the various parameters in Figure 11.11. By now, you may be starting to notice a pattern in the interfaces. There are some small differences in the naming of the various parameters, but you are basically controlling the same thing. The only item that is really changing is the mathematical function (or algorithm) that controls the random behavior of the map.

FIGURE 11.11

The Smoke map's parameters. Notice how closely it resembles other maps discussed in this chapter.

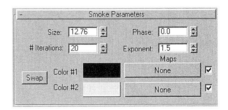

For instance, the Exponent parameter is controlling the threshold between Color #1 and Color #2. For the most part, it works just like the Amplitude parameter of the Water map. The Iterations parameter is very similar to the Iterations of the Splat map. The more iterations you have, the more puffs of "smoke" you'll have.

Dent

Dent, as its name implies, creates a nice, pitted surface on your material when used as Bump map. Ported from an old IPAS plug-in for 3D Studio DOS, the Dent map's functionality has not changed all that much. And like many of the other maps, the parameters are fairly simplistic. Figure 11.12 shows the interface of Dent.

FIGURE 11.12

The Dent map's interface.

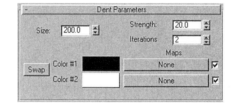

A quick overview is that Size controls the size of the Dent map, Strength is the threshold (predominance) value between Color #1 and #2, and Iterations controls how many dents there are.

The Dent map isn't all that exciting when just being used as a Bump map. Instead of limiting it to the Bump Map channel, try using it with the Self-Illumination Map channel and even Shininess. Dent would also work well as a component of a Mask map for creating splotchy "Shroud of Turin" texture effects. For Dent to look rather good, you'll need to increase the size. The default of 200 produces too small of a dent pattern that almost looks like it's tiling. Instead, increase the size to around 500. You'll notice that the result is much better. Figure 11.13 shows Dent being used in several map channels.

FIGURE 11.13

The Dent map being used in several Map channels of a material. They include Shininess, Shin.Strength, Self-Illumination, and Bump.

Procedural Map Tutorials

In the exercises that follow, you'll apply some of the techniques and maps discussed in this chapter to produce an extra-terrestrial planet surface and an alien to inhabit it. Exercise 11.1 includes using various maps for the planet's surface. Exercise 11.2 uses the same type of maps for creating a nice haze/fog effect. Finally, Exercise 11.3 shows you how to map skin to an alien body.

EXERCISE 11.1: CREATING AN ALIEN PLANET SURFACE

1. Open 11max01.max and render the scene. You'll notice that the file is just a simple terrain model.

2. Click the Material Editor button in the toolbar and select the upper-left material. Rollout the Maps section.

3. Click the None map for the Bump Map channel. Select Noise.

4. In the Noise Parameters section, set the Noise type to Fractal and the Size to 0.5.

5. Use the Go To Parent button to go back up to the Maps rollout. Set the Bump map's Strength to 60.

6. Apply the material to the Planet Surface object and render the scene. Notice how the bumpy look of the terrain surface.

7. Click the None map for the Diffuse Map channel and choose Mix. Set the Mix Amount to 0.5.

8. In the Mix map's parameters, click the None map for Color #1.

9. In the Material/Map Browser's Browse From section, choose Material editor. Select the Noise map that appears in the list to the right. When asked about making a copy or instance, choose Copy.

10. Change the Noise map Size to 1 and alter the color of both Color #1 and #2 to dark shades of brown (R87, G45, B0, and some variation). Note that you should make the two colors somewhat different.

11. You'll now add the Wood map as the other map within the material. Use the Go To Parent button to return to the Mix map's parameters and click the None map for Color #2.

12. In the Material/Map Browser's Browse From section, choose New. Select the Wood map.

13. In the Coordinates section, change the Z Angle parameter to 90.

14. In the Wood Parameters section, set the Grain Thickness to about 18 and change both Color #1 and #2 to darker shades of brown—similar to the Noise map's colors but noticeably different.

15. Rerender the Camera01 viewport. You'll see a much more convincing alien planet surface (see Figure 11.14).

FIGURE 11.14

The results from Exercise 11.1. The planet surface is using a combination of Noise and Wood maps for the surface.

The terrain looks great in Figure 11.14, but the atmospherics are non-existent. To make this look more like a planet, you'll need to add some sort of sky, some haze, and some "clumpy" ground fog. You could use the same type of techniques in the previous exercise to create believable environments in your scene. In the Exercise 11.2, you'll use Noise and Gradient to produce these effects.

EXERCISE 11.2: ADDING FOG TO THE ALIEN PLANET ATMOSPHERE

1. Open the file 11max02.max. This is the completed planet surface from the previous exercise.

2. To add Haze to the Scene, choose Environment from the Rendering pull-down menu.

3. Click the Add button in the Atmosphere section and choose Fog.

4. In the Name field, enter Haze.

5. Set the Color of the fog to a light brown. A value of R192, G149, B66 works well.

6. Set the Far percent to 45 and render the scene. Notice the nice haze now being applied in the distance.

7. Click the Add button again, and add another Fog effect. Name this one Ground Fog.

8. Set the color of this fog to about the same as the Haze effect. Then set the type to Layered. Uncheck Fog Background as well.

9. When the Layered parameters appear at the bottom of the fog interface, set the Falloff to Top, the Top value to 15, and the Density to 75.

10. Turn on Horizon Noise. Set the Size to 5.

11. To create the clumpy Fog effect, click the None map for the Environment Opacity map and choose Noise.

12. First, open the Material Editor, if it isn't open already. Then drag the Noise map from the Environment dialog box to any unused material slot in the Material Editor.

13. When prompted for Cloning options, select Instance.

14. To alter the clumpiness, you'll need to alter some parameters of the Noise map. Set the type to Fractal and the Size to 7.

15. In the Environment dialog box, check Use Map in the Background section. This activates the Alien Sky map already designed in the scene.

16. Rerender the scene. Your alien planet is complete!

FIGURE 11.15

The final rendering from Exercise 11.2. The atmospherics are all generated using Procedural maps and Fog effects.

As you can see, you can use many different settings within the maps discussed to create very convincing effects. Although you didn't create the sky, take some time to analyze how the material was built. You can see that it simply incorporates the compositing of the Gradient Map and the Noise map to produce a sunset and cloud effect.

If you're going to build a great alien planet, you'll need to build a great alien to live on it. In Exercise 11.3, you'll use some of the other maps discussed in this chapter to build the skin on an alien body. Pay close attention to how the maps are being used in multiple channels instead of just one. By copying or instancing one map throughout a material, you can create some great-looking complex surfaces.

EXERCISE 11.3: CREATING AN ALIEN SKIN WITH MAPS

1. Open 11max03.max. Render the scene. This is the right side of an alien's upper body. You'll apply various materials to it to give a more "scaly" look.

2. Open the Material Editor and select the upper-left-hand sample sphere.

3. You'll first build the splattered-looking surface. Rollout the Maps section and click None for the Diffuse map.

4. Select the Splat map. Set the Size of the Splat map to 5 and Iterations to 5. Finally, adjust the Threshold value to 0.27.

5. Alter Color #1 to a dark green and Color #2 to a muted yellow. Use the Go to Parent button to return to the Maps rollout.

6. Click None for the Bump map channel. Select Cellular.

7. Set the size of the Cellular map to 0.2 and then click the Go to Parent button. Set the Intensity Amount of the Bump Map channel to 10.

8. Drag the Cellular map to the Shininess and Shin.Strength map channels, both times making instances of the map. This mutes the shininess in the "grooves" of the scales.

9. At the top of the material's parameters, check SuperSample. This prevents harsh aliasing around the scales. Drag and Drop the material onto the skin object.

10. Render the scene.

FIGURE 11.16

The final rendering from Exercise 11.2. The skin is produced just with the Splat and Cellular maps.

Just by using two maps, you can create a convincing alien skin to apply to just about any object. Another thing to try in this scene is to add a Noise map into the yellow color of the Splat map in the Diffuse channel. This "breaks up" the edges of the splats. You could also mix another map such as Gradient or Wood with the Cellular map in the Bump channel to increase the scaly look. Figure 11.17 shows what happens when you add Noise to the Splat and mix a Gradient map into the Bump channel.

FIGURE 11.17

By adding Noise to the splat colors, you can effectively randomize the color of the splats themselves. Adding a Gradient map to the Bump channel helps add a more scale-like effect.

Illumination Effects

Time to get back to reality—at least a little. In MAX R2, there are actually several new features, material-wise, that help you with illumination. This section talks about how to use various components of both the Standard and Raytrace materials to produce lighting effects from the materials themselves.

Clear and Soft Lightbulbs

Lightbulbs are always a challenge to get just right. They differ so much in size, shape, and intensity that creating a "catch-all" material for all lights just isn't possible. However, there are some basic rules for light bulbs.

- **Use Opacity Falloff.** When a bulb is lit, you can effectively simulate the falloff of light within the bulb by using Opacity Falloff.

- **Use Additive Transparency**. Additive transparency helps when the light source needs to appear to be lit. Basically, it brightens the color of the pixels behind the semi-transparent light. This makes the light appear to be all the more bright. Note that this isn't really effective if the light is not illuminated.

- **Don't use a strong Self-Illumination value.** By keeping Self-Illumination somewhere around 70 to 90, you can retain some of the ambient color of a material. This is very effective for materials that are using Opacity Falloff.

- **Use Reflection Maps.** Reflection maps can seriously brighten your material. Using a map like sky.jpg in the reflection channel works very well. To keep from overpowering a material with a Reflection map, though, you should only use them at about a strength of 10 to 20.

NOTE

If you use a Reflection map for an unlit bulb, remember to use Reflection Dimming! Otherwise, your bulb still appears to be lit—even when you turn Self-Illumination off.

- **Use high Shininess and Shin.Strength values.** Remember, these bulbs are made out of glass. They should be shiny.

- **Use Lens Effects Glow**. Glow helps diffuse the light immediately around the light source—or at least appear to. You'll have to use very subtle values for the Glow effect for it to look proper.

- **Use raytracing only when necessary.** Sure, raytracing looks good, especially on glass. Remember that it adds a great deal of rendering time to your scene and it can actually make light bulbs look worse. Really, the only time you'd want to use raytracing is for an unlit bulb when you're looking at it up close.

Figure 11.18 shows what a good illuminated and non-illuminated light bulb might look like.

FIGURE 11.18

Two light bulbs—one lit, the other unlit. Both are using Standard materials. The main difference, besides the illumination, is that the right light bulb uses a Raytrace map for refraction.

Candles and Other Light Sources

Lit candles are often very difficult to make a material for. For instance, think about a lit candle. The primary problem is that because candle wax is translucent, it appears to be somewhat lit when the wick is lit. There's never really been a way to recreate this in MAX easily—if at all. However, in MAX R2, you have the Translucency value in the Raytrace material to simulate this effect very well. Much like when you're dealing with light bulbs, there are several tips for dealing with Translucent materials.

■ **Lights illuminate Translucent materials.** Remember that if a light source is near a Translucent material it appears to be lit unless you exclude it from the light source. Note that this includes lights that reside within the object with a Translucent material.

■ **Light intensity affects Translucent materials.** The brighter the light is, the brighter the Translucent material will be. Extremely bright lights wash out the subtleties of a Translucent material. Be careful to not overpower your lights.

- **Use darker colors for translucency.** Translucency can be affected by a global color or a map. In either case, you should take care to not use maps that have high brightness values. This overpowers the translucent material.

- **Translucency does not take long to render.** Even though Translucency is part of the Raytrace material, it does not require the calculations that reflections or refractions require. Unless your Translucent material is using either reflection or refraction, your rendering time should not be seriously impacted.

Figure 11.19 shows how you might use translucency to make candle wax appear to be more realistic. Note that two lights are used to get better translucency effects. One light used attenuation, while the other excluded the candle but provided more illumination to the room. Figure 11.20 provides the settings used for the scene. The example is included on your CD-ROM as candle.max.

FIGURE 11.19

You can use a Translucent material on an object, such as a candle to simulate the transmission of light through the wax when the candle is lit.

FIGURE 11.20

The settings in the MAX scene for Figure 11.19. The Translucency color is the same as the Diffuse color. One Omni light is used with attenuation for the translucency effect. Another is used for general illumination.

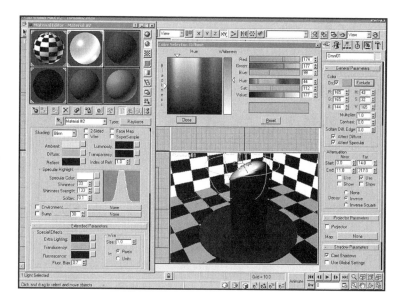

In Practice: Special Effects

- **Use the real-world as a foundation.** A great deal of good source material is available from the world around us for fictional materials.

- **Procedural maps work for organic materials.** Because Procedural maps are random in their effect, they're very easy to use within an Organic material. You can easily create complex, organic surfaces just by using one or a combination of procedural maps.

- **Noise is the undisputed king of procedural maps.** You can use Noise just about everywhere in a scene when there's a call for randomization. Using combinations of Noise within itself or with other maps can greatly enhance a material.

- **Light sources require several steps to build.** There are many things to consider when building a light source material. In this chapter, you saw how you can create both a lit and unlit source just by making minor adjustments to the same material.

- **Use Translucency in the Raytrace material.** Translucency can really make a difference for such objects as lamp shades or candle wax. Anytime you have an object that normally allows some light to pass through it, you should be using the Translucency feature of the Raytrace material.

Chapter 12

ANIMATED MATERIALS

Being a seasoned MAX user, you are well aware of the capability to animate materials. As with anything else in MAX, if it's got a spinner, you can animate it. Furthermore, any animatable parameter within the Material editor can use special animation controllers, as well as the new Motion Capture feature. The animation power of MAX is truly amazing. With this raw power, however, comes unrefined capabilities that you must manipulate to get the effects you desire. Translation: there are no real presets. You can't say, "give me water," and expect MAX to do it wonderfully right out of the gate. You'll need to tweak the values quite a bit to get it "just right."

Like anything else, if you are an animator, computer artist, or both, you need to not only know the tools you have but also how to get the most out of them. When it comes to animating materials, there are quite a few directions to choose from. Before you dive into this chapter, you should be familiar with the animation capabilities of MAX as well as basic material animation concepts. This chapter doesn't cover such basic topics as animating the Diffuse color of a material. Refer to either the MAX R2 hard copy tutorials on the Material editor or to the online MAX R2 reference for more information on basic material editing.

In this chapter, you'll explore topics such as

- Animating naturally occurring materials.

- Animating man-made materials.

- Maps to use with either man-made materials or naturally occurring materials.

T IP

Whenever you're working with animated materials, remember to use the Material Preview function. That way, you can preview the animations of materials in your scene without having to do a full rendering.

Natural Animated Materials

As discussed in Chapter 11, "Designing Fictional and Special Effects Materials," a slew of procedural maps can help you design both fictional and natural organic materials easily. Any one of the Procedural maps that are available for stills can also be used in an animation. Almost all the maps have a Phase value that you can animate. Depending on the map, animating Phase will have a different effect, but it essentially causes any procedural map to move.

In the sections that follow, you'll see what maps to use with various naturally occurring materials. Although several maps are covered, keep in mind that these are just a starting point. Other maps not discussed in this chapter might work for a given natural material. The best way to know for sure is to try one. The possibilities are limited only to your imagination.

Figure 12.1 demonstrates what's possible when using materials with particles to produce a realistic waterfall.

FIGURE 12.1

An animated waterfall created using both natural materials and particle systems. Image courtesy of Kinetix.

Maps to Use with Natural Materials

MAX R2 ships with a host of great maps for building natural-looking materials. The best part is that all the maps, while producing random looks, also can animate just as "naturally." Determining which map works best for you depends on your situation.

Although we'll focus on Procedural materials, note that you can use other maps, such as bitmaps, for natural materials. As a matter of fact, some bitmaps work well for Natural materials, but Procedural materials provide the greatest flexibility for organic surfaces. In the end, the combination of both Mapped materials and Procedural materials look the best.

All the maps discussed here can be animated through the map's Offset, Tiling, and Angle values. You can animate along the world's XYZ axes initially or based upon the UVW Mapping coordinates applied to the object. Using the XYZ method, your map remains oriented to the local coordinate system of the object. If the object transforms, so does the map on the surface. If you use a modifier such as Bend, however, the map remains oriented to the Local Coordinate system of the object. This makes the map appear to "pass through" the geometry as it is bent rather than bending with it.

If you use the UVW map method, you can specify how the Noise map, for example, is applied to the surface of your geometry through Mapping coordinates. This gives you more control over the map, but it also requires you use Mapping coordinates that can often look bad on more complex shapes.

Unlike XYZ mapping, UVW mapping deforms with the object—providing that the Mapping coordinates are applied before the deforming modifier. For most applications, stick with the XYZ method and use UVW only if XYZ doesn't work right or you need more explicit control of the map.

Noise

As mentioned before, Noise is the king of random, organic maps. You can use Noise just about anywhere to get a great, natural-looking material. Animating Noise can be just as much fun. Depending on what the desired effect is, you'll need to animate different parameters. Here are some helpful guidelines:

- **Animate the Offset to "move" the Noise effect.** By animating the Offset values you're just translating the noise along the surface of the object to which you've assigned the material. You'll use this effect later on in the chapter to move the "waves" in water.

- **Animate Blur and Blur Offset to smooth the Noise effect over time.** Blur and Blur Offset just blur the noise effect. If you animate the blurring, however, you can give your material the appearance of getting more distorted over time.

- **Animate Phase for churning.** Phase actually controls the shifting around of Color #1 and Color #2. By animating Phase, you're animating where the two colors exist over time. Where the shift occurs (meaning where the colors go) is completely dependent on the type of noise you have selected.

- **Animate the colors or maps.** This can have the greatest effect of all—especially when you're using Noise in an Intensity Map channel, such as Opacity or Bump. By animating the shifting in colors, you can control the intensity of that channel's effect on the material. By animating the colors along with Phase, you can churn the effect and alter its intensity over time.

Cellular

The Cellular map comes in as a close second to the Noise map as a great one to use for random effects. You can animate the Cellular map for such effects as moving skin on a snake that's crawling around. The primary difference between Cellular and the other maps is that it doesn't have a phase value. This means that you'll have to animate it through Offset, Tiling, Angle, and maps. Although this isn't necessarily a problem, it can prove to be a bit of a hindrance when you just need a quick, random, animated surface. When animating Cellular, follow these guidelines to get the best results:

- **Use maps.** The best part about maps is that you can throw an easily animated value into one of the colors of the Cellular map—even noise. Remember that the map affects only that particular color slot of the Cellular map—such as the Cell color.

- **Animate the Offset values.** By changing Offset over time, you are able to move the cells around the material. Although they move in unison, you can use the previous technique to at least vary the components of the cellular map to get a more random-looking translation along a surface.

- **Use and animate Fractal cells.** The Fractal option gives your cells a more "rough around the edges look." By altering the number of iterations or amount of roughness over time, you can easily add some random animation to the cell's characteristics.

Planet

The Planet map works differently than most of the other maps. Rather than applying some sort of math to two colors to produce a random effect, Planet creates something that looks like a topographical map. Instead of two colors, you have eight. Planet works well when used as a map within other maps. It is not as effective as a standalone map. Figure 12.2 shows the planet interface.

The most obvious way to animate the Planet map is to animate the colors, but this is almost the most inefficient way to animate. If you've ever tried to control colors animating over time, you know exactly how things can get complicated quickly. Each color actually has its own track *and* each track can be broken into three different animatable parameters. That's a total of 24 individual animatable parameters for one map, which can get unmanageable, even for seasoned animators.

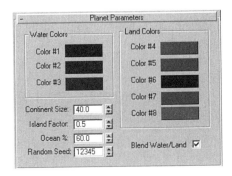

If you're going to use the Planet map in an animation, try animating the Offset and Angle values. Either one produces a great effect. This is mainly because the planet effect morphs as it moves over the surface of the object. (Note that this works only with the Offset field. Angle does not produce this morphing effect.) On the other hand, if you animate the Continent Size value, you can create some interesting fractal patterns. The default value of 40 is good for stills, but if you animate anywhere between 15 and 60, you'll get good results.

Splat

Splat gives great results when animated, but you might not use it in the traditional "splat manner"—meaning you probably won't want to use it to simulate paint splattering against the side of a wall. With Splat, there are a few functions that you'll want to try to animate:

- **Animate the Offset.** Rather than just moving the splat effect around the surface of an object, the Splat map actually "morphs" as it moves, just like Planet. Because Splat has no phase value, this is a way to create churning.

- **Animate Iterations.** The higher this field goes, the more little splats appear. Because this value makes more splats, you could use this as a surface that has tiny water droplets on it. As time goes on, more little droplets show up on the surface.

- **Use Maps.** Like many of the other maps, you can place maps within Colors #1 and #2. Just by placing the Noise map within the map slots, you can randomize the splat pattern even further. As a bonus, you can animate Noise's Phase value.

Smoke

The Smoke map is just begging to be animated. The map itself can be used in about any channel, but there are three main channels where it's most appropriate. Here is a quick way to set up smoke properly:

1. Apply the Smoke map first to the Diffuse map channel. When using smoke in there, the Diffuse colors are affected by the map.

2. Instance the Smoke map to the Opacity channel and turn on 2-Sided. This gives the smoke a transparent look.

3. Instance the Smoke map to the Reflection map.

4. For an enhanced effect, turn on Reflection Dimming so that the smoke appears brighter in direct light.

After you've set up Smoke, there are two main values you can animate to get a good effect. The first is the Offset value. By animating Offset in the direction you want the smoke to travel, you can make it rise, blow sideways, or whatever you decide. As you can with the other maps, you also should animate the Phase value to make the smoke appear to churn. Small Phase changes work well for most situations.

Animated Water

In Exercise 12.1, you'll create a water material from scratch and then animate it. The end result is believable sea water that you can use for many situations.

EXERCISE 12.1: ANIMATING WATER WITH NOISE

1. Open 12max01.max from the CD-ROM. Render the scene first to see what is currently set up. At this point, you basically have a sea object and a sky.

2. Open the Material editor and select the upper-left material in the sample windows.

3. Set the Ambient color to R51, G51, B89 and then set the Diffuse color to pure Black.

4. Set the Shininess to 40 and Shin.Strength to 30.

5. Rollout the Maps section and click None in the Reflection Map channel. Select Bitmap.

6. In the Bitmap Parameters section, click the empty Bitmap button to choose a bitmap to use. Select sky.jpg.

7. Click the Go to Parent button to go back to the Maps level. Set the Reflection Amount to 40.

8. Click None in the Bump Map channel. Select Noise.

9. At this point, you have a decent looking Bump map. Try some further refinements. In the Noise Map parameters section, set the Size to 10 and the Noise Type to Fractal.

10. Turn on the Animate button in the main MAX interface and move the frames slider to frame 100.

11. In the Coordinates section of the Noise map, set the Z Offset value to 20.

12. In the Noise parameters section, set the Phase to 2.

13. Click the Go to Parent button in the Material editor and set the Bump amount to 25.

14. Render the scene to an AVI file to see the animation.

After the animation has rendered, you can see how easy it is to create great-looking water. You can see one frame of the animation in Figure 12.3. The best part is that you don't have to use any raytracing. The only caveat of creating water in this manner is that if an object intersects the water geometry, the illusion is lost. Just to recap, a Bump map only distorts the look of a surface *in a rendering*. It does not actually change the surface. As a result, if two objects intersect each other, the intersection appears to be flat.

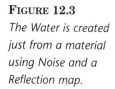

FIGURE 12.3

The Water is created just from a material using Noise and a Reflection map.

Man-Made Animated Materials

Man-made materials are far easier to work with in both creation and animation. Why? Well, if you look around you, you're surrounded with all kinds of ideas for materials in your scene. Some materials are animated; some are not. Whatever the case, you'll find that almost every material that occurs as a result of human intervention is re-creatable within MAX.

Although you can use any of the maps discussed earlier in this chapter to create man-made materials, some other specific maps can assist you in creating more realistic materials.

Maps to Use with Man-Made Materials

When designing a man-made material within MAX, you can use several different kinds of maps. You typically need to be more precise with man-made materials, however, because they are often based on exacting figures. For instance, a steel plate that has bolts around the edges could be easily recreated using a Procedural map like Bitmap in the Diffuse channel. In any case, you'll find that there are certain maps that work well for faithfully reproducing real-world materials in MAX. The first, and perhaps most used, is the Bitmap.

Bitmaps

If you've gone through the tutorials and even through other sections in this book, you've already used the Bitmap Map type. Bitmap essentially allows you to use an image, in one of several supported image file types, as a color or rendering property of a material. Images can include anything from scans of real objects or images to animations from MAX or other programs. Figure 12.4 shows the Bitmap Parameters section.

FIGURE 12.4

The Bitmap map's parameters.

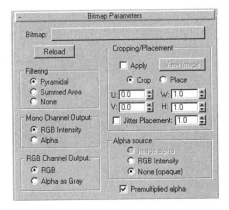

As with many other maps, you can animate Bitmap's values of Offset, Tiling, and Angle. In many cases, animating the offset of a bitmap—especially for decals—is more practical than for Procedural maps.

New to MAX R2 is the capability to crop a bitmap or place it anywhere within a material by scaling it down. The Crop and Place controls eliminate the need for a paint program for cropping and scaling, the only functions many people used them for. Another benefit of using MAX's cropping is that it can be animated. This works well for situations like the one in Figure 12.5. The stripes on the bitmap are straight up and down, but that is easily adjusted with the Angle parameter. Animating the cropping rectangle moves the stripes as if the pole were spinning. The Place feature works by using the entire bitmap. The window, rather than acting as a cropping window, allows you to scale and place the entire map on the surface of an object.

Another benefit of using the Bitmap map type for man-made materials is that you can use animation files, such as AVI or sequential still frames. This means that you can use both computer-generated animations and also high-resolution captured video as a texture for a material. In Exercise 12.2, you'll see how this is accomplished.

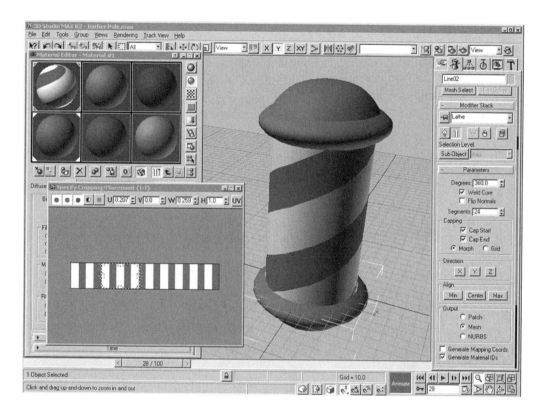

FIGURE 12.5

The pole stripes are animated by using a single bitmap and cropping over time.

Marbles

The Marble map, while procedural, offers a more realistic looking version of its name than some of its bitmap counterparts provide. As of MAX R2, there are now two marble maps, the generic Marble and a new map, Perlin Marble. Figure 12.6 shows both the generic Marble and Perlin Marble interfaces.

The generic Marble is not all that useful as a texture, but it functions very well for Bump maps. Perlin Marble does well as a Diffuse map, an Opacity map, and even as a Bump map if the Levels are set to a low number. In the Color sections of both marble maps, you can use maps versus a solid color to control the colors. You can animate both Marble maps most effectively

when changing the Offset values over time. As with some of the other procedural maps, by animating the Offset values, you're actually changing the
look of the map itself—not just moving it across a surface. Of course, you
can also animate the maps that you're using in the color slots. Just remember to keep the number of extra maps low. The more maps you use in the
material, the more animatable parameters you have to keep track of.

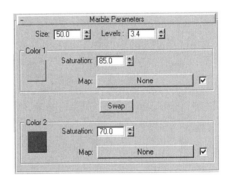

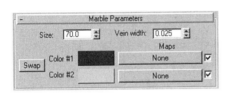

FIGURE 12.6
The Marble (left) and Perlin Marble (right) map interfaces.

Perlin Marble can be used quite well as an Opacity map. By changing Color
#1 and Color #2 to grayscale colors, you can make a nice smoke. By ani-
mating the Z Offset value in a negative direction, you can make the smoke
rise.

The Ballpark Sign

In Exercise 12.2, you will create a material that simulates an animated ballpark sign. The sign will be a progressively lit series of bulbs that have several starting points along the text. The Blend material uses two masks: one
is a still image of the text itself and the other is a line of animated dots. The
dots are in a single line to speed creation and render time only and are tiled
to give the appearance of an array of bulbs. You also use Video Post to apply
a glow to the bulbs.

EXERCISE 12.2: AN ANIMATED BALLPARK SIGN

1. Open the file 12max02 on the CD-ROM. The scene is a painted iron framework with a flat signboard mounted on top. Mapping coordinates have already been applied to the signboard and a paint material is on the framework. The display should look like Figure 12.7.

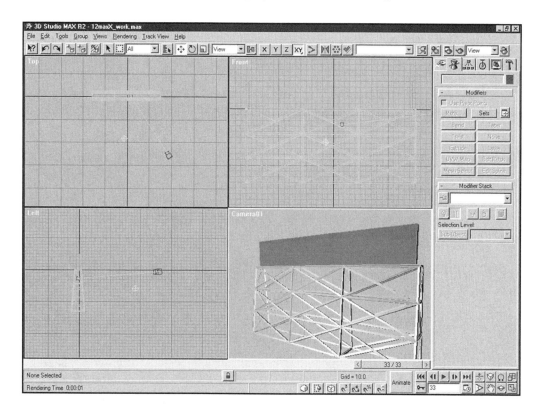

FIGURE 12.7

Basic Ballpark sign.

2. In the Material editor, click the first sample sphere, named DOTS TEXT. Click the Material/Map Navigator icon to open it.

3. Click the Type button and double-click Blend in the Browser list. Click OK for Discard Old Material.

4. Click the Material 1 button and name this material TEXT. In the Basic Parameters rollout, click the gray box to the right of the Diffuse color swatch. Double-click Bitmap in the Browser list, click the Bitmap button in Bitmap Parameters rollout, and find the file on the CD-ROM called ballpark.jpg. Name this level ballpark diff. Click Show Map in the Viewport icon and the map should appear on the signboard in the shaded viewport. In the Coordinates rollout, drag the Blur spinner until the field reads 0.01.

TIP

Neither the sign nor the camera are animated in this scene. Setting the bitmap to minimum blur keeps it crisp at the edges. If there were motion in the scene, however, the edges of the text would show a rolling effect and blur would have to be added.

5. In the Navigator, click Material 2 and name this material DOTS. In the Maps rollout, click None in the Diffuse map slot, double-click Bitmap in the Browser, click the blank Bitmap button in Bitmap Parameters rollout, and single-click the file called DOTS2.AVI from the CD-ROM.

6. While in the Select Bitmap Image File dialog box, after choosing DOTS2.AVI, click the View button to view the AVI file. It is a single row of dots animated from left to right. Close the Viewer, click OK to accept the file, and click the Show Map in Viewport icon.

7. Name this Map level dots diff. Click and hold the Material Effects Channel icon and select 1 from the numbers menu. This Material Effects channel will be used in Video Post to cue a Glow effect.

8. In the Coordinates rollout, enter 0.01 in the Blur field, enter 0.02 in the U;Offset field, enter 2.0 in the U;Tiling field, and enter 12.0 in the V;Tiling field.

9. The DOTS2.AVI file is made of white dots on a black background and you want to change the color of the dots (lightbulbs) in your sign to red. This is the Diffuse map for the dots, so now is the time to change the color. You don't want to recreate the dots animation, however.

10. Click the Type;Bitmap button and double-click RGB Tint in the Browser list. Check Keep Old Map as Sub-Map and click OK. This RGB Tint Map type allows you to change the color of existing bitmaps. Change the green and blue color swatches to black. The display should look similar to Figure 12.8.

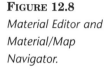

FIGURE 12.8

Material Editor and Material/Map Navigator.

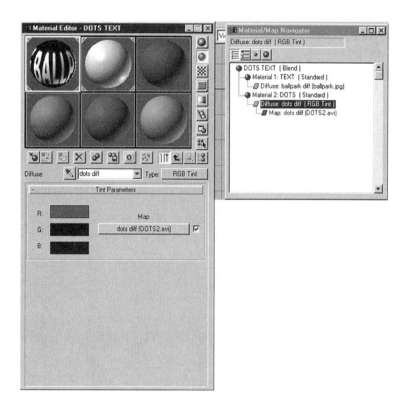

11. In the Navigator, click Material 2:DOTS. From the Navigator, drag and drop Map;dots diff (DOTS2.AVI) to the Self-Illumination slot in Maps rollout. Check Instance in the dialog box and click OK. Drag and drop the new Self-Illumination slot onto the Bump slot, check Instance in the dialog box, and click OK.

12. Enter 200 in the Bump Amount field.

13. In the Navigator, click the top material level, DOTS TEXT (Blend). In the Navigator, drag and drop Diffuse: ballpark diff (ballpark.jpg) onto the Mask slot. Check Instance in the dialog box and click OK. Drag the Frame Slider to frame 17 and the display should look similar to Figure 12.9.

14. Render frame 17 and you should see partial letters on the sign made of red dots and a faint white outline for the letters. Close all dialog boxes.

15. In the Rendering pull-down menu, click Video Post. In the Video Post dialog box, you see a queue set up. Double-click Lens Effect Glow and

click the Setup button in the Edit Filter Event dialog box. You should see the glowing sign in the preview window. If not, click Preview and VP Queue buttons. In the Preferences tab, Size has been set to 8.0 and Intensity has been set to 50.0. Click the Properties tab and see that Material ID is checked and set to 1. This is cueing the Material Effects Channel you set, not any Material ID#s on faces in the scene. Click OK to close the dialog box.

16. In the Video Post dialog box, click the Add Image Output Event icon, click the Files button in the Add Image Output Event dialog box and save the rendering to BALLPARK.AVI on disk. Use the Cinepak codec.

17. Click the Execute Sequence icon. Check Range to render frame 0–33. Click the 320 × 240 button and click Render. When you play the finished animation the glowing red "bulbs" of the sign should light up in waves across the signboard with just a slight, white glow around each letter for accent.

FIGURE 12.9

Material editor and Material/Map Navigator at Frame 17.

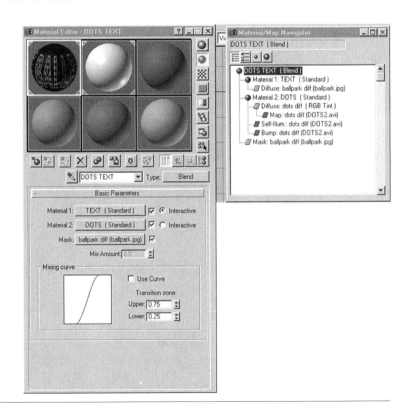

TIP

You can adjust the way the letters light up by changing the U;Offset and U;Tiling of the DOTS2.AVI maps. They should all change the same because they are instances. You can also create a new DOTS2.AVI file by opening DOTS.MAX and making changes to the animation of the dots themselves.

In Exercise 12.2, you created a Blend material using animated and still bitmaps to reveal the underlying materials of the Blend Material type. To make the image more realistic, you used a Material Effects channel to cue a glow in Video Post.

Dropping a Bomb

In Exercise 12.3, you will create a material to be used as a burning fuse on a classic bomb. The material is a complex Blend within a Blend, similar to the material used on text in Chapter 13. The fuse will appear to burn down, while Lens Effect Glow and a particle system will round out the effect.

EXERCISE 12.3: A BURNING FUSE

1. Open the file 12max03 from the CD-ROM. The scene contains a bomb with a fuse. There is also a Particle System, a Particle Array (PArray), and a Combustion Atmospheric apparatus in the scene for special effects. The fuse object is a circle lofted on a helical path with Apply Mapping checked in the Surface Parameters rollout. In this exercise, you focus on creating the fuse material.

2. In the Material editor, click the Material/Map Navigator icon. The first sample sphere is a Blend material type named BURNING FUSE. In the Basic Parameters rollout, click the Material 1: slot and name this material FUSE SURFACE.

3. In the Maps rollout, click the Diffuse color swatch and make it a dark brown color. In the Basic Parameters rollout, check the 2-Sided checkbox.

4. In the Navigator, click Material 2:(Standard), name the material INVISIBLE, click the Type Button, double-click Blend in the Browser

list, and check Discard old material in the Replace Material dialog box. Click OK.

5. In the Navigator, click the new Material 1:(Standard) and name it Invisible. Enter 0 in the Shininess, Shin.Strength, and Opacity fields. This creates a completely invisible material that won't show any specular highlights due to shininess.

6. In the Navigator, click Material 2:(Standard), set Specular, Diffuse, and Ambient color swatches to pure white, and enter 100 in the Self-Illumination field. Click and hold the Material Effects Channel icon and choose 1 from the number menu. In the Basic Parameters rollout, check the 2-Sided checkbox. Name this material GLOWREVEAL. This creates a material to cue a Glow and Highlight effect in Video Post.

7. In the Navigator, click Material 2:INVISIBLE (Blend) and, in the Basic Parameters rollout, click None in the Mask slot. Double-click Bitmap in the Browser list, click the Bitmap slot in the Bitmap Parameters rollout, and get the AVI file called GLOWMASK.AVI from the CD-ROM. In the the Basic Parameters rollout, enter 0.01 in the Blur field. Name this level Glow Mask.

N OTE

If Blur is not set to the minimum in this case, the blurred bitmap is too soft to create the Glow and Highlight effects in Video Post.

8. Click the Show Map in Viewport icon and drag the frame slider back and forth. In the shaded viewport you should see a Particle system moving down the fuse and a thin white line moving up the fuse. You want these two to be in sync with each other, but the GLOWMASK.AVI was created from bottom to top.

9. In the Coordinates rollout, enter 180.0 in the W: angle field and drag the slider. The white line should now stay with the Particle system.

10. In the Navigator, click BURNING FUSE, click None in the Mask slot, and load a Bitmap called MATLMASK.AVI. Name this level Material Mask. Enter 180.0 in the W: Angle field to reverse the direction to top to bottom. Enter 0.01 in the Blur field. The display should look similar to Figure 12.11. Close the Material editor and the Material/Map Navigator.

11. In the Rendering pull-down menu, click Video Post. Video Post has four entries in the queue: the Camera01 viewport, a fuse glow, a fuse highlight, and a Glow effect called smoke that is applied to the Particle system. Click the Add Image Output Event icon, click the Files button, and save to an AVI file called fuseglow.avi to disk. Use the Cinepak codec.

12. In Video Post, click the Execute Sequence icon, check Range, click the 320 × 240 button, and click the Render button.

FIGURE 12.10

Material editor and Material/Map Navigator for BURNING FUSE.

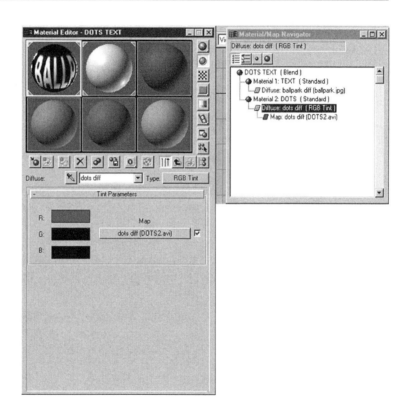

In Exercise 12.3, you created a compound Blend within a Blend material and used animated masks to reveal a material with the Material Effects Channel to cue a glow and a highlight in Video Post. Material 2 in the Blend is a fully invisible material to give the illusion of a burning fuse.

Take the time to analyze the other materials and objects in the scene to see how that bomb object was exploded (PArray) and how the fiery blast was made (Combustion). The smoke material is simply another invisible material with Material Effects Channel 2 to cue the Smoke Glow in Video Post.

Fictional Animated Materials

Fortunately for artists and animators, the realm of fiction is easy to create on the computer. Maybe that's why there have been so many movies about space produced with computer animation software. In MAX, you can plug just about any map into any Map channel and, just by animating it, create some wild effects.

The next exercise focuses on what's possible with the Raytrace material and MAX's maps. You'll find that by just adding Noise to the Luminosity channel, the effect is 10 times greater.

"Plasma Engine" Exercise

In this exercise, you'll use the Raytrace material with various settings to give the plasma engines of a spaceship the appearance that they're actually working as the ship leaves Earth.

EXERCISE 12.4: PLASMA ENGINES USING RAYTRACE MATERIAL AND NOISE

1. Open the file 12max04.max. Render the viewport to see the current scene. Notice that although the engines look okay, they could definitely use some fixing up.

2. Open the Material editor and choose the upper-left material. The material is called Plasma and is a Raytrace material with several colors set already.

3. Set Shininess to 63 and Shin.Strength to 71.

4. Click the Empty button to the right of the Luminosity color swatch. Choose Noise.

5. In the Noise Map parameters, set the Type to Turbulence and the Size to 10.

6. The High Threshold should be 0.525 and the Low should be 0.125.

7. Set Color #2 to a hot pink color, approximately R255, G127, B253.

8. You should have a hot pink, plasma-looking material. The next step is to animate it. Start by turning on the Animate button.

9. Move the Frame slider to frame 100.

10. In the Noise Parameters section, set the Phase value to 0.5. In the Coordinates section, set the Z Angle value to 90.

11. Render out the scene to an AVI file at 320 × 240 resolution.

Figure 12.11 shows the result of Exercise 12.3. By animating just a few values, you can easily create some great fictional materials. When you get the time, examine both the Raytrace material being used and the way the scene is set up. There are actually several elements to this scene—not just the engines—that make it look good.

FIGURE 12.11

The completed rendering from Exercise 12.3.

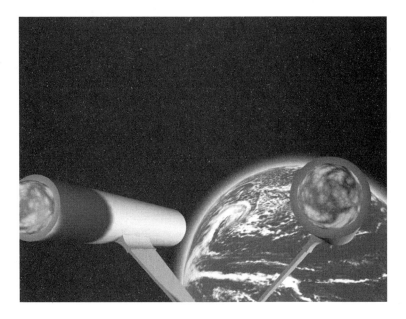

In Practice: Animated Materials

- **Flexibility can often mean complexity.** The greatest thing about MAX's materials is that you can animate everything. It also happens to be the worst quality about it too. Use discretion when creating animated materials. Due to so many possibilities, the material can quickly get away from you.

- **Procedural maps work great for animation.** Procedural maps often have at least the capability to animate the offset. Others also have a Phase value. By animating one or both of these values, you can create wonderful organic-looking materials.

- **Bitmaps are king for man-made materials.** Let's face it, the best way to recreate a man-made material in MAX is to just scan an image of it and use it as a bitmap. There's certainly no shame in doing things the "easy" way. Just remember that you also have the ability to animate many of the values of the bitmap—this includes the new Cropping/Placement function.

- **Fictional materials can use, well—anything.** There's no limit to how you can design a fictional material. The Raytrace material, however, lends itself to creating great fictional materials because there are several new, special-effects parameters that you can use. By working with items such as Translucency and Luminosity, you can design some superb fictional materials.

Chapter 13

Using MAX R2 as a 2D Paint Tool

It happens to everyone eventually. While working with 3D Studio MAX, you need a 2D image for a material bitmap, but you don't have access to paint or imaging software. Don't panic: MAX R2 can be a powerful tool for creating 2D maps, especially animated 2D masks. In this chapter, you use MAX R2 to create four kinds of 2D maps for which you use a program such as Photoshop or Animator Studio normally.

Here are the four scenarios:

- You're doing a demo for an aircraft manufacturer, and they want to see a fuselage detail showing countersunk rivet holes. You have only 3D Studio MAX R2 on the demo computer.

- You have a proposal for a new sailboat, and the colors that you chose for the hull are all wrong. The client wants it fixed *now*!

- You need to represent a lot of small, simultaneous explosions in a scene. Render time is a critical factor in creating the explosions.

- A potential client wants to see what you can do with the logo of a company they just bought. They want the new logo to show the progressive attitude of the new company. You have half an hour.

The Aircraft Manufacturer

You are in the corporate offices of a major aircraft manufacturer, and they want to see a detail of a fuselage showing the countersunk rivet holes. You have a laptop demo computer and no paint or imaging software.

Map Making in the Field

In Exercise 13.1, you use essentially 2D construction methods to create a grayscale map to use as a bump map to simulate rivets and a seam on the fuselage.

EXERCISE 13.1: PAINTING THE 2D MAP

1. Open 13max01.max from the CD-ROM. The file contains a circle named backdisk, a line named rivetcone, and a rectangle named seam. Also in the scene are a strong Omni light set away for even lighting and a Free camera that has the new Orthographic Projection option checked for a distortion-free view.

2. In the Camera01 viewport, pick the circle named backdisk. In the Modify panel, click Edit Stack and choose Editable Mesh from the menu. This converts the 2D circle to a 2D mesh object.

3. Pick the rectangle named Seam; in the Modify panel, click Edit Stack and choose Editable Mesh. Right-click on the Camera01 label, and choose Smooth-Highlight to shade the Camera01 viewport. The rectangle and circle appear as solid mesh objects.

4. In the Camera01 viewport, pick the line named Rivetcone and in Modify panel, click Lathe. In the Parameters rollout, enter 24 in the Segments field. Click Sub-Object to enter Axis mode. In the toolbar at the top of the display, click the Align icon, select the object named backdisk, and check X Position in the Align Position(Screen) area. Click OK to exit the Align Sub-Object Selection dialog box. This step centers the lathe axis with the center of backdisk. Click Sub-Object again to exit Axis mode. You now have a cone, a disk, and a thin rectangle in the Camera01 viewport.

5. In the Material Editor, name the first sample sphere CONE, and set Shininess and Shin.Strength to 0 by right-clicking on the respective spinners.

6. Click on the gray box to the right of the Diffuse color swatch to access Diffuse mapping. Double-click the Gradient map type in the Material/Map browser. Click on the Show in Viewport icon. Right-click on the Blur spinner to set it to its minimum amount of 0.01.

T IP

You can alter the apparent angle of the sides of the rivet hole by adjusting the Color 2 Position spinner. Higher numbers make the sides seem flatter, whereas lower numbers make the sides seem steeper.

7. Drag and drop the sample sphere onto rivetcone in the Camera01 viewport. Click on Zoom Extents All Selected.

8. With rivetcone still selected, click on UVW Map in the Modify panel.

N OTE

Without the UVW Map modifier, the gradient runs around the object in the direction of the lathing. The Planar mapping causes the gradient to run from top to bottom as seen from the Camera01 viewport.

9. In the Material Editor, click on the second sample sphere and name it WHITE. Change the Ambient, Diffuse, and Specular color swatches to pure white, and set Shininess and Shin.Strength to 0.

10. Select backdisk and seam objects, and, in the Material Editor, click Assign to Selection to assign WHITE to the selected objects. The display looks similar to Figure 13.1.

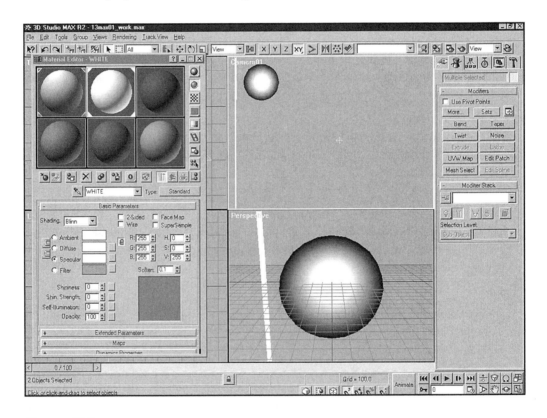

FIGURE 13.1

Black-and-white objects.

11. Right-click in the Camera01 viewport. Click the Render Scene icon, click the Files button in the Render Output area, and save a JPG file called RIVET.JPG to your hard drive. The rendered image should appear similar to Figure 13.2. Save the MAX file to disk with the name 2DRIVET.MAX.

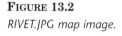

FIGURE 13.2
RIVET.JPG map image.

Applying the Material to the Fuselage

In Exercise 13.2, you apply the bitmap you just "painted" as a bump map in a material. Finally, you assign it to a section of fuselage.

EXERCISE 13.2: APPLYING RIVET.JPG IN A MATERIAL

1. Open 13max02.max from the CD-ROM. This file is a cylinder called FUSELAGE with a camera and one Omni light.

2. Open the Material Editor, name the first sample sphere FUSELAGE, and expand Maps rollout.

3. Click on None in the Bump slot, and double-click Bitmap. Click on the Bitmap slot in the Bitmap Parameters rollout, and double-click on the RIVET.JPG you saved in Exercise 13.1. Name this level rivet bump, and click on the Show Map in Viewport icon.

4. Click on Go to the Parent icon. Click and hold on the Sample Type icon, and choose the Cube sample type. Enter 500 in the Bump Amount field. You see a line and cone in the upper-left of the sample cube's front. They are bumping outward.

NOTE

If the Diffuse color of the material is dark, it may be difficult to see clearly. Change the Diffuse color to a light color for better results.

5. In Material/Map Navigator, go to Bump rivet bump map level. Expand the Output rollout, and check Invert. Invert causes white to become black and vice versa for RIVET.JPG. The line and cone on the sample cube should now be indentations.

6. Drag and drop the sample cube to FUSELAGE in the Camera01 viewport. You should see one repetition of the bitmap on the fuselage object. It should appear similar to Figure 13.3.

FIGURE 13.3

One repetition of Rivet bump map on fuselage.

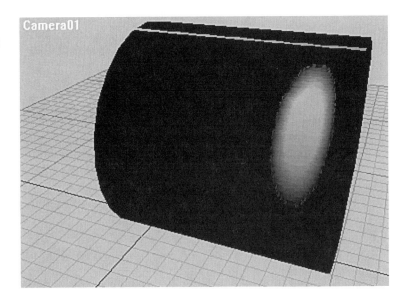

7. In the Coordinates rollout, enter 18.0 in U;Tiling and 8.0 in V;Tiling. Enter 0.015 in the Blur Offset field to soften the bitmap edges. Render the Camera01 viewport. The rendered image looks like a cylinder with overlapping plates and rivet holes.

8. In the Navigator, click on FUSELAGE to get the top material level. Drag and drop the gray Filter color swatch onto the Diffuse color swatch as a copy. Enter 60.0 in the Shin.Strength field. In Maps rollout, click on the Shininess slot, and double-click on Smoke in the Browser list. Name the level shiny smoke and click Go to Parent.

9. Click on the Reflection slot, and double-click Cellular in the Browser list. Enter 20.0 in the Size field of the Cell Characteristics rollout. Check Fractal and name this map level cell reflect. Click the Go to Parent icon, and enter 10 in the Reflection Amount field.

10. Render the Camera01 viewport. The display looks similar to Figure 13.4.

FIGURE 13.4

Rendered fuselage with rivet holes.

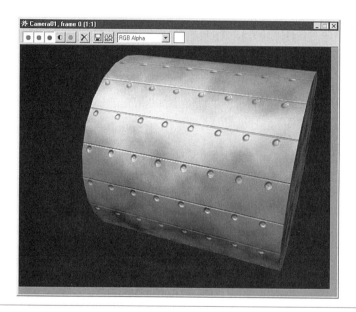

NEW TO R2

You notice some aliasing along the straight seams on the fuselage. You can reduce this effect by checking the new SuperSample option at the top of the Basic Parameters rollout. The seams appear much cleaner but at a significant cost in render time.

Aircraft Project Summary

In Exercise 13.1, you created a scene of simple 2D mesh objects, applied black-and-white materials, and rendered to a bitmap for use in the Material Editor.

In a new scene in Exercise 13.2, you used that bitmap in the Bump slot of a new material to create the illusion of rivet holes in a metal fuselage. No paint software was required and the process didn't take long. You can go back to the 2DRIVET.MAX file and make adjustments to size, spacing, and the Gradient map to get a different effect, and you can use the Tiling features to adjust the position after the material is assigned to an object.

The Sailboat Client

In the second scenario, you need to create a new color scheme for a sailboat you designed. You are at the client's site and do not have access to any imaging or paint software.

A New Paint Job

To start, you create a single bitmap image to be applied to the side of the sailboat defining the bottom paint, the waterline, the hull color, and the deck color. Later, you use the Unwrap UVW modifier to fit the map to the hull.

EXERCISE 13.3: CREATING A BITMAP OF HULL COLORS

1. Open the file 13max03.max from the CD-ROM. The file contains four rectangles and an Omni light.

2. In the Front viewport, select the rectangle named Deck. In the Modify panel, click Edit Stack, and choose Editable Mesh from the menu. Shade the Front viewport. The top rectangle appears as a solid object.

TIP

The following Steps 3 and 4 are a good method to use for the following flat objects:

■ Floors and ceilings

■ Pictures and posters

■ Table tops

- Small, flat ground planes

- Labels and tags

The process works on any closed 2D shape, even those that have been modified, such as a 2D ellipse with a bend modifier. Be aware, however, that for modified objects the result may be unpredictable as MAX R2 tries to create a surface with as few faces as possible. Also, the object will be invisible from the back due to face normals and may require two-sided materials.

3. Convert the other three rectangles to editable mesh objects to create four solid rectangles. The rectangles align edge to edge on top and bottom, but the side edges are not important.

NEW TO R2

If you have multiple objects to collapse to editable mesh objects, you can use the Collapse utility in the Utilities panel. You can select the objects, click Collapse in the Utilities panel, and, for this example, check Multiple Objects in the Collapse To area.

4. In the Front viewport, zoom in until the objects just fill the viewport.

5. Open the Material Editor, and click on the first sample sphere. The material should be named DECK and should be pure white. Drag and drop the DECK material sphere onto the deck and waterline objects in the Front viewport. As an alternate method, you can select deck and waterline and click the Assign to Selection icon in the Material Editor.

WARNING

These materials should be pure color with minimal shininess, and the objects to which they are assigned should be lit with an even light. You want the bitmap created from this file to be flat and free of highlights.

6. Click the second sample sphere called HULL, and drag and drop the blue material to the hull object. Drag and drop the red BOTTOM material to the bottom object in the Front viewport. In the Front viewport, zoom in until the objects completely fill the viewport. The display looks like Figure 13.5.

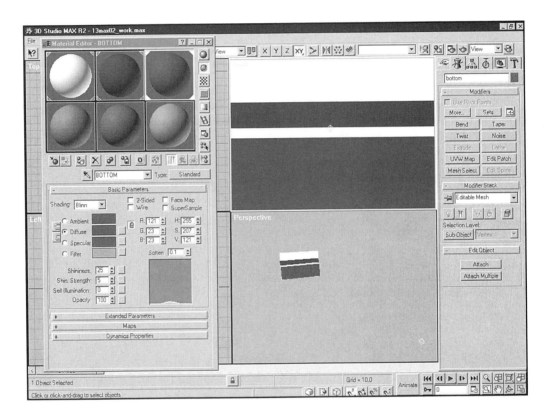

FIGURE 13.5
Rectangles filling Front viewport.

7. Right-click in the Front viewport, if it is not already active. Click on the Render Scene icon. Use the default settings, and save the rendering to a file called HULL.JPG. Save the MAX file to disk with the name HULL.MAX.

Applying the Material to the Hull

In Exercise 13.4, you use the HULL.JPG file created in Exercise 13.3 to make a material for the sailboat hull. You assign the material to the boat and adjust it to fit the lines of the boat better.

EXERCISE 13.4: APPLYING A MATERIAL TO THE HULL

1. Open 13max04.max from the CD-ROM. This file is a scene with a sailboat sitting in calm seas with clouds in the background.

2. In the Material Editor, click on the first sample sphere, which is a gray material called CC36HULL. Enter 40 in the Shininess field and 65 in the Shin.Strength field.

3. In the Maps rollout, click None in the Diffuse slot and double-click Bitmap in the Browser list. Name this level hull diff. Click on the Bitmap slot in the Bitmap Parameters rollout, and choose the file HULL.JPG from Exercise 13.3. Click on the Show Map in Viewport icon. Drag and drop the sample sphere onto the HULL object in the scene. The material shows up on the hull in the shaded viewport but is not correctly mapped.

4. In the Back viewport, select the HULL and, in the Modify panel, click on UVW Map. In the Parameters rollout, click the View Align button, and then click the Fit button. The mapping is now on the side of the hull. You have too much of the white deck material, however, and not enough of the blue hull.

5. In the Modify panel, click More and double-click Unwrap UVW in the list. In the Parameters rollout, click the Edit button.

6. In the Edit UVWs dialog box, click on the Pick Map button. In the Map/Material Browser, check Scene, and double-click hull diff (HULL.JPG) from the list. The display looks similar to Figure 13.6.

7. The Map Coordinate lines in the Edit UVWs dialog box are white and don't show on the white areas of the background map. In the Edit UVWs dialog box, click the Unwrap Options icon, click on the Line Color swatch, and set the color to light gray. Close the Color Selector, and click OK in Unwrap Options. The lines and points are now gray and visible over the entire map.

8. In the Edit UVWs dialog box, click and drag from the upper-left corner to the far right and down approximately one third of the way into the blue stripe. The selected vertices looks similar to Figure 13.7.

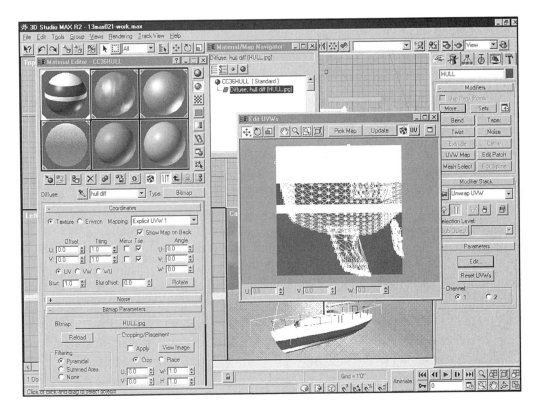

FIGURE 13.6
Edit UVWs dialog box and Map/Material browser.

FIGURE 13.7
Selected points in Edit UVWs dialog box.

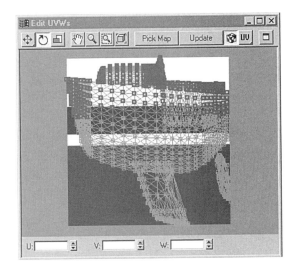

9. Using the Move and Rotate icons in Edit UVWs, move the selected points down and rotate the selected points counterclockwise slightly. When you release the mouse button, you see in the shaded viewport the blue hull material move up and align with the slope of the deck. The moved and rotate selected coordinates look similar to Figure 13.8.

FIGURE 13.8

Moved and rotated selected points in the Edit UVWs dialog box.

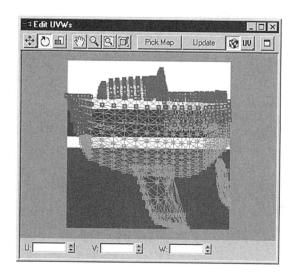

WARNING

Do not move the bottom coordinate points into the white waterline area or the blue/white boundary will become jagged.

10. Save this scene as a file called SAILBOAT.MAX. Close all dialog boxes and render the Camera01 viewport.

Sailboat Project Summary

In Exercise 13.4, you used the HULL.JPG bitmap you created in Exercise 13.3 to create a material for the sailboat hull. You assigned the material to the boat, planar mapping the material to the side of the hull to get a horizontal waterline. You then applied an Unwrap UVW modifier to adjust the coordinate points of the hull so the blue hull color and the white deck color were near the gunwales and followed the slope of the deck. The waterline remained horizontal.

This same method can also be used to create interesting landscape contours. Make as many colored bands as you like and apply planar mapping to the side of a landscape mesh. Use material Blur and Blur Offset settings to blur the color transitions.

The bitmap image does not have to be horizontal bands of color. Use the 2D Line to create odd shapes before converting to Editable Mesh objects.

The Game Client

You are called upon to create an animation showing two rows of five simultaneous explosions and time is of the essence. It would take too long to render a scene with that many Combustion objects on the computer you have available. The answer is a series of mapped 2D explosions.

Anatomy of an Explosion

In Exercise 13.5 you will create an explosion in an empty scene and render that explosion to an AVI file. The AVI file will then be used as a Diffuse and, again, as an Opacity map to create a material to be applied to objects in a new scene. This process will save on overall rendering time.

EXERCISE 13.5: CREATING AN EXPLOSION FOR A MATERIAL

1. Open 13max05.max from the CD-ROM. The scene is set up with an Atmospheric Apparatus with a Combustion atmospheric effect assigned to it. In the center of the apparatus is a small sphere. The sphere has an invisible material assigned to it with G-Buffer Object Channel 1 assigned as a property. This sphere has a MeshBomb spacewarp linked to it. The exploding sphere will be used to cue glow effects for the final explosion.

2. In the Rendering pull-down menu, click Environment and click on Combustion in the Effects list. The Combustion Parameters are default settings, except Flame Type Tendril is checked and, in Explosions area, Explosion is checked and has been set up to start at frame 0 and end at frame 30.

3. A standard combustion explosion is acceptable, but you want a little more interest. In the Rendering pull-down menu, click Video Post.

4. In Video Post, click the Add Scene Event icon, choose Perspective, and click the OK button.

5. Click the Add Image Filter Event, choose Lens Effect Glow from the list, and click OK.

6. Click Add Image Output Event, click the Files button, and name the new file **BLAST.AVI**. Click OK in the Edit Output Image Event dialog box. The Video Post queue looks like Figure 13.9.

T IP

Use the Cinepak codec by Radius for good results with most AVI files.

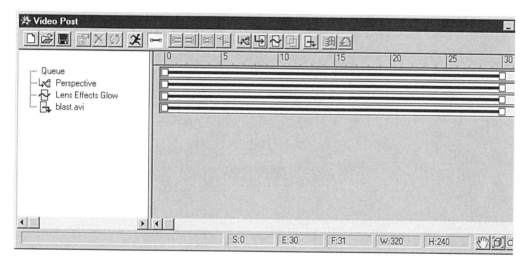

FIGURE 13.9
Video Post queue.

7. Right-click in Perspective viewport to activate it. In the Video Post queue, double-click Lens Effect Glow, and click the Setup button in the Edit Filter Event dialog box. Click the Preview and the VP Queue buttons.

8. Click on the Preferences tab, and check Gradient in the Color area.

9. Click on the Inferno tab, and check Electric. Check Red, Green, and Blue in the Settings area. Go to frame 15, and click the Update button in the Lens Effect Glow dialog box. This glow effect gives electric sparks flying through the explosion. It looks similar to Figure 13.10. Click OK in the Lens Effect Glow dialog box.

FIGURE 13.10

*Lens Effect Glow
Preview display.*

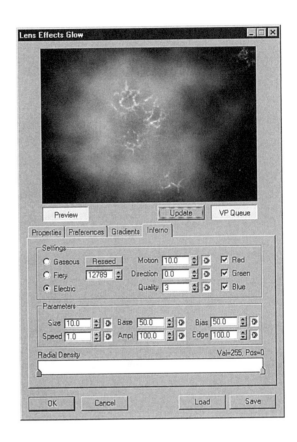

10. In Video Post, click on Execute Sequence. In the Execute Video Post dialog box, check Range and enter **0 to 30**. Click the 320 × 240 button and click the Render button. The file BLAST.AVI will be rendered to disk.

Take a break; MAX may take a while rendering. That's the whole point of this exercise: managing time. Ten explosions in a scene would take much longer. After the file is rendered, you can view it with View File from the Files pull-down menu. Don't forget to save the MAX file as BLAST1.MAX.

Applying the BLAST.AVI as a Map

In Exercise 13.6 you will use Exercise 13.5's BLAST.AVI as a bitmap in both Diffuse and Opacity slots and apply Exercise 13.5's material to flat mesh objects in the scene.

EXERCISE 13.6: APPLYING THE BLAST AS A MATERIAL

1. Open file 13max06.max from the CD-ROM. The scene is a desert planet at night with a stormy sky. In the scene are ten 2D flat planes with LookAt controllers so they will always face the camera. You will add two repetitions of ten explosions over the 60-frame animation. Select the BLAST01 object in the scene, and in the Modify panel, click on UVW Map to add map coordinates. The BLAST01–10 objects are instances so they all get the UVW Map modifier.

2. Open the Material Editor. Name the third sample sphere BLAST, and expand the Maps rollout.

3. Click on None in the Diffuse slot, and double-click Bitmap. Click on the Bitmap slot in Bitmap Parameters, and choose the BLAST.AVI file you saved in Exercise 13.5. Name the map level blast diff. Click on the Show Map in Viewport icon. Drag the Frame Slider to approximately frame 10, and you see the explosion on the sample sphere.

4. Click on the Go to Parent icon, enter 100 in the Self-illumination field. Select BLAST01–BLAST10 in the scene, and click the Assign to Selection icon. You see the blasts in the shaded viewport, which looks similar to Figure 13.11.

5. In the Maps rollout, drag and drop the Diffuse map slot onto the Opacity map slot. Choose Copy, and click OK.

6. Click on the Opacity slot, and rename the map level blast op. In the Bitmap Parameters rollout, check RGB Intensity in the Alpha source area. In the Output rollout, enter 2.0 in the Output Amount field. This boosts the effect of the Opacity map.

7. Close the Material Editor. Click on the Render Scene icon, check Active Time Segment, click 320 × 240, click the Files button, and name the AVI file moonblst.avi. Use the Cinepak codec.

For extra interest, you can add Omni lights synchronized with the blast cycle to give the appearance of a flash from each blast.

FIGURE 13.11

*Blast material assigned
to flat planes.*

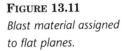

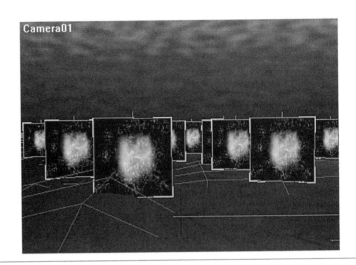

Game Project Summary

In Exercise 13.5, you rendered an AVI bitmap of a combustion effect with electric glow particles to disk. The 30-frame Video Post sequence took a while to render. In Exercise 13.6, you then used the resulting AVI to create a new material to map onto flat planes in the scene. The material used BLAST.AVI as a diffuse color map and as an opacity map to give the planes color only where the explosion occurs and not over the entire flat plane. Each flat plane has a LookAt controller pointing to the camera so if the camera were animated in the scene, the blasts would always face the camera. This gives the illusion that the blasts are 3D, but they render very quickly because the blasts are only a material on a simple plane.

The Logo Redesign

In this final scenario you will redesign your client's logo, adding a sweeping electric glow with highlights across the face of text. The text will be a dull lead material before the glow and a shiny gold material behind the glow. The main objectives of the exercises are

■ Creating animated masks with MAX R2

■ Composing a compound animated material

The masks are purely black-and-white images. One is full-screen to mask the top-level Blend material changing from gray to gold, and the other is just a narrow strip to reveal the lower-level Blend material with Material Effects Channel #1 to cue the glowing and highlighting in Video Post.

Using MAX2 to Create Animated Masks

In Exercise 13.7 you will use MAX R2 to create 2D animated bitmaps that will be used as masks in Exercise 13.8. The lesson shows how easy it is to create complex materials with some very simple masking techniques entirely within MAX R2.

EXERCISE 13.7: CREATING THE 2D MASKS

1. Perform a File/Reset to insure a new MAX R2 session.

2. Click the Time Configuration icon, and enter 120 in the End Time field in the Animation area. Click OK in Time Configuration dialog box.

3. Choose Create Rectangle, and in the Front viewport, click and drag a rectangle to fill the viewport. Enter a Length of 3 units and a Width of 500 units. Name the object glowmask.

4. In the Modify panel, click Edit Stack and convert the rectangle to an Editable Mesh. This step creates a flat mesh object.

5. Zoom in, if necessary, so that left and right edges of the rectangle extend beyond the sides of the Front viewport display.

WARNING

The size of the rectangle is not critical, but it is very important that the object fill the viewport completely when rendering. Any black at the edges of the rendered image will cause artifacts when you use the animation as a mask.

6. In the Front viewport, create another rectangle 500 units long and 500 units wide. Name the object matlmask.

7. In the Modify panel, click Edit Stack and convert the rectangle to an Editable Mesh.

8. In the Front viewport, select matlmask, click Align, and pick glow-mask. Check Y Position, Maximum in the Current and Maximum in the Target to align the top edges of the two objects. Click OK to exit the Align dialog box.

9. Click the Select and Link icon, and click and drag from glowmask to matlmask.

NOTE

To accomplish Step 9, you will find it easiest to press H to select glowmask from the name list, then click Select and Link, and press H again to select matlmask.

TIP

It is important that both objects are animated exactly the same. By linking them you have to animate only one and the other will always have the same motion.

10. In the Front viewport, select the matlmask object, Restrict to Y-axis, and move it downward until it is just out of view. This is easier if you press the Spacebar to lock the selection before moving the object.

11. Move the Frame Slider to frame 10, right-click on the Frame Slider, uncheck Rotation and Scale, make sure that 10 is entered in Source and Destination fields, and click OK. This creates a position key at frame 10 for matlmask. Any subsequent animation will start at frame 10.

12. Click on the Animate button to turn it on, and enter 110 in the frame number field or drag the Frame Slider to frame 110.

13. Select and Move matlmask up in the positive Y direction until the top edge moves off the top of the viewport. After the move, press the Spacebar to unlock the selection. Click the Animate button to turn it off.

14. Open Material Editor, and create a new material with Ambient, Diffuse, Specular color swatches set to pure white (255,255,255) and Self-illumination set to 100. Name this material MASK.

15. Click the Select icon, press H, and choose glowmask and matlmask from the list. In the Material Editor, pick Assign to Selected icon to apply the material to the mesh objects.

16. Pick the Render Scene icon, and render Active Time Segment of the front viewport at 320×240 resolution to a file called MATLMASK.AVI. Use Cinepak codec for good results. This animation shows black frames from 0 to10, then white moving up until frame 110, then all white from frames from 111 to120.

17. In the Display panel/Hide rollout, click the Hide By Name button, and choose matlmask from the list.

18. Click the Render Scene icon, and, using the same settings as in Step 16, render to an AVI file named GLOWMASK.AVI. This will be a thin, horizontal, white strip moving up the screen.

Setting the Logo Scene

In Exercise 13.8, you adjust the material on the logo. The material contains two levels of Blend material, and you will use masking at each level to reveal the underlying material. The large mask will reveal gold under lead and the thin mask will reveal a strip of material that cues a glow effect in Video Post.

EXERCISE 13.8: MASKING THE MATERIALS

1. Open the file called 13max08.max from the CD-ROM. The scene consists of the client's logo. The file contains a logo, several lights, and a camera, and it has a gradient background. A material and a UVW Map modifier are already assigned to the logo. It appears similar to Figure 13.12.

2. Open the Material Editor, click on the first sample sphere, and click on the Material/Map Navigator icon. It looks like Figure 13.13.

3. A look at the Navigator shows that LEADTOGOLD is a Blend material type. Its Material #1 is a dull lead material, which shows on the logo. Its Material #2 is another Blend material made of a gold material and a reveal material that is just a pure white material with the Material Effects Channel set to 1. Neither of the Blend materials has any mix amount or masking, so if you render the scene you will only see the lead material on the text.

FIGURE 13.12
*Client's logo with
a complex Blend
material.*

FIGURE 13.13
*Material Editor and
Material/Map
Navigator for
LEADTOGOLD.*

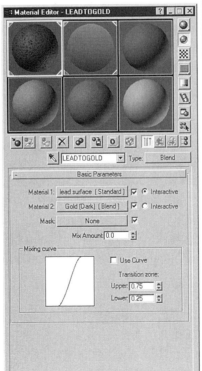

4. In the Navigator, click down the material list to view each material or map and its settings with the Show End Result icon turned off. Turning Show End Result off lets you view the material on the sample sphere.

5. In the Navigator, click on LEADTOGOLD at the top of the list. In the Material Editor/Basic Parameters rollout, click on None in the Mask slot, and double-click Bitmap in the Browser list. In Bitmap Parameters rollout, click the Bitmap slot, and load MATLMASK.AVI, which you saved to disk in Exercise 13.7. Name this level matl mask. Click on the Show Map in Viewport icon. Move the Frame slider to frame 60.

6. The mask appears on the text in the shaded viewport and on the sample sphere, white at the bottom, black at the top. From bottom to top is not the direction you want the mask to travel, however. In the Material Editor/Coordinates rollout, enter 90 in the W: Angle field. The left of the text now appears white and looks similar to Figure 13.14.

FIGURE 13.14
LEADTOGOLD Mask on logo.

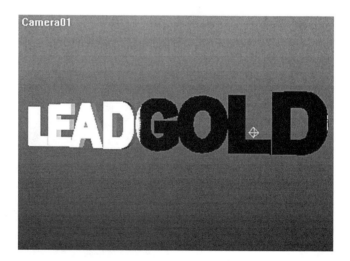

7. In the Navigator, click on Material 2:Gold(Dark). In the Material Editor/Basic Parameters rollout, click on None in the Mask slot. Double-click Bitmap in the Browser list, click on Bitmap slot in the Bitmap Parameters rollout, and get GLOWMASK.AVI, which you

saved to disk in Exercise 13.7. Enter 90 in the W: Angle field to change the mask from horizontal to vertical. Name the map level glow mask. At frame 60, you see the vertical white stripe on the sample sphere.

8. The mask from Step 7 reveals a material called GLOWREVEAL that has a Material Effects Channel set to 1 to cue the glow in Video Post. Render the Camera viewport, and you will see half lead, half gold, and a white strip at the transition of the two materials. It looks similar to Figure 13.15.

FIGURE 13.15
Gold and lead with a white stripe.

9. Close the Virtual Frame Buffer, the Material Editor, and the Material/Map Navigator. In the Rendering pull-down menu, choose Video Post.

10. In the Video Post dialog box, click on the Add Scene Event icon, choose Camera01, and click on OK.

11. Click on the Add Image Filter Event icon, choose Lens Effect Glow from the list, and click OK.

12. Click the Add Image Output Event icon, click the Files button, and name the file LOGOGLOW.AVI. Choose the Cinipak codec, and click OK. Click OK in the Add Image Output Event dialog box.

13. Double-click Lens Effect Glow in the Video Post queue, and click Setup in the Edit Filter Event dialog box. Click the Preview and VP Queue buttons.

14. In Properties tab/Source area, check Material ID. It should be set to 1.

NOTE

The Material ID checkbox in the Properties tab/Source area is not the Material ID # that you can change in Sub-Object level to use with Multi/Sub-Object materials. This refers to the Material Effects Channel in the Material Editor.

15. In Preferences tab/Effect area, enter 5.0 in the Size field, and check Gradient in the Color area.

16. In Inferno tab/Setting area, check Fiery, and check Red, Green, and Blue. The Lens Effect Glow dialog box looks like Figure 13.16. Click OK in Lens Effect Glow dialog box.

17. In Video Post, click the Execute Sequence icon. Check Range, and make sure it is set from 0 to 120. Click on the 320×240 button. Click on the Render button. When the rendering is finished, use File/View File from the pull-down menu to play the AVI file. It should be a bright, burning edge revealing a gold material under the original lead material.

FIGURE 13.16
*Lens Effect Glow
dialog box.*

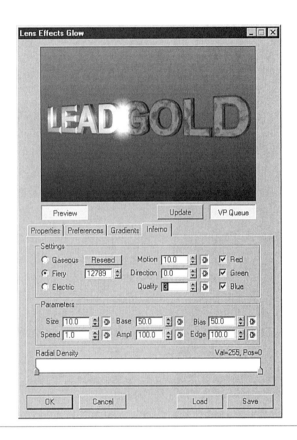

Logo Project Summary

In Exercise 13.7, you used 3D Studio MAX R2 to create two animated black-and-white masks. You used simple 2D shapes with a pure white self-illuminated material sweeping up an orthographic viewport. In Exercise 13.8, you then used the masks in a complex Blend within a Blend material. The large mask revealed one material below another, whereas the thin mask revealed a layer of material with Material Effects Channel 1 to cue a Glow Effect Event in Video Post.

In Practice: MAX as a Paint Tool

■ **Painting black-and-white images**. You can use MAX R2 to create a black-and-white image that you might normally use an expensive 2D paint software for. In the exercises, you created simple 2D and 3D geometry, applied black-and-white materials, and rendered the image to a bitmap to be used in a new scene.

■ **Painting colored images**. Instead of exiting MAX R2 and using other software, you can "paint" a simple colored image with 2D geometry and apply it to a complex object. Thanks to MAX R2's new Unwrap UVW modifier, you can move the mapping coordinate points associated with mesh vertices to distort the mapping for a better fit.

■ **Substituting mapped animated material to reduce render time**. In the exercises, you learned how to render a complex atmospheric blast effect to an AVI file, then apply the AVI as maps in a material to decrease render time significantly with minimal loss of visual effect.

■ **Creating compound materials using animated masks**. You can use MAX R2 to create simple 2D animated black-and-white AVI files to use in a compound material as masks, which reveal underlying maps and materials over time. You used two levels of masking in the exercise, but you have essentially no limit to the complexity possible.

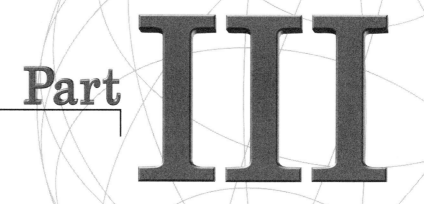

Part III

RENDERING EFFECTS: TAKING MAX TO THE LIMIT

Chapter 14

CAMERAS, CAMERA EFFECTS, AND LIGHTING

Perhaps one of the most challenging aspects of 3D rendering is the proper use of lighting and cameras. All too often renderings or animations remind you that many people simply don't grasp the key concepts of showcasing the virtual world. Sometimes they blame the software they used. MAX had an earlier reputation of producing renderings that looked too "plastic-like," for example. This may have been true, but the fact still remains that as a computer artist, you can stretch the imaginary bounds of the software to obtain the desired effects.

MAX's virtual cameras and lights present you with a host of possibilities for stretching to your virtual world's needs. You need only tap into the potential of the camera and light objects to really achieve great renderings and animations.

If you are familiar with real-world lights and cameras, however, you've got your work cut out for you. Virtually all of MAX's settings and properties for lights and cameras relate to the 3D environment on your monitor, not outside your window. For instance, there is no concept of an f-stop in MAX, but you can easily duplicate the effect of stopping down a camera through the Focus module in Video Post.

To help you make the transition, this chapter seeks to clarify many of the issues and techniques associated with MAX cameras and lights as they relate to their real-world counterparts. It also will explore the many possibilities that exist when you fully exploit the potential of these features. The chapter first looks at real-world camera terminology and how, or if, the features can be duplicated within the virtual world of MAX 2.

Specifically, you'll learn the following techniques:

- Real-world camera terminology and how to translate it to MAX
- Setting up lights in MAX based on traditional techniques
- Specific techniques for simulating certain camera effects

Real-World Cameras

If you look at any camera books, whether on shooting weddings or snapping off shots of nature, you'll find certain common concepts and terms. This section explains what they are and tries to closely map this real-world terminology with features in MAX cameras. Some can be duplicated easily, although others are not as straightforward. Still others are not duplicated at all without the help of a plug-in. If you've never taken a photography class, this section still has relevance. It's not uncommon to discover great techniques in the digital realm while studying real life.

Film-Based Cameras

Film-based cameras record imagery based on a film's exposure to light. The exposed film is then developed and processed. Film-based cameras rely much more heavily on light for proper exposure than a video camera does. Several factors play into the best-captured imagery taken with a film-based camera, many of which you'll explore later. For now, consider the two predominant types of film-based camera used today: still image cameras and motion picture cameras.

Still Image Cameras

Perhaps the most common form of camera is a still image, or still frame, camera—which includes everything from disposable cameras that you pick up from the drug store to professional-grade 35mm cameras. The way they work is simple. You first load in a film that reacts to light. When you're ready to take a picture, you press a button on the camera and it opens a shutter that exposes the film to a certain amount of light for a certain amount of time. We all know what happens when you reach the end of the film. You either bring it in to your local developer to get processed onto paper or—if you're a savvy photographer—you do it yourself. Whatever the case, the end result is a piece of paper with an image on it.

Duplicating a still camera in MAX is, by far, the easiest thing to do. Simulating such effects as film-grain and over exposure, however, is really controlled through a filter in Video Post. In fact, by using a filter in Video Post, you can duplicate many of the special post-processing techniques associated with still life imagery taken with a camera. For instance, you can use Adobe Photoshop filters for many of the effects. The key is knowing where everything is.

Motion Picture Cameras

Acting along the same principles of a still image camera, motion picture cameras capture action through a series of still images called frames. Frames in motion pictures are the exact equivalent to frames in MAX.

For the most part, motion picture films are shot using a wider image aspect ratio than that of video. For instance, your television has an aspect ratio of 4:3 (or 1.33 to 1) meaning that it's not totally square but very close to it. Most films, however, are shot at an aspect ratio of 1.85:1 or 2.35:1, which produces an image much wider than it is tall. In MAX, the aspect ratio is achieved through the Rendering Settings dialog box (more on this will be covered later). Although custom Image Aspect Ratios (IAR) are configurable, several pre-configured preferences enable you to quickly set up your rendering output so that it matches film aspect ratios.

Other common motion picture effects, such as anamorphic flare effects and distortions, can also be achieved through Video Post filters.

Video-Based Cameras

Video cameras work from the same principal as film cameras with respect to capturing a series of frames through a lens, but the way the image itself is processed is quite different. The image, once it passes through the lens, is converted to a digital signal and then processed internally to either a magnetic source, such as a tape, or to a digital storage device, such as a small hard drive.

Video cameras are the easiest to simulate in MAX, because there's virtually no difference in the recorded video versus what you see on the television monitor. Granted, the quality of the videotape itself plays a factor, but by and large the image looks similar. MAX is fairly fine-tuned for output to video. In the Rendering Preferences tab, you can set up your video color checking (a process for finding colors unsuitable for television) as well as field order (how the television updates the screen line-by-line). Even the safe frames were originally designed for video—even though they're just as useful, if not more so, for film.

A Note about Aspect Ratios

You'll notice that when you use the Render Scene dialog box, there are options for rendering to fields, but more important are the Rendering Resolution and Pixel Aspect Ratio settings. Typically, video rendering output resolution hovers right at about 720×480. This may vary depending on the type of device you're outputting to, but they're all pretty close. With the Pixel Aspect ratio setting, you can control how square the pixels are.

For a simple test, render an image out at 720×486 and use the default image aspect ratio. Clone that Virtual Frame Buffer (VFB). Next, render out to the same resolution, but this time change the Pixel Aspect Ratio to 1.0. See how the original image appears squashed, while the more recent rendering looks fine. This is because at a ratio of 1.0, the rendered pixel is exactly square— just like your monitor. If you output the first image to a television monitor, it appears to be fine, because your television "dots" are higher that they are wide. Therefore, your television takes a squashed image from a computer and expands it vertically somewhat. Figure 14.1 demonstrates two different versions of pixel aspect ratios.

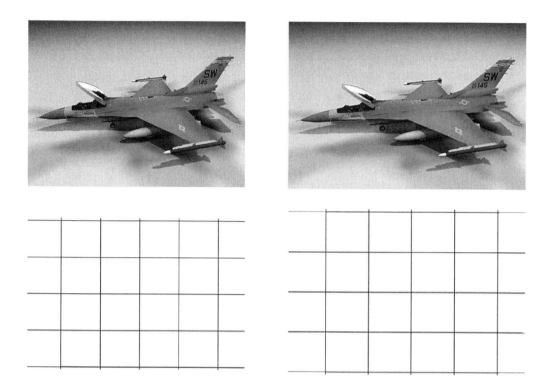

FIGURE 14.1
The image on the left uses a normal pixel aspect ratio whereas the right picture shows the image at a .9 aspect ratio. Note that the grid below is wider than it is tall for the right-hand example.

Film Versus Video Playback Speeds

NTSC-standard video images are captured at 30 frames per second (fps), while film is recorded and played back at a slower rate of 24fps. The 30fps rate typically results in video images that have crisp and lively characteristics. This is not to say that film imagery does not contain those characteristics, it's just very easy to discern the difference between the two.

Try a little test. Watch a TV sitcom, which was more than likely filmed using a video camera. Next, go down to your video store and pick up the latest movie (or have a little fun and actually go to a cinema). Watch the difference. You'll have to watch closely, but the differences are there. Perhaps the most obvious is the film grain, but even the motion appears to be a little less "hectic" in a film versus a videotaped image. This motion-related difference is a direct result of recording and playback speeds. Even a six-frame-per-second difference adds up to 360 frames in just one minute—12 seconds of imagery that's either there or not there depending on which format you're watching.

Fortunately, in MAX, duplicating this effect of film or video playback is easy to set up with the Time Configuration dialog. The default playback rate is 30fps, but you can switch at any time between the different rates. Don't worry, your total animation length may change, but that's normal. MAX is simply adjusting itself to the number of frames necessary to play the animation in your file at the specified frame rate. To test this, try this simple example: With NTSC selected, type in 1800 for Length. Then click Film for playback rate. Notice that the playback rate jumps down to 1440 frames.

Lens Types

Photographers have all sorts of options when it comes to lens varieties. From a normal lens to a fisheye, their choice of lens is usually dictated by the type of subject and the desired effect. A camera lens is constructed of several "elements" (concave or convex pieces of glass) within the lens' encasement. The placement and arrangement of the elements, along with the length of the lens piece, produce the different photograph effects.

Normal Lens

A *normal* lens provides photographers with the most flexibility, photographically speaking. The lens is capable of focusing to many different lengths and is comprised usually of six elements, although some have eight.

All of MAX's cameras use normal lenses. Therefore, you can safely assume that you're matching your rendered image most closely to what a camera with a normal lens would show in real life. MAX cameras, however, don't automatically focus to a specific focal length. This is controlled using the

Lens Effects Focus module. Along those lines, also, are the amounts of lens reflections that you'll see with a normal lens. As mentioned before, a normal lens contains six or eight elements. Therefore, you'll need to have the same number of lens reflections in your scene if you encounter any flares.

All other lens types discussed are modifications of the normal MAX lens through proper post-processing effects using Flare and Focus. Figure 14.2 shows a rendered image using a normal camera lens with a slight amount of depth-of-field blur applied.

FIGURE 14.2

A rendering showing what it looks like to shoot a scene through a normal lens.

Wide-Angle Lens

A *wide-angle* lens enables the camera to fit more in frame than a normal lens. However, this comes usually at a price of focal length. To simulate a wide-angle lens, simply adjust the MAX camera so that it views more of the scene. Adjust the field of view, and then use the Lens Effects Focus module in Video Post to shorten the focal distance of the rendered image. Wide-angle lenses vary in the number of elements, but most use about nine. A rendered example of a wide angle lens is shown in Figure 14.3.

FIGURE 14.3

A wide-angle lens is used to shoot the same scene as in Figure 14.2 from the same position. Notice the amount of blurring now occurring both in the foreground and behind the subject.

Telephoto

A telephoto lens allows the camera to get closer to a subject through a longer lens encasement and the use of special elements. Essentially, you can get closer to a subject with the same focal length. This typically has the effect of making the subject appear to be completely in focus and everything else rapidly out of focus as they exit the maximum focal range of the lens.

To simulate a telephoto lens in MAX, use the focus module with a shorter focal range. That way, objects rapidly blur as they get outside of that range. Telephoto lenses usually have about five elements. Figure 14.4 is rendered with a MAX telephoto lens. Note how blurry the scene is behind the teapot's spout.

NOTE

Focal Range is the area in which subjects appear to be in focus as measured in distance from the subject.

FIGURE 14.4

A rendered image through a telephoto lens. The blur in the background is created with the Lens Effects Focus module.

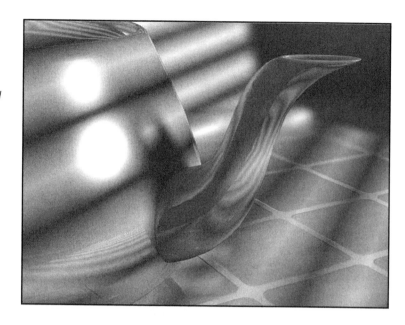

F-Stops

An *f-stop* is a calibrated number that refers to a small device called the *aperture,* which performs the same function for the lens as your iris does for your eye. By altering the diameter of the aperture, you can control both the amount of light and the depth of field of your photographed image. The effect of reducing the aperture's opening is commonly called "stopping down" the lens.

Typically, you would use the f-stop for situations where you either had too much light or not enough and had to correct by either increasing or decreasing the f-stop. Because MAX is capable of adjusting its light sources individually or globally, however, there's no need to simulate this effect through an f-stop parameter. In MAX, you account for light by manipulating the light sources, rather than an f-stop.

On the other hand, altering depth of field is one MAX R2's specialties. This can be easily simulated using the new Lens Effects Focus filter found in Video Post. Although there is no direct correlation to the camera's f-stop and depth of field value within MAX, you can alter the parameters adjusting both Focal Range and Focal Limit within the Focus module itself. See Chapter 17, "Focal Effects," for more information on how to set up depth of field. Figure 14.5 demonstrates the effect of changing focal settings to simulate stopping down a lens.

NOTE

Depth of field is how animators refer to the closest and furthest area where objects in your scene can be rendered "in focus."

FIGURE 14.5

These three images represent the effect of stopping down a lens. The upper-left image simulates a wide aperture setting. Both the upper-right and lower images use smaller and smaller settings respectively to increase the depth-of-field.

Film Speed

Film speeds designate a particular film's sensitivity to light. The faster the film speed, the more sensitive the film is to light. In most parts of the world, the ISO (International Standard Organization) number is used to designate film speed, but the DIN and GOST systems are also used. For instance, when you go to the store, you typically will see film speeds ranging from 100 to 400 for most consumer grade film, but some film can go as low as 25 and as high as 6400.

Slower film speeds are normally best for still life images or images for which there is enough light. Faster film speeds are typically used for darker scenes.

As with f-stops, MAX R2 has no direct correlation to film speed. When you're trying to match or simulate film speeds within MAX, consider two things:

- Higher film speeds tend to be less "contrasty" than slower film speeds.

- Higher film speeds are typically more grainy—especially when blown up.

Fortunately, MAX is capable of reproducing both of these effects rather easily through Video Post filters. You can use the Video Post Contrast filter to alter both the contrast and brightness of the image or animation. For images that appear to be taken at a slower film speed, increase the contrast. You also may need to decrease the brightness slightly. The reverse is true for simulating higher film speeds.

To add film grain, you'll only need a 2D image filter plug-in that simulates this. We use a film grain plug-in that is often used with Adobe Photoshop. In Video Post, you can add the Photoshop filter host into the queue and select the Film Grain filter to get the desired effect. Figure 14.6 demonstrates the usage of both contrast and the Film Grain plug-in to simulate film speeds.

FIGURE 14.6

Using focus, contrast, and film grain settings to simulate film speeds.

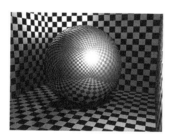
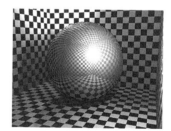
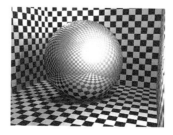

Lens Attachments

Lens attachments in real-life can add effects to the photographed imaged that would not normally be there. For instance, a photographer can add a soft-focus attachment to diffuse the light of a photographed image, thereby softening the lines of the image.

Because even in the real world you must add filters to get effects in your photographs or motion pictures, the easiest way to correlate this with MAX is to use the Video Post filters. A great feature of MAX, however, is that you aren't constrained by the real world, so just about anything is possible. (Two common lens attachments are discussed in the Lens Hoods and Soft-focus Aperture Disk sections.)

NOTE

Not all Adobe-made filters for either Photoshop or Premiere can be used in MAX. Filters designed by third parties, such as MetaTools, can be used without any problem.

Lens Hoods

Photographers typically use lens hoods to shield the lens from intensely bright light sources, such as the sun or bright studio lights. Fortunately, MAX actually must add-in lens reflections, glows, or flares. Basically, you have a lens hood on your camera at all times. In the Chapter 15, "Glows and Lens Flares," you'll see how to add in these effects—essentially removing the lens hood.

Soft-Focus Aperture Disk

The soft-focus aperture disk lens attachment gives intensely bright areas of an image halos. Using it in conjunction with a soft-focus attachment, you can softly defocus your image and have halos surrounding the bright areas for dramatic effects. MAX provides for this functionality via the Glow and Focus filters.

Composition

Computer animators who don't come from an art background are never taught the proper way to compose a scene. Scene composition is perhaps the most critical aspect of computer imagery—much like real life photography. There are several factors to consider. Lighting, camera angle, and FOV (field of view) all play some role in your composition. If your shot involves motion, you must consider other factors. For instance, your composition might look good at frame 0, but be completely off by the end of the sequence. Fortunately, MAX enables you to adjust all of the variables over time that you need to use for composition.

A Starting Point

In the virtual world, however, you are not constrained by real life. This means that rather than having to work with your environment to get the best composition, you make your environment work for you. In the real world, there are concrete factors that we simply cannot change. For instance, an oak desk will always be an oak desk, and to bring out its characteristics, you'll more than likely need to change the lighting in the room. In a way, this makes setting up a shot somewhat less of a challenge. Because there is less that you can change, fewer variables must be tweaked to get the best shot.

In MAX, everything is a variable; you can alter every aspect of your scene. Take the oak desk. If you didn't like the color or grain of the oak, you could make changes to the material itself and leave the lighting alone. In this case, you're altering the material of the object to suit the lighting—not necessarily a real-world adjustment.

Many novice animators get into tweaking everything over and over again thinking that it's the only way to get the best rendered image. If you're just starting out with MAX, stick to what you know at first. If you're experienced with setting up studio lights, set up lights in MAX as you would in real life. Get the lights tweaked just like you want them and *then* start working with the rest of your scene. Once you become a seasoned MAX user, you'll begin to feel more comfortable with adjusting several parameters at the same time, although it's not uncommon for veteran users to stick to adjusting just a few items at a time.

If you have no experience doing anything, start with an area of MAX that you feel comfortable with first. Most beginners tend to pick up camera placement first, mainly because it's something that you can see without having to render. Lighting is, by far, the most difficult concept to grasp and master in MAX, so it's not advisable to begin with lights.

Proper POV

POV, or *point of view*, is the point from which the camera views a scene. Camera placement, whether it be real or virtual, can produce radically different results. When establishing POV, you must think about several things:

- What's the intended subject?

- Are there any items in the scene that could be used to enhance the subject?

- Are there any items in the camera frame that could "steal" from the intended subject?

- If outdoors, where is the light coming from? If indoors, is the lighting good enough or can the position or intensity of lights be altered? (For MAX, the latter is true in both cases because you can actually move the sun if you need to!)

Ask yourself all of these questions prior to determining your POV. Establishing a POV when working in virtual space is far easier, because you can move or alter anything. This is not the case in the real world, however, you can learn a great deal from traditional photography. For instance, sometimes it might be useful to try slightly different POVs and not alter the geometry, but rather use focal effects to accentuate the subject.

Remember that POV can easily enhance or ruin your imagery in MAX. Thankfully, the camera effects that are available in MAX R2 make it extremely easy to set up proper POV. Figure 14.7 demonstrates a good POV to capture the size of the cathedral.

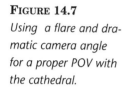

FIGURE 14.7

Using a flare and dramatic camera angle for a proper POV with the cathedral.

A Feel for FOV

While POV determines the perspective from which you view your subject, *FOV*, or *field of view*, determines how much of your subject you actually see and what's around it. Much like POV, FOV can enhance or ruin your scene if too much or too little is captured in the frame.

You can easily test if your FOV is too narrow or too wide by asking someone to view your image or animation. Ask them what they saw. If they didn't notice your intended subject first, then you probably need to alter your FOV (and possibly your POV).

With MAX, you control the FOV through the FOV spinner on a camera or with the FOV button when using a perspective viewport. You can animate FOV through a camera view just by changing the degrees over time. Many novices, however, think that altering the FOV means that you're altering the camera's location, but this is not the case; you're actually altering the viewing area of the camera itself. Altering FOV in MAX also alters the focal length of the lens. That's because, in MAX, both alter the same value. If you want to keep the focal length the same, but have the camera closer to the subject, just use the Dolly button. Keep in mind that the results are very different. Figure 14.8 shows how two different FOV settings can produce completely different results from the same camera position.

Using two different camera FOV settings on the same scene from the same camera position.

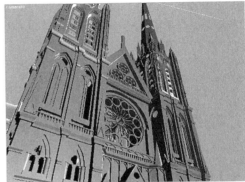

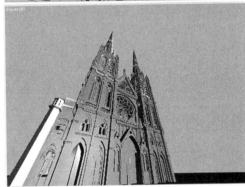

MAX Cameras

So far, this chapter has investigated what real cameras are all about. But the question that most often comes up is "How well can real-world properties be matched up to cameras within MAX?" Fortunately, most effects can be duplicated. Some are easy; some not so easy. It's time to explore some of the key elements necessary for setting up and adjusting your cameras within MAX.

Using the Right Camera

MAX has two camera types built in: *Free* and *Target*. The cameras work nearly identically; there's no fundamental difference in how they view your scene. Both have the exact same controllable settings and both behave the same when their properties are adjusted over time. The difference lies in how they animate.

Target Cameras

A Target camera is a nontraditional real-world camera, but very traditional in the computer world. A Target camera uses a camera object and target object to determine its POV. The camera can be moved independent of the target and vice-versa. Target cameras are great for imagery that involves one or more of the following:

- A fly-around, fly-by, or fly-over

- A tracking shot

- A still

Target cameras have their problems, though. The most common is the *gimbal lock* or *flip-around* scenario. Because the camera always maintains its Z-up axis relative to its target, certain problems occur when passing close to or directly above the target. Most animators call it the whip-lash problem, and it's the telltale sign of a novice animator. Essentially what happens is that the camera whips around the target object as it passes close by—sometimes in only one to two frames, which is completely distracting and unprofessional. Although you can't eliminate the problem of gimbal lock, you can minimize the chances of encountering it.

If your shot involves a fly-by, maintain a safe distance from the target, especially if the camera is above or below the target. Try to remain or be on the same horizontal plane when the camera's near the target. That way, the camera is not rotating along several axes as it passes by the target, but just one.

If you absolutely need the shot from above or below the target, keep your camera slightly left or right of the course so that it doesn't pass directly over the target. Otherwise, your camera will rotate 180 degrees in about one or two frames. Figure 14.9 shows two different possible fly-by paths. The path on the left causes a 180-degree rotation in less than two frames. The right-hand figure's path produces a much smoother fly-by because of path's trajectory arcs away from the camera's target as it gets closer.

When you truck a target camera, you have to move both the camera and its target. While this is not a hassle if you're moving in one direction, it can become quite a pain when you try to follow a winding path—say moving along a windy road that's hugging the cliffs. Although many seasoned animators deal with this nuisance, MAX incorporates another type of camera that eliminates the target: a Free camera.

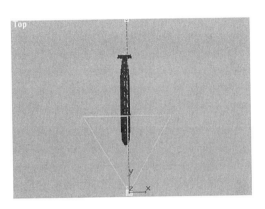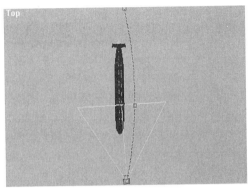

FIGURE 14.9

Using two possible animation paths for a camera. The right-hand trajectory is more desirable.

Free Cameras

Free cameras more closely represent a real-world camera than any of the others. With Free cameras, you basically point a camera object at the subject. Rather than moving a target to an object, you use the Move and Rotate transforms to point the camera where you want to look. For many new users, this might seem to be the more natural approach to setting up a camera. Free cameras work well for:

- Walkthroughs
- Panning shots
- Path-based animation

 The advantage of the Free camera is that it's not constrained by the target's location or the gimbal lock problem. This freedom comes at somewhat of a price because free cameras actually take more time to set up. MAX R2 does incorporate a new feature, however, that enables you to align cameras to the normals of an object. This is really the only way to quickly get a Free camera aligned. From there, any fine-tuning needs to be done through move and rotate. Understanding transform type-ins can be handy when making Free camera adjustments.

Here are some steps to aligning your camera to the normals of an object. First make sure, however, that the face you want to align to is visible in at least one of the viewports:

1. Select the Free Camera.

2. Click and hold on the Align tool, and wait for the flyout to appear.

3. Choose the Align Camera flyout (it looks like a camera with a grid).

4. Click and hold on the object (and face) to which you want to align. Much like the Align Normals tool, you can choose the face that you want to align to specifically by interactively dragging around the selected object.

You can make a Free camera behave like a Target camera by assigning a Look At controller to the Free camera's Transform track. By doing so, you have a tangible target object to work with, but you then are subject to the same problems as a Target camera, mainly the gimbal lock problem.

Matching a Real-World Camera

MAX R2's cameras have been modified to now properly mimic their real-world counterparts with respect to camera lens focal length. This means that a shot taken with a 35mm camera will now properly match up when you composite the live imagery with the virtual scene using a 35mm camera lens. Live-action shots using camera-tracking equipment will now match up properly, as well.

If you don't have a camera-tracking system at your disposal, you can use MAX R2's Camera Match to match up your virtual camera to a photograph or animation. Remember that the Camera Match feature requires that you know the proportions of the subjects taken in the photograph or animation to properly match a virtual camera to the scene. This means that you need to know size and location of the real-world scene. If you don't have this information, Camera Match will likely produce the wrong result.

Simulating Real-World Effects

Many of the effects traditionally created by using lens attachments or through lens manipulation can be duplicated in MAX through the use of

Video Post processes. Unlike real-world cameras where image distortion takes place as the light passes through the lens, MAX photographs the image first and then distorts it through Video Post.

Using Lens Effects Focus

To simulate anything that incorporates a focal effect, you should use MAX R2's new Lens Effects Focus module, within Video Post. All renderings in MAX are focused to infinity. Lens Effect Focus enables you to add real-life focal effects to your rendered image. You can achieve a general scene blur, a radial blur, or a blur based on a focal node (an object that you're focusing on).

As a general rule, almost every scene should have some amount of blur in it, since every photographic work we look at has some amount of focal blur associated with it. Using it in MAX means that your scenes will have an extra sense of photographic realism, which used to require a plug-in. For more information on using Lens Effects Focus, see Chapter 17, "Focal Effects."

Using Photoshop Plug-ins

Using Photoshop plug-ins within Video Post allows you to add custom 2D effects. Previously, you had to do them within Photoshop after you rendered the still image or animation. While Photoshop is a great image-enhancing tool, the application of 2D filters to an image or sequence of images can be done much more easily through Video Post while you're actually rendering out the animation. For still life imagery, Photoshop filters look great.

However, a somewhat serious drawback of using Photoshop filters is that they're evaluated every frame. This can produce animations in which the filters are inconsistently applied over the course of the sequence. For animated sequences, you should consider using Adobe Premiere filters. Premiere filters are also designed for animation and can produce much better results over a sequence of frames. Figure 14.10 shows a rendered image post-processed in Video Post with the Photoshop Filter module. Depending on which plug-ins you have, the effects produced from Video Post—especially when combined—can greatly expand your output options.

As mentioned earlier in this section, one of the easiest techniques to learn first in MAX is setting up a camera. Many animators, however, simply don't follow any one technique consistently enough to document, because there are several guidelines that you can follow when setting up a camera. By following some sort of guideline, you can either develop or fine-tune your technique until you're satisfied with one that works for you consistently.

Framing

Framing is the method by which you position and aim your camera so that your subject is within your camera's *viewing plane* or *frame*. When directors want something to be in frame, they're indicating that they want the object to be within an area that the camera sees.

MAX has some useful tools for determining what's in frame and what's not. MAX has always had safe frames, but with MAX R2, you can now size all the safe frame regions to their own independent values. Plus, you can now mask out the area outside the outermost safe frame. Figure 14.11 shows the usage of safe frames, combined with safe-frame masking at a 70mm aspect ratio. The result is that the Titanic model is framed properly for the "float-by."

FIGURE 14.11

Using safe frames and safe frame masking for a wide aspect ratio shot.

Basic Framing

Simple framing involves positioning and aiming your camera properly so that your subject is in-frame, or at least poised to come in-frame during the animation. When framing your scene in MAX, you should always use safe frames if you intend to go to video. If you're not going to video, you can still use safe frames as a guide for making sure the action or subject is in a consistent location for an animation.

For veteran computer animators, using the transform commands to position a camera and its target is second nature. MAX, however, incorporates buttons in the lower-right corner of the interface, providing all of the necessary commands for controlling a camera. Note that a camera viewport must be active for these buttons to appear. If you're familiar with these buttons, then this might be a good time to explore using the new Expert mode for your camera viewport. By using this mode, you can manipulate your camera or target through keyboard alternate as well as the transform type-in dialog.

Compositing-Based Framing

Composite framing is similar to simple framing, except for the fact that you are framing your virtual scene based on live footage that you want to match.

The footage, whether it is moving or not, requires that you make sure your camera's position, in relation to the background image, is similar to the real camera that photographed the real scene. As mentioned earlier, you can use Camera Matching for this particular operation, especially if precision is needed. Just keep in mind that you'll need to have the proportions of the real photographed scene to be able to match up your virtual scene. Figure 14.12 shows the usage of Camera Matching against a background to produce the illusion of new office buildings in an empty lot.

FIGURE 14.12

Camera matching 3D buildings against an image of a site.

Shot Angles

Shot angles, much like focal effects, can dramatically change the way the audience perceives your scene. Shot angles are usually set up so that the intended subject or point of interest is obvious. With animation, you have the flexibility of moving your camera into position over a series of frames. As a result, the subject gradually comes into frame not only making the audience aware of what it is that they should be looking at, but also building up an anticipation of what it is that they're about to see.

Traditional Angles

Traditional shot angles include the obvious. You can place the camera head on with the subject or slightly off to exaggerate size or location of the subject in relation to the surroundings. A typical camera angle is shown in Figure 14.13 of a carrier's flight deck taken from the bow of the ship.

FIGURE 14.13

A typical camera angle.

Unusual Angles

Sometimes there's a need to grossly exaggerate your subjects through intense camera angles and focal length effects. Say you wanted to make a baby appear to be a giant or a short underpass appear to be a tunnel to infinity. Rather than modeling a scene to mimic these effects, you could just use unusual camera angles instead. Figure 14.14 demonstrates what a normal versus an unusual camera angle does to a close up of the ship's bridge.

Real-World Scene Lighting

In the real world, lighting takes on many different forms from many different sources. Photographers have many options to choose from when lighting their scene. Probably one of the most interesting things about photographic lighting is that it rarely involves the available light. This is not just because the film cannot properly expose without a certain amount of light; photographers often need to change both the location and color of their light to illuminate the subject properly.

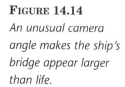

FIGURE 14.14

An unusual camera angle makes the ship's bridge appear larger than life.

With MAX, there is no film, so you aren't necessarily constrained by the limitations of exposure or color reproduction. Proper lighting placement and color, however, most certainly make a difference in the final rendered image. Animators rarely rely on just the default 180-value Omni light to illuminate their scene. They usually employ a mixture of varying intensities and colors, rather than one or two lights of the same intensity and color.

In this section, you'll get a chance to see some real-world light examples and how you might best duplicate them within MAX. Although there is not always a direct one-to-one correlation, you can usually get strikingly similar results.

Studio Lights

Studio lights are standard lights, such as floodlights and spotlights. Depending on the subject, combinations of lights in various locations and brightness are used. As you'll see, you can duplicate most studio-style lighting effects within MAX.

Direct Lighting

Direct lighting involves the aiming of one light, usually a spotlight, from a position off to the side of the scene. Direct light often produces dramatic shadows that actually become an essential component of the scene itself.

With MAX, direct lighting can be duplicated using either a Free or Target spotlight. Most users prefer target spots because they are much easier to aim. You'll want to use shadow maps with them, because raytraced shadows are just too harsh. For a more diffused effect, increase the sample range of the spotlight, which produces softer-edged shadows.

TIP

An important element to remember with respect to shadow maps is that they do use RAM and need to have a proper amount allocated to get the best shadows. Start with the default of 256 and work your way up in 256K increments until you're satisfied with the shadows.

With MAX R2, all lights are now capable of *inverse-squared falloff* or *natural light falloff*. Lights in your scene that use this new feature look much more natural, but inverse-squared falloff is a constant equation that's based on the light's intensity, rather than computer generated attenuation ranges. This means that the light will fall off much more rapidly than you might expect. If you turn on inverse-squared attenuation and your scene becomes excessively dark, increase the multiplier on your light sources gradually until the light is at a suitable level. Figure 14.15 shows the usage of one spotlight to illuminate the subject.

Fill Lights

Fill lights are used to lessen the effect of harsh shadows produced by a direct light source. In Figure 14.15, the shadows produced by the spotlight effectively darkened one side of the teapot.

If you want to simulate light being bounced by a reflector, you should use an Omni light with shadow casting on, but with a high sample range to diffuse the shadows. You probably won't want to use the inverse-squared falloff this time, however, because it could lead to large multiplier values, which, in turn, can produce unnaturally large specular highlights on reflective surfaces.

FIGURE 14.15

Direct lighting being used to illuminate the subject. Notice the harsh dark side of the teapot.

Figure 14.16 demonstrates what happens when you add a fill light to almost the same setup as in Figure 14.15. The darker areas of the image are now brightened somewhat and harsh shadow areas are better illuminated.

FIGURE 14.16

Using a fill light to eliminate darker areas of an image.

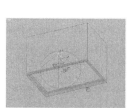

Lighting Areas Other Than the Subject

Filmmakers and photographers often rely on bounced light to provide certain lighting effects when shooting a scene, especially when trying to simulate natural light.

MAX is incapable of automatically reproducing bounced light without the addition of specialized radiosity rendering plug-ins. You can, however, simulate bounced light effects. The most common way to bounce light around is not to actually bounce it, but to exclude objects from receiving light from a light source. For instance, to illuminate a back wall with a spotlight without directly affecting the objects in the scene, you exclude them from receiving the light. Then, to make it appear as if bounced light illuminated the object's backside, you use an Omni light that excludes the wall. Figure 14.17 demonstrates this technique.

FIGURE 14.17

Using several lights to simulate bounced light in an indirect lighting setup.

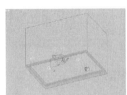

Flashes

Flashes are typically used to provide instant illumination for scenes in which the lighting is insufficient for the photograph. Because this is primarily a limitation of the film, it is not an effect that poses a problem for computer animators. Sometimes, however, you might need to simulate a flash from a camera, strobe light, or lightning bolt. With MAX, you easily can simulate two common types of photography flashes—*direct* and *umbrella*—to produce various effects.

Direct Flashes

A direct flash provides direct illumination from the camera itself. It is an aimed flash that casts light in front of the camera enough to illuminate what is in frame. Direct flashes produce a bright white or bluish light.

Simulating a flash is fairly straightforward. The most common approach is to use a shadow-casting Omni light—a new feature for MAX R2. Set the light's color to pure white with a slight tint of blue and the multiplier to 5 or more. You may also reduce the sample range slightly to produce more hard-edged shadows, but raytraced shadows are still probably too harsh for a flash.

If you have a raytraced, reflective surface, you'll need to use a spotlight instead of an Omni light, because the raytracer reflects the environment around the object. Using an Omni light, your entire scene will be lit by the flash—even behind the camera. The reflective surface will reflect the intensely illuminated objects behind the camera, resulting in overblown specular highlights.

Umbrella Flashes

An umbrella flash produces the same type of flash as a direct flash, but diffuses it so that the end result is much less harsh. Specular highlights are not as blown out and the whole scene appears to have a softer, more general illumination.

Simulating an umbrella flash in MAX is similar to producing bounced light setups. Because, in the real world, umbrella flashes use bounced light to produce their effect, you'll need to do the same through Omni lights. Because of the fact that bounced light diffuses with each reflection, shadows should be diffused accordingly. Try sample ranges from 10 to 15 and shadow map sizes of about 512 to 1024. Once again, if you have reflective surfaces, you may need to use spotlights instead of Omni lights so that you can avoid unnecessary intense highlights. Figure 14.18 shows a bright spotlight used head-on to simulate a flash that might be attached to a camera taking the picture.

Other Flashes

For strobe lights or lightning, the process is essentially the same. For lighting that involves a direct view of the light sources themselves, however, you'll need to use a Video Post filter, such as Glow or Flare, to get the proper effect of a lit light source.

Subject Lighting

Depending on the type of subject you're illuminating, you'll have to use different variations of light types and styles to get the best results. For instance, lighting the interior of a room requires multiple floodlights and perhaps a direct light on the subject. For illuminating a character, you might use a direct light from one side and a dim fill light on the other side to offset the dark shadows. Whatever the case, you'll need to determine where you want the attention to be focused.

For the most accurate realistic lighting in MAX R2, you'll need to enable two features within the lights:

- Shadow casting

- Inverse-squared falloff

If you use these two functions, you're almost guaranteed to have proper amounts of light in your scene. Shadow casting is nearly a must simply because all light casts some amount of shadow if it intersects with another object. The thing to remember is restraint, however. Casting shadows uses RAM, so you should only cast shadows with lights where you need them.

Positioning

Lighting position helps accentuate your subject. Depending on where you place the light, you can evoke different reactions from your audience. The type and quality of the light also plays a role in your final rendering. The images in Figure 14.19 demonstrate the same scene and light with the light in different positions. Note that with the far right image, in which the light is shining directly into the camera, the Lens Effect Flare module is used for realism.

FIGURE 14.19

Three different light positions enhance different features of the subject.

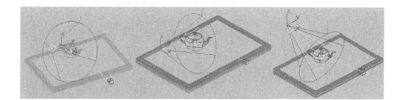

Dramatic Effects

Designed to accentuate certain features of the subject, dramatic lighting, like unusual camera angles, is less representative of reality. A common technique is to light a subject from an extreme angle. Rather than the light looking natural, the subject's features, such as edges and contours, are highlighted through intense shadows. If your shadows are too strong or you're losing too much of the rest of the frame to darkness, use a fill light close by that's relatively low in intensity.

Figure 14.20 shows the subject illuminated through dramatic lighting. As you can see, the effects produced by extreme angle lighting can make a difference when you're trying to stress topographical features of your subject.

Natural Lighting

Natural lighting is something we encounter every day. Although as animators, seeing daylight may be infrequent! Light coming through the windows, skylights, and direct sunlight are just a sampling of effects that can be duplicated in MAX.

FIGURE 14.20

Dramatic top-down lighting on the subject is used to focus attention on a particular area of the subject.

Direct Sunlight

Direct sunlight can be a challenge to work with and it is photographed in many different ways. Outdoor photography enjoys the benefit of having sunlight as a natural light source, but you frequently have to account for dark hard-edged shadows with diffusers or fill lights.

When re-creating sunlight, it's best to use a directional light as your sunlight source, because directional lights cast parallel rays. Although the sun doesn't cast parallel rays, we perceive the rays to be parallel on earth. In MAX R2, a new directional light, *Target Direct*, enables you to define a directional light similar to a spotlight. This takes out most, if not all, of the aiming guesswork.

When creating the light that will act as your sun, remember to think of what time of day it is. Some animators like to use the Sunlight system when building the sun. With the Sunlight system, you can automatically create a sun source that you can adjust based on the time of day, year, and location on the planet. One effect that's not taken into account in MAX automatically is the color of the sun based on the time of day. The real sun rays pass through varying amounts of our atmosphere based on the time of day. You'll notice that the sun is brightest about midday, while it's a deep reddish-orange during the dawn and dusk hours. Recreating this is as simple as changing the color of the sun light source.

You'll probably need to use fill lights as well. Sunlight is very bright, and as a result, a great deal of light is reflected off of various surfaces. In Figure 14.21, you can see that although the sunlight is the primary light source, reflective surfaces on the Lamborghini can be illuminated by reflections of the surrounding scene, most notably the windshield.

FIGURE 14.21

Simulating direct sunlight against a background of an outdoor image.

Moonlight

Fortunately, moonlight isn't all that different from sunlight in its properties. The main difference is the color and intensity of the light itself. You still get much of the same reflection of moonlight on surfaces like you do with sunlight, especially when the moon is very bright.

Much like the sun, moonlight also tends to change color depending on where the moon lies in the sky. However, the moon usually goes from an orange-beige color to a bluish-white color as it reaches mid-sky. Depending on intensity, shadows do exist and can be as intense as sunlight shadows.

MAX Lights

People unfamiliar with a renderer's lighting system might be somewhat confused at first. Rather than defining lights through wattage and bulb type, lights are defined by RGB color schemes as well as a host of other options. If you've been working with 3D programs, however, you'll feel right at home with MAX's lighting system. MAX supports just about every option that you could want—stopping just short of caustics. With a firm grasp of lighting setups, you're ready to explore using MAX's lighting system to its fullest potential.

Using the Right Light

With MAX R2, you now have five lights from which to choose. Granted, many of the functions contained within them are similar, but each light contains at least one characteristic that makes it unique.

As mentioned previously, MAX R2 lights incorporate two types of attenuation and two types of decay. The new attenuation uses a Near and Far value. Near Attenuation is designed to control how far from the light source you begin to see the light. Far Attenuation follows the same principal from the original MAX whereby it controls the distance at which the light's effect is completely diminished in relation to the source.

Using the Right Attenuation

Attenuation is not the best way to control a light's decay for natural lighting. Instead, use the new Inverse or Inverse Squared Decay options. Inverse Decay falls off less quickly than Inverse Squared but is not as close to real life. Recall that Inverse Squared is natural lighting falloff. Inverse gives you similar results with respect to decay but tapers off much less. You could use it if your scene is too dark with Inverse Squared.

Note that using decay with attenuation does work. In this case, it acts much like the Limits parameters of some modifiers. The decay now occurs between the start and end attenuation distances, rather than from the light source to infinity.

Contrast and Soften Diffuse Edges

You now also have the ability to control the lighting's effects on the contrast within the area that it shines. The Contrast spinner goes from 0 (normal contrast) to 100 percent. The result at 100 is a completely "contrasty" image, in which the image appears to be extremely blown out. You can use this feature to your advantage by exaggerating the dominant colors of an image and effectively eliminating its more subtle colors. The main benefit of using this versus a Video Post filter on the entire image is that you control where the contrast is overblown (or not) through the light—just as real life. This can be much more effective and easier to control than applying a filter to the entire image.

The same scene rendered with an shadow-casting omni light. The left hand image is rendered with the light's contrast setting at 100. The right-hand image is rendered with MAX's contrast filter set at 1.0 (and the light's contrast at 0). Notice how the shadow does not appear in the filtered image.

Softening the Diffuse Edge through the spinner of the same name can reduce the sharpness of the region where diffuse and ambient areas meet. At 0, the light produces a normal transition between the ambient and diffuse properties of a surface. At higher values, it can eliminate sharp edges that can appear under certain, harsh lighting conditions.

Note that both the Contrast and Soften Diffuse Edge spinners affect light's illumination characteristics. Although it doesn't actually brighten or darken a light, it does alter the way the light is cast, and this can be perceived as brightness changes. A simple test is to render a scene with the light multiplier at five and then another scene with the contrast at 100. The light looks brighter in either scene, but the results are fundamentally different. This is demonstrated in Figure 14.22.

FIGURE 14.22
The effect of using multiplier in lights versus the contrast value.

Affecting Diffuse and Specular

Finally, you can now control whether or not a light affects the diffuse and specular characteristics of a surface. A great use for this feature is when you want to use a fill light on an extremely shiny or reflective surface. If the light is intended to be diffuse, you should switch the Affect Specular feature off. That way, you can get the nice general lighting of a fill light without the characteristics of reflecting the source of the light in the specular area of a surface.

Omni Lights

Omni lights work well for fill lights. When used with Inverse Squared Attenuation and, a new feature to MAX R2, Shadow Casting, the results are extremely realistic.

One caution about Omni lights—especially when it comes to using multiplier values larger than 1—highly reflective surfaces not only reflect the light but also reflect the effect of the light on any surface close by. This can nearly double the intensity and size of your specular highlight. If you encounter this situation, try using a spotlight with a wide Hotspot/Falloff setting. That way, the light is cast in only one direction, effectively eliminating this problem.

Spotlights

Spotlights, both Target and Free, are useful for directing light and shadows in a specific direction. Spotlights were the original shadow-casting light in the 3D Studio series, so many people have gotten used to using them expressly for that purpose. Although the effect of shadows is useful, you'll now need to evaluate if the situation calls for an Omni light or a spotlight. Spotlights work well as direct lights. Because their area of illumination can be constrained within the cone of the light, you can avoid any messy light spillovers that might occur with an Omni light. Spotlights can also be very effective when used with projector maps (more on these later).

Directional Lights

Directional lights, again both target and free, function similarly to spotlights in many ways. The primary difference between the two light sources is that directional lights cast rays in a parallel direction, but a spotlight's rays are conical. You typically use directional lights for outdoor scenes that include sunlight, in which rays and shadows are typically portrayed as parallel. When you use directional lights with a projector map, however, you can quickly illuminate a scene as if multiple lights were in the room.

 In MAX R2, you can now animate the attenuation of a directional light. This means that other effects, such as laser shots, can be done much more easily.

Simulating Real-World Lighting Effects

When you mimic the real world, one of the most important aspects to consider is the proper type and amount of lighting. This isn't to say that you should build your lighting model exactly the same way as it might occur in real life, however. Doing so has the potential to bring even the most tricked-out PC to its knees. As a matter of fact, you can often duplicate real-life lighting with fewer light sources than required in the real world.

Take an example of an office space that's illuminated by several fluorescent ceiling lights. A common technique is to project an image of several light, soft-edged rectangles through a spot or directional light. The end effect is light that is believable but by no means similar to the real-life counterpart.

To take this scene a step further, you could use another light from the bottom of the scene to cast a light similar in color to your floor's surface color. This would produce an effect similar to radiosity, albeit faked. An example of this is shown in Figure 14.23.

FIGURE 14.23

A room illuminated using a projector-mapped light, as well as another light to produce a reflected light on the walls near the floor.

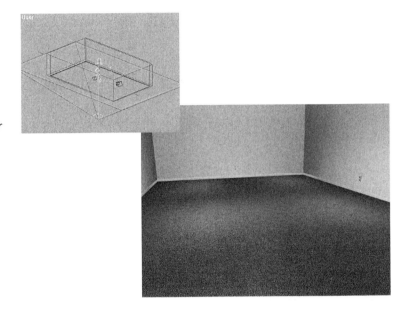

Lighting Techniques

There are literally hundreds of different techniques for illuminating your scene. A whole book could be devoted to just demonstrating lighting options. While it is not possible to cover all lighting techniques here, there are some hard and fast techniques that work well.

Building Up Your Light

A common mistake is to pound all the lights you think you need right into a scene. This might work if you build similar scenes all the time and have discovered a lighting method that works best all the time. Because most animators build and work with all sorts of different scenes, often little commonality exists between lighting setups.

Many users start lighting a scene without considering the materials they intend to use. They instead rely on MAX's default coloring system to give themselves some sense of surface properties. This technique rarely works in the end, though. Your lighting typically changes when you assign the actual material you intend to use. Usually, it's best to first assign your initial (first draft) materials before you begin with your actual lighting design. You can then later tweak materials in conjunction with the lights until both look right. Of course, some animators find other methods work best for them, which may differ from our suggestion.

When your scene involves multiple light sources, start by introducing one light source at a time. It's usually best to start with lighting the subject by its primary light source. Once you've added a light, render the scene. This way, you can check to see if the light is both positioned properly and that its settings, such as color and intensity, are right. Then add another light source. Each time, you're rendering and checking the effect on your scene. Note that you may have to go back and adjust some of the intensities of lights that you set up earlier. If you're trying to compare the effect of two or more lights on an area of your scene, turn off all other lights. That way, you can properly judge the lights involved and their effect on the scene.

Light Colors

Most of the light that we encounter is tinted with a color. Indoor lighting, especially fluorescent lighting, is usually perceived to be white, whereas incandescent lights are perceived to be a bright beige color. Note that this is the color that is perceived if you are inside looking in. If you were staring into a building at night that was illuminated by fluorescent lights, they would appear to be more bluish-green. This is due to the colors your eye perceives based on the light entering it. Remember, even at nighttime some amount of light enters your eye, which can affect the color of the lights you see as a result. If the light you're setting up just doesn't look right, try to observe the same light design in the real world—closely. Your brain knows that the light is white, but what do you actually see?

When setting up lights, color is always a critical factor. White light rarely works for all situations. MAX provides you with a default light of 180 in the R, G, and B channels. This is designed as a quick way to get your scene illuminated, but you shouldn't rely on it as your sole color for illuminating your scene. If you're having trouble with your scenes looking flat, try varying the color and intensity of your lights, so that the colors you want to accentuate stand out and other colors are muted. A blue surface completely absorbs all red and green light, and reflects the blue to the viewer's eye, which in this case is the rendered image. Thus, a light shining on a blue object must have some blue in it for the object to appear anything but black.

Lighting Options

When deciding how to illuminate your scene, you must consider several points first. If you know the types of materials that you want to use for a scene, then you're one step closer. If not, you should probably determine the types and colors of the materials you intend to use. If you're working in an environment where others are designing the materials for you or you simply are unable to assign the materials, then assign a wireframe color to the object that most closely represents what the probable material will look like. You will probably have to tweak the lighting once the actual material has been assigned because you can't always account for such effects as reflectivity or bumpiness, but at least it's a little less work than if you had not assigned a similar wireframe color at all.

After you've got your model and either your materials or a close representation of them ready, you can begin determining which type of lighting option you should go with.

Balanced Light

Balanced light is simply a lighting option that involves the usage of multiple light sources to evenly illuminate a scene. Essentially, this option works well for illuminating a space, such as a room or area in which there is no particular spot that you intend to focus the audience.

You can use a combination of Fill and Direct lights to evenly illuminate your scene. Balanced light typically involves many rendering passes to get it right. For the best effect, make sure there are not "hot-spots" (overly lit areas) or shadow spots. An effective light covers the entire scene evenly.

Large Room Lighting

Because you'll usually want to illuminate a larger room using Inverse Squared Decay, you may need to illuminate the room with more light sources than usual. The technique mentioned previously in which you actually use less lights (in favor of more Omni lights) will usually not work unless the light is cast in some sort of pattern that can be easily duplicated in a 2D image.

Large room lighting first requires that you set up the room as it would normally be lit. This is typically darker than is acceptable. You now have two options as this point:

- Increase the normal lighting of the room via multipliers. Note, with MAX R2, you can now globally increase the lighting through the Global Lighting setting located in the Environment dialog.

- Add lights that emanate from around the camera and point towards the camera's POV. The lights themselves don't need to be full brightness, so just make them bright enough to properly illuminate your subject.

Profile Lighting

Profile lighting is typically used for dramatic effects on profiles of characters. Profile lighting can either completely darken a subject against a very bright or white light or light a subject through unusual angles, as discussed earlier.

The technique of illuminating a subject from behind and having the profile cast a shadow onto a surface introduces a whole new topic: translucency. Translucency is a function of the new raytrace material (see Note). By applying a translucent material to a thin surface, say a box with 0 height, you can accurately reproduce the effect of a projected shadow profile. Simply aim a shadow casting light source at your surface and place the object which you want to profile somewhere in between the light and the surface you're projecting on. Figure 14.24 shows how the raytrace material can simulate the effects of translucency, which is needed for realistic profile lighting.

NOTE

Translucency is the transmission of light through an object. A lit candle illuminates the wax near the flame, for example. As the distance between the stem of the candle and the location of the flame increases, the amount of light transmitted through the wax is diminished. So, the correlation between the thickness of a surface and the amount of translucency plays a role in how much light actually passes through it. Light, because it is passing through a surface, will also become tinted from the color of a surface.

Until MAX R2, this effect was not possible. With the new raytrace material, you can now simulate the effect of translucency through a color or a map. The color of the map controls the color that is tinted in a translucent surface.

FIGURE 14.24

Using a translucent, raytrace material to reproduce a profile light setup.

Interior Lighting Simulations

Many times you'll actually be looking at or have a light source somewhere in frame. In such cases, you'll need to create the proper material and light. You'll also have to use the proper post process effect, such as Flare or Glow, to best simulate a light type. This section describes two common lighting simulations: daylight and interior light (or light fixtures). It doesn't cover setting up the right material or post effect, however. For more information on setting up light effects via a material or post process effect, please see Chapter 11, "Designing Fictional and Special Effects Materials," or Chapter 15, "Glows and Lens Flares."

Simulating Daylight

Simulating daylight requires that you know where your outdoor light is coming from. Because this is obviously a fictional outdoor light source, you have three possible situations to deal with:

- The point at which the light entering the room is in frame.

- The point at which the light entering the room is out of frame.

- The point at which the light entering the room is both in frame and out of frame.

In any of the situations, the light perceived entering the room is often a different color than what is perceived outside, so you'll have to make color adjustments appropriately. For instance, sunlight entering a room when the point of entry is in frame is often perceived to be more bright or intense than it actually is. This is mainly due to the major illumination differences between inside and outside.

If the point of entry is out of frame, you have free reign with respect to the intensity of the light. You can also use projector maps to fake the projection of blinds or other objects blocking the daylight's point of entry. Figure 14.25 shows how easy it is to simulate morning light breaking through the kitchen window just by using a projector-mapped spotlight and a fill light to reduce the darker areas.

Simulating Light Fixtures

The light casting portion of a light fixture can be represented in many ways. For an example that utilizes new features, examine a lamp with a lamp shade. Creating a realistic light source like this with the original MAX would have been next to impossible.

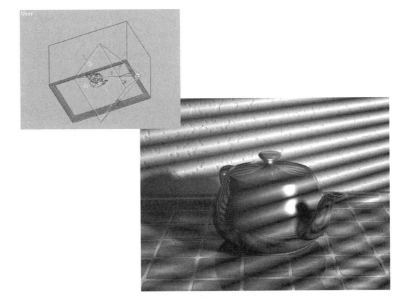

First of all, the lampshade is open at both ends. To get the right amount of light cast both on the ceiling and floor or table surface, you'd need to use two spotlights, one pointing up, the other down.

Next, to create a lamp shade that appears to be illuminated from within, you need to play with the Self Illumination values of the shade's material in the original MAX. With Translucency, you can easily mimic a realistically lit lamp shade. Because the light itself is not actually transmitted but rather simulated as transmitted, you are still required to add another light source that does not cast shadows in order to illuminate the space. Figure 14.26 demonstrates this new functionality.

All in all, interior lighting has become much easier in MAX R2. You'll find that all the new controls available—most of which are discussed in this chapter—will greatly increase the realism and overall believability of your rendered images and animations.

FIGURE 14.26

A lampshade illuminated by using a translucent raytrace material—an effect previously impossible in MAX.

In Practice: Cameras, Camera Effects, and Lighting

- Traditional Camera types, terminology, and techniques. You can take those traditional concepts and apply them to MAX cameras.

- Special lighting techniques and how to best simulate real-world setups. With the new lighting capabilities of MAX 2, setting up lights has become far less painful, but still requires a great deal of attention in order to get it "just right."

- How to use Video Post even when it might not seem obvious to simulate renderings that might use a specific f-stop or film speed. With the right filter, nearly any photographic effect can be simulated within MAX.

- How to produce traditional camera and lighting methods, which tend to generate the most realistic rendering effects.

Chapter 15

GLOWS AND LENS FLARES

3D Studio MAX R2 introduces a new level of realism in rendering with its new Lens Effects module. Artists and animators can now easily simulate camera flare effects using this new feature. Oddly enough, the effects simulated by the Lens Effects module are usually considered undesirable artifacts in traditional filmmaking or photography.

This chapter takes you through simulating various effects using the Flare and Glow modules of Lens Effects, such as:

- Applying glows to neon signs
- Using Glow for backlighting effects
- Using the Raytracer with Glow
- Using Flare for a sunrise effect

If you're unfamiliar with the Glow and Flare interface, take some time to go through the introductory tutorials provided by Kinetix with every copy of MAX R2.

Natural Glow and Flare Causes

Glows and camera lens flares are often caused by your perception—that is the way you view a subject. For instance, if you were to look at the sun (don't do this, by the way), you would perceive to see rays and an intense glow around it. However, if you were to look at the sun through a camera, you would perceive the sun to have sharper rays along with small discs-like halos, called *lens reflections*. In actuality, the sun looks much differently up close and personal. It doesn't appear to be the same when perceived from Earth at all.

Flares are caused by light emanating from a source reflecting in the lens elements of a camera. Flares are actually composed of several elements, one being the lens reflection. The number of reflections is dependent upon the number of elements in the camera lens itself. (Chapter 14, "Cameras, Camera Effects, and Lighting," discusses several lens types as well as the number of elements within each lens.) Other components of a lens flare such as the star, ring, and rays are all dependent on the light source's intensity, as well as its location within the frame of the camera. Lens Effects Flare makes it easy to duplicate flare effects. The trick is knowing what type of flare you want or what camera effect you're trying to simulate.

Glows are caused by bright light sources illuminating the surface of the object. Depending on the type of surface and the intensity of the light source, the glow can range in size and shape. Furthermore, atmospheric conditions can affect your perception of a glow. For instance, a chrome bumper on a car can have an intense glowing halo if it is illuminated by bright lights. That same bumper can appear to be just chrome in a normal or dimmer light situation. Sunlight is an example where glows are perceived differently depending on the atmospheric conditions. For instance, the sun on a hazy day appears to have a rather large glow around it, whereas on a clear day, its glow is much tighter and intense. Glows are typically perceived at the source as well. Lens reflections happen at the camera lens, but a glow occurs at the source object in almost every situation. Lens Effects Flare accounts for this, but it also enables you to glow the source in a 2D fashion—that is, the glow is not occluded by objects that block the rays caused by the light source.

Glows rely heavily on the intensity and color of the light source itself. For instance, a bright white light such as a car's headlight produces a more intense glow than a cool, blue, backlit sign. In either case, you need to alter not only the color and density of the glow, but also the size and softness in order to get the proper glow effect.

Many aspects affect how you perceive subjects in real-life. In the upcoming sections, you see how to mimic your real-world perception of glows and flares using the Lens Effects Glow and Flare modules.

FIGURE 15.1

Examples of both naturally occurring lens flares and glows.

Glow Keying Elements: Sources

The Glow module of Lens Effects is a great way to glow geometry, rather than light sources, which are the Flare module's specialty. The secret to making a glow look correct, however, is by keying off of the right elements. MAX R2 enables you to key your glow off one of several components—or sources—within a scene. In this section, you explore the common elements to key from, as well as why you would and should use them. Figure 15.2 shows the Source Select area of the Glow interface.

FIGURE 15.2

The Source Selection area in the Lens Effects Glow module.

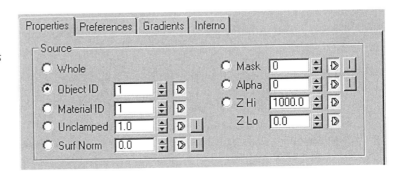

Glowing Objects

The Glow module enables you to glow objects based on their object (or G-buffer) ID. The main benefit of glowing objects based on their ID is that you can easily select one of several *whole* objects to glow. Essentially, you can pick and choose the exact objects to glow through the G-buffer ID assignment. Through G-buffer assignment, glows can be occluded by other geometry. The most common problem with Glow using G-buffer assignment is that G-buffer data is not passed behind objects utilizing fully or semitransparent materials. This means that if your glowing object passes behind a pane of glass, the object will render, but the glow will disappear. A solution for this, however, is through the X-ray plug-in from Digimation. X-ray allows G-buffer data to essentially pass through transparent geometry. An example of X-ray is shown in Figure 15.3.

FIGURE 15.3

An example of Glow with and without X-ray. Because the G-buffer data does not pass through transparent objects, the X-ray plug-in must be used to use object IDs as sources.

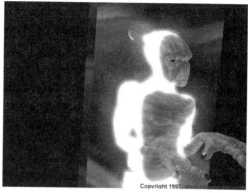

Glowing specific objects works for most situations. An example of where you might use an object as your keying source might be a neon sign. The sign itself is a piece of geometry that prevents you from using the Flare module for two reasons.

- Although Flare has a glow section within it, you can only glow light sources.

- The glow effect in the Flare module is always circular (except for when you use squeeze; then it becomes oval in shape). This means that you cannot produce a glow that adheres to the contours of the neon sign.

Most neon tubing color is constant. If it isn't, then you might consider using a glow based on a Material ID, discussed in the next section.

EXERCISE 15.1: GLOWING NEON ON A DINER SIGN

1. Load 15max01.max from the CD-ROM.

2. Render the Perspective viewport.

3. Notice how the neon tube around the sign is assigned a self-illuminated material. A pink Omni light is also used to give the appearance of the neon tube emitting light on the sign's post. To glow the neon tube, you need to change its Object G-Buffer ID. First, select the Pink spline that runs around the edges of the sign.

4. Right-click on the spline and choose Properties.

5. In the G-Buffer Object Channel field, enter 1 and then click OK.

6. Choose Rendering/Video Post to call the Video Post module.

7. Double-click on the Lens Effects Glow entry in the Video Post queue, and then click the Setup button.

8. Enable the preview option in Glow by clicking Preview and then VP Queue.

9. At this point, the neon tube should be glowing. However, the glow is too large and intense to be believable. To make the neon a bit more believable, reduce both size and intensity. Begin by clicking on the Preferences tab.

10. In the Effect section, set the Size to 3.0.

11. In the Color section, set the Intensity to 75.

12. Click OK to exit the Glow dialog box. Then render the scene from Video Post.

The end result is a neon tube that has a nice, subtle glow on it. In succeeding exercises, you see how to make the sides of the reflective sign glow as well. The final rendering from this exercise is shown in Figure 15.4.

FIGURE 15.4

The final rendering from Exercise 15.1. Notice how the glow is not overly intense— just enough to indicate that the neon tubing is illuminated.

Glowing Material IDs

Glow also enables you to glow objects using the Material Effects Channel. In the Material Editor, you can assign a material or sub-object material a specific channel from 0 to 15.

FIGURE 15.5

The Material Channel Assignment area of the Material Editor. Use it to assign Material Effects Channels to any material in your scene. Note that you can have up to 16 Material Effects Channels in one scene.

The main benefit of glowing materials over objects is that you don't necessarily have to glow the entire object. Many advanced materials contain several material definitions through, say, a Multi/Sub-Object material. With a glow based on a Material Effects Channels, you can pick and choose the elements you want to add the effect to.

WARNING

The Material Effects Channel is misnamed in the Glow Module as Material ID. In actuality, Material ID's are used with Multi/Sub-Object materials for face-level material assignment. The Material Effects channel is for Video Post purposes such as Glow.

Another, more hidden benefit of glowing by Material Effects Channel is that you can also glow reflections of materials when using the Raytrace material or map. The Raytrace map is capable of transmitting Effects Channels in reflections or refractions. As a result, the glow can now occur in areas of your rendering that were previously impossible.

In the next exercise, you see how to glow not only the neon tube in Exercise 15.1's diner sign, but also the sign's chrome frame.

EXERCISE 15.2: USING MATERIAL IDs WITH GLOW

1. Load 15max02.max form the CD-ROM.

2. Click on the Material Editor button.

3. Click on the first (upper-left) sample slot with the Pink Neon material in it.

4. Click on the Material Effects Channel button, and set the channel number ID to 1.

5. Now that you defined the Neon material to be a channel of 1, you can set that as your source within the Glow module. Select Rendering/Video Post.

6. Double-click the top Lens Effects entry in the Video Post queue, and click the Setup button.

7. Click the Preview button followed by VP Queue.

8. Choose the Material ID source option and confirm that the ID is set to 1.

9. Click OK to exit the Glow dialog box. Render the scene from within Video Post to see the glow effects.

Your neon tubing is still glowing, but so is its reflection in the frame of the sign! Try experimenting with different size and color settings. You notice that using different colors can produce different glows in the reflection itself. When you finish, render out the sequence to .AVI or to a real-time playback device to see the results. Figure 15.6 shows the completed result.

FIGURE 15.6

The final rendering from Exercise 15.2. Although it is similar to the final output of Exercise 15.1, you can now see the glow occurring on the reflection of the neon tube. This is due to using Material IDs instead of Object IDs for sources.

Glowing Unclamped Colors

Unclamped colors represent the pixels in your rendered image that are brighter than pure white. MAX always renders images at 64-bits but displays them at 24-bits of color. Other information—unclamped color values, Object ID, Material ID, Z-buffer, and such—might be stored within the image, but MAX does not display it unless explicitly told to do so. Now, unclamped colors values will be used *much* more within MAX R2 thanks to the program's new Raytrace material. The Raytrace material benefits from the fact that MAX R2's new Shininess and Shin.Strength (shininess strength) settings are unclamped to values of 200 and 10000, respectively. Metals and glass are now much more realistic as a result. This feature is available only in the Raytrace material.

In previous versions of MAX, an intense light created an intense specular highlight and usually caused a small glow on the surface of an object. Using the Unclamped color region in MAX R2, you can now easily glow these specular areas, as well as any other areas that are brighter than pure white.

In the following exercise, you add a subtle glow effect to the specular highlights of a Martini glass and cocktail shaker. The intense specular highlights are a result of using the Raytrace material.

EXERCISE 15.3: GLOWING CHROME AND GLASS

1. Load 15max03.max from the CD-ROM.

2. Choose Rendering/Video Post.

3. Double-click the Lens Effects Glow entry in the queue, and then click the Setup button.

4. When the Glow dialog box appears, click Preview and then VP Queue.

5. Set the Source to Unclamped and the amount to 1.5.

6. Click on the Preferences tab, and set the Effect Size to 3.

7. Change the Intensity from 100 to 75.

8. Click OK to exit the Glow dialog box.

9. Click the Material Editor button in the main toolbar.

10. Click on the lower-left material sample.

11. Scroll down to the Raytracer Controls section, and click on the Options button.

12. Enable the Global Enable Raytrace check box.

13. In Video Post, click the Execute Sequence button to render the scene.

Exercise 15.3 gave you a chance to see how using the Unclamped color region for glows can enhance renderings with intense specular highlights. It also shows how the Raytrace material is ideal for creating these intense highlights. Figure 15.7 shows the final rendering from the exercise.

TIP

When using Raytrace materials with glows, turn off the Global Raytrace option before previewing your rendering in the Glow dialog box. This will speed rendering time without eliminating the specular highlights.

FIGURE 15.7

The Final rendering from Exercise 15.3. The specular highlights contain Unclamped colors that can be used as sources for glows. This technique gives metals and glasses a more natural look under bright light conditions.

Additional Glowing Source Options

Although not as significant as the major glowing source options (G-Buffer ID, Material ID, and Unclamped colors), the remainder of keys available makes it painless to add glow effects to other areas of your scene or geometry. In this section, you see some brief examples of how you might use these other keying methods.

Mask

The Mask source option uses a Mask map that's determined by the Mask button within the Edit Filter Event dialog box. You can pick the areas you want to glow by using, say, the Alpha channel of an image. The spinner value for this source is a cutoff point. Basically, any pixel values in the mask that are higher than the ones dialed in on the spinner will be glowed.

Although this source is not very common to use, you might find it useful from time to time—especially if you want to give your rendered image the appearance of having a glowing image projected onto it.

NOTE

The Mask source option usually requires that you set your Glow Size relatively low, usually less than 5.

Z Hi/Low

Z Hi/Low enables you to glow a rendered scene based on Z-depth. Two values, Hi and Low, work together. The difference between them is the area of your rendered scene that is glowed. Z Hi is the maximum distance from the camera and Z Lo is the distance closest to the camera.

Using this option can produce a great "scanner" effect in which a beam of light appears to pass through a room and illuminate the edges of the objects as it crosses over them.

Surface Normals

The Surface Normals option enables you to glow faces of an object in your scene whose normals are within a certain threshold determined by the spinner value. Any faces whose normal is between the spinner value and 90 degrees will be glowed.

You can use this source option fairly effectively on flat surfaces, such as a cut diamond. As the diamond rotates and the flat surfaces became more and more perpendicular to the camera, they glow more.

Glow Effect Restrictions and Controls

Using glow in a scene enables you to effectively communicate brightness. However, a crucial element is controlling the amount of glow and where it occurs in the scene. The Glow module in MAX R2 enables you to constrict the effect of the glow to specific areas of the keyed source. Although it isn't essential to constrain the glow, you can enhance the realism of your scene by using the glow effect in moderation. In this section, you get a chance to see how the Glow module enables you to limit the effect and how the limits work. Figure 15.8 shows the Glow module's Filter Options section. (Note that not all options will be discussed.)

FIGURE 15.8

The Filter options section in Glow. Using these options, you can specify where the glow effect occurs on your source.

Glowing the Whole Source: The All Filter

When using Glow, there might be times when you intend to glow the entire keyed source. This is, perhaps, the most common way to glow an object and the one you'll use most. When you use its All filter, the Glow module places the glow effect on the entire source from the center of the source outward. As a result, the size of the glow effect relates to the glow's start at the center of the object. This is different from the way other filters, such as Perimeter, work.

In Exercise 15.4, you use Glow's All filter and some fine-tuning to better simulate the appearance of fluorescent light tubes in an office or lab environment.

EXERCISE 15.4: A GLOWING FLUORESCENT LIGHT FIXTURE

1. Load 15max04.max from the CD-ROM.

2. Select Rendering/Video Post.

3. Double-click the Lens Effects Glow entry in the queue, and then click Setup.

4. Set the Source to Material ID 1.

5. Make sure All is selected as the filter. At this point, the glow looks okay. However, the intensity, color, and size of the glow are wrong. In the next few steps, you change the settings to make the tubes appear to be actually glowing.

6. Click on the Preferences tab.

7. Set the Size of the effect to 2.

8. Change the color from Pixel to Gradient.

9. Set the Softness value to 15.

10. Click the Bright and Size buttons in the Distance Fade section.

11. Check the Lock check box on.

12. Change the number in either the Bright or Size fields to 2000.

13. Click OK to exit the Glow dialog box and then render the scene from within Video Post.

At this point, the glow looks much better. The process of adding Distance Fade adds realism to your rendering, especially for scenes where the objects fade into the distance over the course of an animation. For further control of the effect, you might alter both the radial color and transparency. Figure 15.9 shows the completed rendering.

FIGURE 15.9

The completed light fixture with glow added. Not only was Material ID used as a source, but also the Distance Fade options were set so that the glow subsided as the light's tube gets further from the camera.

Glowing the Perimeter

Glowing the perimeter, either with Perimeter or Perimeter Alpha, can give your keyed source the appearance of being backlit. This is because the glow effect does not appear on the object itself, but rather along the edges.

When using either Perimeter or Perimeter Alpha, the Glow module analyzes the specified source and glows just around the edges of it. Using the Perimeter filter is great for producing backlit signs. You can also use it to create halos around your geometry or materials. Be aware of a few pitfalls, however, when using the perimeter options. The first pitfall can occur rather easily on scenes without Alpha channel information. Alpha channel information is the area of your rendered image that involves transparency.

Perimeter Versus Perimeter Alpha

The difference between the two perimeter options is how they determine where the glow starts. The Perimeter Alpha option essentially uses the Alpha channel to determine where the glow is going to start. Because the Alpha channel contains antialiasing information, the glow will also be antialiased around the edges of your source. The rendered result is great. However, you have times when your image does not contain alpha information or your image is pure opaque—meaning a pure white Alpha channel. Therefore, Glow cannot determine where the edges of your source start and result in an inaccurate or heavily aliased glow.

This is exactly what the Perimeter option is for. Although not as precise as Perimeter Alpha, Perimeter can give you similar results without having to rely on alpha information. The main problem is that the resultant glow is often not what you want. So what do you do in this situation?

You have no perfect way around this problem. You can, however, minimize it by tweaking different variables within Glow to reduce the amount of aliasing around an edge. For instance, you can soften the glow effect. If you use the Gradient color option, you can reduce the radial transparency near the center of the glow by changing the first flag to a dark gray and placing another, lighter flag somewhere to the left of the first flag. Although not perfect for every situation, this band-aid solution works much better for animations because still images are often subject to close scrutiny.

Working with Backlit Signs

When using either perimeter option for backlit signs, you must take care if you plan to view the sign from different angles, especially in an animation. The primary reason is that the glow effect does not actually back-light the sign, but rather places a glow around its perimeter. Although this works great for most viewing angles, the more your view changes to looking at the sign's side, you see the problem. The glow effect appears to glow the whole sign from the side.

Exercise 15.5 shows this problem but in a situation where it is more acceptable. You use the same diner sign as before but glow the "MAX's" portion of the sign using the perimeter function.

EXERCISE 15.5: GLOWING THE PERIMETER OF THE MAX LOGO

1. Load 14max05.max from the CD-ROM.

2. Choose Rendering/Video Post.

3. Double-click the second (bottom) Lens Effects Glow entry in the Video Post Queue.

4. Click the Setup button.

5. Choose Material ID as the source, and set the value to 2.

6. Click on the Preferences tab.

7. Set the Size of the glow to 3.

8. Set the Color of the glow to User.

9. The glow will more than likely be too red. Click the color swatch next to the User option, and increase the brightness slider on the red color just enough so that it increases the glow's intensity. A setting of approximately R255, G7, B7 should work.

10. Click the OK button to exit the Glow dialog box and then render the scene from within Video Post.

FIGURE 15.10

Usage of the Perimeter filter on the MAX logo. The Perimeter option in this example gives the MAX logo the appearance of being illuminated from within.

Exercise 15.5 shows a situation for which using Perimeter works well. Figure 15.10 shows a final rendering. At times using either Perimeter or Perimeter Alpha backfire. In certain backlit sign situations—especially where the sign is mounted against some surface—there can often be a great deal of aliasing when using Perimeter Alpha or inaccurate glows resulting from using Perimeter. Figure 15.11 shows such a scenario.

FIGURE 15.11

A case where neither Perimeter nor Perimeter Alpha works well. In the image on the left, Perimeter Alpha produces aliased edges. The image on the right, which uses Perimeter, produces a softer but less accurate tracing of the perimeter of the logo.

To counter this, make a copy of the object that you are currently glowing using the Perimeter option. Scale down the copy along the depth of the object so that it is not as deep as the sign itself. Next, place the copy right behind the sign. Make sure that it is not encased within the original object. Finally, set your source to be the copy's Object or Material ID. The result is convincing and is easy to animate if you want. Exercise 15.6 shows you how to use the object copy technique.

EXERCISE 15.6.1: CREATING A BACKLIT SIGN WITHOUT USING PERIMETER

1. Load 14max06.max from the CD-ROM.

2. Select the MAX 2 logo object.

3. Click the Move button in the toolbar.

4. While holding down the Shift key, click and move the MAX 2 logo object up in the Top viewport.

5. Select Copy at the Clone Options dialog box.

6. Go to the Modify panel, and click the More button.

7. Choose Xform.

8. Click and hold the Scale button in the toolbar.

9. Choose the Non-Uniform scale flyout.

10. In the top viewport, scale down the logo on the y -axis until it appears approximately ⅛ the size of the logo.

11. Turn off the Sub-object button in the Modify panel.

12. Use the Move command to move the thin logo directly on top of the original logo in the Top viewport. At this point, you have a scaled copy of the original logo sitting directly behind it up on the wall.

13. Choose Edit/Properties.

14. Set the new logo's G-buffer ID to 1.

15. Choose Rendering/Video Post.

16. Double-click the Lens Effects Glow entry in the queue.

17. Click Setup.

18. Click the Preview button followed by VP Queue.

This will take some time to render on slower computers because quite a bit of raytracing is being used in the scene. At first glance, you have quite a few adjustments that need to be made. First of all, the glow effect is not being reflected on the wall. This is a problem that you can easily correct by altering the Material Effects Channel assigned to the object and using that as the source.

EXERCISE 15.6.2: Switching the Glow Source

1. Click the Material Editor Button in the toolbar.

2. Assign the "Light" material (upper-left material) to the cloned logo.

3. In the Glow dialog box, click the Update button to rerender the scene. (This allows glow to get all the new scene settings such as Material Effects Channel assignments.)

4. Set the source to Material ID 1.

5. Click on the Preferences tab and set the size to 1.

The color of the glow is fine right behind the sign. However, the reflection of the glow is a dull white. This is because Glow is currently glowing a color based on the pixel colors. If you specify a color or range of colors (using gradient), you can set the exact color that you want the glow to be—regardless of the color of the pixels generating the glow.

EXERCISE 15.6.3: Adjusting the Glow's Color

1. In the color area, select Gradient.

2. Click on the Gradients tab.

3. Double-click the left flag of the Radial Color gradient.

4. Set the color of the Flag to a light blue or cyan.

By making a slight change to the color of the gradient, the back-light effect is much more believable. The Exercise 15.6 series demonstrates two key concepts:

- Instead of using either perimeter option for backlight effects, create a copy of the object and glow the copy.

- When using Material ID's for Glow, you probably need to use a specific color or gradient to better control the color of the glows in any reflection or refraction.

The final rendering is shown in Figure 15.12.

FIGURE 15.12

The final rendering from the Exercise 15.6 series. The effect of a back-light can be achieved with glow, but using a smaller copy of the original object as the source instead of the Perimeter filter.

Gradient Design and Control

Gradient design is, by far, the most powerful aspect of the Glow module; it's what makes the entire Lens Effects module so useful. With gradients, you can design the most intricate glow effects that can be used in both still images or animations. However, it takes a bit of practice.

In Glow, you have four different gradients—two color and two grayscale—that you use in conjunction with each other to produce the various glow effects. The color gradients control the color of the glow, and the grayscale gradients control the transparency of the glow and are commonly called *transparency* gradients.

The first step in understanding gradients is to learn the terminology. Several terms within the gradients can make your life miserable unless you understand what they mean. The next two sections both explain and demonstrate the common terms used when working with gradients.

NOTE

You must be using the Gradient color option—defined in the Preferences tab of Glow—to see the results of changing any gradient.

Radial Versus Circular Uses

Glow incorporates two types of gradient definitions: Radial and Circular. They are used for both color and transparency. Both radial and circular can be used independently or in conjunction with each other to produce different styles of glows.

Radial gradient definition is determined from the center point of the glowed source outward. The left side of the gradient is the center of the glowed source and the right side is the outermost extents of the gradient that is determined by the glow's size (both by gradient and numerical). Figure 15.13 shows the glow effect with different radial transparencies.

Circular gradient definition works by controlling the glow as it travels along the perimeter of the object. You can alter where the glow takes as well as its color around the object by varying grayscale intensities or adding colors to circular gradients.

The trick for circular gradients is that they work based on the direction of the edges of an object. This means that if an object has several faces that point in the same direction along its edges, they all have the same glow effect on them if they fall within the right threshold. Figure 15.14 shows how the circular gradient works.

FIGURE 15.13

How a Radial gradient works. The left-most part of the gradient is the center of the radial cross-section. The right-most part of the gradient represents the effect at its extents.

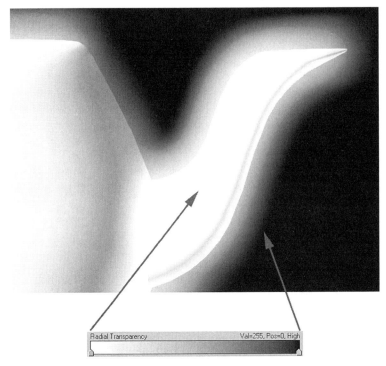

FIGURE 15.14

How a circular gradient works. The left side of the gradient represents the 0° mark. As you progress from left to right, the gradient's effect travels clockwise around the source object.

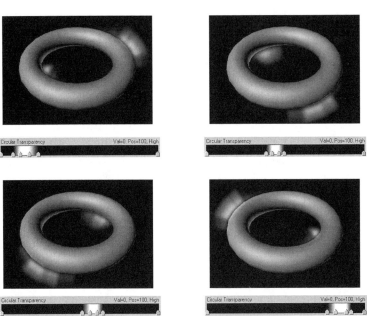

Gradient Composition Techniques

Both circular and radial gradients can be combined to add, average, or subtract their values and produce a hybrid gradient as a result. Color gradients are paired up with each other as well as Transparency gradients.

To control how gradients are combined, just right-click over a gradient itself. Toward the bottom of the pop-up menu, you see several options for combining glows. Depending on which gradient you click over, you'll also be defining how its corresponding gradient (for example, circular color and circular transparency) is defined.

Five combination methods exist for gradients:

- **High Value** Compares the values of the two gradients and selects the higher RGB value to determine the glow.

- **Average** Averages the two RGB values of the gradients—basically (RGB1+RGB2)/2. The resultant value determines the color of the glow.

- **Low Value** Similar to High Value but with the opposite effect. Instead of using the high RGB value, MAX uses the low value to create the glow.

- **Additive** Adds the RBG values of the gradients. RGB1+RGB2=Glow. You need to exercise caution here because adding some values together can result in pure white.

- **Subtractive** The opposite of using Additive. The lower value is subtracted from the higher value resulting in more dull glows.

NOTE

Nearly every module of Lens Effects uses gradients. All gradients use the same definition and combination methods. Refer back to this section when using gradients in other modules.

Building a Glow

Designing convincing glows consistently takes practice. Don't expect your first few attempts to be completely successful. One of the greatest things about the Lens Effects modules is that they are flexible. One of the worst things about the modules is that you can spend a considerable amount of time tweaking your settings until you get the "perfect" glow or flare. Fortunately, you can take some steps that can serve as a foundation for most of your glows. You can then build about that foundation to produce a customized look.

In the end, what counts is that the glow looks good. The following sections help if you've had little experience with using glow.

Determining the Source

The first item that you must consider is the source of your glow. What type of object is it, and what sort of material is it made of? A common thing for novices to do is to glow every light source or self-illuminating object in their scene. These sort of things don't happen in real life.

As stated earlier in this chapter, most glows happen as a result of atmospheric conditions. If it's hazy or smoky, glows are much more prevalent. If it's a clear day or room, usually only the brightest of objects appears to glow.

If it's possible to observe a real-life counterpart of your source, take advantage of it. Better yet, take a picture and tape it to your monitor. That way, you can more accurately build the glow when it comes time to mimic the real source in your scene. (Remember to use high-speed film if you plan on taking a picture of a source at night.)

Glows that occur much more frequently, usually subtle ones, are often left out by most animators. They can, however, make a world of difference in a scene's realism. For instance, a polished, brass drawer handle in direct light often gives off a very subtle glow in the bright specular highlights. For effects such as this, it's best to use Unclamped as your source and set the size of the glow small enough so that it's noticeable, but not overpowering for the scene.

Determining the Color

The color of a glow depends, once again, on the atmosphere around your source as well as the source itself. If for instance, you have a sun rising over a lightly foggy city, the color of the fog should be included as part of the color of the glow along with the bright yellow color of the sun. Unfortunately, MAX has no way of doing this automatically. A script, however, can help automate some of this process.

Determining the Intensity

The intensity level of a glow is usually caused by the intensity of the source, although atmospherics do play some role. A simple example is a light bulb in a room. If the light bulb is illuminated in a clear room, the glow's intensity is relatively low. However, if that room were to be filled with some smoke and the light bulb were lit at the same intensity, the glow's intensity would increase because the smoke particles would now also be illuminated. If you increased the level of smoke to the point where it was difficult to even see in the room, the glow would again be diminished. It would, however have a similar halo around it as in the mildly smoky room, just not as intense.

Building a Flare

Using Lens Effects Flare for the first time might seem a bit daunting. The interface contains so many elements that it's a wonder how anyone manages to build a lens flare—much less animate it!

Because you've already gone through the MAX tutorials to build a lens flare, let's take a look at some of the variables that might make the lens flare a little more realistic or complex.

Much like building a glow, building a lens flare can take practice. You have several ready-made lens flares that ship with MAX R2. A good practice is to try building your own lens flare from these. That way, you at least have some sort of starting point. (They're also very useful if you need a quick lens flare, and you don't have the time to build one yourself.)

The final exercise of this chapter deals with using some of Flare's commands to produce a sun-generated lens flare at dawn. You'll use a combination of Flare's effects to produce the overall lens flare. After the exercise, you'll also see what other options you can use to refine the lens flare.

EXERCISE 15.7: CREATING A BETTER FLARE

1. Open 15max07.max from the CD-ROM.

2. Choose Rendering/Video Post.

3. Double-click on the Lens Effects Flare entry in the queue.

4. Click the Setup button.

5. In the Flare dialog box, click the Node Sources button.

6. In the Select Object dialog box, choose Sun and then click OK.

7. Click the Preview button, followed by VP Queue.

8. Click the Apply Hue Globally check box on.

9. Set the Hue spinner to approximately 85.

10. In the Render column, set Auto Sec and Star to on.

11. Click on the Glow tab, and set Glow Size to approximately 100.

12. Click on the Star tab, and set Size to 200, Angle to 20, and Qty. to 4.

13. Exit the Flare dialog box, and click the Execute button in Video Post to render the image at a higher resolution. Figure 15.15 shows the final rendering.

FIGURE 15.15

The final rendering from Exercise 15.7. This shows the use of several Flare settings to create a more realistic flare—even from the default flare.

At this point, you have a nice sun flare in your rendering. As an added effect, you can also use Axial Transparency to fade the flares on one side. This produces a more realistic flare in the end because most lens elements are either concave or convex. The resulting flare on the element is not even across the lens but rather more prominent on one side or the other.

TIP

For quick, sure-fire flare fade, set the left-most flag on the Axial Transparency to black. Then turn on all the Fade check boxes for every secondary you want to fade. Figure 15.16 shows an example with Axial Fade on.

FIGURE 15.16

Axial Fade on the secondary flares. For Axial fade to work, you must use both the Axial Transparency gradient as well as the Fade check boxes for either the manual or automatic secondary flares.

If you like building from scratch, though, you can follow these quick tips for building a flare that might save you some time:

- **Turn off the elements that you don't need.** For example, if you're building the glow portion of a flare, turn off the secondary lens flares. You don't need them, and they force the glow into the upper-left corner of the Lens Flare interface anyway. When you're ready to move on to other elements of your flare, you can either leave your current element on or shut it off.

- **Copy and Paste!** Every flag in a gradient can be copied and pasted somewhere else. At least a few elements of your lens flare often share the same color. It's a pain to redefine unusual colors all the time. Copying and pasting helps alleviate this hassle. Obviously, this isn't much of a problem if you use pure reds, blues, or greens.

- **Use the Hue of your source.** This is a new feature added to the Lens Effects package for MAX R2 that makes defining a lens flare's color much easier. Rather than having to build a lens flare's color based on your arbitrary gradient settings, Apply Hue Globally uses the hue of the light source and applies it to every color definition of your lens flare's elements. For more control over the mixture of your light source's hue and the hue of your flare's elements, use the Hue spinner for each element.

- **Use Multiple Sources.** In Flare, you can choose to flare as many light sources as you want. Just use the multiple selection commands that you normally use (Shift or Ctrl) to select as many sources as you want. Flare will then flare all the sources with the same settings. This works very well for arrays of lights that have the same properties, such as runways or lights on a spaceship.

If you take some time to think about these guidelines when building flares, you'll save a great deal of prep-work that can eat up costly production time.

Determine the Source

Determining the flare's source is easy—it's a light. Unlike the Glow module that glows objects, materials, and a host of other items, Flare is designed to glow and flare just lights. In a way, this makes it easier for you to determine what your flare is going to look like.

The trick is now to make the lens flare look good for the light source. Sometimes, it just needs to be simple, such as a dimly lit light bulb. In other cases, it might need to be dramatic, such as an alien sun breaking from around a planet.

Because lens flares incorporate so many elements, they tend to be more artistic than glows or highlights. If you're just starting out building your own lens flares, the best thing to do is to observe flares you see—whether it be in real life or through various media. Science fiction movies and television programs are often great sources for ideas. You can also take just about any camera outside on a nice day and point it toward the sun—just be careful not to look right into the sun! You can observe not only the effect the sun's light has on a camera, but also how the flare moves when you move the camera.

Account for the Environment

Much like a glow on an object, the characteristics of a flare depend a great deal on the kind on environment in which the flare is occurring. For instance, in space, a flare might be perfectly crisp because you have no real atmosphere with which to interact. If you try to simulate looking at the sun from the surface of Earth, the atmosphere determines your flare's "crispness." By altering the Flare Soften value, you can adjust how crisp the flare is. A note about using Soften, though: Using Soften too much actually makes the flare look blurred, as if you're looking through a lens with some film residue on it. Typically, you use a combination of increasing both Soften and the size of the glow to simulate flares in hazy conditions. Figure 15.17 demonstrates a softer flare with a larger glow.

FIGURE 15.17

A more diffused lens flare using the Soften parameter. Use this to simulate a flare on a more hazy day or through a dirty lens.

Account for the Camera Type

One other element that most people don't think of is the type of camera that you use—or, more appropriately, try to simulate. For instance, cameras can have several types of lenses attached to them. Different lenses have different numbers of elements in them. As a result, the number of secondary flares change. Granted, this might be considered to be a bit nit-picky, but too many secondary flares can often be distracting and too few can often go unnoticed. Refer to Chapter 14, "Cameras, Camera Effects, and Lighting," for more information on lens types and numbers of elements.

Lastly, if you are either going to film or simulating film output, you should use the Squeeze parameter. If you change the rendering aspect ratio of your scene to a film aspect ratio, the flare does not automatically alter itself. To squeeze the flare into a more "anamorphic" look, use the Squeeze spinner along with the check box for the corresponding flare element that you want to squeeze.

FIGURE 15.18

An anamorphic flare from using the Squeeze parameter. Use this parameter for output to film—or simulating output to film.

In Practice: Glows and Lens Flares

This chapter demonstrated several concepts and techniques associated with using the Glow and Flare modules of Lens Effects.

- **Glow and flare causes.** In an effort to produce the best computer-generated flares and glows, it helps to understand that their real-life counterparts are caused by atmospheric effects.

- **Glowing sources.** The Glow module gives you many options for choosing sources. Your choice is often dictated by the type of scene and objects with which you work. Object ID is ideal for light bulb objects or neon tubing. Material ID is ideal when Raytrace reflections or refractions are present in the rendered image.

- **Filtering glows.** At times, you need to control where the glow effect occurs on the object. Through options such as Perimeter, Perimeter Alpha, and All, you can effectively define where a glow will occur on your selected source.

- **Determining sources for glows.** Glows can occur because of many situations but are usually the result of various atmospheric conditions. When you're concerned with how a glow should appear, just observe a real-life situation in which the glow occurs. If you're not simulating real-life, use artistic license coupled with real-life knowledge.

- **Determining sources and camera types for flares.** Because both the atmosphere and the type of camera lens you look through cause flares, you need to use some of the more advanced features of Flare. Use Hue values for taking on the color of the flare source. Soften, when used with Effect Size, is best for simulating hazy conditions. And use Squeeze primarily for film output or simulating the "anamorphic" squeeze effect associated with outputting to film.

Chapter 16

Designing a Scene for Highlights

When you stare down a city street at night or casually glance at a pond illuminated by the setting sun, chances are you've seen a highlight. Highlights are multi-pointed streaks that emanate from an intense light source or reflection of a light source on a shiny surface. In 3D Studio MAX R2, you can simulate this effect very easily using the Lens Effects Hilight or Lens Effects Flare module in Video Post. Much like the Glow module, Hilight and Flare enable you to add effects to many components of your scene. This chapter will show you how to navigate both the Hilight and

Flare interfaces to quickly add highlights to either objects or lights in your scene. For example, you'll learn:

- Controlling the location of the highlight effect
- When to use Hilight versus Flare
- How to use color with Hilight
- The advantage of combining Hilight with Glow
- Techniques to simulate candlelight

Hilight effects in MAX are 2D; however, their distance from the camera can control their size and intensity. The primary reason for this is that highlights actually occur within the eye. The highlight is not generated on the object. Candlelight is a good example. The moisture in your eyes causes the light from the candle to be refracted somewhat, and therefore your brain perceives the light has a highlight. Notice that the candlelight really doesn't have a highlight, but you perceive that it does. You'll need to remember this information later on when you begin designing your scene for highlight effects.

Highlights can often have a dramatic effect when used in moderation, but on the other hand, they can be quite distracting when used in excess. The key to building a scene with which you plan to use the Hilight module is to determine which objects or light sources you want to accentuate with highlight effects. This is not typically something that you do *while* building a scene but is usually an afterthought during the rendering phase of your project. You can save yourself some time, though, by thinking early in your project about what objects you might add effects to. This is especially true with shiny surfaces. Because material design can and does occur at many stages throughout an animation's production, you'll need to keep in mind that some materials might produce too many or too few highlights for your scene.

NOTE

You don't use the Hilight module for light objects, but rather the Flare Module. Hilight is only intended to work with geometry.

Working with Hilight

Hilight doesn't work much like Glow or Flare—in the sense that the modules are not set up the same way. Highlights are, by far, the most difficult to control of any of the Lens Effects module effects. The primary reason for this is that you have to set up your scene for highlights rather than setting up highlights for your scene—the way every other module of Lens Effects works. If you want highlights in your scene, you'll usually end up adjusting both lighting and materials to the point where your highlights show up in the right place. The Place Highlight command, when used with lights, works well for determining where the Hilight module places the highlight.

With that thought in mind, there are some things you can do both before and even after you've started to work with Hilight to ensure that your highlights end up where you want them:

- **Use shiny surfaces.** Hilight is designed to make shiny surfaces appear to be extremely shiny under bright conditions. The new Raytrace material works very well for this because of its expanded shininess capabilities.

- **Use bright lights.** Bright light sources bring out the specular highlights of your materials. The brighter the light is, the more intense the specular highlight will be and, consequently, your highlights will be more focused on the areas of your surface.

- **Use Place Highlight.** Place Highlight enables you to pinpoint where the brightest light will hit on the geometry. With this command, you can specify exactly where you feel the highlights should be.

Hilight uses the same type of source components and filters as Glow does. Hilight's Geometry tab, however, does contain some specific commands that differ from Glow—namely in its Effect and Vary sections (see Figure 16.1).

Using Hilight's Effect Section

Effect contains three commands: Angle, Clamp, and Alternate Rays. Angle is fairly self-explanatory, but how do you determine the angle that the highlights should be at? Typically, highlights' angles are dependent on the angle at which you're viewing the highlighted source. This is purely subjective, however, because the angle can differ between looking at the source with the naked eye versus a camera. It is safe to say that if you're viewing a source with several highlights on it, they all should be at the same angle; otherwise, the effect starts to become distracting.

FIGURE 16.1

The Effect, Distance Fade, and Color sections of the Hilight module.

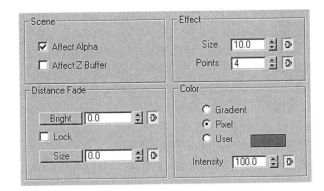

Clamp enables you to control how many highlights show up on a source. Think of it as a threshold value. You're controlling how many pixels Hilight is skipping over before it adds another highlight to the source. The higher the value is, the fewer highlights appear. This number becomes *very* important when you're highlighting an entire object and only want a few highlights on it, instead of everywhere.

Alternate Rays (or Alt Rays) enables you to alternate the size of every other ray in a highlight. The spinner value represents a percentage difference from the maximum size value of the highlight. Because this effect is repetitive and not random, you should limit your usage of it—it looks very computer generated when used in excess. Also, the effect works best when used with a point value at eight or higher, which is set in the Preferences tab.

Using Hilight's Vary Section

The commands available in the Vary section of Hilight attempt to randomize the size or angle, or both, through a random seed value. The default is just to vary the size. If you turn on the vary option for Angle, you will see why it defaults to off. When you randomize the angle, especially on scenes with only a few highlights, it looks very strange. Use this option only if you have a scene where there is already a ton of randomness—such as a rendering of a table covered with diamonds.

Color Usage with Hilight

Hilight uses the same color options as Glow, but your highlights may do just fine with using the default of Pixel color. The reason for this is that Hilight works off the intensity of a surface's color. Typically, the color of the highlight is the color of the surface.

You can use Gradient, however, to produce nice feathered tips that are a different color from the center of the highlight. Furthermore, you might also want to add many colors around the highlight. For instance, let's say you're rendering the surface of a CD. Typically, the highlights are rainbow-colored either from the center out or around the highlight itself.

To add colors to the gradient, simply click anywhere on the gradient itself. Hilight then places a small marker, called a *flag*, at the point where you clicked. If you then double-click the flag, you can change its color. Hilight allows for up to 100 flags on a gradient. If you'd like to delete a flag, just click the flag and drag it beyond the extreme left or right side of the gradient.

Using Flare versus Hilight

Although this chapter is about creating highlights, you need not use just the Hilight module to produce them. As a matter of fact, the only way to get highlights on light sources is to use the Flare module. The examples you'll explore in this chapter will show the usage of both modules to produce the most desirable effect. However, there are two rules you should follow when creating highlights:

- Use the Hilight module for creating highlights on objects.

- Use the Flare module when creating highlights on light objects.

In this chapter, you'll get a chance to explore three different scenarios in which highlights are used.

Combining with Glow

When you're using the Hilight module—such as when you're highlighting objects—you'll often find that combining it with the Glow module works well. When you have shiny metals under an intense light, for instance, there is often a soft, diffused glow around the specular highlights. If you place a small, controlled glow around the Unclamped color region, the shininess of the metal looks a bit more dramatic—and the highlight enhances it even further. For more information on how to use the Glow module, refer to Chapter 15, "Glows and Lens Flares," or the MAX R2 documentation. Figure 16.2 shows how adding a glow just to the specular highlights on shiny metals is a great setup for placing highlights on top.

FIGURE 16.2

Three examples of the same shiny-surfaced scene. The upper-left figure is the rendering without any effects added. In the upper-right figure, just Glow is used. In the lower, middle figure, both Glow and Hilight are used.

Shiny Surfaces

Shiny surfaces, such as metals or glass, are usually part of most renderings. When designing a shiny material, you'll often find yourself struggling to get the shininess to render just right. More often than not, you can easily make a surface look shinier just by adding a subtle glow and highlight. Even just the addition of a highlight can make a surface appear to be more shiny—without changing the material. Of course, there are times when it is the material itself. You may need to alter the material's shininess or shininess strength properties. For more information on designing materials, both shiny and dull, refer to Part II, "Designing Convincing Materials."

In Exercise 16.1, you'll use the combination of Glow and Hilight to create the same rendering as shown in Figure 16.2 on a brass door handle. You'll first start by preparing the glow, and then you'll add the highlight. The scene is using the Raytrace Material, new to MAX R2, for adding the intense specular highlights to the brass handle.

EXERCISE 16.1: ADDING HIGHLIGHTS TO SHINY METALS

1. Load 16max01.max. Click the Render Scene button to see the scene without any highlights.

2. Choose Rendering/Video Post.3. Double-click the Lens Effects Glow entry in the queue and then click the Setup button.

3. To see your rendered scene in the Hilight module, click Preview, followed by VP Queue. (Note that this may take a few moments on slower computers.)

4. Set the source to Unclamped and the value to 1.2.

5. Click the Preferences tab. For Size, enter 2.0; for Intensity, enter 50.0. This produces a soft glow on the specular highlights of the handle.

6. Click OK to exit Glow.

7. Double-click the Lens Effects Hilight entry in the queue. Click the Setup button.

8. Click Preview, followed by VP Queue.

9. Set the source to Unclamped and the value to 2.0. Set the filter to All.

10. Click the Geometry tab.

11. Set the Clamp to 35.

12. Click OK to exit the Hilight dialog.

13. Render the scene from Video Post at 640 × 480

14. Save your completed scene to a new filename.

FIGURE 16.3

The completed rendering from Exercise 16.1. For shiny surfaces, it's often a good idea to use both Glow and Hilight to properly accentuate the specular highlights on a surface.

At this point, you have a brightly lit brass door handle with a soft glow and highlight applied to it. You could add or remove some of the highlights by altering the Clamp setting in the Hilight Geometry tab. Figure 16.3 depicts the final result from Exercise 16.1.

Notice that your 640 × 480 rendering does not look the same as the preview in the Hilight module. Although this isn't the result of a bug, the difference does point out a limitation of using the Preview function. Hilight is based on pixels; therefore, the fewer pixels it has to work with, the fewer overall highlights there will be. The same rendering at 320 × 240, by the way, looks identical to the preview in Hilight. There's no real way around this limitation other than to render out your scene at full resolution to test your Hilight settings.

Candlelight Highlights with Flare

Candlelight, like other light sources, looks different when viewed with the naked eye versus through a camera lens. When you view it with the naked eye, you typically see the flame and perhaps a very subtle glow or highlight right around the flame. Looking through a camera lens presents a bit more of a challenge, though. The glow is usually accentuated, there is a streak running through the center of the flame, and you may even have lens element flares.

Adding highlights to a lit candle usually does not involve using the Hilight module. You may use Hilight to add an effect to a surface illuminated by the candle, but not on the candlelight itself. Instead, you'll find yourself using the Flare module and the trick of using it is not to go overboard. By default, Flare adds rays and all kinds of secondary flares, which is usually wrong for candlelight. You'll find yourself doing a good deal of tweaking to get the highlight just right. One of the best ways to simulate candlelight is to look at a lit candle through a camera and with the naked eye. Look at the candle from different angles and in different ambient light situations. You'll find that the results of the highlight can differ significantly.

If you don't have a candle or a camera, then don't worry. Exercise 16.2 takes you through the steps of building a possible situation with a lit candle. Before you start the exercise, take some time to take a look at how the scene is set up. Here are some key items:

- **The Omni light used:** The light used is a shadow-casting light that is tinted a shade of orange-yellow. It is also set to Inverse-squared decay. The result is that the light emitted looks more natural.

- **The candle wax material:** The candle wax is a Raytrace material with the Extra Lighting feature used. Although Translucency may work here, Extra Lighting with a gradient intensity map works better.

- **The Combustion setting:** To produce some sort of flame, combustion must be used. Although video captured flames may work, combustion already comes with MAX. With a little time spent, you can animate combustion easily.

In this next exercise, you'll use a rather unconventional method for adding a highlight to a scene—with Flare. To properly highlight light sources, you must use Flare. The effect does work, but you need only use a few components of Flare to get it right. As a matter of fact, overusing Flare can be very distracting.

EXERCISE 16.2: HIGHLIGHTING A CANDLE

1. Load 16max02.max and render the scene.

2. Choose Rendering/Video Post.

3. Double-click the Flare entry and click the Setup button.

4. In Flare, click the Preview button, followed by VP Queue.

5. Check the Apply Hue Globally checkbox on, and set the Hue value to about 80.

6. Set the Soften value to 4.

7. Uncheck the Render option for Ring and Rays, then turn on the Render option for Streak. Note that these are the checkboxes in the lower right-hand portion of the Flare interface—not the small preview window checkboxes.

8. Right-click the Axial Transparency gradient.

9. Choose Load Gradient and load axial.dgr.

10. Click the M Sec tab. (Make sure the settings for Man Sec 3 are being displayed. You can determine this by looking to the right of the "< >" arrow buttons.)

11. Right-click the Radial Transparency gradient. Choose Load Gradient and load flare3.dgr.

12. Set the size of the secondary flare (M Sec) to about 110, set the Plane value for the secondary flare to about 50, and check the Fade checkbox on.

13. To create the other secondary flare, click the Advance Flare button (it looks like a ">") to go to Man Sec flare 4.

14. Right-click the Radial Transparency gradient. Choose Load Gradient and load flare4.dgr.

15. Make the second flare smaller than the first, by setting the size of the secondary flare to about 25. Set the Plane value for the secondary flare to about 20, and check the Fade checkbox on.

16. Click the Streak tab and set the Size to 200, the Angle to 90, and the Width to 15.

17. Click OK to save the changes and exit Flare and render out the scene from Video Post. You'll now see a subtle but effective highlight on the flame.

This exercise focused on the use of Flare to produce a highlight effect. To produce this exercise, Jeremy spent time analyzing a real candle through both the naked eye and a camera's lens and the results of Exercise 16.2 are based upon his observations. Although nearly every highlight or flare effect is subjective, this exercise gives you an excellent idea of what it takes to produce an accurate, realistic highlight effect. The results from the exercise are displayed in Figure 16.4.

FIGURE 16.4

The final result of Exercise 16.2. When using Flare to create highlights on light sources, you only need a few components to make the effect look convincing.

Using Hilight on an Entire Object

There will be times when you'll want to add highlights to the entire surface of an object, not just in the bright areas. You may want to scatter highlights, for instance, across a surface made out of glitter or sequins. There will be other occasions where using Unclamped may be unsuitable because other shiny or bright surfaces exist in the rendering—surfaces to which you don't want to add highlights. An example of this would be a character in a sequin gown and the brass section of a big band behind the character. You might want to add highlights to just the gown and not the shiny brass horns. The best option is to highlight by Object ID, and use both the Brightness filter and Clamp threshold to control the amount for highlights added.

The final exercise of this chapter explores adding highlights to a morning sunrise over the water. You'll use the techniques described in this section to add highlights across the surface of the water. As before with other exercises, take some time to look at the way the scene is set up—primarily the location of the light source and the material being used for the water.

EXERCISE 16.3: SUNRISE ON GOLDEN POND

1. Load 16max03.max. Render the Environment viewport.

2. Choose Rendering/Video Post.

3. Double-click the Lens Hilight entry in the queue and click the Setup button.

4. Set the Source to Object ID 2.

5. To create highlights based on the brightness of the sun's reflections, choose the Bright filter, and set the value to 200.

6. Click the Geometry tab and set the Clamp value to 60.

7. Click the Preferences tab.

8. In the Distance Fade section, turn on both Size and Bright, and click the Lock checkbox on.

9. To reduce the brightness of the highlights that are far from the camera, set either the Bright or Size value in the Distance Fade section to 1000.

10. Click OK to exit the Hilight dialog box.

11. Render the scene.

After the scene renders, you can see how well placed the highlights are on the surface of the water. Once again, you might try experimenting with the settings of the highlight to see how well (or badly) the effect adjusts. For an added treat, go the Rendering/Environment dialog, and activate the Clouds environmental effect that is currently disabled. The rendering time will be longer—but well worth it. Figure 16.5 shows the end result with Clouds turned on.

FIGURE 16.5

The final result from Exercise 16.3, plus Clouds. Notice how the highlights are evenly distributed across the illuminated areas of the water's surface. This is due to the usage of the clamp feature within Hilight.

In Practice: Highlights

- **Hilight works differently than most of the Lens Effects modules.** Instead of designing a highlight for a scene, the reverse is usually the case. More often than not, you'll find yourself figuring out ways to build a scene to take advantage of the Hilight module.

- **Hilight is for Geometry and Flare is for light sources.** Remember that when you plan on highlighting a light source, you'll need to use the Flare module. Hilight is intended to work with geometry and materials.

- **Use Glow and Hilight together.** When highlighting shiny surfaces, it's a good idea to enhance the effect of a highlight by also adding in a glow on Unclamped color regions.

- **Use only portions of Flare for highlighting lights.** Flare has many components to it. To use Flare as a highlight-like effect, you need only use Glow, Secondary Flares, and Streak.

Chapter 17

FOCAL EFFECTS

If you've ever worked with a real camera before, you know about focus. Even if the only camera you've ever owned had auto-focus, you at least know that someone or something had to focus in order for the photograph to turn out nice and crisp. When you pick up your pictures from the developer, you often see the effects of focus. Some of your pictures are nice and in focus, some are completely out of focus, and in others part of the picture is in focus and the rest isn't.

All these effects were, believe it or not, impossible to accomplish in MAX 1 without a plug-in. Most of its resulting images looked computer-generated for one reason: no focal effects. If you've ever done a close-up shot of something using MAX, you've probably noticed that everything is in focus. Although this is nice, it doesn't accurately represent what you see in real-life or what a real camera would see.

The Lens Effects Focus module within Video Post makes it easier for you to simulate camera focal effects by blurring the scene based on scene elements, such as focal points, or distance from the center of the frame out. In any case, focus helps add a bit more realism to your rendered scenes. The Lens Effects interface is shown in Figure 17.1. To get a better idea of how focus works in MAX R2, you'll explore the following:

■ Focus terminology

■ The three types of focal blurs

■ Adjusting and controlling the focus ranges

Focus Terminology

Several terms describe both how a camera focuses and what the resultant effects are. However, traditional labels don't always match up with what programmers call items in their interfaces. In Focus, you have three main terms (with concepts) that you must first understand before diving into the module.

The next three sections take you through those three elements. Where possible, parallels have been drawn to real-world terminology for those who've had some photography experience. Note that you can do many things with the Focus module to simulate focal effects, but it doesn't have any equivalents to such items as f-stops or focal length (with respect to focal properties).

Focal Loss

The Focus module's Focal Loss settings provide for the amount of blur occurring in the scene. The higher the focal loss, the more blurry your scene will be. The two settings Horiz Focal Loss (for horizontal blur) and Vert Focal Loss (for vertical blur) enable you to blur more on one axis than the other. This capability is useful if you're trying to simulate, for example, looking through a pair of glasses and then taking them off. Several animators have actually complained that it's difficult to look at the Focus module's preview window when they are blurring more on the horizontal axis than the vertical—it looks too much like they're not wearing their corrective lenses!

FIGURE 17.1

The Lens Effects Focus module's interface. Notice how simple the interface is—only one panel and just a few settings. Mastering those settings, however, can be a challenge.

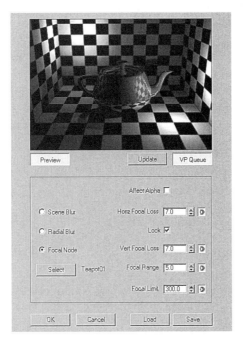

The key thing to remember about focal loss is to use it in moderation. The default setting of 30 is too high for anything except a general scene blur. However, lower settings—those under 10—produce much better depth-of-field effects. Depth-of-field refers to where the camera's focal point is (referred to as a Focal Node in the interface) and how much or how little areas in front of and behind the point are out of focus. (For more information on depth of field, refer to Chapter 14, "Cameras, Camera Effects, and Lighting.") Figure 17.2 shows appropriate and inappropriate settings for Horiz and Vert Focal Loss when using a focal point.

FIGURE 17.2

The left image shows a proper amount of focal loss for a scene when using a focal point. The right image shows the same scene with Focal Loss settings that are too high.

Focal Range

Focal range is the distance from the point of interest outward before focal loss begins to take place. It's best thought of as the "hot spot" area for Focus. The closer the Focal Range value is to 0, the less distance you have before Focus begins to blur the scene. However, rather than the distance being projected from the focal point outward in a spherical fashion, it is calculated based on the viewing plane of the camera (the Z-Axis, or Z-Buffer, of the rendered scene). The viewing plane is the plane that is perpendicular to the viewing axis of the camera. Figure 17.3 shows what a viewing plane looks like.

You might wonder why the effect uses the camera's viewing plane. Because Focus is a post-processed effect, it is applied after the scene is rendered. Focus relies on the Z-Buffer to perform its operation. The Z-Buffer is an invisible layer of data that accompanies the rendered image to represent a distance from the viewing plane for each point in the image—in other words, how far away from the camera is a rendered portion of the scene. Because Focus is acting on only a rendered image and has no interaction with the 3D objects in your scene, it relies on this Z-Buffer to determine how much to blur any portion of your rendering. The Z-Buffer gives Focus the capability to quickly blur a scene. However, it also means that blur is calculated planar to the camera—which can be a problem when focal loss is set high. At higher focal losses, you see a noticeable "blurred wall" that is actually your Focal Limit plane (refer to Figure 17.2). This is a rather undesirable effect for most cases. If you get a blurred wall, try reducing the amount of Focal Loss. At the very least, it makes the wall less noticeable.

FIGURE 17.3

A viewing plane in MAX. Both Focal Range and Focal Limit are dependent on this focal plane, or Z-depth, to work. The plane that intersects the teapot is the focal plane. The plane farthest from the camera represents the Focal Limit. The distance between the plane closest to the camera and the Focal Limit is the Focal Range.

T IP

If you see the focal planes in your rendering, try reducing both Focal Loss settings in Focus. Although it does not eliminate the focal plane problem, it minimizes it as much as possible. The right image in Figure 17.2 is a good example of too much focal loss.

Focal Limit

The Focal Limit setting, similar to Focal Range, represents the distance between the maximum Focal Range value and the point where the blur reaches its maximum strength. Again, the best way to think of this is as a falloff value of the blur in relation to the hotspot. (Although, the blur is actually becoming stronger, not falling off.) You cannot set Focal Limit to be less than or equal to Focal Range. Figure 17.4 shows where the various focal areas might exist in a sample image.

FIGURE 17.4

A visual representation of the focal areas in the Focus module. The distance between the Focal Node and the Focal Range plane contains no blur. The distance between the Focal Range planes and Focal Limit planes is where the blurring occurs. As you reach the Focal Limit planes, the image is blurred at the maximum amount.

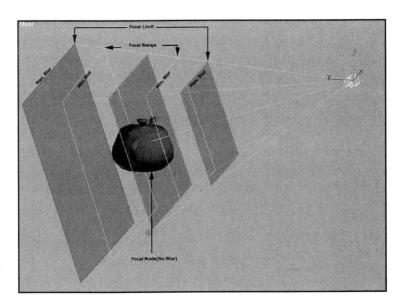

Also much like the Focal Range setting, Focal Limit is dependent upon the Z-Buffer data of the rendered image. This means that it is subject to the same limitations of having a "planar" look when focusing on a point. Focal Limit should always be a generous number higher than the Focal Range, primarily because a quick ramping of no blur to maximum blur is extremely noticeable and distracting.

It's important to point out that both Focal Range and Focal Limit behave very differently when used with the Radial Blur method of Focus. (See the upcoming section, "Radial Blur," for more information on how it works.) They have no effect when Scene Blur is selected.

General Focal Effects

Two settings provide a nice, general scene blur when using Focus: Scene Blur and Radial Blur. Both blur the scene but in very different ways.

Although these two methods of blur are used much less frequently than the Focal Node option (more on that coming up), they can be used for a number of situations.

Scene Blur

Scene Blur applies a general blur to the entire rendered image unless it is used with a mask. A mask enables you to specify where the rendered image will be blurred by using the grayscale values of an image. Darker areas are treated as transparent; lighter areas are opaque. When using Scene Blur, the only settings that work in the Focus interface are the Focal Loss settings, as well as the Lock and Affect Alpha check boxes.

Scene Blur, like any other blurring method, offsets all of the pixels in your rendered image the distance specified in the Focal Loss settings. Because sometimes you might want to blur a background while keeping your foreground sharp, this is a useful and quick option.

Radial Blur

Radial Blur creates a blur from the center of the image outward. This is where the hotspot/falloff thinking pays off. With Radial Blur, you need to use both the Focal Range and Focal Limit settings. With only a little difference between both Focal Range and Focal Limit, you see a noticeable "edge" between focused and blurred. For best results, use a larger difference. Set the Focal Range to approximately 10 and the Focal Limit to approximately 100 to 130. This produces a nice soft-corner blur that is good for dream sequences or *Abyss*-like effects. Furthermore, animating these two values can be an eye-focusing experience. Figure 17.5 shows the settings of Radial Blur and the resultant rendering.

NOTE

Both Radial and Scene Blur happen in 2D space, and do not rely on the Z-Buffer to produce their result. This means that Focal Range and Focal Limit are 2D parameters. When used with the Focal Node setting, they become 3D parameters.

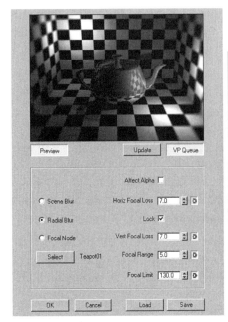

FIGURE 17.5
Radial Blur settings and resultant rendering. With proper Focal Range and Focal Limit settings, you can get nice, "soft" corners on your renderings.

Determining the Focal Point

Depending on your scene, you'll probably focus on one or more subjects, especially during the course of an animation. This is when you'll start to use the Focus module's Focal Node option.

Before using Focal Node, however, you must select a *focal point*. A focal point could be anything—a person, an object, the corner of a building—that you want your viewers to concentrate on. After determining what you want to focus on, you need to determine if you're going to animate that focus item over time. If so, consider a few options:

- **You can animate the camera's target location.** If that is the object you focus on, then your camera will always be focused on its target.

- **You can create a dummy and animate it.** If you simulate a focal shift for dramatic effects, this is often done without moving the camera or its target. By focusing on the dummy, you need not worry about the camera's target, just where the dummy exists.

- **You can animate the Focal Range and Focal Limit values.** This is perhaps the most tedious way to animate focus. Although feasible, it's not practical because it can be very difficult to keyframe and you have no visual reference of where the Focal Node is in the viewports.

Once you determine how your focal point is going to behave, then you can begin to use the Focal Node Blur option.

Focal Node Blur Uses

Focal Node blur relies on some object in your scene to determine where the camera focuses. That object, as mentioned earlier, is usually where you intend to have the focus of your scene all of the time—throughout the course of an animation.

The Focal Node option actually focuses on the geometry itself and not the pivot point (see Figure 17.6). Although a great deal of information in MAX relies on the location of pivot points, this is not the case with Focus. Because Focus is based on Z-Buffer information, the object's pivot-point location is not a factor in a rendered image. When using a focal node, make sure to set the Focal Range to a setting high enough so that the whole object is in focus. Otherwise, some portion of your object might be blurred, which is typically not a desired effect.

Focus Shift

Enough theory, you're now ready to try some focal effects of your own. In Exercise 17.1, you use the Lens Effects Focus module in Video Post to replicate a film camera move used to draw the viewer's attention from one specific character or object to another. The method you use here shifts the focus from a distant object to a foreground object, forcing the viewer to see something that might normally be lost in a busy scene. Focus changes are an important part of cinematic storytelling and should be considered in computer animation as well. Pay close attention to focus the next time you go to the cinema or rent a video.

FIGURE 17.6

The same scene with the three different blurring methods. Notice that both Scene (left) and Radial (right) are 2D effects. The Focal Node (middle) demonstrates how Focus works in 3D space.

A Cityscape in Focus

Exercise 17.1 is a night street scene in a cityscape. First, you direct the viewer's attention to the car by throwing the background and foreground out of focus. Next, you animate the camera to move a small amount up and to the right to signal a change. An animated Field of View change fills the display with the new foreground object while keeping the out-of-focus background object large and in the viewer's consciousness. You will use an animated dummy object as the focus node.

EXERCISE 17.1: COMBINING FOCUS SHIFT WITH A CAMERA MOVE

1. Open 17max01.max from the CD-ROM. In the Rendering pull-down menu, click Make Preview and click Create in the Make Preview—Camera02 dialog box to accept the default setting. This renders a thumbnail of the Camera02 viewport.

2. After the preview renders, click Rendering View Preview and click the Play button in the Media Player to see the camera movement and field of view change. The entire viewport renders in focus so your eye is not drawn to any particular object or area in the display.

NOTE

You can also render the Camera02 viewport to an AVI file for more detailed materials and atmospherics, but for the purposes of this exercise, you can see the effect of having the full screen in focus during the animation in the preview.

3. In the Rendering pull-down menu, click Video Post.

4. In the Video Post dialog box, click the Add Scene Event icon, choose Camera02, and click OK to exit the dialog box. Click the Add Image Filter Event icon and choose Lens Effects Focus from the list. Click OK in the Edit Filter Event dialog box to close it. Click the Add Image Output Event icon. Click the Files button and save the file to an AVI file on your hard drive. Use the Cinepak codec. The Video Post dialog box should look like Figure 17.7.

5. In the Video Post dialog box, double-click Lens Effect Focus, and click the Setup button in the Edit Filter Event dialog box.

6. Make sure the Frame Slider is set to frame 0. In the Lens Effects Focus dialog box, click on the Preview and VP Queue buttons. The Preview window should be a completely blurred view of the scene.

7. Check the Focal Node option, and click the Select button. Double-click BlurDummy01 in the Select Focal Object list. All blurring is determined from the center of the dummy object now. Remove the check from the Lock button, and enter 6.0 in Horiz Focal Loss, 3.0 in Vert Focal Loss, 35.0 in Focal Range, and 600 in Focal Limit. The

BlurDummy01 focal node is in the middle of the car and with a Range of 35, the whole car is in focus. 600 in the Focal Limit softens the edge between in focus and out of focus. The Lens Effects Focus dialog box should look similar to Figure 17.8.

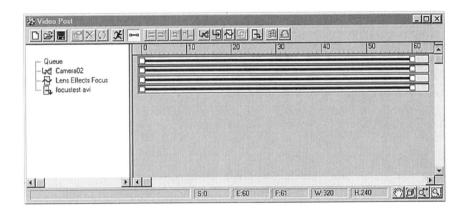

FIGURE 17.7
Lens Effects Focus in Video Post queue.

TIP

The blurring effect tends to look a little more realistic if you unlock Horiz and Vert Focal Loss and adjust the entries to something nearer to the aspect ratio of the rendered image size. Rounding off to a Width:Height ratio of 2:1 is a good starting point.

8. Click the Animate button to turn it on, and enter 50 in the frame field or drag the Frame Slider to frame 50. Click the Update button in the Lens Effects Focus dialog box.

NOTE

Anytime you make a change in MAX R2, click on the Update button to reflect the MAX changes in the Preview window.

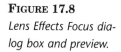

FIGURE 17.8

Lens Effects Focus dialog box and preview.

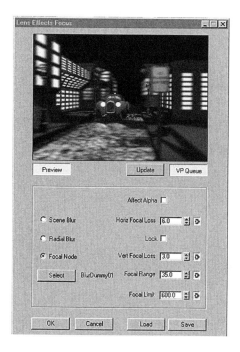

9. Enter 8.0 in Horiz Focal Loss, 4.0 in Vert Focal Loss, and 335.0 in the Focal Range field. Click the Animate button to turn it off. These settings bring the sign into focus, throw the car out of focus, and increase the blurring slightly. The display should look similar to Figure 17.9. Click the OK button in Lens Effects Focus dialog box to close it.

10. In the Video Post dialog box, click the Execute Sequence icon. Make sure Range is checked and 0 to 60 is entered in the range fields. Click the 320 × 240 button and click Render. On slower machines this may take a while to render.

11. After the scene is rendered, click on Files/View File and play the animation back. You can see how the animated focus draws your attention from one object to another. In the Preview from Step 1, you had no idea what you should be looking at in the animation. Now it is quite obvious that the car is important at the start and the sign is important at the end of the animation. Close the Media Player after playing the animation, and close Video Post.

FIGURE 17.9

The sign is now in focus and the car is out of focus.

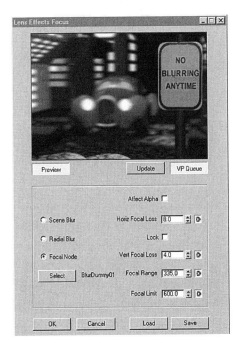

12. In the Rendering pull-down menu, click Environment. Click each entry in the Effects list and check its Active check box to turn it on. Close the Environment dialog box. This activates some fog in the scene and volume effects on the streetlights and car headlights.

13. In the Rendering pull-down menu, click Video Post and double-click the last queue entry to change the Image Output Event to a new AVI file. Click the Execute Sequence icon to render the new scene to disk.

14. When the new scene is rendered, play it back and notice the moving black line at the curb in front of the car, the lines near the driver's side tire, and the flashing in the grill. In both animations, you see a slight flash at the edge of the street sign in the last few frames.

TIP

Use Lens Effects Focus in MAX R2 to add impact to the storytelling of your animation, but use it on short sequences and study the test renders carefully to avoid unwanted artifacts, especially when using Focus in conjunction with atmospheric effects. You can try moving the Focal Node in the scene or changing the Focal Range slightly, or increase the Focal Loss settings to correct these anomalies. Be aware, however, that it is difficult to make Lens Effects Focus work with atmospheric effects.

In Exercise 17.1, you set up a Video Post queue using Lens Effects Focus to animate a focal blurring in a scene. You set the Horiz and Vert Focal Loss amounts to something more in line with the rendered output aspect ratio. This keeps the effect from being more blurry at the top and bottom than at the sides.

Lens Effects Focus can be a powerful tool in drawing the attention of the viewer to specific objects to enhance a point in the story, but watch for artifacts created by the blur.

In Practice: Focal Effects

- **Focus adds focal effects through blur.** The Focal Loss parameter enables you to add more or less blur to the scene. By unlocking Horiz and Vert Focal Loss, you can blur the rendered image more or less along a specific axis.

- **Use general blur settings for nonfocal point effects.** You can use both Scene Blur and Radial Blur to blur a scene without depending on the Z-Buffer. Scene Blur blurs the entire rendered image, and Radial Blur blurs the scene from the center of the rendered image outward.

- **Focus is based on Z-depth.** Because of this "feature," focus begins and ends focal effects based on a planar range rather than spherical. At higher Focal Loss settings, this becomes very noticeable.

- **Use dummy objects when simulating focal shifts.** Rather than using the target of the camera, create a dummy object for your Focal Node. This enables you to create focal shifts without moving the camera or its target.

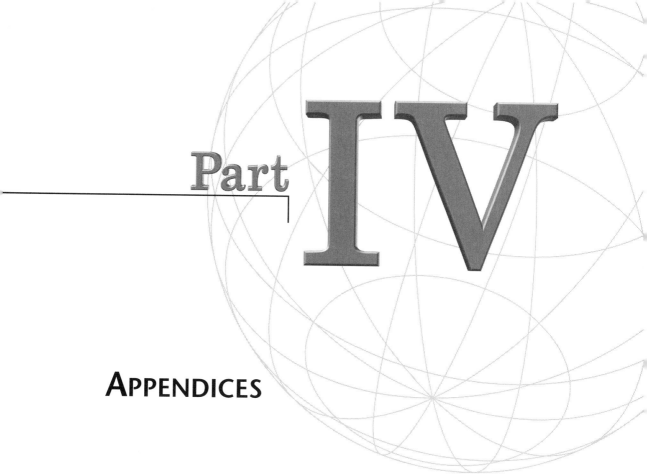

Part **IV**

APPENDICES

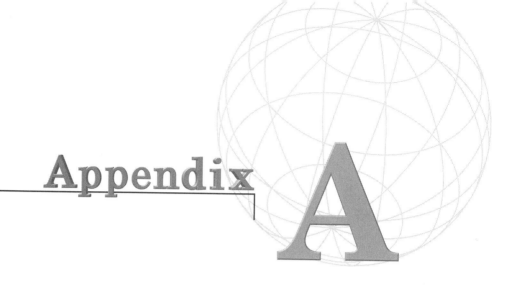

Appendix A

AutoCAD and 3D Studio MAX: Getting Them to Talk

Many 3D Studio MAX R2 users are also AutoCAD users or

they work with individuals who create 2D and 3D drawings

in AutoCAD. Alas, the process of transferring models between

3D Studio MAX R2 and AutoCAD is not always as seamless

as you would like to expect. In this appendix, you will

- Learn the options available for importing AutoCAD drawing files into 3D Studio MAX R2 and how those options can affect the way you work.

- Learn what type of objects 3D Studio MAX R2 translates AutoCAD entities into, and learn tips for making the process more flexible.

- Other import/export file types and their uses for those users with older versions of AutoCAD or users with other CAD or modeling software.

NOTE

For more information on working with MAX R2 and AutoCAD see Chapter 2, "Architectural Modeling."

Why Doesn't 3D Studio MAX R2...?

A common question that long-time AutoCAD users often ask is, "Why doesn't 3D Studio MAX do this or that the same way AutoCAD does?" This is usually followed by the statement, "I've invested a lot of time learning AutoCAD and I don't want to have to learn new software."

Well, 3D Studio MAX *is* new software! Historically, both programs developed from totally different sources that had little to do with each other. AutoCAD is an engineering tool, by engineers for engineers, intended to create working, dimensioned drawings and models to be used in manufacturing objects. 3D Studio MAX is a presentation tool, by artists for artists, intended to create realistic renderings and animations to tell a story or present an idea.

In the past few years, Autodesk, Kinetix, and the Yost Group have put a lot of effort into making the two programs pass data in a predictable and efficient manner. Tools have been included in MAX R2—such as Snaps, the Sun Locator, and parametric doors and windows—that have come from discussions with architects and engineers. You can expect the trend to continue in future revisions.

In the meantime, analyze your office work methods and use the talent you have available to make the process as smooth as possible. There are no hard-and-fast rules. Start the process with simple files and work your way into more complex projects, remembering that AutoCAD is a drafting/engineering tool and MAX is a presentation tool.

The File Import Options

3D Studio MAX R2 offers several options for importing files from other 2D and 3D sources. The current file types that can be imported into MAX R2 are

- 3D Studio Mesh (.3DS, .PRJ)

- AutoCAD (.DWG)

- AutoCAD (.DXF)

- 3D Studio Shape (.SHP)

- Stereolithography (.STL)

- Adobe Illustrator (.AI)

This appendix will focus on importing AutoCAD drawing files (.DWG), as it is generally the most commonly used option for AutoCAD/MAX users. The DWG file import has the most intelligence built into the translation process, resulting in more logical and editable objects in MAX R2.

N OTE

Visit www.ktx.com for any information on updated DWG import files.

When you choose Import/AutoCAD (.DWG) from the file's pulldown menu, you are presented with a series of dialog boxes: first, the Select File to Import dialog, then the DWG Import, and finally the Import AutoCAD DWG File. The Select File to Import dialog lets you choose the file type and pick the file to import. The DWG Import dialog and Import AutoCAD DWG File dialog are explained below.

AutoCAD DWG Import Dialog

The following options are available in the DWG Import dialog:

- **Merge objects with current scene:** Use this option to keep the existing MAX R2 scene intact and merge the new AutoCAD models into it. The new objects use the AutoCAD coordinate system for positioning.

- **Completely replace current scene:** This option deletes all objects currently in the MAX R2 scene and imports the AutoCAD objects into an empty scene. This also uses the AutoCAD coordinate system for positioning.

FIGURE A.1

DWG Import dialog.

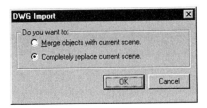

Tip

If you are importing from an AutoCAD drawing that uses Civil Engineering units derived from State Plane Coordinates, and so on, your objects could be hundreds of thousands of units from the 0,0,0 MAX R2 coordinate. You may want to move all objects in AutoCAD to be near 0,0,0 before importing.

Import AutoCAD DWG File Dialog

The Import AutoCAD DWG File dialog contains several options that will be described below in more detail. Familiarize yourself with the options and then test the import process on your own files, preferably starting with smaller imports and working your way to larger projects.

FIGURE A.2

Import AutoCAD DWG File dialog.

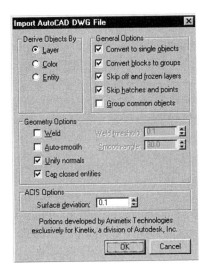

Derive Object By

The Derive Object By section offers three choices:

- **Layer:** Object names are derived from the AutoCAD layer name. For example, objects on an AutoCAD layer named Floor would be named Floor.01, Floor.02, and so on in MAX R2. Deriving objects by layer is the most common method of importing from AutoCAD because it offers the most user control.

T IP

Importing 2D AutoCAD entities and making them into 3D objects in MAX R2 is a very efficient method of capitalizing on the accuracy of AutoCAD and the flexibility of MAX R2. Often, because of their placement on various AutoCAD layers, shapes imported into MAX may need to be edited. Attaching or detaching shapes is a very common technique to produce logical compound shapes. Familiarize yourself with MAX R2 Sub-Object editing methods, such as those found in Chapter 2, especially those on how to attach and detach 2D splines to create compound shapes in MAX R2.

- **Color:** Object names are derived from the AutoCAD system color number. An AutoCAD object that has the color red comes into MAX R2 named Color001.01. This makes it very difficult to tell what object is what because the names have no logical association to the object.

- **Entity:** This method of importing from AutoCAD is rarely used. The objects have such names as Arc.01, 3Dface.01, and so on. Not only do the names not have any association to the object, but they can result in unmanageable numbers of individual objects.

General Options

The General Options checkboxes are:

- **Convert to Single Objects:** This option works in conjunction with Derive From: Layer, Color, Entity to make similar AutoCAD objects into one MAX R2 object. For example, all circles with the same thickness on a layer named TANK would be combined as a number of MAX R2 circles with one common Extrude modifier.

- **Convert Blocks to Groups:** Block objects in AutoCAD are converted to a MAX R2 group with the same name as the block. Multiple block inserts in AutoCAD become instance objects in MAX R2.

- **Skip Off and Frozen Layers:** AutoCAD objects that are on frozen or off layers are ignored in the import process. Common AutoCAD layers to freeze are Text and Dimension layers.

- **Skip Hatches and Points:** AutoCAD hatch patterns and point entities that are imported can overwhelm a MAX R2 scene with unusable data. Always have this checked on.

TIP

You can create useful 2D polyline information in AutoCAD by using the BHATCH command with the advanced option called Retain Boundaries checked. This creates a solid polyline of the area defined by the hatch pattern. You can then import just the boundary into MAX R2 as a spline. The resulting AutoCAD R14 hatch pattern would *not* be imported during the process, regardless of the Skip Hatches setting.

- **Group common objects:** Imports all AutoCAD objects that are on the same layer, have the same color, or are the same entity type into a MAX R2 Group.

Geometry Options

The Geometry Options include:

- **Weld:** Globally welds adjacent vertices of AutoCAD objects into a single MAX R2 vertex based on the Weld Threshold distance. This works only when objects are imported with the Convert to Single Objects option mentioned above.

TIP

Global welding can be problematic. Global welding with too high a Weld Threshold setting can cause smaller details to collapse in Mesh objects. You should definitely uncheck Weld for all ACIS solid models from AutoCAD and from surface models if you are having any sort of problem. You get more predictable results from Welding objects manually after they are imported into MAX R2.

- **Weld Threshold:** Range = 0.0–999999.0. The Weld Threshold amount is in system units. If two or more vertices are within a distance less than or equal to the setting, they are welded into one vertex.

WARNING

If you have something such as window trim that projects two inches from the façade and the Weld Threshold is set to two inches, all trim collapses unpredictably.

- **Auto-smooth:** Auto-smooth assigns smoothing group numbers to faces based on the angle they meet at a shared edge. If adjacent faces share a common smoothing group number, the edge appears smoothed. If faces do not share a common group, the edge appears sharp.

TIP

Smoothing problems can show in imported DWG files along with welding problems. They manifest themselves as faces that appear darker or lighter than their neighbors. Make sure a MAX R2 object is properly welded, next remove all smoothing group numbers, and then manually apply Auto-smooth or specific smoothing group number assignments.

- **Smooth Angle:** Range = 0–90. Smooth Angle determines at which angle faces must meet to receive a common smoothing group number.

- **Unify Normals:** With Unify Normals checked, the import process tries to make all face normals point in the same direction relative to the center of the object. Flipped face normals appear as "holes" in the MAX R2 mesh object. ACIS solid models already are unified and should have Unify Normals unchecked.

TIP

Flipped faces are a fairly common problem with AutoCAD objects and improperly welded faces can be a cause of flipped faces. First, weld the mesh and then render the object either with a two-sided material applied, or by checking the 2-Sided option in Views/Viewport Configuration. If faces are flipped, they appear rendered, but if they are missing completely, you still see the hole. If faces are flipped, use the Normal modifier or edit the mesh at Sub-Object/Face and flip them individually. If faces are missing, you can build new faces or use a Cap Holes modifier.

- **Cap Closed Entities:** Applies a MAX R2 Extrude modifier to all closed AutoCAD entities and puts capping faces at each end. Closed AutoCAD entities with no thickness have an Extrude modifier with a height of 0 and appear as flat faces. When the Cap Closed Entities is unchecked, entities with thickness are still extruded, but no end caps are applied. Entities with no thickness are imported as MAX R2 2D shapes.

ACIS Options

The final section of the Import AutoCAD DWG File dialog box, ACIS Options, offers one setting:

- **Surface Deviation:** Range = 0.001–999999.0. This is the maximum distance in system units from the surface of an AutoCAD ACIS solid model and the Mesh object in MAX R2. Smaller numbers make a tighter fit or a more accurate Mesh object.

Warning

Small Surface Deviation settings can create very complex Mesh objects in MAX R2. Large settings can cause lost detail in a model.

AutoCAD DWG and 3D Studio MAX R2 Entities Translation

The process of translating entities and objects from AutoCAD to MAX R2 and back requires that each software package translate from one object type to another. Tables A.1 and A.2 list the entity or object from one program in the first column and its corresponding object type after translation.

TABLE A.1

AutoCAD DWG to MAX R2 Objects

AutoCAD Entity	3D Studio MAX R2 Object
Point	Point Helper
Line	Spline Shape
Arc	Arc Shape
Circle	Circle Shape
Ellipse	Ellipse Shape
Solid	Closed Spline Shape
Trace	Closed Spline Shape
2D Polyline	Spline Shape
3D Polyline	Spline Shape
Polyline Donut	Donut Shape

AutoCAD Entity	3D Studio MAX R2 Object
Spline	Spline Shape
MLine	Spline Shape
Text (using TTF or PFB)	Text Shape
3D Face	Mesh Object
Polyline Mesh	Mesh Object
Polyface Mesh	Mesh Object
ACIS Object	Mesh Object
Region	Editable Mesh with 0 thickness
Blocks	Objects or Group by option
UCS Definition	Grid Helper
DView (perspective)	Target Camera
Point Light	Omni Light
Spotlight	Target Spot
Distance Light	Directional Light
Thickness Property	Extrude Modifier
Polyline Width	Spline Outline
Color	Object Color by option

TABLE A.2

MAX R2 Objects to AutoCAD DWG Entities

3D Studio MAX R2 Object	AutoCAD Entity
Circle Shape	Circle
Donut Shape	Donut Polyline
Ellipse Shape	Ellipse
Text Shape	Text (using Standard style)
Spline Shape (one straight segment)	Line

continues

TABLE A.2 CONTINUED

MAX R2 Objects to AutoCAD DWG Entities

3D Studio MAX R2 Object	AutoCAD Entity
Spline Shape (coplanar linear segments)	2D Polyline
Spline Shape (non-linear or 3D)	Spline
3D Surfaces	PolyFace Mesh
Cameras	Named DView
Omni Light	Point Light
Spotlights	Spotlight
Directional Light	Distant Light
Grid Helper	Named UCS
Point Helper	Point

Although exporting from MAX R2 to AutoCAD is not as common as importing objects from AutoCAD, it would be easier, for example, to create convincing screw threads in MAX R2 than in AutoCAD.

TIP

An excellent tool included in MAX R2 is the Section option found in the Create/Shape panel. It cuts a 2D section shape through 3D objects on any plane and converts the section to a 2D shape that can be exported to AutoCAD for dimensioning or to be used in creating AutoCAD solid objects.

Other Import/Export Format Options

Users who do not have access to AutoCAD Release 14 drawings or have problems with the DWG import process can use several other import file types available.

3D Studio 3DS, PRJ

Files that are created in 3D Studio DOS Release 4 or earlier end with .3DS (Meshes) or PRJ (Project files). AutoCAD Release 13 and 14 have a

3DSOUT command that writes the 3DS format. The 3DS, PRJ formats are for 3D objects only.

Adobe Illustrator AI

Although it is not an AutoCAD or 3D Studio file type, you can import Adobe Illustrator (AI88) files into 3D Studio MAX. This allows you to use 2D vector objects created in Adobe Illustrator, CorelDRAW!, or any other software that uses the AI88 format.

T_{IP}

CorelDRAW! has a Trace feature that traces 2D bitmaps with vectors that can be saved in AI format. This is a method to automatically trace logos or unusual fonts.

When importing AI88 files, 3D Studio MAX converts polygons to Shape objects.

W_{ARNING}

AI files created with Corel Trace can have large numbers of vertices and may need optimizing in Corel or, manually, in MAX R2.

AI Import Options

You choose an option in the Shape Import dialog to set how the shape objects are created:

- **Single Object:** All polygons in the AI file are converted to Bézier splines and are placed inside a single Composite Shape object.

- **Multiple Objects:** Each polygon in the AI file is converted to a Bézier spline and is placed inside an Independent Shape object.

AutoCAD DXF

DXF files are used to import and export objects to and from AutoCAD (and other programs that support this file format). See Figure A.3 for the Import DXF File dialog.

FIGURE A.3

Import DXF File dialog.

TIP

Keep the following in mind when you are creating your DXF geometry and when you are deciding whether to convert by layer, color, or entity:

- With AutoCAD Release 12, if you are using the AutoCAD Advanced Modeling Extension (AME), use the SOLMESH command on your AME models prior to saving the DXF file.

- After importing a DXF file, you might want to divide the resulting 3D Studio MAX objects into smaller objects by editing at the Sub-Object/Face level and detaching sets of faces into new objects.

Entities that are frozen or turned off are ignored, yet the successful unification of face normals depends on the welding of coincident vertices. Sometimes, depending upon the precision of the model created in AutoCAD, the vertices may not be close enough to be considered "coincident." They will not be welded and the faces will not be properly unified. In this case, increase the Weld Threshold value in the Import DXF File dialog.

Converting by layer can result in objects consisting of many elements. In certain cases, some of these elements may have all their face normals flipped the wrong way. Use the Normal modifier to correct this.

If, for some reason, you do not want to flip normals with a Normal modifier, you can either use two-sided materials, or turn on the Force 2-Sided option in the Render Scene dialog.

If you are loading a large scene containing thousands of entities (such as 3D faces) and have chosen to load an object by entity, the conversion can take a long time. It also produces a huge number of objects to handle in 3D Studio MAX. To avoid this, organize your DXF file so that these kinds of entities are grouped by layer, then make the conversion by layer rather than by entity.

Derive Objects from Options

The first section of the Import DXF File dialog, Derive Objects From, offers three choices:

- **Layer:** Each layer with a unique name is converted into a separate object.

- **Color:** All entities of the same color are converted into a single entity.

- **Entity:** Each entity is converted into a separate object.

Weld Vertices

The Weld vertices control how coincident vertices in the DXF file are welded into single vertices in the 3D Studio MAX mesh. They are

- **Weld Threshold:** Determines the size of the area that vertices must occupy to be welded.

- **Weld:** Turns on the Weld Vertices function.

NOTE

See the AutoCAD DWG import section earlier in the book for more information on vertex welding.

Auto-Smooth

Auto-Smooth applies smoothing groups to the geometry based on the smoothing angle set by the Smooth Angle spinner. Edges between faces that have an angle between them that is greater than the specified smoothing angle appear faceted in the rendered image. Edges between faces that are below the specified angle are smoothed. To activate Auto-Smooth, use

- **Smooth Angle:** Sets the angle at which smoothing occurs.
- **Smooth:** Turns the smoothing on.

NOTE

See the AutoCAD DWG import section earlier in the book for more information on smoothing.

Arc Subdivision

In the Arc Subdivision section, you can make two settings:

- **Polygon Degrees:** Specifies the number of degrees between each vertex of any imported curvature that's converted to a mesh object in 3D Studio MAX. An example might be an extruded spline.

- **Spline Degrees:** Specifies the number of degrees between vertices in an imported curvature that's converted to a Bézier spline (a shape) in 3D Studio MAX. This could be an arc or a non-extruded spline, for example. Unlike Mesh objects, Bézier splines contain their own curvatures, so you don't need as many vertices. The default setting of 90 degrees is usually adequate.

Miscellaneous

The final section of the Import DXF File dialog offers three checkboxes:

- **Remove Double Faces:** Removes one of the pair wherever two faces are occupying the same location.

- **Fill Polylines:** Converts closed 2D polylines into mesh objects. Closed, planar, 3D polylines are capped. If the 2D polyline is open, it is imported as a spline shape.

- **Unify Normals:** Forces the normals of all faces on each object to face the same way (usually out).

NOTE

See the AutoCAD DWG import section earlier in the book for more information on face normals.

3D Studio SHP

You can import 3D Studio R2–R4 2D Shape files with the Import (*SHP) option. They are imported as MAX R2 2D shapes.

3DSIN and 3DSOUT

3DS is the 3D Studio Release 4 mesh file format. You can import and export 3DS files from 3D Studio MAX. PRJ is the 3D Studio Release 4 project file format.

When you import a 3DS or PRJ file, you can merge the imported objects with the current scene or replace the current scene completely. If you choose to merge the objects with the current scene, you'll be asked whether you want to reset the length of the animation in the scene to the length of the imported file (if the imported file contains animation).

When you import a 3DS file, the following information is imported:

- Backgrounds (solid, gradient, and bitmap).

- Fog, Layered Fog, and Distance Cue.

- Ambient light level.

- Subtractive transparency is converted to 3D Studio MAX "Filter" transparency and the filter color is set equal to the Diffuse color.

- Transparency falloff settings.

- All Map channels that are enabled. Map channels that are turned off in the 3DS file do not import into 3D Studio MAX.

- All Map parameters, including UV transforms, Negative, Mirror, and Rotation. Some Map parameters such as Blur, Luma, RGB, and Alpha work much differently in 3D Studio MAX. These values are converted to new values that produce a similar effect.

- Mask bitmaps are imported as a 3D Studio MAX mask texture.

- When materials with both Texture 1 and Texture 2 are imported, a composite texture is created and added to the Standard material's Diffuse channel.

- Reflection maps, auto-cubics, and mirrors.

- Automatic Reflection map Nth frame and Map Size settings.

- SXP translation for Marble and Noise materials.

- 3DS/DOS IK Joint parameters.

- 3D Surfer Patch data.

When you import a 3DS file, the following information is not imported:

- Morph keys

- Keyframer instances

- Map channels that are turned off

- Custom .cub-format cubic maps

- Decal transparency using the RGB color of the upper-left pixel of the map

- When you import a PRJ file, all of the above items are imported, plus Shapes.

When you export a 3DS file, the following information is exported:

- Position, Rotation, and Scale animation. If the controller is a TCB controller, the TCB, Ease In, and Ease Out values are also saved. If the controller is any other type of key controller, the keys are saved, but the tangent information is lost. If the controller is not a key controller, only the object's transformation at frame 0 is saved.

- Basic material color/parameters from the Standard material.

- Single maps with their amount, offsets, scales, and so on.

- Auto-cubics and Mirrors.

- Target cameras, target spotlights, and Omni lights.

- Most "static" parameters for cameras and lights, and animation tracks for Roll, Falloff, Hotspot, and FOV.

When you export a 3DS file, the following information is not exported:

- Composite and procedural maps.

- UV mapping coordinates.

- Grouped object transformations. There's no concept of group hierarchy in the 3D Editor. Groups export to the Keyframer because the Keyframer understands hierarchies.

- Global shadow parameters.

When you export a 3DS file, the following occurs:

- All non-mesh geometry, such as procedural primitives and patches, are collapsed to meshes before export.

- Objects are exported as they exist on the frame 3D Studio MAX displays at export time. If you want to output morph targets, go to each frame and export the target to a different filename.

- Meshes are saved with edge display information and smoothing groups.

- 3D Studio MAX instances are saved as Keyframer instances.

- Modifier and morph animation is frozen at the current frame, collapsed, and exported as a simple mesh.

Warning

A known problem in 3D Studio MAX Release 1 is that 3DS files created by the 3D Studio Release 4 Save Selected method do not import correctly. To work around this problem, reload the file created with Save Selected into 3D Studio MAX and create a new file with the Save command. Then import this file into 3D Studio MAX.

Stereolithography STL

A new import/export file type in MAX R2 is the stereolithography (STL) file format. In order for a Mesh object to be used as a stereolithography object, it must have a very high surface integrity. Models can often be imported via STL from high-end CAD packages.

The stereolithography files are intended for use with software that slices Mesh objects into thin layers of descriptive information and then translates it into a 3D model by "plotting" the layer with a laser.

Tip

MAX R2's new modifier, STL-Check, highlights any potential invalid STL features in a MAX R2 Mesh object prior to exporting. If you are having trouble with imported objects from any source, STL-Check can highlight an offending open edge or coincident faces so you can correct the problem.

Import STL File

The Import STL File dialog includes nine options:

- **Name:** Accepts a name for the 3D Studio object created from the STL file. The default is the filename (without extension) or the name saved internally in the STL file.

- **Weld Vertices:** Welds coincident vertices in the STL file into single vertices in the 3D Studio mesh.

  - **Weld Threshold:** Determines the size of the area that vertices must occupy to be welded. Vertices with distances equal to or less than this value are welded into a single vertex.

  - **Weld:** Turns on the Weld Vertices function. In most cases, you should leave this box selected because unwelded objects cannot be unified or smoothed.

  - **Use Threshold:** Instructs STL import to use the standard 3D Studio Welding method. This can be a very slow process.

  - **Quick Weld:** Instructs STL import to use a welding algorithm optimized for the STL format. This is up to 30 times faster than standard 3D Studio welding and is highly recommended.

- **Auto-Smooth:** Applies smoothing groups to the geometry based on the smoothing angle set by the Smooth Angle spinner. Edges between faces that have an angle between them greater than the specified smoothing angle appears faceted in the rendered image. Edges between faces that are below the specified angle are smoothed.

- **Remove Double Faces:** Removes one of the pair wherever two faces are occupying the same location. This step is recommended.

- **Unify Normals:** Forces the normals of all faces on each object to face the same way (usually out). If, when you render your 3D Studio scene, the face normals are pointing in the wrong direction, use the Normal modifier to flip them. For best results, leave this box selected.

FIGURE A.4

Import STL File dialog.

Note

See the AutoCAD DWG import section earlier in the book for more information on vertex welding, smoothing, and face normals.

In Practice: AutoCAD and 3D Studio Max

- **Follow correct procedures.** A big step in making the AutoCAD to MAX R2 file translation as smooth as possible is to make sure your AutoCAD operators are well trained in correct AutoCAD procedures, such as layer management, knowledge of thickness and elevation, and ACIS solids versus surface models.

- **Use vertex welding and smoothing carefully.** Understanding MAX R2 vertex welding and smoothing group controls is essential to fine-tuning the models imported into MAX R2. Be aware that global welding on import can collapse small details if the Weld Threshold is set too high for the size of the objects.

- **Transfer with 3DS to save materials and mapping.** The 3DS file format is the only format that carries material and mapping information back and forth from MAX R2 to AutoCAD.

- **Choose 3DSOUT for ARX transfers.** AutoCAD's 3DSOUT export option can transfer ARX information from AutoCAD to MAX R2.

- **Translate 2D shapes and splines**. This is an efficient method of exchanging data between AutoCAD and MAX R2.

- **Try STL import and export.** The new STL import/export is a reliable method of transferring 3D data between AutoCAD, as well as other CAD programs, and MAX R2.

Appendix B

DESIGNING WITH PLUG-INS

As a MAX user, you have one of the greatest advantages over users of other 3D software—the ability to expand. Through the use of the plug-in technology built into MAX, you can extend, enhance, or add features to the base product. Although MAX is capable of doing many things, some areas of the software could be enhanced or replaced by a good plug-in.

Believe it or not, MAX is actually made up of plug-ins. There is a central program called the *core* and everything else is essentially plug-ins. With R2, you can now see plug-ins initializing in the startup or *splash* screen. Along the bottom of the splash screen, you should see "Initializing...". As plug-ins are initialized, their names appear. This process occurs rather quickly. What's happening here is that MAX is looking for plug-ins, but *not* necessarily loading them into RAM. MAX wants to know what's available so it can present it to you, the user, when the main interface appears. It's not until you try to use the plug-in does MAX actually load it into memory fully. The end result is memory usage only when MAX needs it.

T IP

Although this isn't a plug-in tip, you can change MAX's startup screen by renaming any *BMP* file *splash.bmp* and placing it in the root MAX R2 directory. Just make sure it's small enough to see the rest of the Windows interface!

Plug-In Names

MAX's plug-ins show up as DLL files within your plug-ins directory as well as anywhere else you might place them on your hard drive. (DLL stands for Dynamic Load Library.) Plug-ins, depending on their type, will have a different last letter (at least) in the extension. Table B.1 lists the extension changes.

TABLE B.1

Plug-In Extensions Defined

Extension	Meaning
.DLO	Objects found in the Create Panel
.DLM	Modifiers
.DLT	Materials found in the Material Editor
.DLC	Animation controller plug-ins
.DLR	Rendering plug-ins
.DLE	Plug-ins located in the File/Export command
.DLI	For plug-ins located in the File/Import command
.DLU	For "other" plug-ins found in the Utility Panel
.BMI	Raster file (bitmap) plug-ins

A few other plug-in types exist, but Table B.1 shows the major ones. The reason for this list is not just to show how many types there are, but also to show you where you might find a plug-in in MAX after you've installed it. All too often, users download plug-ins from a developer or on a Web site, only to be unable to figure out where the plug-in is located or what it is actually supposed to do.

NOTE

Although scripts are plug-ins, they have a .ms extension and must be loaded via the MAXScript plug-in or through the Windows NT command line.

Plug-In Sources

This Appendix does not focus on specific plug-ins or developers. It is designed, rather, to give you an idea of how various plug-in types work and how they might assist you in your day-to-day production life within MAX. It also focuses on plug-ins that are directly related to the subjects contained within this book. Therefore, you'll find information on modeling, material, and rendering plug-ins. For the most up-to-date information, you can refer to two places on the Internet:

- **The Kinetix Web site:** Go to www.ktx.com for the latest information on MAX from Kinetix. There is also other information on other Kinetix products, such as 3D Studio VIZ and Character Studio.

- **The Kinetix Support Forum:** There are actually two locations for this currently. You can log on to the Kinetix forum of CompuServe, GO KINETIX, or you can go to the new Kinetix Web support forum, support.ktx.com (note there is no www in the address).

Plug-ins are frequently updated, so check at least once a month on your favorite sites for updated versions.

To Pay, or Not to Pay?

An issue that comes up often with users is whether to pay a developer for a plug-in or to just use a free one (or shareware) available on the Internet. Unfortunately, there is no clearcut argument for preferring either one.

Pay

A few things can be said for commercially developed plug-ins. First off is that most good developers have technical support. If you run into a problem, chances are they'll be able to get you out of it quickly. Another is that they have dedicated testing environments. Although some developers test more thoroughly than others, most spend a considerable amount of time developing and testing a plug-in before releasing it for general consumption. As a result, MAX runs much more smoothly because poorly developed or unstable plug-ins can wreak havoc on MAX's overall stability. (See the section "Unplugging Plug-Ins" for remedies.)

Also, developers provide plug-ins for business. That means that they have dedicated resources, meaning money and people, to develop quality plug-ins. As new versions of MAX come out, commercial developers are closely in touch with Kinetix to make sure that their plug-ins work with the new release. Lastly, commercial developers are obligated just by the nature of the industry to provide documentation. Free plug-in documentation is sparse at best. No matter what anyone tells you, trying to figure out a plug-in without adequate reference material and tutorials is both time-consuming and frustrating.

Don't Pay

On the other hand, free plug-ins have a major benefit over commercial plug-ins: They're *free*. To many people, that's the best price that they'll pay for a plug-in. Free plug-ins are usually developed by hobbyists who love MAX and love to program. This is *not* indicative of their programming skills, however. Many free plug-ins provide excellent and useful features for MAX. They're often full-featured and completely stable. However, don't expect this to be the case for everything. There will be the occasional rogue plug-in that will completely destabilize MAX.

Whether you choose to go with commercial, free, or both types of plug-ins, remember that that's the power of MAX. You can add to it whenever you need to increase the features or functionality of the base package.

Objects and Modifier Plug-Ins

Whenever you download a plug-in that contains a .dlo or .dlm extension, it's going to show up either in your Create or Modify panel. These plug-ins can allow you to create new objects or edit objects in a completely new way.

If an object plug-in is designed correctly, it will normally show up in its own category within one of the seven types of creation categories. Where it appears and what name it has depends on how the developer wanted it. Object plug-ins can greatly decrease development time of certain types of geometry. For instance, if you find yourself frequently making trees by hand, try one of the several plug-ins that create various types of foliage automatically. 3D Studio VIZ, a design Visualization product from Kinetix, proved the usefulness of being able to have new object types when it introduced Door and Window objects for architects in its first release. It should be pointed out that many other object plug-ins can extend the Create panel, including objects such as lights and helpers. Figure B.1 shows the MAX interface with a few objects created with object plug-ins.

FIGURE B.1

A few objects created using object plug-ins available for MAX R2.

Modifier plug-ins work along the same lines as object plug-ins, but they work by being applied to various types of objects. Modifiers can alter the shape of the geometry but can also edit the geometry at the root level.

For instance, the Physique plug-in that is part of the Character Studio package from Kinetix allows you to edit an object at the vertex level. Figure B.2 shows the MAX interface with a few objects modified with modifier plug-ins.

FIGURE B.2

MAX R2 modifier plug-ins available from third-party developers.

Material Editor Plug-Ins

When it comes to extending the Material editor via plug-ins, there are two options: as a complete material or via a Map type. Complete materials usually function much like the Standard material. They are often specialized to enhance existing features or to extend MAX's material and rendering capabilities. Many times, new material plug-ins require a new or enhanced rendering engine. The new Raytrace material is an example of how a plug-in material type might work. (Rendering engines are discussed in the next section.) If the plug-in is designed to add a Map type, then it appears in the listing of maps available when you click a map slot within the Material editor. Considering the Raytrace material again, you can see how it is also plugged in to MAX as a map as well. Most plug-in renderers work this way because they need special materials to work inside the plug-in rendering engine. Figure B.3 shows a rendering made with both material and map plug-ins available for MAX.

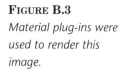

Rendering and Special Effects Plug-Ins

Many developers have added to these categories of MAX features. Since MAX R1, several plug-ins have been released that enhance or replace the default Scanline Renderer built into MAX. Although this was almost a necessity for MAX R1, the need has become less apparent with the addition of raytracing in the MAX renderer—however, it's almost certain that developers will improve upon it as well. Special effects plug-ins can include anything from Lens Flares to environmental effects. Again, MAX R2 ships with Lens Effects, but other Lens Flare plug-ins out there will more than likely have new or improved features over the standard MAX Lens Effects. Figure B.4 shows an illustration that was created using a specialized rendering engine.

Other Plug-Ins

Several other plug-in types are actually available for MAX R2. As a user, it's up to you to go out and find ones that work best for your needs. This means that you'll spend quite a bit of time looking at and experimenting with all types of plug-ins. Plug-ins can range from the more common types mentioned in this appendix to the more unusual, such as a plug-in designed to allow you to print from the Rendering dialog box. Fortunately, many discussion forums often review plug-ins as they become available. Just check the Kinetix support forum to see what's the latest in plug-in technology. Take advantage of this resource as it's not uncommon for several hundred plug-ins to be available for MAX at one time!

FIGURE B.4

A rendering of a MAX scene using a specialized rendering engine.

Unplugging Plug-Ins

Eventually, you are bound to run into poorly developed plug-ins, plug-ins in beta, or rushed to market plug-ins that should still be in beta. These plug-ins can destabilize MAX. Before you go pointing the finger at MAX for being unstable, check into the plug-ins you have loaded. Sometimes a plug-in can cause MAX to be unstable even if it's not being used.

If you frequently download from the Internet, the threat of a destabilizing plug-in is always present. So you may want to take some preventive measures to allow yourself to easily "unplug" a plug-in by removing it from MAX's plug-in paths. The best rule of thumb is to organize your plug-ins into major sub-directories. From there, you can create even more sub-directories for each plug-in if you like. Figure B.5 shows how a directory structure might appear for your plug-ins. Notice how beta plug-ins are organized in their own separate directory. Figure B.6 shows how the resulting plugin.ini file would look. Plugin.ini is a simple text file that you can edit yourself if you feel comfortable doing so. Within it are the direct paths to your plug-ins and a description of what they are. There are also entries for the online help system. These appear in the Help/Additional Help pulldown menu in MAX.

FIGURE B.5

A directory structure that allows you to pull certain plug-ins out of MAX if they're causing trouble or simply not needed.

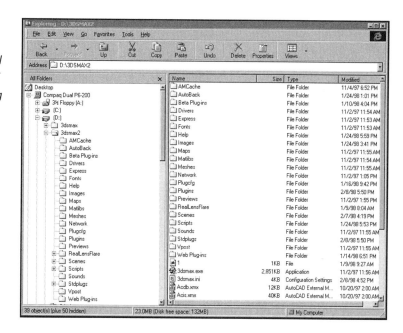

FIGURE B.6

The plug.ini file located in the root 3DSMAX directory. This text file is editable by you in Notepad, but you can access its entries the same way through the Configure Paths option in the File pull-down menu.

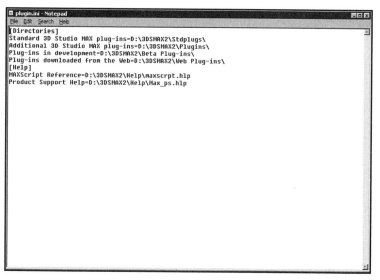

MAX also has the capability to load using an alternative plug.ini file. You can specify which plug-ins to load using this method rather than using one INI file and moving or removing plug-ins and entries in the INI file. Here are the steps for doing this:

1. Copy your plugin.ini file to something, such as allplugs.ini.

2. Create a copy of your 3DSMAX R2 shortcut and edit its properties.

3. Change the command to 3DSMAX.EXE –p allplugs.ini.

4. Configure this one to have *all* your plug-ins and leave the original plugin.ini alone.

In Practice: Designing with Plug-Ins

- **Take note of a plug-in's file extension.** Plug-ins appear in various places in the MAX interface. MAX is designed so that plug-ins won't "stand out" from the rest of the product. Although this is great from a usability standpoint, it can sometimes be a hassle when trying to search for where a newly installed plug-in might reside. Use Table B.1 to help locate where a plug-in might exist in MAX.

- **The decision to pay is yours.** Plug-ins come from many sources throughout the world. Some are commercial; some are freeware. If you are going to buy a plug-in, remember that it's often a safe bet. It's even better if you can try it out in a "demo" version first. If you're going the free route, just be careful. Sometimes plug-ins can wreak havoc on MAX if they're not designed properly.

- **Take out plug-ins when MAX appears to be unstable.** If MAX appears to be crashing way too much, then a plug-in is probably to blame. Set up MAX so that it doesn't load any third-party plug-ins and then begin adding them back, one-by-one. Eventually, you'll find the offending plug-in.

Index

Symbols

S